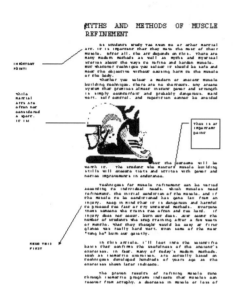

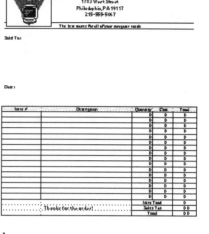

To use clipart, custom drawings, charts, and graphs, see Chapter 5.

To use columns and tables to create newsletters, spreadsheets, and ruled-forms, see Chapter 7.

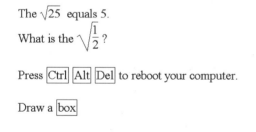

The $\sqrt{25}$ equals 5.

What is the $\sqrt{\dfrac{1}{2}}$?

Press Ctrl Alt Del to reboot your computer.

Draw a box

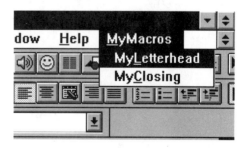

To create equations and use special characters and symbols, see Chapter 6.

To create macros, and customized toolbars and menus, see Chapter 8.

For every kind of computer user, there is a SYBEX book.

All computer users learn in their own way. Some need straightforward and methodical explanations. Others are just too busy for this approach. But no matter what camp you fall into, SYBEX has a book that can help you get the most out of your computer and computer software while learning at your own pace.

Beginners generally want to start at the beginning. The **ABC's** series, with its step-by-step lessons in plain language, helps you build basic skills quickly. Or you might try our **Quick & Easy** series, the friendly, full-color guide.

The **Mastering** and **Understanding** series will tell you everything you need to know about a subject. They're perfect for intermediate and advanced computer users, yet they don't make the mistake of leaving beginners behind.

If you're a busy person and are already comfortable with computers, you can choose from two SYBEX series—**Up & Running** and **Running Start**. The **Up & Running** series gets you started in just 20 lessons. Or you can get two books in one, a step-by-step tutorial and an alphabetical reference, with our **Running Start** series.

Everyone who uses computer software can also use a computer software reference. SYBEX offers the gamut—from portable **Instant References** to comprehensive **Encyclopedias**, **Desktop References**, and **Bibles**.

SYBEX even offers special titles on subjects that don't neatly fit a category—like **Tips & Tricks**, the **Shareware Treasure Chests**, and a wide range of books for Macintosh computers and software.

SYBEX books are written by authors who are expert in their subjects. In fact, many make their living as professionals, consultants or teachers in the field of computer software. And their manuscripts are thoroughly reviewed by our technical and editorial staff for accuracy and ease-of-use.

So when you want answers about computers or any popular software package, just help yourself to SYBEX.

For a complete catalog of our publications, please write:

SYBEX Inc.
2021 Challenger Drive
Alameda, CA 94501
Tel: (510) 523-8233/(800) 227-2346 Telex: 336311
Fax: (510) 523-2373

SYBEX is committed to using natural resources wisely to preserve and improve our environment. As a leader in the computer book publishing industry, we are aware that over 40% of America's solid waste is paper. This is why we have been printing the text of books like this one on recycled paper since 1982.

This year our use of recycled paper will result in the saving of more than 15,300 trees. We will lower air pollution effluents by 54,000 pounds, save 6,300,000 gallons of water, and reduce landfill by 2,700 cubic yards.

In choosing a SYBEX book you are not only making a choice for the best in skills and information, you are also choosing to enhance the quality of life for all of us.

Word 6
for Windows
Secrets & Solutions

Word 6
for Windows™
Secrets & Solutions

Alan R. Neibauer

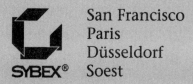

San Francisco
Paris
Düsseldorf
Soest

Acquisitions Editor: Joanne Cuthbertson
Developmental Editor: Sarah Wadsworth
Editor: Alex Miloradovich
Project Editor: Valerie Potter
Production Editor: Carolina Montilla
Technical Editor: Horace Shelton
Book Series Designer and Production Artist: Suzanne Albertson
Screen Graphics: Cuong Le
Typesetter: Deborah Maizels
Proofreader: Rhonda Holmes
Indexer: Matthew Spence
Cover Designer: Archer Design
Cover Photographer: Mark Johann

Screen reproductions produced with Collage Plus.
Collage Plus is a trademark of Inner Media Inc.

SYBEX is a registered trademark of SYBEX Inc.

TRADEMARKS: SYBEX has attempted throughout this book to distinguish proprietary trademarks from descriptive terms by following the capitalization style used by the manufacturer.

SYBEX is not affiliated with any manufacturer.

Every effort has been made to supply complete and accurate information. However, SYBEX assumes no responsibility for its use, nor for any infringement of the intellectual property rights of third parties which would result from such use.

Library of Congress Card Number: 93-87708
ISBN: 0-7821-1392-3

Manufactured in the United States of America

10 9 8 7 6 5 4 3 2 1

Dedicated to the memory of Harry Cutler

Acknowledgments

Every book is a group effort and I was lucky enough to have the SYBEX group on my side.

My appreciation to Alex Miloradovich, for performing his usual editing magic to get this book into shape. Joanne Cuthbertson, acquisitions editor, and Sarah Wadsworth, developmental editor, successfully organized the overall project. Project editor Val Potter coordinated our efforts, somehow keeping everything on track.

My thanks to technical editor Horace Shelton for his careful attention to detail and helpful suggestions. Also, thanks to production editor Carolina Montilla, typesetter Deborah Maizels, proofreader Rhonda Holmes, and indexer Matthew Spence. The efforts of designer Suzanne Albertson translated the concept of this new format to reality. Thanks also to Dr. Rudolph Langer, as well as the other people at SYBEX whose efforts contributed to this book.

Barbara Neibauer served as my in-house editor, assistant, time-keeper, and friend. She kept her sense of humor through some late nights. She continues to amaze and charm me, even as we approach our 28th year as husband and wife.

Contents at a Glance

Contents

xix

9 WordBasic Programming

Introduction

Word is not an ordinary word processing program; it is a powerful tool. By learning how to use Word's true capabilities, you can increase your personal productivity. The secrets and solutions presented in this book are practical answers to very real problems.

Word offers a complete range of information processing capabilities to automate office operations and enhance the decision-making process. Because this book is designed from the user's perspective, it is quite unlike any other you will find. It shows you how to tap into Word's capabilities, get things done, and accomplish your objectives. It will also, hopefully, stimulate your creativity and inspire you to develop your own set of powerful productivity tools.

What This Book Contains

This book assumes you already know how to use Word for Windows to edit and format text, and it gets right to the business of teaching you effective techniques for performing sophisticated tasks.

 **N o t e**   Throughout this book, you'll find features such as this Note. They contain valuable information to enhance or expand your knowledge and use of Word for Windows.

We've divided the book into six parts.

◆ **Part 1: The Basic Word**—shows you how to apply Word's features in unique and powerful ways. In Chapter 1 you'll learn about features new to Word 6 for Windows that automate your work, such as AutoText, AutoCorrect, and AutoFormat, and using Word Wizards to produce completely formatted documents and business letters. You will also learn how to use sections to apply different formats to pages within a document, and how to control the appearance of the Word screen. Chapter 2 describes the frequently overlooked and underused resources of styles and templates. You'll learn to master these resources to streamline text entry and formatting. Chapter 3 covers the formatting and printing of envelopes and labels. In addition, you will learn how to use labels for special documents, such as business cards, tickets, brochures, folders, greeting cards, place cards, and folded booklets.

◆ **Part 2: The Published Word**—covers desktop publishing and graphic techniques. In Chapter 4, you will learn how to add graphic lines, boxes, and page borders, and how to work with frames. You will also learn how to use WordArt to create special effects with True-Type fonts. Chapter 5 describes how to work with graphic images, custom drawings, charts, and drop capitals. Graphic characters, symbols, and equations are discussed in Chapter 6. Chapter 7 is about columns and tables. You will learn how to create newsletters and booklets, and even how to create brochures that contain both landscape and portrait text. Not only will you learn how to create spreadsheets, you will find out how to create invoices that automatically compute sales tax and totals, questionnaires, graphics, and calendars.

◆ **Part 3: The Word on Macros**—is devoted to unlocking the powerful secrets of macros. Chapter 8 covers the fundamentals of macros, and how to customize Word's toolbars, menus, and keystroke combinations. You will learn how to record, edit, and write macros using the powerful WordBasic macro language. Chapter 9 covers advanced macro programming, such as input, conditional, and repetition commands. You will learn how to write macros for automating your work, such as filling in invoices and forms. In Chapter 10, you will learn special macro applications, including how to create your own custom dialog boxes. In addition, you'll learn how to harness new Word features, such as dynamic dialog boxes and preview windows.

 **Tip**

Tips like this one describe shortcuts and handy ways to use Word more efficiently and effectively. Read these and put them into practice.

◆ **Part 4: The Merging Word**—reveals solutions to creating form documents, envelopes, labels, and database reports. In Chapter 11 you will learn to use Word's new Mail Merge Helper, how to handle blank fields, and how to use math to create derived columns. You will also learn how to create interactive merges for adding information and selecting records as the documents are created. In Chapter 12 you will learn how to use macros and merge files to manage mailing lists and databases. You'll see how to use macros to delete records, select specific records for completing invoices, automatically mark duplicate records for deletion, and sort records.

S E C R E T S

Revealing Word's Secrets

This feature tells you about unique ways to use Word for Windows, and about powerful—often ignored or misunderstood—techniques.

Here are some examples of the Secrets revealed in this book:

◆ Zooming the Word Display
◆ Using the Shortcut Menus
◆ Assigning a Shortcut Key
◆ Style Tips and Tricks
◆ Template Tips and Tricks

- ◆ WordArt Tips and Tricks
- ◆ Macro Command Tips and Tricks

Each Secret is enclosed in a shaded box like this one and employs numbered steps, illustrations, and listings as needed to fully explain the topic at hand.

◆ **Part 5: The Well-Managed Word**—covers advanced document assembly using sophisticated, practical applications. In Chapter 13, you will learn how to combine macros and merge files to automate the creation of documents and database records. You will even automate a receivables system, including updating client records in the database when an invoice is completed. Chapter 14 covers document management techniques for the busy office. You will develop a file management system for automatically naming and saving documents in multiple directories. The system will maintain an index of files and allow you to search for, open, and delete specific files. You will also learn to use document variables to track your editing sessions, create sequential access files for storing information and working with text files, and make your own INI files just like those created by Windows.

S O L U T I O N S

Solving Difficult Challenges

This feature details practical, often fun ways to apply Word. You'll find step-by-step techniques for solving some tough word processing problems, or learn the best ways to create those difficult documents.

Here are some of the many Solutions you'll find in this book:

- The Style Gallery
- Using the Replace Command
- Positioning Paper in the Printer
- Laying Out Text in Two Orientations
- Creating Drop Caps
- Creating Watermarks
- Using the Equation Window
- Word's Sample Macros

Look for these and many more Word Solutions in shaded boxes like this one.

- **Part 6: The Professional Word**—focuses on powerful applied techniques. Chapter 15 describes the creation and use of on-line forms, including text fields, checkboxes, and drop-down lists. There is also a special section all about Word's fields. Chapter 16 shows you how to create a system that records billable time and produces summary reports for each client. A section devoted to the legal profession shows you how to automate standard forms, such as pleadings and legal notices. A section on academic Word covers templates that standardize reports and dissertation formats, including footnote layouts. You will also learn to use merge techniques to prepare tests and answer keys. A hypertext system using bookmarks, fields, and macros is presented, as well as a section on using sound and music in documents.

 **Warning** This is a warning, letting you know of some potential problem area or error that may occur. It may warn you of actions that can result in lost data or other serious consequences.

How to Use This Book

Although a mouse is not absolutely necessary for using Word for Windows or other Windows applications, it is highly recommended. The instructions in this book assume that you have a mouse, or are already familiar with using the keyboard to access menu bar options and work with dialog boxes.

This book uses the following method to streamline the selection of Word's options:

Select File ➤ Page Setup ➤ Paper Size

The ➤ symbol is used to separate items that you must select. So this instruction means: "Select the File menu, select the Page Setup option, and then select the Paper Size option from the dialog box that appears." Do not select the ➤ character.

Quick and Easy Macros

Many of the special techniques discussed in this book use macros to automate their operation. All of the macros are completely listed and thoroughly explained. If you do not want to type the macros yourself, however, you can download them from the SYBEX forum on the CompuServe information network.

You will find the macros in a compressed archive file named 1392-3.EXE in the WORD PROCESSING library. The file also contains invoice forms used in several chapters, complete reference listings of WordBasic statements and functions, and a discussion that expands on techniques discussed in Chapter 16.

Once you log on to CompuServe, use the GO SYBEX command to reach the SYBEX forum. Download the self-extracting compressed file and copy it into your WINWORD directory. Then decompress the file by typing **1392-3**. After decompressing the archive, read the README.DOC file for additional information.

A Note from the Author

You are now ready to capture the potential of this truly powerful and versatile program. You will find that Word has capabilities you may have never imagined. Take control and use them.

PART
one

The Basic Word

1
Harnessing Word's
New Features

2
Styles and Templates

3
Envelopes, Labels,
and Small Documents

CHAPTER 1

Harnessing Word's New Features

USING THE SECRETS AND SOLUTIONS presented in this book, you'll be able to go far beyond basic word processing to a much greater level of efficiency and satisfaction. But before delving into these techniques, let's review some of the new and unique features of Word 6.0 for Windows and how you can use them to realize an immediate increase in productivity. The fundamental concepts presented in this chapter lay a foundation for some of the more advanced chapters that follow.

Working with AutoText

AutoText provides a fast way to insert text into a document by entering an abbreviation. You can enter a name by typing the person's initials, or a difficult to spell word by entering its first several letters. With AutoText, you can insert any amount of text—a word, a boilerplate paragraph, an entire table, or a graphic such as your company logo.

 **N o t e**   AutoText replaces, and improves upon, the Glossary feature included in previous versions of Word for Windows.

S E C R E T S

Styles and Templates

Any discussion about Word for Windows must include styles and templates. While these will be discussed in detail in Chapter 2, you'll see references to them in this chapter as well.

A *style* is just a collection of formats. You can have a style called "Headline," for example, that contains the Times Roman 12-point bold format and the $1/2$-inch indentation format. When you want to create a headline, you *apply* the style so the text takes on its formats. When you start Word, it applies a style called Normal to your text.

A *template* is a document containing a collection of styles. You can create templates for each type of document that you produce, such as a memo template for memorandums, a fax template for fax cover pages, an invoice template for invoices. When you want to create a specific type of document, you use the appropriate template, then apply the styles in the template to paragraphs, headlines, and other elements on the page.

A template can also contain text, custom macros, menus, keyboard assignments, and toolbars that you can use to complete that type of document. When you start Word, it uses a template called Normal, which contains all of Word's default formats.

Creating an AutoText Entry

To create an AutoText entry, select the text that you want to be able to insert. Then, select Edit ➤ AutoText, or click on the Insert AutoText button in the standard Toolbar, to see the dialog box shown in Figure 1.1.

FIGURE 1.1

AutoText dialog box

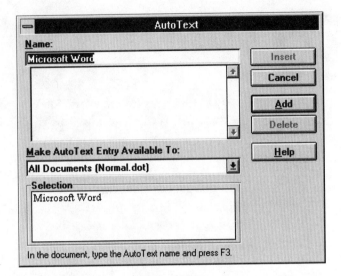

 **Tip**   When you select the text, include the blank space that follows it. Then, when you insert the text using AutoText, the space will automatically appear so you can continue typing without entering the space yourself.

The first several characters of the selected text will appear in the Name text box, and the entire selection appears in the Selection box. You use the Name entry to later insert the selection in a document. You can select Add to accept the name shown, or you can type another identifying name (up to 32 characters) and then select Add. Use AutoText names that are short, convenient to type, and clearly describe the text.

 **Note** By default, the AutoText entry is stored in the Normal template. This means that it will be available to every document. If you are using another template, you can also select to store the entry in that template. From the AutoText dialog box, pull down the Make AutoText Entry Available To option and select the desired template. The AutoText entry will only be available for use with documents based on AutoText designated templates. Refer to Chapter 2 for more information on templates.

Follow these steps to create an AutoText entry:

1. Type and then select your full name in a Word for Windows document.

2. Select Edit ➤ AutoText, or click on the Insert AutoText button.

3. In the Name text box, type your initials.

4. Select Add to save the entry and return to the document window.

5. Type and select the word **carbon.**

6. Select Edit ➤ AutoText, type **C** in the Name text box, and select Add.

7. Press Enter, type your initials, then press F3. Word replaces your initials with your full name.

8. Press Enter, type **C** and press F3 to insert the word carbon.

 **Note** AutoText names are not case sensitive. If you type c or C and then press F3, Word will insert the word carbon. The inserted entry appears in the same case as it was when you selected it.

Saving and Printing AutoText Entries

To save paragraph formats with the text, select the paragraph mark at the end of the paragraph. Word stores formats such as line spacing and indentations in the paragraph mark. (That's why deleting the paragraph mark removes the formatting.) By including the mark in the selection, the formatting is saved with the AutoText entry, and reapplied when you insert the text.

To print a list of your AutoText entries, select File ➤ Print, pull down the Print What list, select AutoText Entries, then click on OK.

Inserting an AutoText Entry

To insert an AutoText entry, type the name that you assigned it, then press F3 or click on the Insert AutoText button. Word will replace the name with the complete entry. If you hear a beep, it means that Word does not recognize the text at the insertion point as an AutoText entry.

 **Tip**

> You do not have to type the complete AutoText name, only enough characters to identify the entry. For example, if you have only one AutoText entry that starts with the letter B, just type B and then press F3.

The AutoText name must be preceded by at least one space and can be followed by any number of spaces or one hard return. For example, if you name the AutoText entry CO, Word will not insert the entry if you type NCO and then press F3. You can, however, type CO, then press the space-bar or the Enter key, and press F3. Multiple returns and tab spaces cannot be used.

You can also insert an AutoText entry using the AutoText dialog box. Select Edit ➤ AutoText, choose the name of the entry you want to insert, then click on Insert.

By default, Word inserts AutoText in the same font, size, and other character attributes it had when it was saved as an entry. You can also select to insert the text without formatting. When you display the AutoText dialog box without selecting text first, the Formatted Text and Plain Text options replace the Make AutoText Entry Available To option. Select Plain Text to add the text unformatted so it assumes the formats of the current paragraph.

 **Note** Don't be surprised if you hear Word's warning beeps when you are first learning how to use AutoText. When you click on the AutoText button, you'll hear a beep if no text is selected and if the text to the left of the insertion point is not an AutoText name. When you select Edit ➤ AutoText, you'll hear the beep if no text is selected and no AutoText entries exist.

Editing and Deleting AutoText Entries

While AutoText entries are retained from Word session to session, they are not carved in stone. You can delete an AutoText entry, rename or edit it, and even move it from one template to another.

To delete an entry, select its name in the AutoText dialog box, then click on Delete.

To change an entry, insert it into a document, edit the text as desired, then select the text again. Click on the Insert AutoText button, or select Edit ➤ AutoText. Next, choose the entry's original name in the list box (or type it in the text box) and select Add. A message box will appear asking if you want to redefine the entry. Select Yes.

Use the same procedure to replace an entry with another of the same name. (To rename an AutoText entry, or to move it to another template, see Chapter 2.)

Working with AutoCorrect

The AutoCorrect feature takes the concept of automatically inserting text one step further. With AutoCorrect, Word will insert an entry automatically: you do not have to press F3 or click any buttons. In fact, you might have already seen AutoCorrect in action when you type.

AutoCorrect makes the following corrections as soon as they occur:

◆ Change "straight quotes to" "smart quotes," the curly quotation marks used by typesetters

◆ Correct two initial capitals, replacing a second uppercase letter in a word with lowercase

◆ Capitalize the first letter of sentences. This option may initially be turned off

◆ Capitalize the names of days

◆ Replace text as you type—AutoCorrect changes the following:

REPLACE THIS	WITH THIS
(r)	®
adn	and
don't	don't
i	I
incl	include
occurence	occurrence
recieve	receive
seperate	separate
teh	the

AutoCorrect makes the replacement when you press the spacebar, tab, or Enter key after typing the incorrect word. For example, if you type **i did not recieve the order**, AutoCorrect will display the sentence correctly as **I did not receive the order.**

 **Note**

If you type the word, then press an arrow key or move the insertion point with the mouse, the entry will not be corrected.

You can use AutoCorrect to insert frequently used words and phrases from typed abbreviations. AutoCorrect can also be used to correct words you know you frequently misspell. For example, suppose you usually misspell paragraph as paragragh. You can set Word to correct the mistake as you type.

 **Tip**

You can automatically create an AutoCorrect entry to correct a common misspelling during the spell check process. When Word stops at a word that you often misspell, make sure the proper spelling is in the Change To box, then click on AutoCorrect.

Creating an AutoCorrect Entry

To create an AutoCorrect entry, select Tools ➤ AutoCorrect to display the dialog box shown in Figure 1.2. In the Replace box, type a normal misspelling or an abbreviation for an automatic entry. In the With box, type the correct spelling of the word, or the full text you want displayed with the abbreviation. Select Add, then Close.

If you select text before displaying the dialog box, the text will automatically appear in the With box. You can also choose to insert the text as Plain or Formatted.

FIGURE 1.2

AutoCorrect
dialog box

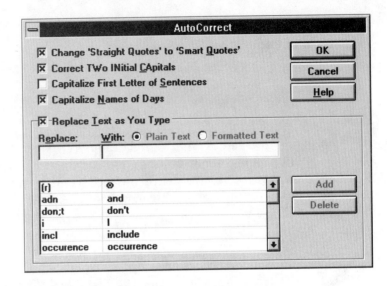

To create an AutoText entry:

1. Select Tools ➤ AutoCorrect to display the AutoText dialog box.

2. In the Replace text box, type **hc**.

3. In the With box, type **hydrocarbon**.

4. Select Add. Selecting Add in the AutoCorrect box does not close the box.

5. In the Replace text box, type **nacl**.

6. In the With box, type **Sodium Chloride**. Begin each word with a capital letter.

7. Select Add.

8. In the Replace box, type **paragragh**.

9. In the With box, type **paragraph**.

10. Select Add, then Close.

 **Note**

The case of your AutoCorrect entries is important! If you enter the Replace and With entries in all lowercase letters, Word will replace the text to match the case of the replacement text. For example, if you create an entry to replace s with sulfur, word will also replace S with SULFUR. However, if you use any uppercase letters in either string, Word will match them exactly. If you enter the S in the Replace box, Word will not replace a lowercase s in the text. Likewise, if you enter SULFUR in the With box, the AutoCorrect replacement will always appear in uppercase.

Using AutoCorrect

To use an AutoCorrect entry, type the abbreviation, press the spacebar or the Enter key, and the full text will appear. If you misspell the word as specified, the correct word will appear.

 **Note**

Like AutoText, an AutoCorrect entry must be preceded by at least one space. However, you can type a punctuation mark after the name, and Word will still display the full entry when you press the spacebar, Tab, or Enter key.

To use the AutoCorrect entry you created earlier:

1. Type **hc** and press Enter to insert the word hydrocarbon.

2. Type **HC** and press Enter to insert HYDROCARBON in all uppercase letters.

3. Type **nacl** and press Enter. The words Sodium Chloride appear just as you entered them into the AutoCorrect dialog box.

4. Type **NACL** and press Enter. Word displays Sodium Chloride!

5. Type **Paragragh formats.** Word corrects the spelling when you press the spacebar.

AutoCorrect Tips and Tricks

While AutoCorrect is very useful, it can be downright annoying. For instance, suppose you need to type HCl, the abbreviation for hydrochloric acid. When you press the spacebar at the end of the word, AutoCorrect changes it to Hcl.

To reverse an AutoCorrect action, select Edit ➤ Undo AutoCorrect. You can also turn a particular AutoCorrect feature on and off by clicking its checkbox in the AutoCorrect dialog box. Deselecting the Replace Text As You Type box, for example, will prevent AutoCorrect from changing misspelled words or expanding abbreviations.

You should be careful when creating AutoCorrect entries using single letters or very short Replace names. If you define the replacement of carbon for the letter c, Word will replace the letter even if it is used as a person's middle initial. Entering a period after the initial will not prevent AutoCorrect from changing it.

If you want to use single letters to quickly insert text, use the letter as an AutoText name. You'll have the option of pressing F3 to expand the entry.

 **N o t e**

The smart quotes inserted by AutoCorrect are special symbols not found on the keyboard. If you save your document in a format other than Word for Windows, Word will convert the quotes as necessary. For example, if you save the document in WordPerfect format, Word will record the quotes using the appropriate WordPerfect character set. If you save the document as ASCII text, Word will change the smart quotes back to straight quotes.

S O L U T I O N S

AutoText vs. AutoCorrect

AutoText and AutoCorrect are both useful features. While they have similar capabilities, however, they can be used quite differently.

Use AutoCorrect to correct common misspellings and for frequently used words. Make certain that the Replace phrase will not result in unintentional changes, such as changing Adam C. Chesin to Adam CARBON. Chesin.

Remember, AutoCorrect expands an abbreviation or corrects a word automatically. If it takes effect, you can always select Edit ➤ Undo AutoCorrect. Word will not make the AutoCorrect change if you move the insertion point before you press the spacebar or the Enter key.

With AutoText, you can press the F3 key, click on the Insert AutoText button, or use the AutoText dialog box. AutoText is best for less frequently used boilerplate entries, or when you want to use an abbreviation that could result in unintentional AutoCorrect results.

For example, if you study chemistry, you could assign the name of each element to an AutoText entry using its symbol as the name, and still be able to refer to yourself with the pronoun I without replacing it with Iodine every time. To enter Iodine, type I and press the F3 key.

Word's New Formatting Tools

Word for Windows has all of the standard formatting capabilities. You can change fonts and font sizes, arrange the layout of paragraphs and pages, and add lines, patterns, and graphics. In the following sections, we'll discuss some special new features.

Using the Format Painter

To copy a format, place the insertion point in the text that contains the format you want to copy, then click on the Format Painter toolbar button. The mouse pointer changes to a small paintbrush and an I-beam. Select the text you want to apply the format to, and when you release the mouse button, Word applies the format.

To use the keyboard to copy formats, place the insertion point in the text containing the format you want to copy, and then press Ctrl+Shift+C. Select the text you want to format, then press Ctrl+Shift+V.

 **Tip**

To copy a format to more than one selection, double-click on the Format Painter toolbar button. When you are done copying the formats to other text, press Esc or click on the Format Painter button again.

The AutoFormat Feature

You can format an entire document in one click of the mouse using Word's AutoFormat feature. AutoFormat applies a built-in set of styles, and you can even select from a gallery of additional styles. (In Chapter 2, you will learn more about styles and templates.)

How AutoFormat Works

To use AutoFormat, click on the AutoFormat button in the standard toolbar. Word will scan your document, identifying certain formatting elements, such as titles, subtitles, and lists. It will then make the following changes:

◆ Apply built-in styles to titles and subtitles (titles start with uppercase letters, end with returns, and precede blank lines)

**Note**

> The first title in the document is assigned the style Heading 1, which is Arial 14-point bold in the default template. Any other titles having the same format as the first will also be changed to the Heading 1 style. For example, if the first title on the page is bold, then every bold title will be converted to Heading 1. The next title that has a different format is converted to the Heading 2 style, the next to Heading 3 style, and so on. There are nine different heading styles.

◆ Apply the body text style to other text on the page (the style depends on the template)

◆ Remove extra paragraph marks (usually inserted by pressing Enter at the end of a line)

◆ Replace spacebar and tab key indents with paragraph indents

◆ Insert bullets in place of asterisks, hyphens, or other characters used to highlight bulleted lists (Word removes numbers or symbols you added yourself)

◆ Insert copyright, registered trademark, and trademark symbols in place of (C), (R), and (TM)

◆ Replace straight quotes with smart quotes

**Tip**

> If you change your mind after applying the formats, select Edit ➤ Undo AutoFormat.

Confirming AutoFormat

You can apply AutoFormat and review the changes before accepting them. Select Format ➤ AutoFormat, then select OK from the dialog box that appears. Word will format your document then display the dialog box shown in Figure 1.3.

FIGURE 1.3

AutoFormat
options

The box gives you the options of accepting the changes, rejecting them all, reviewing and confirming each, or displaying a list of other style templates. If you select to review each of the changes, Word highlights the first text that was changed and displays the dialog box shown in Figure 1.4.

The text is automatically displayed with the following revision marks:

MARK	INDICATES
Blue paragraph mark	a new paragraph style
Red paragraph mark	a deleted paragraph mark
Red strikethrough	deleted text or spaces, replacement of tabs and spaces with indentation
Blue underline	inserted underlines
Change bar	revised formatting or style indicated by a vertical line in the left margin

You can select these options from the dialog box:

◆ **Reject:** undoes the changes to the highlight text.

◆ **Find →:** moves to the next affected text.

◆ **Find ←:** moves to the previous affected text.

FIGURE 1.4

Review AutoFormat
Changes dialog box

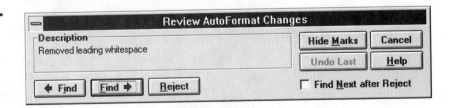

- ◆ **Hide Marks:** removes the revision marks.
- ◆ **Undo Last:** reverses the last rejected text to the auto format.
- ◆ **Find Next after Reject:** automatically locates the next revised text when you select Reject.

S O L U T I O N S

The Style Gallery

The formats applied by AutoFormat are styles in the current template. You can apply other styles by selecting another template from the Style Gallery. Select Format ➤ Style Gallery to display the dialog box shown here. (You can also select Style Gallery from the AutoFormat box.)

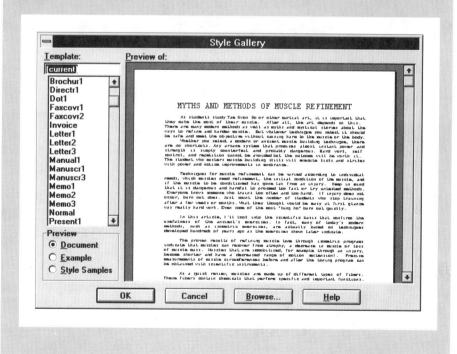

The list box contains the names of the available templates. The preview window shows your document with the template's styles. Select a template to see how your document looks, and scroll the preview window to see the styles applied to other sections of the document. You can also click on Example to see a sample document that uses the full potential of the style, or select Style Samples to see samples of all of the template styles.

When you find a format you like, select OK. If you have already used the AutoFormat command, Word will replace the formats of the applied styles with those from the selected template. Otherwise, click on the AutoFormat button to format the document. (If you change your mind, select Edit ➤ Undo Style Gallery.)

To format just a section of text, select it before clicking on the AutoFormat button.

Customizing AutoFormat

AutoFormat can make some sweeping changes to a document. If you've already manually formatted some elements, such as headlines and lists, you can adjust AutoFormat to only change selected elements. This way, you can retain certain formats while changing others.

To customize AutoFormat, select Tools ➤ Options ➤ AutoFormat, or Format ➤ AutoFormat ➤ Options to display the dialog box shown in Figure 1.5.

You can make the following choices:

◆ **Preserve:** retains styles that you specifically assigned, only changing text that has not been formatted using a specific style.

◆ **Apply Styles To:** sets the elements you want AutoFormat to affect—headings, lists, and other paragraph styles.

FIGURE 1.5

AutoFormat
Options dialog box

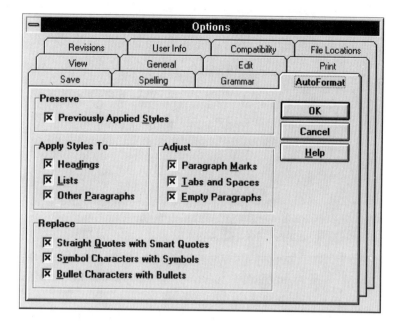

◆ **Adjust:** selects to add or delete paragraph marks, replace spaces with tabs and remove unnecessary spaces, or remove blank lines between paragraphs and headlines.

◆ **Replace:** chooses the automatic replacement style—straight quotes to smart quotes, symbols for characters (such a register and trademark), and bullets on numbered lists.

Working with Wizards

A Wizard takes you step-by-step through the design of a document. Word will let you select design elements, prompt you for the necessary information, and insert it automatically in the document. For fax cover pages and other documents, Word will even use the name and company that you inserted when you installed Word.

Here's a list of the Wizards that come with Word:

Agenda Wizard

Award Wizard

Calendar Wizard

Fax Wizard

Letter Wizard

Memo Wizard

Newsletter Wizard

Pleading Wizard

Resume Wizard

Table Wizard

Using a Wizard

To use a Wizard, select File ➤ New to display the Template dialog box. Double-click on the Wizard you want to use, or select the template, then click on OK. (Templates contain styles but are not interactive. See Chapter 2 for more information on using templates and styles.)

A prompt in the status bar will ask you to insert information, or one or more dialog boxes will appear requesting formatting choices or text to insert into the document. Enter the information requested, select options from the dialog box, or enter text in text boxes. Select Next to move to the next box. Select Finish after completing the final dialog box.

 **Note** Before the first dialog box appears, Word may have to set up the format, load a file, or perform another operation. Watch the status line for a report on Word's progress.

Select Cancel to stop the procedure, or select <Back to return to the previous dialog box in the series. When the last dialog box is displayed, the Next button will be dimmed.

 **Tip** | In any dialog box, you can click Finish to bypass remaining dialog boxes and to display the document with the options selected and text entered to that point.

The Letter Wizard

The Letter Wizard gives you a quick way to create and format letters. You can even select from prewritten letters that already contain text. Let's use the Letter Wizard now to see how Wizards operate.

1. Select File ➤ New, then double-click on Letter Wizard. A dialog box appears with the following options:

◆ **Select a prewritten business letter:** lets you choose from a list of 15 letters that already contain the basic text. All you have to do is edit the letter with some specific information.

◆ **Write a business letter:** creates a formal letter with options such as the typist's initials, client account number, and notations for enclosures and attachments.

◆ **Write a personal letter:** creates a more informal layout.

2. Choose Select a Prewritten Business Letter, then click on Next. A dialog box appears listing the prewritten letters that are available, as in Figure 1.6.

3. Select Collection letter: 30 days past due, then click on Next. A dialog box appears with the options Letterhead stationary and Plain paper.

4. Choose Plain paper, then click on Next. A dialog box appears requesting the recipient's name and address, as shown in Figure 1.7.

5. Delete the text in the top box and enter the following mailing address:

```
Adam M. Chesin
Pickwick, Inc.
508 West Street
Ventnor, NJ 08745
```

6. Check the name and address in the bottom box. If your complete address does not appear, select the box and enter it now.

FIGURE 1.6

The Letter Wizard

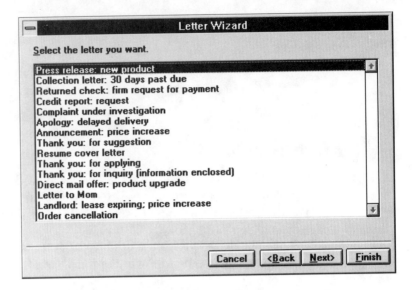

FIGURE 1.7

Letter Wizard
address
information

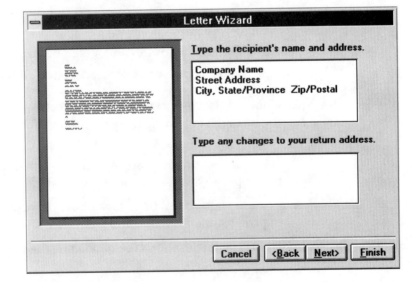

Once you enter your address and complete the letter, your address will be saved and used automatically with all of Word's Wizards.

7. Select Next. A dialog box will appear listing three style options—Classic, Contemporary, and Typewriter.

8. Select a style option, then click on Next. Word now presents you with three options. You can select to create an envelope or mailing label, display the help system as you complete the letter, or just display the letter.

9. Select Just display the letter, then select Finish.

Note If you select to create an envelope or label, a dialog box will appear with additional options. See Chapter 3 for more information.

The letter appears in Figure 1.8. You must replace items that are surrounded by square brackets—such as [Company]—and underlined text with your own information. Complete the letter, then print and save it.

Note If you receive an error message when you try to use a prewritten letter, it may not have been installed when you installed Word. Exit Word, run the Word Setup program, and select the Complete/Custom option. Refer to your Word manual for more information.

FIGURE 1.8

A letter ready to be completed

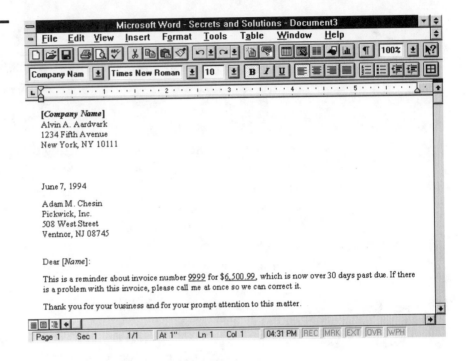

Using Word's View Modes

Word has four view modes—Normal, Outline, Page Layout, and Master Document. When you first start Word, it will be in Normal view. You can type, edit, and format documents in all four views.

Here are the four views and their basic characteristics:

◆ **Normal view:** shows you fonts and graphics, but not headers, footers, page numbers, and margin areas. Graphics do not always appear in their exact position in relation to the text, and multiple columns will not appear side-by-side.

◆ **Page Layout view:** shows you the document exactly as it will appear when printed. A ruler will appear down the left side of the screen.

◆ **Outline view:** creates outlines and helps you organize documents.

◆ **Master Document view:** helps you work with large documents that are divided into sections.

To change views, pull down the View menu and select the option desired. You can also use the three buttons on the left of the horizontal scroll bar to change views.

 **Tip**   If you find the toolbars and other screen elements distracting, you can remove them all in one step by selecting View ➤ Full Screen. The title and menu bars, toolbars, ruler, status bar, and scroll bars will be removed. A small icon labeled Full will appear in the bottom right corner. Click on the icon or press Esc to return the screen to its normal display.

S E C R E T S

Zooming the Word Display

The default display magnification is set at 100%. This means that text and graphics appear about the same size on screen as they do on the printed page. To change the magnification, select View ➤ Zoom to display the Zoom dialog box shown here.

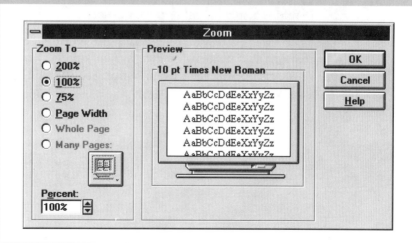

Select a percentage, then click on OK. The options are 200%, 100%, 75%, Page Width, Whole Page, and Many Pages. You can also set a custom magnification between 10% and 200%. Page Width adjusts the magnification so you can see the full line of text on the screen. Full Page displays an entire page on screen.

The Whole Page and Many Pages options are dimmed in Normal view. In Page Layout view, select Many Pages to display a thumbnail display of two or more pages on the screen. Click on the icon of the monitor, then drag the mouse down and to the right to determine the number of pages displayed. (The number of pages depends on the size of your document.)

You can also zoom by using the Zoom Control button in the standard toolbar. The options are 200%, 175%, 100%, 75%, 50%, 25%, 10%, and Page Width. In Page Layout view, the list also includes Whole Page and Two Pages.

Working with Sections

If you are a new Word for Windows user, one of the most confusing elements may be sections. A *section* is a portion of a word document that contains a specific set of page formats.

If your entire document uses one set of page layouts, such as the same margins and page numbering system on every page, then it contains only one section. You'll see the notation Sec 1 in the status bar no matter what page you are on.

 **Note** You only need to be concerned with sections when you want to use different page layouts in the same document, such as single columns on one page and double columns on another, or different margins or page sizes. When you want to change the format of a single page (or on a part of a single page), you must insert a section break.

Formatting in Page Layout

To format an individual page, place the insertion point at the start of the page and select File ➤ Page Layout. Change the page size or margins, pull down the Apply To list, select This Point Forward, then select OK. Word will insert a section break that also serves as a page break, as in Figure 1.9. (The section break line does not appear on screen in Page Layout view.)

FIGURE 1.9

Section break lines

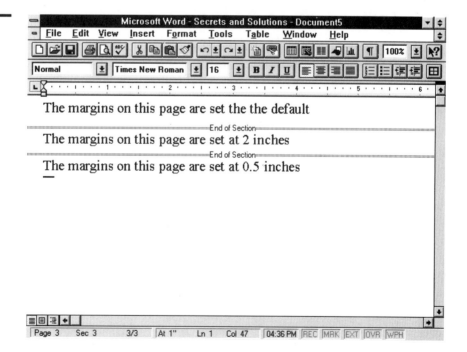

The page size and margins will apply from the start of the page following the section break until the end of the document, or until the next section break. Delete a hard page break if it appears immediately before the section break line. Otherwise, a blank page will print between the page and section break lines.

 **Note**

When you change the settings in the Page Layout menus, use the Apply To list to determine how to apply the formats. Select Whole Document to apply the layout to every page. Select This Point Forward to insert a section and a page break. If the insertion point is already within a section, you can also select This Section to change the settings of the current section.

Formatting by Section

You can also insert a section break and then choose the formats for the section. Select Insert ➤ Break to display the Break dialog box. The dialog box has the following options:

◆ **Next Page:** inserts a combination section break and page break. The new section formats will begin on a new page.

◆ **Continuous:** inserts a section break without a page break. Use this option when creating a page with both single and multiple-column text, or to change the left or right margins of text on the same page.

 **Note**

Any other format changes applied to the new section, such as page size, numbering, and top and bottom margins, will begin on the next page—these formats cannot be combined on the same page.

◆ **Even Page:** begins the next section on an even-numbered page (to start chapters on even-numbered pages, for example).

◆ **Odd Page:** begins the next section on an odd-numbered page.

Removing Section Formats

When you, or Word, insert a section break, the break line contains the formats of the text above it. In essence, the section break line says: "This is where the current formats end and new formats begin."

Warning

> If you delete a section break line between two pages (by selecting it and pressing Del), you are actually removing the formats from the first page. The page size and margins that you gave to the second page will now apply to the first page as well. This may not be what you intended to do.

The best way to remove the section formats is to click on the Undo button in the toolbar and select Page Setup. As an alternative, you can cut the section break line and paste it at the end of the second page. The original formats of the first page will now be applied to all of the text above the pasted section break.

Customizing Word

For further control over the Word environment, select Tools ➤ Options to display the Options dialog box. Select the tab referring to the item you want to change, and then select from the options that appear. Select OK to modify the settings (see Table 1.1).

TABLE 1.1: The options on the Options dialog box

TAB	PURPOSE
View	Changes the appearance and display of elements in windows, including the display of fonts, graphics and drawings in view modes
General	Determines the common default settings, including the units of measurement, background pagination, and the number of documents listed in the File menu
Edit	Controls editing settings, such as typing to replace a selection, allowing drag and drop, using the Ins key to paste text, smart cut and paste to add or delete extra spaces, and adding accents to certain uppercase letters
Print	Sets printing defaults, such as formatting during draft output, reverse printing order, update fields and link when printing, and background printing a document
Compatibility	Controls the display of documents created with other word processors, such as font substitution, balanced columns, page and column breaks displayed in frames, line spacing at the start of the page, and alternating page margins
Save	Sets options for saving documents, including the creation of backup copies, prompt for summary information, prompt to save the normal template, embedding TrueType Fonts, automatic backups, and password protection
Revisions	Determines the color and symbols used when making revisions
User	Identifies the user name for the document summary, the initials for annotations, and address for envelopes and labels
File Locations	Determines the default path for documents, graphics, and templates
Spelling	Sets options such as suggesting alternate spellings, ignoring uppercase words and numbers, and setting the custom dictionary
Grammar	Determines the style rules for checking documents
AutoFormat	Controls the styles and formats applied during AutoFormat

 **Note**

For more information on customizing Word's menus, toolbars, and the keyboard, see Chapter 8.

S E C R E T S

Using the Shortcut Menus

Word provides shortcut menus for frequently used menu options. A shortcut menu appears when you point to a particular area of the screen and press the right mouse button. For instance, to copy a section of text to the clipboard, select the text, point to the selection, then click the right mouse button. Select Copy from the shortcut menu shown here.

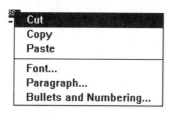

To paste the text in a new location, point where you want to insert the text, click the right mouse button, then select Paste from the shortcut menu. (To display a shortcut menu with the keyboard, press Shift+F10. Close the menu by pressing Esc.)

Styles and Templates

T HIS CHAPTER IS DIVIDED INTO two major sections, Styles and Templates. However, both subjects are so interconnected it's difficult, if not impossible, to discuss one without mentioning the other. So before jumping into either subject in detail, let's get a general idea of the relationship of the two, and of the underlying concepts.

Word's Sense of Style

The style Word uses by default is called the Normal style. It defines the font and font size, the line spacing, and text alignment. So when you first begin Word, your text will appear in 10-point Times Roman, single-spaced, and left justified.

 **Tip**

To change the default page size, margins, paper source, or overall layout, click on the Default button in any of the Page Setup dialog boxes.

The Normal Template

All of Word's default format settings are stored in the normal template, a file called NORMAL.DOT in the Template subdirectory. The normal template contains any macros, AutoText entries, menus, keyboard key assignments, and toolbars that you create. These items are called *global* because they are automatically available to you unless you specifically replace them with items from another template.

 **Warning**

If you delete the NORMAL.DOT file from the disk, it will be recreated when you start Word. It will contain the original default values supplied with Word for Windows, but any custom items that you added, such as AutoText entries and macros, will be lost.

There are also about 75 styles in the normal template. The styles cover the formats of every built-in feature that you can create using Word, such as tables of contents, indexes, annotations, lists, and captions. When you create a footnote for example, Word formats the note according to two of these styles—the footnote number is formatted using the footnote reference style, the text of the note by the footnote text style.

Paragraph and Character Styles

There are two types of styles, paragraph and character. A paragraph style may contain any format that affects the appearance of text, such as font and size, or which can be applied to an entire paragraph, such as line spacing and text alignment.

A character format may contain any of the formats selectable from the Font dialog box. You can apply both a character and paragraph style to the same text.

The Body Text Style

Many of the other styles in the template are based on the normal style. For example, the style called Body Text is defined as: Normal+Space After 6 pt. This means it uses all of the formats applied to the normal style, but also adds a 6 point space (about one half of a line) between paragraphs.

You would use the body text style to automatically add extra space between paragraphs and items in a list. Each time you press Enter, Word adds the extra 6 points in addition to the current line spacing.

Other Style Templates

While the styles in the normal template are the most common, Word has designed other styles and makes them available in templates other than NORMAL.DOT. These templates are also in the Template subdirectory. Most of the styles in these templates have the same names as those in NORMAL.DOT, but they may contain different formats. For example, in the template named PRESREL3.DOT, the normal style uses the Courier font, rather than Times Roman.

The body text style is defined as: Normal+Indent: First 0.5", Line Spacing Double, Space After 6 pt. This means the style will contain all of the normal formats, but text will be double-spaced, with an extra 6 points between paragraphs, and the first line of every paragraph will be indented ½ inch.

 **N o t e**   The template named PRESREL3.DOT represents Press Release 3, one of three layouts you can use for press releases. The template names may appear strange because they can only include 8 characters, in addition to the DOT extension.

Automatic Reformatting

One of the most powerful features of styles is their ability to automatically reformat text. For example, suppose you manually format 20 subtitles in Arial 14 point. If you wanted to change the headings to another point size or font, you would have to select and reformat each one.

If you formatted the subtitles by applying the Heading 1 style, however, you could change all 20 subtitles by simply modifying the style. All 20 subtitles will instantly change to reflect the new formats.

AutoFormat Revisited

When you apply an AutoFormat, Word scans your document looking for elements that can be formatted according to the styles in the current template. It applies the body text style to paragraphs, heading styles to titles and subtitles, and the list bullet style to lists.

When you select a template in the Style Gallery, you are choosing another set of styles that can be applied, but you are not executing AutoFormat. However, the styles in the new template will replace those with matching names in the original document template. The normal style in the new template will automatically replace the normal style, the heading 1 style will replace the heading 1 style, and so forth.

Text already formatted using a style will change to reflect the new formats. Every title you formatted with the heading 1 style, for instance, will automatically change to the new heading 1 style. If you have not yet run AutoFormat, or have not applied any styles yourself, selecting a template from the Style Gallery will only affect text using the normal style format.

The Power of Styles

Styles are often underused and misunderstood by casual Word users. It's a pity because styles offer such immense potential. The use of Wizards and AutoFormat compensates for some of this oversight because they apply styles for you automatically. But an understanding of styles can give you much more flexibility and efficiency.

Applying Built-In Styles

To take advantage of Word's styles without really worrying about templates or styles themselves, use the Style list box on the left of the formatting toolbar. Here's how:

1. Select the text you want to format using a style.

   ◆ To apply a paragraph style to a single paragraph, or a character style to one word, place the insertion point anywhere in the paragraph or word.

   ◆ To apply a style to more than a paragraph or word, select the text.

2. Pull down the Style list to display a basic set of the styles in the normal template. To display all of the styles, hold down the Shift key while you pull down the list. With the keyboard, press Ctrl+Shift+S, then press the ↓ key. (Paragraph styles will appear in boldface, character styles in normal text.)

**Note**   When you first start a document, unless you hold down the Shift key while pulling down the Style list, the list will contain only five common styles. As you apply, create, or modify other styles, they will be added to the list.

3. Click on the style you want to apply, or highlight the style and press Enter. You can scroll the list by typing the beginning characters of the style name.

You can also apply a style to text you are about to type. Select the style from the list, then type your text. To return the normal, or some other style, select it from the Style list.

In some cases, a style will remain in effect when you press Enter, and subsequent text will appear in the same format. In other cases, a style ends when you press Enter and Word reverts to the normal style.

After typing a title or subtitle in any of the nine heading styles, for example, Word automatically reverts to the normal style when you press Enter. This saves you the trouble of changing to the normal style to continue typing the text of your document.

 **T i p**

To immediately apply the same style to other text, select the text and press Ctrl+Y. To apply styles from another template, select Format ➤ Style Gallery, select the template from the list, then choose OK.

Keyboard Shortcuts

You can use the following shortcuts to apply styles with the keyboard:

STYLE	PRESS THESE KEYS
Normal	Ctrl+Shift+N
Heading 1	Alt+Ctrl+1
Heading 2	Alt+Ctrl+2
Heading 3	Alt+Ctrl+3
List	Ctrl+Shift+L

The Style Dialog Box

You can also apply a style by using the dialog box displayed in Figure 2.1. Select the text you want to format, then select Format ➤ Styles or press Ctrl+Shift+S twice. Select the style in the list box on the left, then choose Apply.

When you select a style, its definition appears in the Description box, and a sample paragraph and text appear in the preview windows. Reading the style description is a good way to learn how Word structures styles.

FIGURE 2.1

Style dialog box

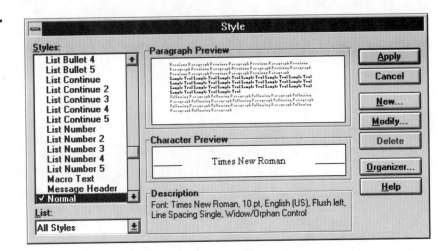

 **Tip**

Use the drop-down list to select which types of styles you want displayed. The options are All Styles, Styles in Use, and User-Defined Styles.

Removing Styles

Removing a style removes its formats from the text. There's more than one way to remove a paragraph style, and each may have a different result.

◆ If you did not perform any other action since applying the style, select Edit ➤ Undo Style. The text will appear in the format it was before you applied the style. For example, if you applied the heading 2 style to a title already formatted as a heading 1, the title will again appear with the heading 1 formats.

◆ You can also select Style from the Undo button in the toolbar. If you recently applied a number of styles, the word Style will appear several times in the list. Select the first occurrence to remove the most recently applied style, the second occurrence for the next, and so on.

◆ Select the text and apply the normal style. The text will use the normal formats no matter how it appeared before you applied the style.

◆ Delete the paragraph mark at the end of the paragraph. This will combine the text with the text that follows it, and apply its style. For example, if you remove the paragraph mark from body text followed by a heading 1 title, the text of the paragraph will be added to the title.

To remove a character style, select the text, then press Ctrl+S. You can also select the style named Default Paragraph Font, which contains the font and font size attached to the current paragraph.

Tip

If you use the Font dialog box to change fonts within a paragraph, you can quickly return to the original font by selecting this style.

S O L U T I O N S

Using the Replace Command

You can also remove a style, or assign another style to text using the Replace command dialog box. If you want to apply a different style to text, however, it must be a style already used somewhere in the document. For example, if you want to reformat all heading 1 titles to heading 2, the heading 2 style must be used in the document at least once. If it is not, place the insertion point on a blank line and apply the style. You will then be able to select it as the replacement style.

Select Edit ➤ Replace. Delete any text that may appear in the Find What text box, pull down the Format button and select Style. A list box will appear showing the names of the styles used in the document. Select the style that you want to replace or remove, then choose OK.

Next, delete any text in the Replace With box. If you want to re-move the style, without replacing it, click on the No Formatting button if any format appears under the Replace With text box, then select Replace All. If you want to replace the style with an-other, select Format ➤ Style, select the style you want to insert, then select OK. Select Replace All to make the replacements.

The Style Area

As your documents become more sophisticated, you might find your-self using a greater number of styles. If you forget which style you applied to a paragraph, place the insertion point in the paragraph and look at the Style text box in the formatting toolbar.

 **Note**   If text is formatted using both a paragraph and character style, the paragraph style will appear in the text box when the text is not selected, the character style will appear when the text is selected.

You can also display a style name area along the left side of the screen. This is a vertical pane that shows the name of the style used for each para-graph, as shown in Figure 2.2. To display the style area, select Tools ➤

FIGURE 2.2

Style area

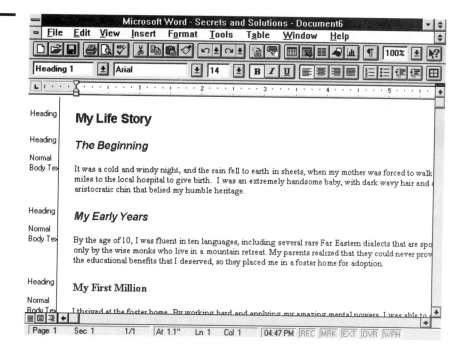

Options ➤ View, select Style Area Width, then enter a measurement greater than 0.

To adjust the size of the style area, place the mouse pointer on the line separating the area from the text. The pointer will change to a double vertical line, with arrows pointing to the left and right. Drag the split line with the mouse. (With the keyboard, enter a new measurement at the Style Area Width prompt in the Options dialog box.)

To close the style area, drag the split line off the left edge of the screen, or enter 0 at the Style Area Width prompt.

Changing Word's Styles

By changing a style, you are altering the formats that it applies to text. When you change a style, any text formatted by it in the active document will automatically reflect the new formats. You can change a default style so it will not affect the styles in other documents, or you can make the change so it is saved in the normal template. You modify a style using the Style dialog box or a technique called style by example.

 **Warning**

Changing one style may automatically affect a number of other styles. Remember, for instance, that most styles are based on the normal style. They use the attributes of the normal style, then add additional spacing or other formats. If you change the format of the normal style, every style based upon it will be changed as well.

Style by Example

The quickest way to change a style is by example. Select text that has been formatted by the style you want to change, making sure that the style name appears in the Style text box in the toolbar. Then, change the formats using the toolbar, menus, or shortcut keys.

Next, pull down the Style list in the toolbar and select the same style. The Reapply Style dialog box will appear as shown in Figure 2.3. Select OK to redefine the style.

FIGURE 2.3

Reapply Style
dialog box

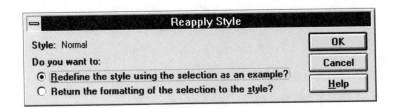

 **Note**

> If text is formatted by a character style, and you only modify a paragraph setting, the Reapply Style dialog box will not appear when you select the character style from the list. To change a character style, you must change a character format.

Using the Dialog Box

You can change any style, whether or not you've actually used it in a document, through the Style dialog box. Select Format ➤ Style. A checkmark will appear next to the character style applied to the text at the insertion point, and the applied paragraph style will be selected. Select the style that you want to modify, then click in the Modify button to display the Modify Style dialog box, shown in Figure 2.4.

FIGURE 2.4

Modify Style dialog box

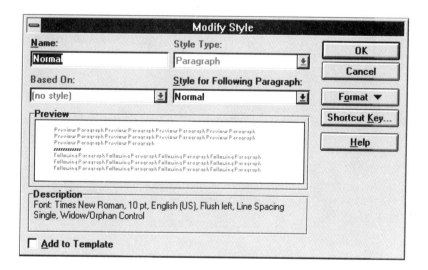

S E C R E T S

Assigning a Shortcut Key

By assigning a shortcut key to a style, you can apply the style without moving your hands from the keyboard. This is particularly useful if you are a touch typist and need to enter a great deal of text as quickly as possible.

To assign a shortcut key combination to a style, select the style in the Style dialog box, click on Modify, then click on Shortcut Key. Click on the Keyboard tab, if it is not already selected, to display the dialog box shown here.

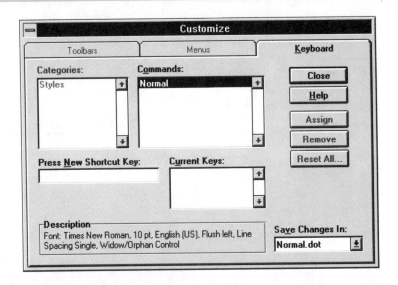

Select the Press New Shortcut Key text box. Press the key combination that you want to assign to the style. Click on the Assign button, then close the dialog box. Select OK to close the Modify Style dialog box.

You can press any combination of the Ctrl, Shift, and Alt keys along with one letter or number. The only combination not allowed is the Shift key by itself with a letter or number—these are reserved for typing punctuation marks and uppercase letters.

The combination appears in the text box, such as Ctrl+Shift+J. Word displays a message under the text box reporting the current function assigned to that keystroke, such as:

```
Currently Assigned To:
Bold
```

If you continue to assign the keystroke to the style, you will not be able to perform the built-in function with that key combination.

 **Note**   You cannot modify the style named Default Paragraph Font. To change the default font, modify the normal style. Also, you cannot change the name of a built-in style. If you enter a new name in the Name text box, it will be added to the end of the default name.

Pull down the Format list and select the type of format you want to modify. The options are Font, Paragraph, Tabs, Border, Language, Frame, and Numbering. Change the settings in the dialog box that appears, then select OK to return to the Modify Style box. Repeat the process until you change or add all of the formats desired, select OK to return to the Style dialog box, then select Close.

 **Note**   Most of the other options in the Modify Style dialog box will be discussed in the section on Creating Custom Styles later in this chapter.

Changing the Normal Template

Modifying a style only changes the style in the current document. The modified style will not affect new or any other existing documents. If you want to use your modified style globally—that is, apply it to other documents as well—you have to save the changes in the template.

Do this by selecting the Add to Template checkbox in the Modify Style dialog box. When you select OK to exit the dialog box, Word adds the changed definition to the template.

If you changed the style by example (as described earlier in this chapter), select Format ➤ Styles, select the style from the list, then select Modify to display the Modify Style dialog box.

Applying Modified Styles

The modified styles will be available with every new document. However, they will not automatically be applied when you open an existing document. To apply the styles, open the document, select File ➤ Templates, click on Automatically Update Document Styles, then select OK.

Saving Modified Templates

Word doesn't actually save the modified template on the disk until you exit Word, or until it performs an automatic save operation. Unlike previous versions of Word for Windows, when you exit Word, no dialog box will appear asking if you want to save the template. It is saved automatically.

Restoring Default Values

If you make a number of changes to the normal template, then want to restore all of the original default values, delete the file NORMAL.DOT in the template directory. Word will remake the template using the factory default values the next time you start the program.

Creating Custom Styles

You may decide not to modify the built-in styles but to create your own. You can use your own custom styles for special documents, and still rely on the default formats for standard documents.

You create your own styles in much the same way as you modify an existing style, using the Style menu or by example.

Style by Example

To create a style by example, type and format a paragraph using the settings you want to record in the style. Select the paragraph, click in the Style box in the toolbar, type a name for the style, then press Enter.

 **N o t e**
When you click in the Style list box, or press Ctrl+Shift+S, the style name already there will become selected. Typing the new name automatically deletes the selected text, but it does not delete the style.

The paragraph formats of the text will be saved in the style. The font, font size, and other character attributes of the first selected character will also be added to the style. For example, if you only select an italic word in a paragraph of otherwise regular text, the italic attribute will be added to the style. Once you press Enter after naming the style, the entire paragraph will appear in italic.

 **Note**
Creating a style by example does not save it in the template. You must select the style and choose the Add to Template box.

After you create a style by example, you can assign it a shortcut key, add it to the template, or modify the style as explained previously.

 **Note**
You cannot create a character style by example. To create a character style, you must use the Style menu command.

Using the Dialog Box

You can create both paragraph and character styles using the Style menu command. Select Format ➤ Style ➤ New to display the New Style dialog box, which has the same options as the Modify Style dialog box.

◆ **Name:** lets you type a style name. Style names are case-sensitive, so HEADLINE, Headline, and headline will be considered three different styles. The name can contain up to 253 characters, letters or punctuation marks—except backslash (\), opening and closing braces ({}), and the semicolon (;).

◆ **Style Type:** lets you select either Paragraph or Character. If you select Character, you can only include font and language formats.

◆ **Based On:** lets you select a style that you want to use as the basis for your style. For example, suppose you want to create a heading style that looks just like heading 1 but centered on the screen. Selecting the heading 1 style as the base will begin the definition of your own style as Header 1 +. You can then complete your style by selecting centered alignment from the Paragraph dialog box.

◆ **Style for Following Paragraph:** lets you select a style to take effect when you press Enter after typing text in your new style. By default, the option will contain the same name as your new style.

◆ **Format:** lets you select the formats you want applied with the style. Pull down the list, choose the classification of format, select options from the dialog box that appears, then select OK.

◆ **Shortcut Key:** lets you assign a key combination to the style.

◆**Add to Template:** lets you save your style with the template for use with other documents

S E C R E T S

Style Tips and Tricks

When you create and apply character styles, you have to be aware of the interaction of some format options. In most cases, formats that you apply as part of a style are added to other formats. If you apply an underline style to characters that are already bold, the text will be both bold and underlined.

Remember that toolbar buttons such as bold, underline, and italic act as toggles. If you select bold text and click the bold button, the bold attribute will be removed. The same will occur if you apply a bold character style to text you've already bold-faced. When you apply the style, the bold attribute will actually be toggled off.

Styles Step-by-Step

Now, let's practice creating and using styles. The following steps show you how to design styles for titles and subtitles:

1. Select Format ➤ Style ➤ New.

2. Type Main Title as the style name.

3. Pull down the Style for Following Paragraph list, scroll the list, and select Normal.

4. Select Format ➤ Font.

5. Choose the Arial font in 18 point bold, then select OK.

6. Select Format ➤ Paragraph.

7. In the After text box in the Spacing section, enter 18 pt.

8. Select Alignment ➤ Centered, then select OK.

9. Select Shortcut Key, then press Alt+T.

10. Click on Assign, then Close.

11. Click on OK to return to the Style dialog box. Figure 2.5 shows the complete description of the new style.

12. Select New, and type **Subhead** as the style name.

13. Pull down the Style for Following Paragraph list, scroll the list and select Normal.

14. Select Format ➤ Font.

15. Choose the Arial font in 14 point italic, then select OK.

16. Select Format ➤ Paragraph.

17. In the Before text box in the Spacing section, enter 12 pt.

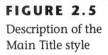

FIGURE 2.5

Description of the Main Title style

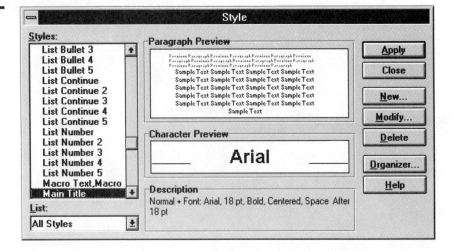

18. In the After text box, enter 6 pt, then select OK.

19. Select Shortcut Key, then press Alt+S.

20. Click on Assign, then Close.

21. Click on OK, then Close to return to the document window.

Automatic Reformatting

Now, let's use the styles, then see how Word automatically reformats text when you change a style.

1. Press Alt+T, then type **Last Will and Testament.**

2. Press Enter. The style will be turned off and the normal style applied to the new text.

3. Type the following sentence, then press Enter twice.

```
Being of sound mind and body, I hereby make this my Last Will
and Testament, and revoke any and all prior Wills and/or
Codicils.
```

4. To insert the subheading, press Alt+S.

5. Type **Bequeaths,** then press Enter twice.

6. Type the following sentence, then press Enter twice.

```
I give and bequeath my estate as specified below.
```

7. Press Alt+S, type **To My Beloved Spouse**, then press Enter twice.

8. Type the following sentence, then press Enter twice.

```
For the years of love and loyalty, I give and bequeath my
spouse the sum of $500.
```

9. Press Alt+S, type **To My Beloved Cat,** then press Enter twice.

10. Type the following sentence, then press Enter twice.

```
For the years of love and loyalty, I give and bequeath my cat,
Lovejoy, the remainder of my estate.
```

Modifying a Style

Now, let's modify one of the styles to see how Word reformats the text.

1. Place the insertion point in any of the subheadings.

2. Select Format ➤ Style. The style at the position of the insertion point is selected in the style list. If this were not the style you wanted to change, highlight the style before continuing.

3. Select Modify.

4. Select Format ➤ Font.

5. Choose Times New Roman in 14 point.

6. Select Underline ➤ Single, then select OK.

7. Select Format ➤ Paragraph.

8. Select Alignment ➤ Centered, then select OK.

9. Select OK, then Close to return to the document window.

The subheadings automatically change to reflect the new formats in the applied style.

Working with Templates

When you are preparing to do a job, you gather all the tools, equipment, and supplies you'll need before you begin. A template does just that. It contains all the styles, text, AutoText entries, toolbars, menus, and macros required for a specific type of document.

 **Tip**   By adding text to a template, you can avoid typing repetitive boilerplate text that appears in every copy of a certain type of document. For example, you should create a template that contains your letterhead. Then, just use the template when you want to send a letter.

When you save the document that uses the template, the Save As dialog box will appear so you can save the document with a new name. This way, you cannot accidentally overwrite the template with the completed document.

How you use a template, however, depends on which of its resources are available to you. For example, you can use a template so only its styles can be accessed, but not any text or other elements. In fact, you are doing just that when you select a template from the Style Gallery. You are applying the styles in the template but none of its other elements.

Starting a Document

When you want to use every element in a template, you use the template as the base for a new document. Select File ➤ New to display the Template dialog box, select the template you want to use as the basis for the document, then select OK.

 **Tip**

> Use a Wizard to select a template and design a document interactively. Use the Style Gallery to preview the styles of a template before you use it. See Chapters 1 and 14 for more information.

Any text in the template will appear on screen, as well as any custom menus or toolbars. Use the styles, AutoText, and other resources of the template to complete the document.

Attaching a Template

Once you start a document, it is not too late to use the resources of another template. You can make the styles, macros, AutoText entries, custom menus, and other command entries of another template available by attaching a template to an existing document.

To attach a template, select File ➤ Templates to see the Templates and Add-Ins dialog box shown in Figure 2.6. Click on Attach, select the template from the list box that appears, then select OK to return to the dialog box.

Any macros and AutoText entries in the original template that have the same name as those in the attached template, will be replaced. The styles in the attached template, however, will not automatically replace like-named ones in the original, nor will they be available for selection in the Styles dialog box.

To make the styles available, and reformat text already formatted with styles, select Automatically Update Document Styles in the Templates and Add-Ins dialog box. The styles in the attached template will reformat text already using similarly named styles from the original template.

Attaching a template will not change or add any text in the document. If you attach a template containing the standard letterhead, for example, the letter will not appear on screen. The attached template will also not affect the page setup, such as margins, paper size, and orientation.

FIGURE 2.6

Templates and
Add-Ins dialog box

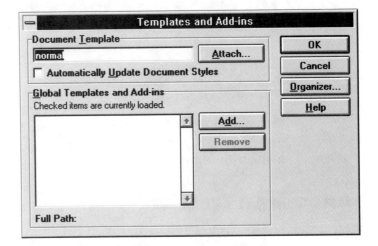

 **Tip**

If you type a letter using the normal template, and then decide you want to add text or a letterhead from another template, start a new document using the template, then copy the text of the letter onto it.

Using Global Templates

There may be times when you want to use a macro, AutoText entry, or other item in another template without its styles. By making a template global, you have access to its macros and AutoText entries without replacing those with matching names in the document's current template.

To designate a global template, select File ➤ Templates ➤ Add. Select the template from the Add Template dialog box, then click on OK. The name of the template will appear in the Global Templates and Add-ins list with a selected checkbox, as shown in Figure 2.7. This means that any macros and AutoText entries of the template will be available for use in the document. (You can add as many global templates as you need.)

FIGURE 2.7

Global Templates
and Add-Ins list

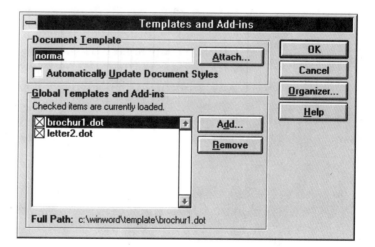

 **Note**

When you exit Word, the list of global templates will be recorded in the WINWORD6.INI file, so they will appear automatically the next time you start Word. However, the checkboxes next to the template names will be unselected. Select the checkbox to make the global template's resources available.

If you no longer need the global resources, select the template in the list box, then click on Remove.

S E C R E T S

Template Tips and Tricks

Here's a handy summary of the differences between basing a document on a template, an attached template, and a global template.

◆ When you base a document on a template using the File ➤ New command, all of its text and resources are applied.

◆ When you attach a template, you replace macros and AutoText entries with matching names, but you must select Automatically Update Document Styles to replace or access styles.

◆ When you create a global template, you add macros and AutoText entries, without replacing those of matching names. Styles are not available.

When there are matching item names, Word will use the items in an attached template, then those in the normal template, then those in any global templates in alphabetical order. Any document template in the Startup directory will become global automatically when you start Word.

Creating a Template

While the templates provided with Word are quite useful, you may want to design your own templates for documents that you produce periodically. The following sections explain the various methods you can use.

Basing a Template on a Document

Suppose you've already created a document that you'd like to use as a template for other documents. For example, perhaps you've designed a newsletter that you want to use as the basis for regular publications. Open the newsletter and delete any text that you do not want to appear with other editions. Retain common items, such as the newsletter name and masthead, special graphics, and column bylines.

Then, select File ➤ Save As, pull down the Save File as Type list and choose Document Template. Word will automatically select the Template subdirectory in the Directories list box. Type the template's name in the Filename box, then select OK.

When you are ready for the next publication, start a new document using the template as its base.

Designing a New Template

You can design a totally new template either as a document, using the method just described, or by opening a new template window. To open a template window, select File ➤ New, click on the Template button in the New section, then choose OK.

Add the elements that you want the template to contain:

◆ Formatted text that you want in every (or most) documents using the template

◆ Page size, orientation, margins, and layout selections from the Page Setup dialog box

◆ Custom styles

◆ AutoText entries

◆ Macros

◆ Custom menus, toolbars, and shortcut keys

When you are satisfied with the template, select File ➤ Save, enter the template name, then select OK.

Modifying an Existing Template

You can also create a template by modifying one of those provided by Word, or one that you've already created. Select File ➤ Open, then select the Template subdirectory. Pull down the List Files of Type list and choose Document Templates (*.dot). Double-click on the template you want to modify, or select its name and choose OK.

Modify any of the text or other elements in the template, then select File ➤ Save.

Modifying a Document's Template

You can also modify a template while you are working on a document based on that template. To change the default font or page setup, choose your options in the Font or Page Setup dialog boxes, then click on the Default button in the dialog box.

When you create a style and select the Add to Template box, the style will be saved with the template. When you create a macro, AutoText entry, menu, toolbar, or keyboard, you must specify that you want the item saved in the template, rather than the Normal template.

◆ For macros, pull down the Macros Available In list and select the name of the template.

◆ For AutoText entries, pull down the Make AutoText Entry Available To list and select the Documents Based On option followed by the name of the template.

◆ For keyboards, menus, or toolbars, pull down the Save Changes In list and select the name of your template.

When you save the document, or close it before you save it, a dialog box will appear asking if you want to save the template. Select Yes.

 **Note** To change the text in a template, you must display it with the File ➤ Open command.

Copying Template Styles

You can easily copy elements from one template to another. For example, suppose you modify several styles and save them in one of your custom templates. If you later decide that you'd like to use one of the styles in the normal template, you can copy the style from one template to the other.

Copying an item from one template to another replaces an item having the same name. You can copy macros, styles, AutoText entries, and custom toolbars. To copy an item:

1. Select File ➤ Templates ➤ Organizer to display the dialog box shown in Figure 2.8.

FIGURE 2.8
Organizer
dialog box

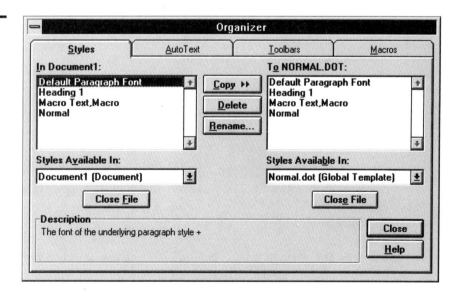

2. Select the tab for the type of item you want to copy—a macro, style, toolbar, or AutoText entry.

3. List the resources and the destination templates in the left and right list boxes.

**Note**

It doesn't really matter which template is listed in which box; you can select and move an item from either box. You can even transfer an item even if you are not currently using one of the templates. However, the process will go faster if you start by opening a document using either of the templates.

4. If the name of one of the templates is not shown above the list box on the left, pull down the Styles Available In List.

5. If the template is listed, select it. If the template is not listed, click on the Close button, and then click on the Open button that replaces it.

6. Select the template containing the item, then click on OK. (Word will display a list of the items in the template.)

7. Next, using the options in the right side of the dialog box, repeat the same procedure to list the name of the other template.

8. Select the item you want to move. (When you select an item from one of the lists, the template becomes the In template, and the other becomes the To template. The triangles in the Copy button will point in the direction of the To list, the destination template.)

9. Click on Copy to copy the item from one template to the other.

**Note**

Choose Delete to delete the selected template item. Choose Rename to change its name.

Templates Step-by-Step

Now, let's create a simple template to review these procedures. The template will include the text of your letterhead.

1. Select File ➤ New ➤ Template ➤ OK.

2. Click on the Center text button in the toolbar, or select Format ➤ Paragraph ➤ Alignment ➤ Centered ➤ OK.

3. Select Format ➤ Font.

4. Select Times New Roman 18 point bold, and then OK.

5. Type your name, address and telephone number, so it appears as a letterhead, then press Enter twice to insert a blank line.

6. Select Insert ➤ Date and Time.

7. Select the fourth data format.

8. Click on the Insert as Field checkbox, then select OK.

9. Press Enter.

10. Click on the Align Left button in the toolbar, or select Format ➤ Paragraph ➤ Alignment ➤ Left ➤ OK.

11. Select File ➤ Save, type **LHEAD** and select OK.

12. Select File ➤ Close.

 **Tip**   Inserting the date as a field ensures that when you use the template, the current date will appear, not the date the template was created.

13. To use the template, select File ➤ New.

14. Select the LHEAD template, then OK.

When your letterhead appears on screen, you can complete the text of the letter.

 **Note**

The template created in this chapter only illustrates the most fundamental uses of Word templates. As you learn how to create macros, toolbars, forms, and other elements later in this book, you'll learn how to create truly powerful templates.

Envelopes, Labels, and Small Documents

T HIS CHAPTER SHOWS YOU HOW easy Word makes it to work with envelopes and labels. In fact, you can create an envelope and print labels with a few clicks of the mouse. You can also take advantage of the labels feature to create and print small documents, such as business cards, tickets, and announcements.

 **Tip**

See Chapter 11 for more information on printing envelopes and labels using Word's merge techniques. To learn how to create brochures and folded booklets with columns, see Chapter 7.

Creating Envelopes

When you need to print an envelope, you don't have to worry about setting the page size and margins. Word has a built-in feature that formats and prints envelopes for you, even showing you how to feed the envelope into your printer.

You can create an envelope by itself, or combine it with a letter or other document in the active window. For example, if you have a laser printer, you can combine the letter and envelope in one multipage document. The letter prints using portrait orientation on letter-size paper; the envelope prints landscape. You can print the envelope using manual feed, or one of your paper trays.

S O L U T I O N S

Positioning Paper in the Printer

Certain printing techniques require you to know which side of the page your printer prints on. If you have a dot matrix printer, you always insert paper so the side to be printed on is facing the printhead. The paper position depends on how your printer handles paper.

For example, if you insert the paper in the back, behind the roller, you'd place the printing side away from you so it will face the printhead when it rolls around. If you feed continuous paper up through the bottom, the printed side should face you.

With laser printers, the position of the paper depends on the printer model and whether or not you are inserting it in a paper cassette or manually. With a printer such as the LaserJet III, for example, you feed paper in the cassette or manually with the side to be printed facing up, the top of the page in first. You feed envelopes with the top edge toward the left.

However, not all laser printers feed paper the same way. To see the recommended way for feeding envelopes with your printer, select Tools ➤ Envelopes and Labels, then click on the Envelopes Tab. You'll see a graphic similar to the one shown here.

To test your printer and learn how it feeds paper before you print, use the following steps:

1. Write the word "Cassette" on several pieces of paper, and the word "Manual" on some others. Then, write the words "Face Up" on one end of each sheet.

2. Start Word and type *Printed Side*.

3. Insert the sheet of paper marked "Cassette" in the tray so the words "Face Up" are facing up and go into the printer first.

4. Print one copy of the document. (If the printed text is at the same side and end as your written words "Face Up", you know you feed the paper with the printed side up and the top of the sheet in first.)

5. On a label (use a diskette label if you have one), write "Print side up, top in first" and stick it somewhere visible on the paper cassette.

6. If the words are not on the same side, insert another sheet of paper into the cassette so the words "Face Up" are facing down but still going into the printer first.

7. Print another copy of the document. (If the words align now, write "Print side down, top in first" on the label and stick it to the cassette.)

8. Repeat the same procedure with the sheets marked "Manual" but feed the paper into the manual input tray. When you discover how the paper feeds, write it on a label and place it near the manual input area. The cassette and manual tray may or may not feed paper the same way.

Combining Letters and Envelopes

Let's use the envelope feature to print a document.

 **Note** If you want to print an envelope by itself, without a letter, start a new document window, then select Tools ➤ Envelopes and Labels. Continue with the procedure at step 2.

1. Start Word and enter the following letter. If you are already in Word and have a document on screen, click on the New button in the tool-bar, or select File ➤ New ➤ OK.

```
January 2, 1994

Miss Daisy Renaldi
3467 West Palm Avenue
Palm Court, FL 81029

Dear Miss Renaldi:

    We have received your order and will ship the materials
by the end of this week. Thank you for your business.

Sincerely,

Alvin A. Aardvark
```

2. Select Tools ➤ Envelopes and Labels to display the Envelope dialog box, shown in Figure 3.1. Click on the Envelopes tab if the Labels box is in the foreground. (If your letter has more than one address, select the mailing address before choosing Tools ➤ Envelopes and Labels.)

The preview panel shows the default envelope size, and the feed panel illustrates the recommended position for inserting the envelope into your printer. In Figure 3.1, for example, the envelope is shown being fed face up in the center of the tray, with the top edge of the envelope toward the left.

FIGURE 3.1

Envelopes and
Labels dialog box

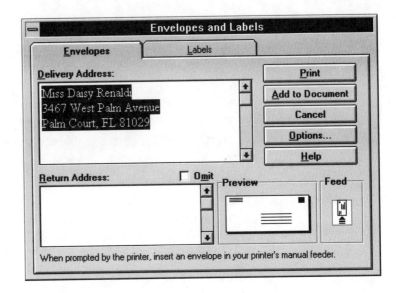

3. The mailing address should appear in the Delivery Address box. If the address is incorrect, select the box and edit the address.

 **Note**

> If you changed the return address, a dialog box will appear after step 5 asking if you want to make it the new default. Select Yes or No. If you select Yes, the address will appear again when you create an envelope. The address will also be displayed in the User Info tab when you select Tools ➤ Options. You can change the return address in the User Info tab as well.

4. To include your return address, select the Return Address box and type your address. Your name and address may already appear here. (To print an envelope with a preprinted return address, click on the Omit check box.)

5. Select Add to Document to place the envelope at the beginning of your document, separated from the text with a section break. (If you want to print the envelope by itself without the letter, select Print to print the envelope immediately.)

 **Note**

If you are in Normal view, the return and delivery addresses will appear separated by only one line break. Don't worry, the addresses will print in the proper positions—change to Page Layout to see the printed locations.

6. Select File ➤ Print ➤ OK.

7. Insert an envelope into the manual feed tray, then click on OK.

 **Tip**

You can use bookmarks to insert the delivery and return addresses automatically. Select the delivery address in the letter, and then select Edit ➤ Bookmark. Type: *EnvelopeAddress* and click on Add. Select the return address, and then select Edit ➤ Bookmark. Type: *EnvelopeReturn* and click on Add. The selected addresses will appear when you display the Envelope dialog box.

Setting Envelope Options

The settings in the Envelopes dialog box reflect the most typical business envelope format and the recommended paper feed for your printer. You can customize the settings to use a different envelope size and printed font, to print bar codes, and to adjust the position of the addresses. You can also change the envelope feed and direction.

 **Note**   Only change the direction of feed setting if your printer is not fully supported by Windows and requires a non-standard feed method.

Changing Envelope Settings

To customize the size and appearance of the envelope, click on the Preview pane in the Envelopes and Labels dialog box, or select Options, and then the Envelope Options tab to display the box shown in Figure 3.2.

FIGURE 3.2

Envelope Options
dialog box

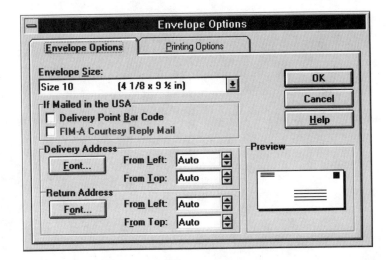

◆ Check the envelope size. If it is incorrect, pull down the Envelope Size list box and select from the defined envelope forms for your printer. You can also select Custom Size and enter a new width and height.

◆ To print a POSTNET bar code on your envelope, select the Delivery Point Bar Code box. The code will appear just above the address, using the zip code at the end of the delivery address. If you select to print a POSTNET bar code, you can also select the FIM-A Courtesy

Reply Mail option. The code identifies the front side of the envelope for automated presorting.

◆ If you want to print the delivery or return address in a font other than that used for the normal style, select the appropriate font button, choose a font from the dialog box that appears, then click on OK to return to the Envelope dialog box.

◆ To change the position of either address, set the measurement in the appropriate From Left and From Top boxes.

Setting the Envelope Feed

To change the paper source or feed settings, click on the Feed panel in the Envelopes and Labels dialog box, or select Options, and then the Printing Options tab to display the box shown in Figure 3.3.

FIGURE 3.3
Printing options

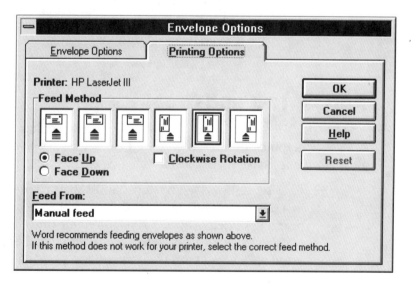

One of the Feed Method boxes will be selected, illustrating the recommended orientation and position for feeding envelopes in your printer.

◆ To change the position and direction of feed, click on one of the six feed method buttons. Each button illustrates an orientation and direction. The first three buttons represent feeding the envelope using portrait orientation, on the left, center, and right side of the tray. The last three buttons represent landscape orientation on the left, center, and right side of the tray.

◆ Click on the face down button if your printer requires you to feed envelopes face down.

◆ If you feed envelopes for landscape orientation, you can click on the Clockwise Rotation button to change the leading edge position.

◆ To change the feed tray, choose from the Feed From list.

◆ Click on Reset to return the settings to your printer's defaults.

 **Tip**

When you create a letter using the Letter Wizard, you will be given the option of printing an envelope at the same time. If you choose Yes, Word will display the Envelope dialog box for you to select options.

Adding Text and Graphics

Before printing an envelope, you can enhance it with additional text, graphics, or lines. If you want to use the design elements with every envelope, make them special AutoText entries.

Use the Tools ➤ Envelopes and Labels command to insert an envelope in a document. Add any text or graphic in the position you want it to appear on your envelopes. Select and name one element as the AutoText entry EnvelopeExtra1. Select and name the second element as EnvelopeExtra2. Word will record both the content and position of the entries.

When you create an envelope using the Tools menu, Word automatically inserts the two AutoText entries. You do not have to insert them yourself. (You'll learn more about using graphics and rotated text in Chapters 4 and 5.)

Manual Formatting

The Envelope feature should work well with all Windows-compatible printers. If you experience problems, try adjusting the position of the addresses, or the envelope feed and direction. Try various envelope sizes, or create a custom size, if needed.

If you still experience problems, you can format and print envelopes manually. The solution is to format a standard $8\frac{1}{2}$ by 11 inch document size so the address prints in the proper place when you feed an envelope into the printer.

First, decide if you need to print the address in portrait or landscape orientation. With laser printers, for example, you will usually use landscape orientation, so use the File ➤ Page Setup ➤ Paper Size command to select the landscape option for an $8\frac{1}{2}$ by 11 inch page size.

Next, set the page margins to place the address at the correct location. This will depend on the position you feed the envelope in the tray. For example, if you feed the envelope in the center of the tray, start by setting a 4.5" top margin, 0.5" right and bottom margins, and a 6" top margin.

Type an address and print it using a sheet of $8\frac{1}{2}$ by 11 inch paper in the manual tray. After it is printed, place an envelope on the sheet with the right edge of the envelope at the top of the page, and in the position where you would feed the envelope onto the printer.

 **Tip**

If you feed envelopes in the center of your tray, place the envelope centered between the right and left margins. Trace around the envelope, then measure how far the printed address is from the position it should appear. Adjust the margin settings to position the address, then print another sample.

Working with Labels

As with envelopes, Word has popular label sizes already defined for you. Definitions are supplied for both laser (individual sheet) and tractor-fed labels. They include mailing address labels as well as those for diskette labels, video cassette labels, name badges, file folders, index cards, and other stock label forms. You format labels by simply selecting one of the predefined sizes. You then type an address, or other label information, and press Tab to move to the next label.

 **Note**   When Word inserts a label design into a document, it is actually creating a table. Each label is just a table cell. Word calculates the row height and column width so the cells are the proper label size. In Chapter 7, you will learn how to use table techniques to overcome some of the limitations of the label feature, and how to customize your labels even further.

Making Name Badges

As an example, suppose you are planning a conference or convention and want to prepare name badges for those attending. We'll use the label feature to create the badges, and format the badges to automatically center the label text horizontally and vertically.

1. Click on the New button, or select File ➤ New ➤ OK.

2. Select Tools ➤ Envelopes and Labels, then click on the Labels tab to display the dialog box shown in Figure 3.4.

The Label options dialog box offers the following choices:

◆ **Full Page of the Same Label:** when selected, any text in the Address box will print on every label on the page.

◆ **Use Return Address:** prints a set of return mailing labels with your own address.

◆ **Address:** lets you type the contents of each label manually.

FIGURE 3.4

Labels options

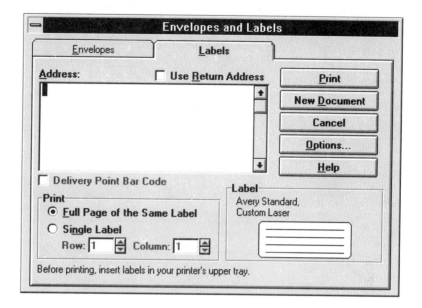

◆ **New Document:** lets you insert the blank label form into a document.

◆ **Single Label:** lets you enter the text in the Address box and print an individual label on a sheet of labels.

◆ **Row/Column:** lets you designate the specific label you want to print. When you select this option, the New Document button will become dimmed. You cannot display the label in a document window, just print it directly from the Labels dialog box.

◆ **Preview Panel/Options:** lets you select a label size.

3. Select Full Page of the Same Label, if it is not already selected.

4. Click on the preview window or select Options to display the dialog box shown in Figure 3.5.

FIGURE 3.5

Label Options
dialog box

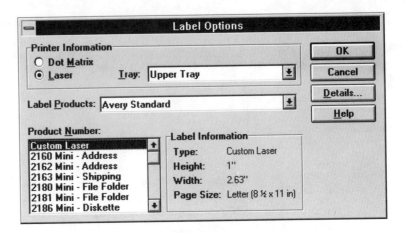

 **Note**   Word classifies labels as either Laser or Dot Matrix. Dot Matrix labels are on continuous fanfold stock; laser labels are on individual carrier sheets. You can use a laser label with any printer that accepts individual sheets. Dot Matrix labels are inserted into a document with a page break between each, so they cannot be used on laser printers—a sheet will be ejected after each label. You can list either type by selecting the radio button in the Printer Information box.

5. If the paper source is incorrect, select the proper source in the Tray list.

6. If necessary, click on the Laser button.

7. If necessary, select Avery Standard from the Label Products list. Other options are Avery Pan European and Other.

8. Scroll the Product Number list box to select the label marked Avery 5095 Name Tag. The Label Information box will describe the layout of the label sheet and the layout will be illustrated in the graphic of the page.

9. Select OK, then New Document to display the labels outlined on the screen, as in Figure 3.6.

FIGURE 3.6

Labels on the
screen

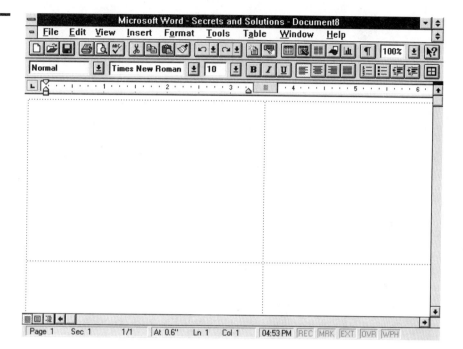

10. To format and enter the first name, select Format ➤ Font.

11. Choose the Arial font in 18 point, then click on OK.

12. Select Format ➤ Paragraph.

13. Select Alignment ➤ Centered.

14. In the Before box in the Spacing section, type 72, then select OK.

15. Type the text of the first label: **William Watson.**

16. Select the contents of the label—point to the space to the left of the name and click the mouse button, or press F8 then Ctrl+Home.

17. Select the normal style in the style list, then select OK to reassign the style.

18. Press Tab to reach the next label, then type the next name: **Madge Bolivar.** (Continuing typing labels, pressing Tab after each, until you have a label for each participant.)

19. Select File ➤ Print ➤ OK to print the sheet of labels.

 **Tip**

Using the Before spacing option places the text of the label at the correct location, but it limits the label text to one line. A more efficient method is to use form fields. With form fields, you can control the position of several lines of text and automatically move the insertion point from label to label by pressing Enter. See Chapter 15 to learn how to automate labels using form fields.

Defining Custom Label Forms

You can create a custom label form by selecting the Custom Laser or Custom Dot Matrix option from the Product Number list. However, if there is a predefined label that is close in size and specifications to the label you want to create, select it from the list instead. Then, select Details to display the dialog box like the one shown in Figure 3.7.

FIGURE 3.7

Custom Laser
Information
dialog box

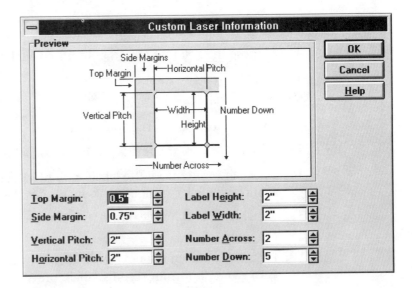

 **Note** If you selected a predefined label from the list, its name will appear in the title bar of the dialog box. When you change a setting, however, the title changes to Custom Label Information, so you cannot change the built-in label, just create a custom one.

Set the options to fully describe the labels you are using, then select OK. The preview at the top of the box illustrates each of the settings, and it will change as you enter measurements. As you set options in the box, check the effects in the preview window.

◆ **The Top Margin/Side Margin:** tell Word the exact location of the first label on the page. Enter the distance from the top of the page to the top of the first label, and from the left side of the page to the left edge of the labels.

◆ **Vertical Pitch:** sets the distance from the top of one label to the top of the next. It is the total of the label height plus the distance between labels. You cannot enter a vertical pitch if there is only one label per page. (Set the Number Down option to greater than one before changing the vertical pitch.)

◆ **Horizontal Pitch:** sets the distance between the left edge of one label and the left edge of the next. You cannot set this option if there is only one label across the page. Set Number Across to greater than one before changing the horizontal pitch.

◆ **Label Height/Label Width:** set the height and width of the individual labels.

 **Tip** To create labels without any space between then, set the vertical pitch equal to the label height, and set the horizontal pitch equal to the label width.

◆ **Number Across/Number Down:** set the number of labels across and down the page.

When you select OK, a dialog box will appear asking if you want to save the custom label form. Select Yes.

Note

Word will display a dialog box if you specified an arrangement of labels too large to fit on the page. Select OK to return to the dialog box and correct the settings.

S E C R E T S

Label Tips and Tricks

You cannot change the label sheet size in a Custom Label dialog box. Before selecting Details, check the Paper Size in the Label Information box. If the size is not the same as the paper size you want to use for the custom form, check the predefined sizes to see if there is a sheet that matches your labels. For an $8^{1}/_{2}$ by 11 inch page size, select the Avery Standard 5165 Full Sheet label or another $8^{1}/_{2}$ by 11 inch form.

None of the built-in label sizes are designed for landscape orientation. If you try to create a series of labels wider than $8^{1}/_{2}$ inches, you'll see a warning when you select OK from the Custom Information dialog box. It won't help to set the page size to landscape before you create the label, nor to change the default page layout to landscape.

Fortunately, you can still print labels in landscape by changing the page and label sizes after you have a label grid displayed on the screen. To do this, you'll need to use some of Word's table handling techniques, such as setting the height of rows and the width of columns. You'll learn more about this in Chapter 7. Just remember that there is a solution to creating landscape labels and printing labels on custom page sizes.

Word can only retain two custom label forms, one laser and one dot matrix. Once you change and save a custom laser label, for example, the previous custom laser definition is lost. However, changing the definition will not affect a document already formatted using the previous specifications. The label definition is not a style, but a description of a custom table.

To set up and use several different custom labels, create a custom label form, add it to a new document, then save the document as a template. To use the labels, begin a new document with the template as its base. The label grid will appear unchanged, even though the custom label definition may have been changed.

If you already entered text in the labels, delete the text before you save the template. Do not use the Edit ➤ Select All commands and press Del, because the label grid will be deleted as well. Instead, drag the mouse over the text and then press Del. Save the empty labels as a template.

See the section on Making Custom Folders with Templates later in this Chapter for an illustration of using two different label forms for one document.

Working with Small Documents

Instead of wasting paper printing small documents one per page, you can format them as labels. Using this method, you can print multiple copies per page, then cut them into individual pieces when you're done.

Designing Business Cards

Suppose you want to create your own business cards. A business card is 2 inches by 3.5 inches, so you can print 10 on each sheet of paper. Let's start by creating a label form for laying out 10 cards per page.

1. Select File ➤ New.

2. Select Tools ➤ Envelopes and Labels.

3. Click on the Labels tab, then select Options.

4. Scroll the list and select Custom Laser.

 **Tip** Confirm that the Paper Size is $8^1/_2$ by 11 inches. If not, scroll the Product Number list and select a label that has an $8^1/_2$ by 11 inch carrier sheet.

5. Select Details.

6. Set the top margin at .5, and set the side margin at .75.

7. Set the vertical pitch at 2, and the horizontal pitch at 3.5.

8. Set the label height at 2, and the label width at 3.5.

9. Set the number across at 2 and the number down at 5. Figure 3.8 shows the settings.

10. Select OK twice to save the custom size.

11. Select OK, then New Document to insert the label grid into a new document window.

FIGURE 3.8

Label settings for
business cards

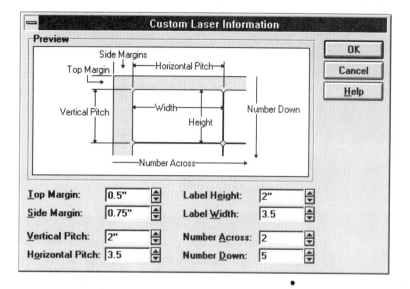

S E C R E T S

Text Tips and Tricks

In our business card example, we have created and inserted the labels. We now need to enter formatted text into the first label on the page, select and copy the text, and then paste it onto the other labels on the page. We're using this technique because we want to include two different font sizes in the text of the business card.

Could this be accomplished faster by typing the text of the label in the address box? (Any text entered in the box appears on each label of the sheet.) Unfortunately, not. You cannot select font or other format options from the Labels dialog box. The text in the address box will appear in the font of the normal style.

You could complete the label, then apply one font to all of the text by selecting Edit ➤ Select All, then choosing a font and font size. You can also change the font in the normal style and then create the label. But neither of these techniques will automatically format the labels in more than one font.

Applied character and paragraph styles are ignored when Word inserts the text into a label. In addition, if you select and copy formatted text in the window, you can insert it into the address box by pressing Ctrl+V. But again, Word inserts the text in the normal style.

To use several different fonts or sizes you'll have to select and format text manually. Copying and pasting the text from one label to the next is really no great hardship. If every label on the page contains the same information, you only need to fill one page of labels. Then, print as many pages as you want by setting the Copies option in the Print dialog box.

You can save yourself the work of copying text on to each card by using a macro (see Chapter 8). You can also include graphics and boxes as explained in Chapter 5.

Entering Text

To enter the text into the first label, make sure the insertion point is in the first label, then follow these steps:

1. Select Format ➤ Paragraph, set the Spacing Before option at 0, then select OK.

2. Click on the second line in the label, or press the down arrow, then press Enter.

 **Note**   If you just press Enter in the first line of the label, Word inserts a blank line before the label and moves the insertion point there. Placing the insertion point in the second line of the label allows you to enter another blank line by pressing Enter.

3. Click on the Center button in the toolbar, or select Alignment ➤ Centered from the Paragraph Indents and Spacing dialog box.

4. Select the Arial font at 14 point.

5. Type the following, then press Enter three times.

```
Aardvark Antiques
111 Alwood Avenue
Albany, AL 10923
```

6. Select the Arial font at 12 point.

7. Select the Italic button in the toolbar.

8. Type **If It Is Old, We Got It.**

9. Select the text of the label, then select Edit ➤ Copy.

10. Click in each of the next cards on the page (or press Tab to reach the card), then press Ctrl+V.

11. Select File ➤ Print ➤ OK to print a page of the cards.

Figure 3.9 illustrates how the cards might appear when printed. The dotted lines represent the trim lines—where you would cut the sheet to produce the individual cards.

FIGURE 3.9

Sample printout
with trim lines

Tip

To print trim lines, add dotted inside and outside border lines. See Chapter 7 to learn how to add lines to tables.

Printing Your Cards

Business cards printed on thick paper look more professional. Although most printers cannot handle card stock, you should be able to find a heavier weight paper that your printer can feed. If necessary, adjust your printer so the paper feeds along a straight path. You might want to print one camera-ready copy, then have a commercial printer duplicate it on card stock and cut the individual cards.

Creating Numbered Tickets

If you are planning a special event for which you would like numbered tickets, you can use a label form to format the tickets, and a special field code to number them consecutively. Tickets that are 2 inches by

4 inches are the same size as the Avery 5163 label. However, to precisely control the spacing of the tickets so they can be easily cut, let's create a custom label form using the Avery label as a base.

1. Starting from a blank window, select Tools ➤ Envelopes and Labels ➤ Options.

2. Select the Avery Standard label named 5163 Shipping, then select Details. (Note that the dialog box will be titled Shipping 5163 Information, but will change to Custom Label Information when you change one of the settings.)

3. Next, set the side margin to .25 and the horizontal pitch to 4. These are the only changes necessary.

4. Select OK three times, then New Document.

5. Enter the text of the first ticket.

6. Select appropriate fonts and font sizes—just make sure the text does not exceed the label size—as shown in Figure 3.10.

FIGURE 3.10
Ticket text

You Are Invited To Attend
The Annual Masked Ball
Presented By
Aardvark Computers
Sunday, June 3, 1994, 7 P.M.
345 West Franklin Street
Philadelphia, PA 19101

Ticket:

Ticket Numbering

Before you select and copy the text of the ticket, you should insert a ticket number. Using numbers helps you keep track of ticket sales and avoid counterfeiting. You can also use the numbers for door prizes, seating arrangements, and other purposes.

Note

In order to number the tickets, we'll use a special feature called a field. As you work with Word, you'll use fields more and more, especially for producing form letters and other business forms. A field is a special code that tells Word to insert certain information into a document. For example, when you select Insert ➤ Date and Time ➤ Insert as Field, the date is added as a code. When you print the document, Word inserts the date of printing, not the date that the field was actually inserted.

The field we'll use to insert the date is called SEQ, for *sequence*. The sequence acts as a counter. Each time Word locates the sequence in a document it increases the number by one. For example, we'll use a sequence called ticket. The first sequence field named ticket in the document is displayed as the number 1, the second sequence field is displayed as 2, and so on.

To insert the sequence numbering, follow these steps:

1. Place the insertion point in the first ticket where you want the number to appear.

2. Select Insert ➤ Field to display the dialog box shown in Figure 3.11.

3. Select the Field Codes box and delete the equal sign (=) that appears there.

4. Type **SEQ TICKET.** This creates a sequence field called ticket.

Note

You can use any name you want for the sequence field. Ticket simply identifies the purpose of the document. Sequence names are case sensitive.

FIGURE 3.11

Field dialog box

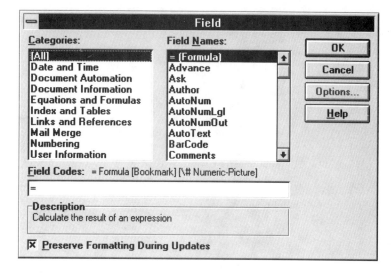

5. Press Enter. The number 1 will appear at the position of the insertion point.

6. Now, copy the entire contents of the first label to the other labels on the page. You'll notice that every ticket is numbered 1. We'll take care of that now.

7. Select Edit ➤ Select All, then press F9. Figure 3.12 shows a page of numbered tickets.

The F9 keystroke updates the contents of every field. In this case, it consecutively numbers each occurrence of the ticket field. You must have a field selected before pressing F9.

 **Tip** You can update a specific field by selecting it, then pressing F9. When you select a field, it appears reversed on a gray background instead of the black background of regular selected text. To delete the field, select it and press Del.

FIGURE 3.12

A page of
numbered tickets

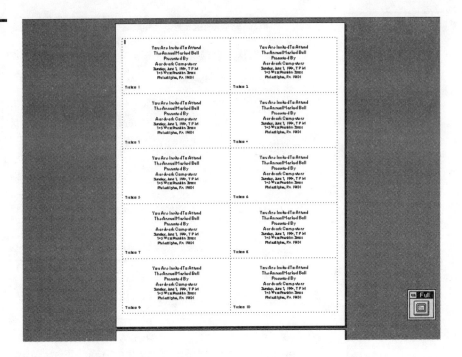

Printing Multiple Pages

If you print multiple pages of labels by setting the Copies option in the Print dialog box, Word will not increment the sequence on each page. Every page will have tickets numbered 1 through 10. Instead, you must select and copy the page as many times as needed.

Follow these steps:

1. Select Edit ➤ Select All, Edit ➤ Copy, then click the mouse to deselect the text.

2. Press Ctrl+Home to move the insertion point to the top-left corner of the first label.

3. Press Enter to insert a blank line above the label.

4. Press Ctrl+V for each additional page of tickets you want to print.

5. To have Word update the sequence fields when you print the tickets, select File ➤ Print ➤ Options.

6. Select Update Fields in the Printing Options section, then select OK twice to print the tickets. Word updates the fields, incrementing the sequence numbers and printing the pages of tickets.

S E C R E T S

Field Tips and Tricks

When you insert a field, Word displays the results of the field—the number or other value that the field represents. For instance, Word displays a number when you insert a SEQ field, or the date when you insert the date as a field.

You can also select to display the field codes themselves. Select the results of the field you want to display, or choose Edit ➤ Select All to display every field, then press Shift+F9. You'll see the actual code inserted by word. The sequence code, for example, will appear as {SEQ TICKET *MERGEFORMAT}.

Shift+F9 serves as a toggle. Select the text again and press Shift+F9 to display the results. If a field is not selected when you press F9 or Shift+F9, you'll hear Word's warning beep.

You can insert more than one sequence of consecutively numbered fields in the same document. Just use a unique name for each in the Insert Field dialog box. For example, each of the tickets shown here has two numbers, one on the stub and one on the ticket itself. The field used on the stub was named SEQ STUB; the field on the ticket is SEQ TICKET. On the first ticket, SEQ STUB and SEQ TICKET appear as the number 1. One the second ticket, they appear as the number 2, and so on.

```
                 The Masked Ball          You Are Invited To Attend
                 Aardvark                 The Annual Masked Ball
                 Computers                     Presented  By
                 Sunday                    Aardvark Computers
                 June 3, 1994           Sunday, June 3, 1994, 7 P.M.
                                           345 West Franklin Street
                                           Philadelphia, PA 19101


                 Ticket:  1        Ticket:  1
```

The tickets in our example use landscape orientation. Each ticket is actually on two labels—one for the stub and one for the ticket. You'll learn how to create this format in Chapter 7.

Formatting Place Cards

A place card can be formatted with a label form, then folded in half so it can stand on its own. A place card is actually similar to a name badge, except the label size is larger and the Spacing Before option is set to position the name on the lower half of the label.

To create place cards that are 4 inches wide and $1\frac{1}{2}$ inch high after being folded, set these label specifications:

Top Margin	1
Side Margin	.25
Vertical Pitch	3
Horizontal Pitch	4

Label Height	3
Label Width	4
Number Across	2
Number Down	3

In the Paragraph Indents and Spacing box, set the Before option at 180 points, about 2½ inches. Type each name, centered, on a separate label. After printing, cut the page on the trim lines as shown in Figure 3.13, then fold each card so it can stand on its edge, as in Figure 3.14.

FIGURE 3.13

Place cards with trim and fold marks

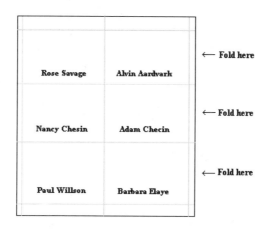

FIGURE 3.14

A finished place card

S O L U T I O N S

Laying Out Text in Two Orientations

In the labels discussed so far, all of the text is printed in the same direction. But, there are some special layouts, such as greeting cards, that require text to print in two different orientations. The trick is to use a label form that positions the text at the proper position on the page. You enter and print the inside pages, then turn the page around, and enter and print the outside pages.

To create the labels for cards, set up an $8^1/_2$ inch by 11 inch label sheet with these specifications:

Top Margin	6
Side Margin	0
Vertical Pitch	0
Horizontal Pitch	4.25
Label Height	5
Label Width	4.25
Number Across	2
Number Down	1

In the label on the left, type the text you want to appear on the back cover. In the label on the right, type the text for the front cover. Print one or more copies of the page, depending on the number of greeting cards you want to mail. The 6 inch top margin will cause the text to print on the bottom section of the page, starting $^1/_2$ inch below the fold line.

Using the same page of labels, type the text for the inside left page in the left label, and the inside right page in the right label. Remove the printed pages and feed them into the printer so the blank section of the page will be printed. Do not turn the pages over but turn them so the opposite edge enters the printer first. If your printer accepts the top of the sheet in first, insert the printed side in first. The inside pages will print on the bottom blank section of the sheet.

Here's an example of a printed, unfolded card. Fold the card into quarters, with the blank side facing in.

Inside Right	Inside Left
Back Cover	Front Cover

Making Custom Folders with Templates

The greeting card uses one custom label for both the inside and outside pages. The top margin setting is the same for both sides. Other formats, however, require different settings for the two sides of the page, so a single custom label form cannot be used for both.

For example, look at the ticket folder shown in Figure 3.15. A small section of the page is folded up from the bottom, then the page is folded in half like a booklet. When opened, the small folded section serves as a pocket to hold a ticket or other material.

FIGURE 3.15

Ticket folder

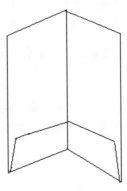

You can format text or graphics to print on the front and back covers, as well as on the flap of the pockets on the inside. As with a greeting card, all of the text is printed on the same side of the sheet, but it is rotated on one end so it appears in the correct position when the page is folded.

You need two label designs for this format—one for the cover and one for the flap. Since you can only have one custom form at a time, design the label for the outside cover, insert it into a blank document, then save the document as a template. After you change the label form for the inside pages, you can still type and print the cover by starting a new document using the cover template.

 **Warning**   If you do not save a document or template with the inserted label grid lines, you'd have to recreate the custom form if you designed another in the interim.

To create a packet that can hold a ticket up to 4 inches by 10 inches, start with a $8\frac{1}{2}$ inch by 11 inch label sheet with these specifications for the cover:

Top Margin	.25
Side Margin	.25
Vertical Pitch	0
Horizontal Pitch	4
Label Height	8.25
Label Width	4
Number Across	2
Number Down	1

Select New Document to insert the labels on a page. Next, select File ➤ Save As, select Document Template from the Save File As Type list, then enter the name COVER. Close the window and start a new document.

Next, create the labels for the flap using these specifications:

Top Margin	9
Side Margin	.25
Vertical Pitch	0
Horizontal Pitch	4
Label Height	2
Label Width	4
Number Across	2
Number Down	1

Select New Document to insert the labels on a page, then save the document as the template named FLAP.

Now, start a new document using the template COVER. The label grid lines will appear. Type the text of the back cover in the first label on the page, the text of the front cover on the second, then print the document.

Next, start a new document using the template FLAP. Type the text of the left-hand flap in the first label on the page, the text of the right-hand cover on the second. Reinsert the printed cover, rotated end to end so the small blank section will be printed, then print the page. Finally, fold the flaps in first, then fold the page in half.

PART
two

The Published Word

Lines, Borders, and WordArt

WITH WORD'S DESKTOP PUBLISHING FEATURES, you can create sophisticated, professional-looking documents of all types. In later chapters, you will learn how to work with pictures, graphics, equations, and columns. In this chapter, you will learn how to quickly improve the visual appearance of your documents with lines, boxes, and borders. You will also learn how to create special effects with TrueType fonts.

Lines and Boxes

In Word, lines and boxes around text are paragraph oriented. This means you should place the insertion point in the paragraph you want to highlight with a line or a box, or select multiple paragraphs.

You add lines, boxes, and shading using either the Borders toolbar or the Borders and Shading dialog box. To display the Borders toolbar, use either of these techniques:

◆ Select View ➤ Toolbars ➤ Borders ➤ OK

◆ Point to one of the displayed toolbars, click the right mouse button, then select Borders from the shortcut menu that appears

Use the list box on the left of the toolbar to select a line type. The options are shown in Figure 4.1. You can select the line style before you apply it to text, and you can change the style after you've added a line to a document.

FIGURE 4.1

Line styles

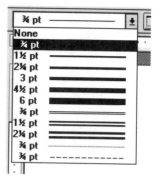

The buttons following the list box determine the position of the line in relation to the paragraph, as shown in Table 4.1.

TABLE 4.1: Borders toolbar buttons

BUTTON	NAME	FUNCTION
	Top	inserts a line above the paragraph
	Bottom	inserts a line below the paragraph
	Left	inserts a line along the left margin
	Right	inserts a line along the right margin
	Inside	inserts lines between selected paragraphs
	Outside	surrounds the text in a box
	No	removes all of the lines

Adding Horizontal and Vertical Lines

Use the first five buttons in the toolbar to insert horizontal and vertical lines around text. The buttons are toggles—select a button once to insert the line, a second time to remove the line. For example, to place a horizontal line above a paragraph, place the insertion point anywhere in the paragraph, then click on the Top Border button. The button will appear pressed down when the insertion point is in the paragraph. To remove the line, click on the button again.

Horizontal lines extend from the left to the right indentation positions. With the default paragraph format, the line will extend from margin to margin, even if the paragraph contains a single word centered on the page. To create a narrower line, drag the indentation markers on the ruler, or change the indents in the Paragraph Indents and Spacing dialog box.

Vertical lines appear down the left or right side of the text at the indentation position.

 **Tip**

If you place a left border next to text that has paragraphs of different indentations, the lines follow the contour. Instead of one continuous vertical line, separate lines appear at each indentation level. To place a solid line down the left margin, or at the one indentation level, use a single cell table, as explained in Chapter 7.

To change the type of line applied to text, place the insertion point in the text, then choose a new line style from the list box. The buttons that were pressed down, indicating the positions of any applied lines,will now appear unpressed. Click on the border buttons to apply the newly selected line style.

Surrounding Text in a Box

To enclose a paragraph in a box, place the insertion point anywhere in the paragraph, then click the Outside Border button. To remove the box, click on the No Border button.

To surround several paragraphs in a single box, select the paragraphs and then click on the Outside Border button. Click on the Inside Border button if you also want to add lines between paragraphs. The Inside Border button is also a toggle, so you can click it again to remove the lines.

 **Note**

When you click on the Outside Border button, it will not appear pressed down. Instead, the four individual line buttons in the toolbar will appear to be pressed down. You can remove a specific line by clicking on one of the buttons. Clicking on the outside border button, then the top line button, for example, will leave lines on the sides and below the text.

The height of the box will adjust automatically as you insert and delete text within it. However, the only way to change the width of the box is to change the left and right indentations. As with lines, the box extends from the indentation positions, no matter how few words are actually on the line.

When you apply a box, the left border will also follow the contour of the indentations. When paragraphs have several indentation levels, the left border will not appear as a continuous vertical line. To create a box around text of various indentations, use a single cell table, as explained in Chapter 7.

Using Background Patterns

The list box on the right of the toolbar sets a background fill pattern. The options are shown in Figure 4.2. Note that the choices include a number of gray shades as well as lines and other patterns. Fill shades 80%, 90%, and 100% will result in reverse text, with white characters on a dark background. If you want reverse characters with other fill patterns, select the text, then select Format ➤ Font ➤ Color ➤ White.

FIGURE 4.2

Fill shades and patterns

 **Note**   When you apply most of the pattern backgrounds, such as horizontal and vertical lines, the text may be difficult to read. The light horizontal, and up and down vertical patterns cause less distraction, but can still make reading difficult.

You can use a background pattern whether or not you surround the text in a box. Without lines, the pattern will create a rectangular area the same size as an outside border, but without any lines at the edge of the fill.

To remove a background pattern, select Clear from the list.

SOLUTIONS

Looking at Lines, Boxes, and Patterns

Here are some examples of how to apply lines, boxes, and patterns. The headline across the top of the page has a 30% fill without any border lines. The line beneath the headline has a 6 point bottom border applied to a blank paragraph.

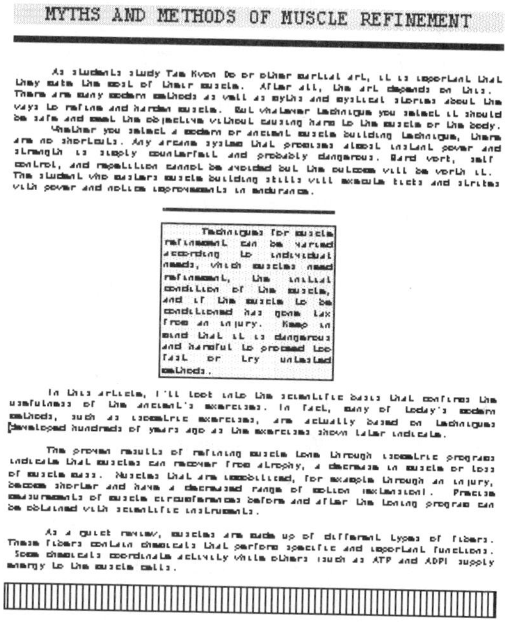

MYTHS AND METHODS OF MUSCLE REFINEMENT

As students study Tae Kwon Do or other martial art, it is important that they make the most of their muscle. After all, the art depends on this. There are many modern methods as well as myths and mystical stories about the ways to refine and harden muscle. But whatever technique you select it should be safe and meet the objective without causing harm to the muscle or the body.

Whether you select a modern or ancient muscle building technique, there are no shortcuts. Any arcane system that promises almost instant power and strength is simply counterfeit and probably dangerous. Hard work, self control, and repetition cannot be avoided but the outcome will be worth it. The student who masters muscle building skills will execute kicks and strikes with power and notice improvements in endurance.

Techniques for muscle refinement can be varied according to individual needs, which muscles need refinement, the initial condition of the muscle, and if the muscle to be conditioned has gone lax from an injury. Keep in mind that it is dangerous and harmful to proceed too fast or try untested methods.

In this article, I'll look into the scientific basis that confirms the usefulness of the ancient's exercises. In fact, many of today's modern methods, such as isometric exercises, are actually based on techniques developed hundreds of years ago as the exercises shown later indicate.

The proven results of refining muscle tone through isometric programs indicate that muscles can recover from atrophy, a decrease in muscle or loss of muscle mass. Muscles that are immobilized, for example through an injury, become shorter and have a decreased range of motion (extension). Precise measurements of muscle circumferences before and after the toning program can be obtained with scientific instruments.

As a quick review, muscles are made up of different types of fibers. These fibers contain chemicals that perform specific and important functions. Some chemicals coordinate activity while others (such as ATP and ADP) supply energy to the muscle cells.

The line and filled box in the center of the page were positioned by changing the left and right indentations. The box at the bottom of the page was created by selecting two blank lines, clicking the Outside Border button, then applying a light vertical pattern.

Placing Lines in Headers and Footers

You can place a line in a header or footer to create a visual element or to separate it from the text on the page. Select View ➤ Header and Footer. In the header panel, click on the Bottom Border button to place a horizontal line below the header text. In the footer panel, click on the Top Border button for a line above the footer text.

By adjusting margins and the paragraph settings of the header, you can place a vertical line or an entire border on every page of the document.

 **Note**

> In this chapter, you will learn how to use a header to create lines down and borders around a page. You'll learn how to create the same effects using drawing tools in Chapter 5.

Creating a Vertical Line

To place a vertical line down the left side of the page:

1. Select File ➤ Page Setup ➤ Margins.

2. Set the top margin at –.5 and the bottom margin at 0.8. (The negative top margin will allow text to appear on the same page as an expanded header.)

3. Set the From Edge setting for the Footer to 0, and then select OK in the Page Setup dialog box.

4. Select View ➤ Header and Footer. (You'll notice that the header window, usually only three lines high, now extends all the way to the footer at the bottom of the page.)

5. Select Format ➤ Paragraph.

6. Set the left indent at –.5, then set the Line Spacing at Exactly and 720 points. (The negative indent places the line in the left margin

area so it does not interfere with the text on the page. The line spacing setting creates a single 10-inch paragraph.)

7. Display the Borders toolbar and click on the Left Border button.

Putting a Border around Every Page

Use the following techniques to place a border around every page:

1. Set the top margin at –.75, the bottom margin at 0.8, and the From Edge footer setting at 0.

2. In the header, set the left and right indents at –.5, and the Line Spacing at Exactly and 696 points.

3. Click on the Outside Border button in the Borders toolbar.

4. Select a light fill pattern if desired.

 **Note**

You may have to experiment with the margin and spacing settings to create a pleasant-looking box. Your printer and fonts may effect the appearance of the text in relation to the box lines.

S O L U T I O N S

Applying a Vertical Text Banner

You can also use the header to display a vertical text banner down the side of every page. To create this effect, set the top margin to –1, then select View ➤ Header and Footer. Select Format ➤ Paragraph and set a negative left indentation at least the same size as the font you want to use.

For example, if you will be using a 24 point font, set the left indent at least –24 pt. Then, select the font and font size, and type the text of the banner, one letter on each line, pressing Enter after each.

The notation pt following a number indicates that the measurement is given in points. There are about 72 points to an inch. (If you want to enclose the banner in a box, use a frame as explained later in this chapter.)

Borders and Shading

You can create borders and shaded rectangles using the Format menu. To apply a line or border, select Format ➤ Borders and Shading, then click on the Borders tab to display the dialog box shown in Figure 4.3.

FIGURE 4.3

Paragraph Borders
and Shading
dialog box

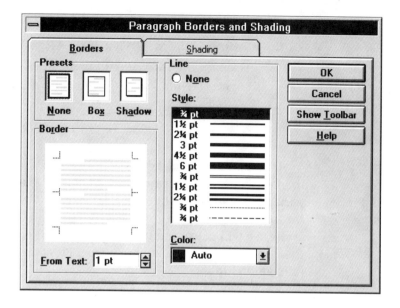

Using Preset Borders

Use the preset boxes to quickly insert a box or shadow box, or select None to remove all lines. A shadow box has thicker lines on the bottom and right to give the impression of a shadow. In the Line section, select the line thickness or style. Select None to remove the lines.

Notice the illustration of a page of text in the Border section of the dialog box. The horizontal lines in the illustration represent the paragraph at the insertion point, or the selected paragraphs. Click on the location where you want to add or delete a line.

For example, to insert a line at the top of the paragraph, click on the top of the text in the diagram. To insert or remove a line along the left of the text, click on the left of the text in the diagram.

Note You cannot insert a line if the None button is chosen in the Line section. Clicking on the None preset will also select the None line button. If the button is selected, choose a line type from the Style list first.

If you are using the keyboard, press Alt+R to choose the Border option, then press any of the arrow keys. As you press a key, small triangles will alternately appear on either side of the lines. When the triangles appear at the line you want to insert, press the spacebar. At one point, pressing an arrow key will place triangles around all of the outside border lines, and then on the inside border line as well. Press the spacebar to add all of the lines at one time.

The From Text Setting

You use the From Text setting in the dialog box to determine the distance of the line from the text. By default, lines will appear 1 point away from text. Increase the setting for extra space, or lower it to 0 for a tighter fit. You can increase the setting up to 31 points.

Tip Increasing the From Text setting adds space in all four sides of the text, extending the box into the margin areas, if necessary.

The From Text setting also affects the appearance of the background fill pattern. A fill pattern surrounds the text up to any line around it. Where there is no border line, the pattern only extends the default 1 point distance, regardless of the From Text setting.

For example, if you set From Text to 6 points, then apply only a left border line and fill pattern, the pattern will extend 6 points to the left line, but only 1 point on the top, right, and bottom. If you remove the line on the left, the pattern will snap back to the 1 point distance.

Tip   If you want to extend the pattern but not display a line, apply the lines but select the color White from the Color list in the Border dialog box. The line is technically in place, but just cannot be seen or printed.

S O L U T I O N S

Aligning Borders with Margins

The lines on the left and right actually extend into the margin areas. You may want to align the lines precisely with the margin, or with other different thickness lines in a consecutive paragraph.

For example, if you apply a ¾ point box to one paragraph, and a 6 point box to another, the sides of the two boxes will not align evenly because the lines extend further into the margin.

To align the border with the margins, adjust the left indentation of the paragraph to accommodate the thickness of the line and the space between the line and the text. For example, if you select a 6 point line and use the default 1 point spacing, the line extends 7 points into the margins. By changing the left and right indents of the paragraph to 7 points, the text shifts over so the edge of the line is at the margin, not beyond it.

Be sure to type 7 pt in the indent text box. Word will convert the setting to its approximate decimal equivalent 0.1. If you type 7, Word assumes you mean 7 inches.

The Shading Dialog Box

To set the background pattern, select the Shading tab in the Paragraph Borders and Shading dialog box. The dialog box is shown in Figure 4.4.

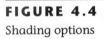
FIGURE 4.4
Shading options

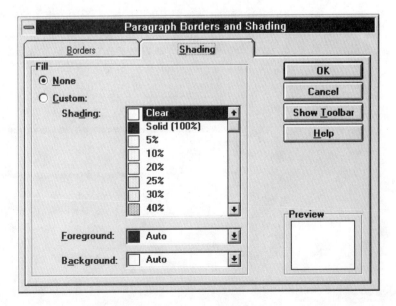

Select a pattern from the list, and if desired, change the foreground and background colors. A sample showing your custom style will appear in the preview panel.

Working with Frames

A border is an actual line around text, just as if you draw a border on a sheet of paper. A frame is a conceptual line. When you enclose text in a frame, you make the text it surrounds an independent object, separate from other paragraphs on the page.

As an object, you can move and position the frame, and thus the text it encloses, anywhere in the page, just as you can move a chess piece around the chess board. You can also change the size of the frame and select to have other text flow around it.

Selecting Text

Select the text you want to include in a frame, then select Insert ➤ Frame. If you are in Normal view, you'll see a dialog box asking if you want to change into Page Layout View. Select Yes. If you select No to remain in Normal view, Word will insert a border line around the text, but you will not see or be able to work with the frame. You must be in Page Layout view to work with frames.

 **N o t e**   If you select less than an entire paragraph, Word separates the text from the paragraph in which it was located and makes it a separate paragraph.

Word displays the frame as a crosshatched box around the selected text, and inserts a single line border. Around the frame are eight sizing handles, indicating that the frame is selected and ready to be manipulated, as in Figure 4.5.

FIGURE 4.5

Framed text

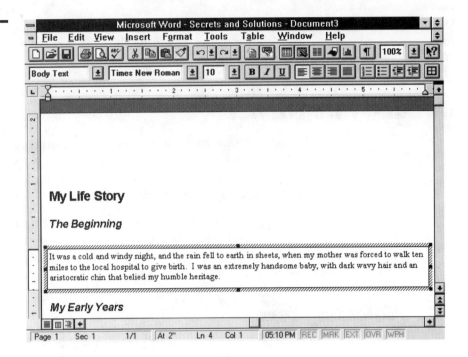

If you selected a paragraph which has lines ended by wordwrap, the frame extends from the left and right margins, or the width of the column if you are using a column layout, even if the text is indented. If the text is indented, however, the single-line border will only extend from the indentations, not the full width of the frame.

If you selected a single sentence that ends in a carriage return, such as a title, the frame extends just to the end of the text. Text of the paragraph following the frame will shift up to start on the same line to the right of the frame, as in Figure 4.6.

Editing Framed Text

When the frame is displayed on the screen, click inside the frame to edit the text. The handles will disappear, but the frame will still be displayed. The height of the frame will increase to accommodate your text. Click outside the frame to remove it from the display, but not remove the border line or the frame itself.

FIGURE 4.6

Framed and
shifted following
text

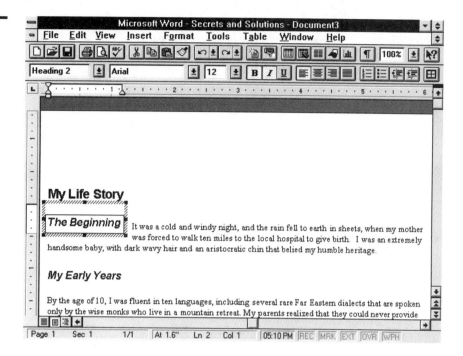

Customizing a Frame

You can work with a frame in several ways, but you must select it first. When the frame is not displayed, you select it in two stages. (With the keyboard, use the arrow keys to move the insertion point to the frame.)

Click on the framed text to display the cross-hatched frame border. This places the insertion point within the frame so you can edit or insert text. You can also change the border style, remove the lines altogether, or select a fill pattern. Border lines and shading will follow the indentations of the text, not the frame boundaries.

 **N o t e** **Removing the border line by clicking on the No Border button does not remove the frame, just the printable line around the framed text.**

To change the size or position of the frame, point to a border line or crosshatch frame line so the mouse pointer appears with a four-directional arrow, then click the mouse to display the handles. To change the position of the frame, drag the four-directional mouse pointer to the desired location. To change the size of a box, drag any of its eight handles as follows:

◆ Drag the center handle on the left or right border to change the width of the frame

◆ Drag the center handle on the top or bottom border to change the height of the frame

◆ Drag a corner handle to change the width and height

Formatting Framed Text

You can format text within a frame just as any other text in a document. Selecting paragraph alignment effects the position of the text in the frame, not in relation to the page. For example, selecting Centered alignment centers the text within the frame, it does not center the frame on the page.

Removing a Frame

To remove the frame, select it in Page Layout view, then select Format ➤ Frame ➤ Remove Frame. If you select a frame and then press Del, the frame and its contents will be deleted.

Wrapping Text around a Frame

When a frame does not extend the full width of the margins, Word wraps other text around the frame, as in Figure 4.7. The text will remain .13 inches from the edges of the frame. Think of this as water flowing around a large rock in a river. If you move the rock, the water will flow around it at another location in the river. The same applies to frames. If you move the frame, the surrounding text will also adjust to flow around it.

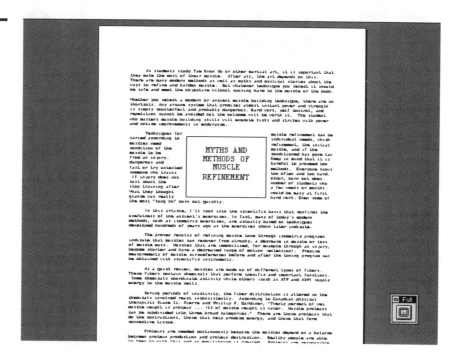

FIGURE 4.7

Text wrapped
around a frame

You will only see how text wraps around the frame in Page Layout and Print Preview modes. In Normal view, the frame will appear in its own paragraph.

Using Frames as Placeholders

If you are laying out a page for publication, you may want to reserve space for a picture or other element that will be added later on. You can do this by drawing an empty frame and positioning it in the space you want to reserve, as shown in Figure 4.8.

Select Insert ➤ Frame without selecting any text. Drag the mouse to draw a box the size of the desired frame, then release the mouse button. Then, change the size and position of the frame to reserve the space, or enter any desired text in the frame. The height of the frame will increase to accommodate your text, but not the width.

FIGURE 4.8

A shaded frame as
a placeholder

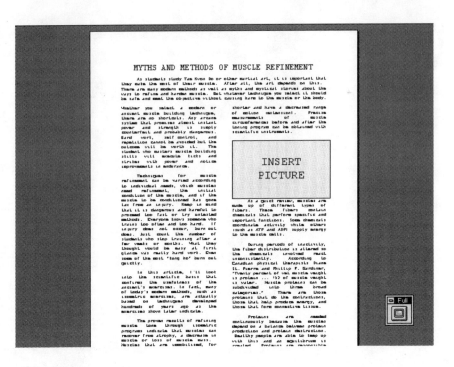

The Frame Dialog Box

If you have a mouse, it is easy to adjust the size and position of the frame by dragging. However, unless you have a very steady hand and sharp eye, it may be difficult to place the frame in an exact position, such as dead-center on the page, or make it a specific size.

For an exact size and location, and to control other aspects of a selected frame, use the Frame dialog box shown in Figure 4.9. Select the frame you want to customize, then select Format ➤ Frame.

 **Tip** You can also display the Frame dialog box by clicking the right mouse button on the frame border, then selecting Format Frame from the shortcut menu that appears. Select Borders and Shading from the shortcut menu to add a border or fill pattern.

FIGURE 4.9

Frame dialog box

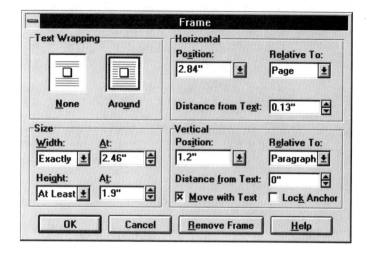

◆ **Text Wrapping:** determines how text flows around a frame. Select None to place the frame on its own line; select Around to flow text around the sides of the frame. Text will flow on the left or right as long as there is at least one inch between the frame and the margin.

◆ **Size:** sets the width and height of the frame. The text boxes will show the current size of the frame. Change the settings to an exact size, or select Auto to make the frame just large enough for its contents.

◆ **Horizontal:** determines the position of the frame in relation to the edge of the paper, margin, or column, as selected in the Relative To list. You can enter an exact position or select from Left, Right, Center, Inside, or Outside. Selecting Center relative to the page, for instance, positions the frame in the exact center of the page. You can also set the distance of the frame from wrapped text on the left and right.

◆ **Vertical:** determines the position of the frame in relation to the top or bottom edge of the page, margin, or the paragraph. You can enter an exact position, or select Top, Bottom, or Center relative to the margin or page. You can also enter a distance from the text above and below.

Anchoring Frames

A frame is anchored to its nearest paragraph. Locking an anchor to a paragraph forces Word to print the frame on the same page as the paragraph. If editing or formatting moves the paragraph to another page, the frame will move along with it.

To display the anchor, as shown in Figure 4.10, click on the ¶ button in the toolbar then select the frame. To lock the anchor, select Edit ➤ Frame ➤ Lock Anchor. The anchor icon will now include a small icon of a padlock.

FIGURE 4.10

Frame anchor

You can also change the anchor position to link the frame with another paragraph on the page. Select the frame, then unlock the anchor by selecting Lock Anchor again from the Frame dialog box. Point to the anchor, drag it to the paragraph you want to link with the frame, then lock the anchor in that position.

For example, suppose you have a sidebar that explains a particular section of text. You want the sidebar to print at the bottom of whatever page contains the section of text. Select the frame, set its position at the bottom relative to the page, then lock the anchor to the section of text.

 **N o t e**   Once you lock the anchor to another paragraph the anchor will no longer appear. To see the anchor, select the frame, unlock it, then drag the frame slightly.

If you want the frame to remain in a specific position, regardless of the text, unlock the anchor and deselect the Move with Text option in the Frame dialog box.

SOLUTIONS

Looking at Frames in Action

The following illustration shows the relative placement of frames. The two frames at the top of the page are set left and right relative to the page. The next frame is set centered relative to the page, and the bottom frames are set left and right relative to the margins.

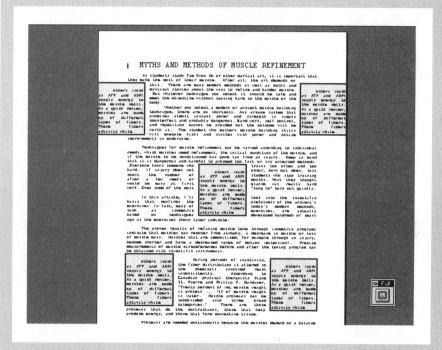

If you change the margins, the position of the two frames at the bottom of the page will change as well. The other frames will not change because they are set relative to the page itself and are independent of the margins.

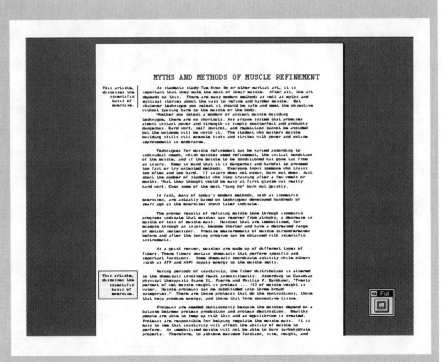

Here, the left margin was increased to 1.5 inches, then frames moved into the margin to illustrate margin notes. Use margin notes to highlight sections of text, add references, or small explanatory notes. The line between the frame at the top of the page and the text is a right border line. The frame at the bottom has a full border and shade pattern.

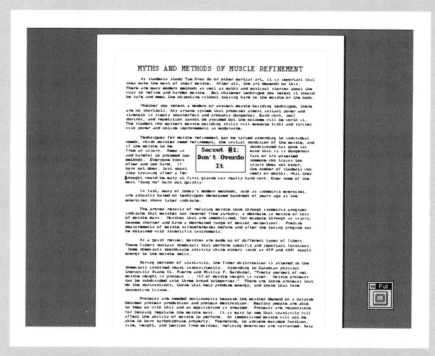

This document has two frames. One frame is placed in the center to highlight an important point. You can use a frame like this in newsletters to point out an important article in an inside page. The border around the page is a frame in the header. To create a page border with a frame, set the top margin at −1, view the header, and draw a frame around the entire page from the top of header to top of footer. Draw the frame wide enough so it does not interfere with the text on the page.

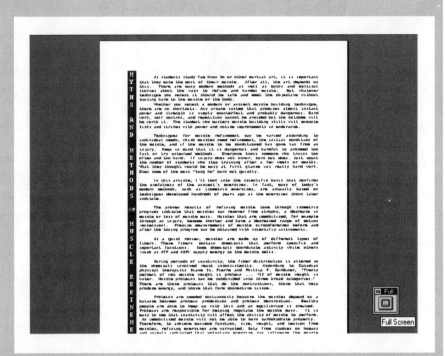

Here, a frame is used to print a vertical banner in reverse down the side of the page. A frame was inserted, the paragraph format within the frame set at centered alignment, then each 16 point letter of the banner typed on its own line. The size of the frame was then set at 18 points, and a solid 100% fill pattern was added. To repeat the banner on every page of the document, select and cut the frame, then paste it into the header.

Working with WordArt

When you want to create a special effect with text, use WordArt. With WordArt, you can create slanted, curved, filled, and rotated text for use in headlines, watermarks, eye-catching graphics, and even buttons. You can include the art in frames, even add it to a header or footer to repeat it on every page.

Creating Text Effects

To create a text effect, select Insert ➤ Object, click on the Create New tab if it is not already selected, then select Microsoft WordArt 2.0. A dialog box appears where you enter the text, and the WordArt toolbar replaces any other toolbars already displayed, as in Figure 4.11. (You will learn about other object's you can insert in Chapter 5.)

FIGURE 4.11

WordArt toolbar and text box

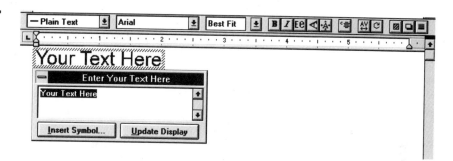

◆ In the Enter Your Text Here box, type the text that you want to format using WordArt.

◆ Select the shape of the text in the first list box on the toolbar. Shape options, and a sample of one applied to text, are shown in Figure 4.12.

◆ Select a TrueType font and size of the text in the next list boxes.

◆ Select the special effects for the text using the remaining toolbar buttons. The options are listed in Table 4.2.

◆ Click on the Insert Symbol button to display the characters available in the current font. Select the Wingdings font for graphic characters and symbols.

FIGURE 4.12
WordArt shape
options

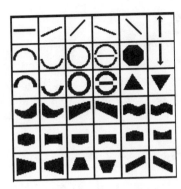

TABLE 4.2: WordArt toolbar buttons

BUTTON	NAME	FUNCTION
B	Bold	bolds all text
I	Italic	italicizes all text
Ee	Even	makes all characters the same height regardless of case
◁	Flip	rotates text on its side
⬧	Stretch	stretches text vertically and horizontally
⬦	Alignment	sets text position in the graphic box
AV	Spacing	adjusts the amount of space between characters
↻	Rotate	rotates and slants text

TABLE 4.2: WordArt toolbar buttons (continued)

BUTTON	NAME	FUNCTION
	Shading	displays options for fill patterns and colors
	Shadow	displays options for creating shadow characters
	Border	displays options for border thickness and style

To see how the text appears, click on Update Display in the dialog box. When you are satisfied with the effect, click in the document window to remove the dialog box and WordArt toolbar. The original toolbars reappear.

Editing WordArt Text

Word inserts the text into the document as a picture box. When you select the text, a single-line, non-printable, border appears around it with eight handles. You can change the size of the box, and thus the text within it, by dragging the handles. To change the box's position, or wrap text around it, enclose it in a frame by selecting Insert ➤ Frame.

 **Note** You'll learn more about working with picture boxes in Chapter 5. However, to save you some frustration, you cannot add a fill pattern to the background of a picture box. To add a printable frame around the box, select it and click on the Outside Border button.

To edit the text or change its style, double-click on the WordArt text, or click the right mouse button on it and select Edit WordArt 2.0 from the shortcut menu. Word starts the WordArt application, displaying the text in the Enter Your Text Here box. Make your changes, then click in the document.

S E C R E T S

WordArt Tips and Tricks

The WordArt shortcut menu also includes the option Open WordArt 2.0. This opens WordArt as a separate dialog box, rather than a toolbar on the document window. Enter the text, select options, then select OK to insert the WordArt picture box into the document. Select Apply to insert the picture box and remain in WordArt.

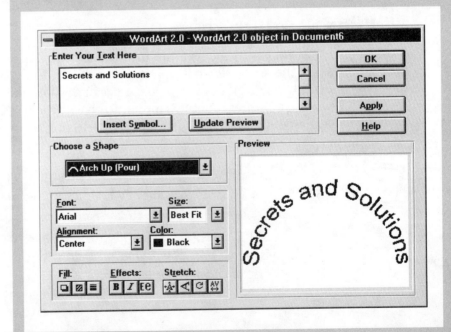

You can also display the dialog box by selecting the Display As Icon option in the Object dialog box, and then starting Word-Art. However, when you exit the dialog box, Word displays the WordArt icon in the document, rather than the formatted text itself.

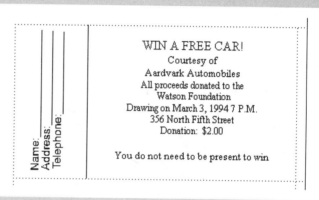

Take advantage of WordArt to create rotated text, such as land-scape text in a portrait oriented document. The raffle ticket, shown here, was created using labels in portrait orientation. The width of the labels were adjusted using table functions. The stub was formed on a narrow label, with WordArt rotated 90 degrees. The line between the stub and the ticket is a right border line on the stub label. You cannot place a frame on a label, but you can use rotated WordArt to print a return address down the side of an envelope.

READ AND DESTROY

This document uses WordArt to create a watermark repeated on every page. The WordArt was created while in a header, using a light background pattern and rotated 45 degrees. A frame was inserted around the WordArt picture box, dragged to the center of the page, and then enlarged. In Chapter 5, you'll learn how to create watermarks that contain graphics.

Secrets and Solutions   Secrets and Solutions

Secrets and Solutions   Secrets and Solutions

WordArt was used here to create the text of a button, then copied onto 2 inch by 2 inch labels. For a special event, create and print your own button message, then find a local company that will cut the labels into individual pieces and make the buttons for you. If you have trouble adjusting the size of the WordArt picture box, see Chapter 5.

CHAPTER

5

Pictures, Charts, and Graphics

C HAPTER 4 DESCRIBED HOW TO work with frames. This chapter explains techniques for inserting and manipulating graphic images, as well as creating freehand drawings, charts, and graphs.

Working with Pictures

To display a list of graphic images you can insert into your documents, select Insert ➤ Picture. Word will display a dialog box listing .WMF graphic files in the Clipart subdirectory. To display other graphic types, select the type in the List Files of Type list, or select another drive or directory

 **Tip**

If you want to see what a picture looks like before retrieving it, click on the file name and then click on the Preview Picture option. Continue clicking on file names until you find the one you want. You can also type the name of the file in the File Name text box. As you type, Word will select and display files automatically, even if you do not enter the file extension. Word can display files in all common formats, such as PCX, TIF, BMP, and WPG.

Inserting a Picture

Double-click on the name of the picture file you want to insert, or select it and then choose OK. The image appears in the document at the position of the insertion point, as shown in Figure 5.1. The dimensions of the figure are based on the size of the graphic image.

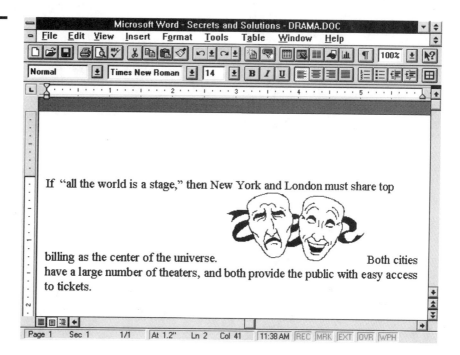

Picture Boxes

A graphic is inserted in a picture box, much like WordArt text. When you select the picture, a box appears around it with eight sizing handles. To change the position of the box, drag it to another location using drag and drop.

You can also enclose the picture in a frame, then drag the frame. Use a frame when you want text to wrap around the picture. To frame a picture, select the picture then choose Insert ➤ Frame, or select Frame Picture from the shortcut menu.

 **Note**

> When you use drag and drop to move a picture that has not been framed, you can only position the picture in existing text—at a location where you could normally place the insertion point. When the picture is framed, you can move it to any location on the page, even below the endmark.

Adding a Border

Add a printable border around the picture using the borders toolbar or dialog box. Display the dialog box using the Format menu, or by selecting Borders and Shading from the shortcut menu. You cannot add a shading pattern to the picture background because Word treats the picture as opaque.

Resizing a Picture

To change the size of the picture, drag one of the handles. Use a corner handle to enlarge or reduce the picture while maintaining the original proportions. Use a handle on the side, top, or bottom to change just the width or height.

As you drag the mouse, the word Scaling will appear in the status line followed by the percentage increase or decrease width and height.

Tip Remember that pictures look best when kept in their original proportions. If you place a frame around the picture, changing the size of the frame also changes the size of the picture.

Cropping a Picture

To crop a picture, hold down the Shift key while you drag a handle. The word Cropping will appear in the status line, along with an indication of the area being cropped (top, right, bottom, or left) and the amount being cropped. A negative number indicates you are adding to the picture box, a positive number means you are reducing it.

Cropping adds extra white space around the picture, or reduces the amount of the picture displayed. Figure 5.2 illustrates the difference between scaling and cropping.

FIGURE 5.2
Scaled and
cropped pictures

 **Note** Cropping the picture smaller does not delete any of the picture, it just hides it from being seen. You can later crop the picture larger to reveal more of the original picture. Changing the size of a cropped picture will not display more, just change the size of the cropped image.

The Picture Dialog Box

You can also crop a selected picture and change its size by choosing Format ➤ Picture to see the dialog box shown in Figure 5.3. In the Crop From section, enter a positive number to reduce the amount of the picture displayed, enter a negative number to add white space around the picture. As you crop the picture, the height and width settings will adjust to show the resulting picture size.

Change the size of the picture using the Scaling or Size settings. Use the Scaling boxes to change the picture by percentage, such as entering 125 to increase a dimension by 25 percent. Use the Size boxes to set a specific height or width, to fit the box into a selected area, for example.

FIGURE 5.3

Picture dialog box

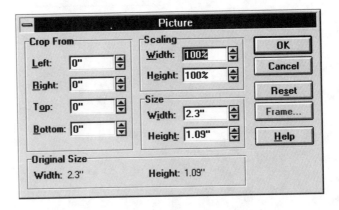

Tip You can use the same dialog box to scale or resize a selected WordArt picture.

Click on Reset to return the picture to its original size. Click on Frame to display the Frame dialog box.

Adding Picture Captions

If you have several pictures in a document, you might want to add captions. A caption identifies a picture so you can refer to it in the text. (You can also use captions for tables, equations, and other objects.)

To add a caption, place a frame around the picture, select the frame, then choose Insert ➤ Caption, or right-click and select Caption from the shortcut menu. Word will display the dialog box shown in Figure 5.4.

FIGURE 5.4

Caption dialog box

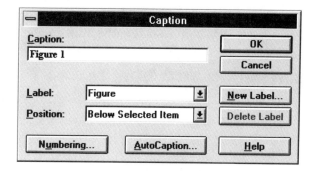

 **Note** When you add a caption to a framed picture, the caption will be included in the same frame. If you later move the frame to reposition the figure, the caption will move with it. If you do not place a frame around the picture first, the caption will appear near the picture but it will not be linked with it, and it will not move when you move the picture. If you add a caption before inserting and selecting the frame, delete the caption and try again.

Default and Custom Labels

The Caption box shows the default label, the word "Figure", and a number. You can change the number, or add additional text to the label, but you cannot edit or delete the label itself. If you want another label, pull down the Label box and select from Figure, Equation, or Table.

To create a custom label, click on the New Label button, and then enter a new label name. To delete a custom label, select it and click on Delete. You cannot delete the built-in Figure, Equation, and Table labels.

Positioning and Numbering

Use the Position setting to determine if the caption appears above or below the picture.

Word automatically increments the caption number as you add captions. The first object labeled Figure will be numbered 1, the second will be numbered 2, and so on. Each label name—Figure, Table, and Equation—has a separate sequence.

To change the numbering method, click on Numbering to display the dialog box shown in Figure 5.5.

Pull down the Format list and select the type of number you want added to the current label. Options are Arabic numbers (1, 2, 3), lowercase letters (a, b, c), uppercase letters (A, B, C), lowercase roman (i, ii, iii), and uppercase roman (I, II, III).

FIGURE 5.5

Caption
Numbering
dialog box

Including Chapter Numbers

You can also number objects by chapter. Select the Include Chapter Number checkbox in the Caption Numbering dialog box. By default, Word assumes a new chapter begins with a title formatted using the heading 1 style. The figure following the first heading 1 text will be labeled Figure 1-1, the second Figure 1-2. The figure after the second heading 1 title will be labeled Figure 2-1.

**Note**
To include chapter numbers, you must be using the automatic heading numbering function. Select Format ➤ Heading Numbering to display six numbering styles. Choose the style you want, then select OK. Word will automatically add a chapter number at the start of each line using the Heading 1 style.

The AutoCaption Feature

If you plan on adding captions to all of your pictures, use the Auto-Caption feature. Word will insert the label and next caption number as soon as you insert the picture.

In the Caption dialog box, select AutoCaption to display the dialog box shown in Figure 5.6. The list box contains the various objects that

FIGURE 5.6
AutoCaption
dialog box

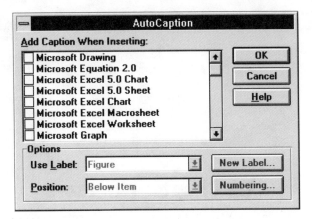

you can insert in a document. To caption picture boxes automatically, select the Microsoft Word 6.0 Picture checkbox. Choose the label and position desired, or create a new label, choose numbering options, and then select OK.

S E C R E T S

Picture Tips and Tricks

Remember, if you frame and select the picture before creating the caption, the caption is included in the frame. Without the caption, the frame and the picture box are the same size—you cannot select or move each individually.

With a caption in the frame, however, you can select just the picture or just the frame, and then select and place a border around each. If you add shading to the selected frame, the pattern will fill in the portion not covered by the picture box, as shown here.

Figure 1

You can move the entire object—the picture, caption, and frame—by dragging the frame. You can also select and move just the picture, but you can only move it out of the frame to another location in the document. You cannot move the picture to change its position within the frame.

Pictures seem to be connected to the top-left corner of the frame. You can drag a handle to add extra space between the right side and bottom of the picture and the frame border, but you cannot add space between the top and left side of the picture and the border.

Linking Pictures with Documents

Suppose you want to print a graphic image in a document, but there is a chance that the image will later be changed in some way. You can ensure that the most recent version of the graphic file prints with the document by *linking* the file to the document.

To link a graphic file as you insert it, select the file in the Insert Picture dialog box, click on the Link to File button, then select OK. If you later change the picture, you can update the link to display the edited version.

Storing Linked Files

By default, a complete copy of the picture file is also stored with your Word document. For example, if you have a picture file that is 62,000 bytes large, your document will increase in size by that amount.

By deselecting the Save Picture in Document check box, only the link to the picture is actually saved in the document. (The option is only select-able when you choose to link the picture, otherwise it is the default value and cannot be changed.) Your document won't be much larger than it was without the picture.

 **Note**   If you choose not to save your picture with the document it's linked to, each time you scroll the picture into view, Word has to retrieve it from the file to display it on screen. This may slow down Word's response somewhat, especially when working with large documents and picture files.

If Word cannot find the file named in the link, it will display a blank rectangle where the picture should be. If you do not save the picture file with your document, you must take extra precautions to make sure the file is saved to a disk. For example, suppose you want to take the file into the office from your home computer. Be sure to copy the picture file to the floppy disk as well.

Tip

As an alternative, both link the file and store it in the document. When you copy the file to the floppy disk, the latest updated version of the linked file will be saved along with it. You can also work with the file as a link at home, then save the picture to the document before copying it to the floppy disk. You'll learn how to do this in the next section on Updating and Changing Links.

Updating and Changing Links

After you create a link, you can change the way Word links the files. Select Edit ➤ Links to display the dialog box shown in Figure 5.7. (The Links option will be dimmed in the Edit menu if the document contains no linked objects.) The box will list the name and type of all linked files, as well as the type of update.

FIGURE 5.7

Links dialog box

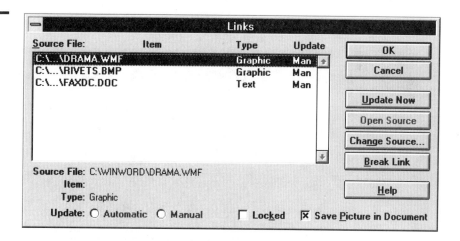

Automatic and Manual Updating

By default, all links created with the Insert Picture command are set to be updated manually. If you change the file, you must select the picture in the Source File list, and then click on Update Now. You can also insert a picture by Selecting Insert Object Create From File. Pictures linked with this command are set to update automatically, so the newest version of the file will be displayed when you open the document. You can change the update method to manual in the Links dialog box.

Multiple Updating

To update several files at one time, press Ctrl while you click on the source file names, then select Update Now.

Locking a File

Select the Locked checkbox to prevent a file from being updated. For instance, you may be planning on editing a picture, but still want to use the original version in the document. Rather than removing the link, in case you decide to update it later, select the source file name and choose Locked. Word will not automatically update the link, and you cannot update by choosing Update Now.

You can also lock and unlock a link from within the document. Select the object and press Ctrl+F11 to lock it. Press Ctrl+Shift+F11 to unlock it.

S E C R E T S

Links Tips and Tricks

Here are some other ways to use the options on the Links dialog box:

◆ *Open Source*: starts the application used to create the selected linked file, with the file ready to be edited. For example, if you created and linked a Paintbrush picture, selecting the source file and clicking on Open Source will run the Paintbrush application.

- *Change Source*: lets you specify the source file. If you re-named or moved a linked file to a different directory, for instance, Word will be unable to locate it. To reestablish the link, select the file name in the Source File list, then click on the Change Source button. Type the path and name of the file you want to establish the link with and press Enter, or use the Drives and Directories list to locate the file and double-click on it.

- *Break Link*: removes the link between the object in the document and the source file, without removing the object from the document. To break a link using the keyboard, se-lect the object and press Ctrl+Shift+F9.

- *Save Picture in Document*: maintains the link with the origi-nal file and also inserts it into the document. Use this op-tion before copying the Word document to floppy disk to insure the picture file will be available.

Word internally stores the date and time stamp of the linked file. When it automatically updates a link, or you update it manually, Word checks the date and time of the file on disk against its internal record. It only updates the file if the date of the disk file is later than the recorded date.

If you are transporting a linked file between computers, such as from the office to home, make sure the computer clocks of both machines are set correctly. If you have an older copy of the file, but it contains a later date because of the way the computer clocks are set, it could actually replace a more recent version.

 **Tip**　To update the links when you print the document, select Tools ➤ Options ➤ Print ➤ Update Links.

Using Word's Drawing Tools

Word provides comprehensive tools for creating your own pictures. You don't have to be an artist, but you do need a steady hand and a good eye for perspective and design. You can even modify a WMF picture file from the clipart directory, WPG files, or other graphic files.

The best way to become proficient with the drawing tools is to practice. In the following sections, you'll learn what each tool does and the general principles of creating and editing pictures.

Creating and Editing Drawings

To create a drawing, you have to display the drawing toolbar, shown in Figure 5.8. Use any of these techniques:

◆ Click on the drawing button in the standard toolbar to display the drawing toolbar and to change to page layout mode.

◆ Select View ➤ Toolbars ➤ Drawing, or select Drawing from the toolbar shortcut menu. If you are not in Page Layout mode, you will be asked to switch to it when you draw the first object.

Drawing Objects

The five buttons on the left of the toolbar create objects—lines, boxes, ellipsis, arcs, and freeform shapes. Click on the tool you want to use, then drag the mouse on the window to draw the object.

FIGURE 5.8

Drawing toolbar

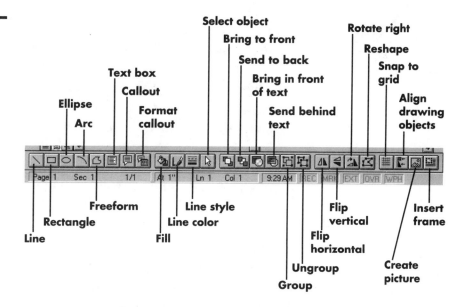

Tip

Hold down the Shift key while you drag to draw a straight line when using the line tool, a square when using the rectangle tool, and a circle when using the ellipse tool.

When you release the mouse, the object will appear with handles, which you can use to move or change the size of the object.

Selecting Objects

After you draw an object, you can select it to change its shape, position, color, or other aspect.

To select an object, place the pointer on it until the pointer is accompanied by a four-directional arrow, then click the mouse button. Handles will appear around, or along the object. You can then drag the object to change its position, drag handles to change its size, or select other options from the drawing toolbar. (You can move the object anywhere in the document, even below the endmark.)

Tip   To select several objects, hold down the Shift key while you click on each. You can also click in the Select Drawing Objects button, then drag the pointer to form a box around the objects you want to select. Once you surround an object in a frame, you cannot select it and change it with the drawing toolbar. Remove the frame if you want to manipulate it as a drawing object. Refer to the section on Creating and Editing Pictures later in this chapter.

Freeform Shapes

A freeform shape is a series of connected line segments. Click where you want to start drawing, then drag the mouse to draw freeform shapes. To create a line segment, move the pointer to the end of the line and click again. The position where you click or release the mouse button becomes the starting point for the next segment. Continue adding other segments, then double-click when done.

Reshaping Objects

You can change the shape of a freehand object after you double-click. Click on the object to select it, then click on the Reshape button. Handles appear at each of the intersections of the lines. Drag one of the handles to change the shape. To add a new handle, in the center of a line for instance, press Ctrl and click on the location.

Note   A drawing toolbar button remains in effect until you release the mouse button, or double-click to end a freehand drawing. Once you complete an object, the toolbar button appears unpressed, and the mouse reverts to its selection function. To draw two or more consecutive objects, you must click the toolbar button for each one.

Working with Text Boxes

A text box is similar to a framed paragraph, but it can overlap other text on the page. Click on the text box tool on the drawing toolbar, and then drag the mouse to form a rectangle the size of the box desired. When you release the mouse, the box will be selected.

Type the text in the rectangle, then click outside of the box. Text boxes have a default single line border, which you can change using the Borders dialog box or the toolbar.

S O L U T I O N S

Creating Drop Caps

Word has a special feature for creating drop capitals, as shown here. A drop capital is a large initial letter that begins a paragraph. Drop capitals are used in books, annual reports, and other publications to attract the reader's attention.

As students study Tae Kwon Do or other martial art, it is important that they make the most of their muscle. After all, the art depends on this. There are many modern methods as well as myths and mystical stories about the ways to refine and harden muscle. But whatever technique you select it should be safe and meet the objective without causing harm to the muscle or the body.

Whether you select a modern or ancient muscle building technique, there are no shortcuts. Any arcane system that promises almost instant power and strength is simply counterfeit and probably dangerous. Hard work, self-control, and repetition cannot be avoided but the outcome will be worth it. The student who masters muscle building skills will execute kicks and strikes with power and notice improvements in endurance.

Techniques for muscle refinement can be varied according to individual needs, which muscles need refinement, the initial condition of the muscle, and if the muscle to be conditioned has gone lax from an injury. Keep in mind that it is dangerous and harmful to proceed too fast or try untested methods. Everyone knows someone who trains too often and too hard. If injury does not occur, burn-out does. Just count the number of students who stop training after a few weeks or months. What they thought would be easy at first glance was really hard work. Even some of the most "kung ho" burn out quickly.

In this article, I'll look into the scientific basis that confirms the usefulness of the ancient's exercises. In fact, many of today's modern methods, such as isometric exercises, are actually based on techniques developed hundreds of years ago as the exercises shown later indicate.

To create a drop capital:

1. Place the insertion point at the start of the paragraph so the letter you want dropped is to the immediate right of the insertion point. (To drop more than a single character, select them first.)

2. Select Format ➤ Drop Cap to display the Drop Cap dialog box.

3. Select Dropped to place the capital within the paragraph, or select In Margin to position it in the margin area to the left of the text.

4. If you want the letter to appear in a font other than the one already used, select a font from the Font list.

5. In the Lines to Drop text box, enter the number of lines high you want the character.

6. Use the distance option in the Drop Cap dialog box to set the distance of the letter from the text.

7. Select OK when you're done.

If you are in Normal view, a dialog box appears asking if you want to change to Page Layout view. Select Yes. In Normal view, the drop capital will appear on a line separate from the text; however the document will print correctly.

Word displays the drop capital in a frame, so you can adjust the size and position if you desire.

Here are some other points to keep in mind:

◆ Text boxes have an internal margin of 5 points. If you add a shade, the pattern extends 1 point beyond the text, not to the edges of the box.

◆ Text boxes do not automatically increase in size as you enter text. To display more text, select and enlarge the box.

◆ Text boxes are transparent, so they can be superimposed over other text or pictures.

◆ You can layer a text box over or behind other objects.

◆ Text you enter will be formatted according to the normal style.

Adding Callout Lines

A *callout* is a text box without a border, but with a line, called the callout line, pointing to the text. Use a callout to add notes or references, using the line to point to a related picture, table, or other object, as shown in Figure 5.9.

FIGURE 5.9

Callouts

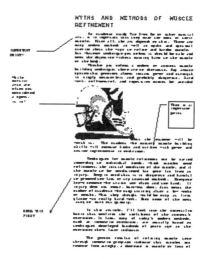

Using the Callout Tool

To add a callout line, choose the callout tool. Point to where you want the callout line to begin, usually at the text or object you want to reference, then drag the mouse to where you want to type the note or reference. Drag the mouse straight to create a straight callout line, or up or down for a segmented line.

When you release the mouse button, the insertion point will appear in the callout box. Enter the text desired, then click outside of the box.

Tip

To add arrows to the end of callout lines, see the sidebar on Changing Drawing Object Formats later in this chapter.

Editing Callouts

To change the appearance of the box or line, select the callout and click on the format callout tool. A dialog box will appear where you can change the type of line, the distance between the line and the text, and place a border around the text. (You cannot select the callout line and box separately.)

Color and Fill Patterns

Three drawing toolbar buttons allow you to change the type and color of lines, and the color or shade of objects. The buttons effect any new objects you draw, or any selected objects.

Use the fill button to select a pattern or color. The options are shown in Figure 5.10. You'll soon learn how to use this option to create watermarks.

FIGURE 5.10

Fill options

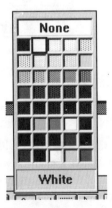

Click on the line color button to display color options, and on the line style button to select a line thickness or to place arrowheads on the ends of lines.

 **Tip**   Select More from the Line Style list to display a dialog box of style options. See the sidebar on Changing Drawing Object Formats later in this chapter.

These settings remain in effect until you change them again. If you select a color to draw a specific object, reset the option if you do not want it applied to other objects. For example, if you select a solid fill pattern, every circle and rectangle that you draw will be solid black. Change the fill pattern to white for open circles and rectangles.

Layering Objects

Layering is the process of positioning objects in relation to each other. Picture the screen as consisting of three layers of transparent plastic. The text you see on the screen is in the middle layer. When you create a drawing object, it appears on the top layer, obscuring the text below it.

To place an object in the bottom layer, below the text, click on the send behind text button. The text will now appear over the object. Click on the bring in front of text button to return the object to the top layer.

 **Tip**   The layering options are also available in the shortcut menu displayed by clicking the right mouse button on a selected drawing object.

Individual objects can also be layered over each other. If you draw one object over another, it partially obscures the bottom object. To place one object under another, select it, and click on the send to back button. Click on the bring to front button to return it to the foreground. Figure 5.11 illustrates layered objects.

FIGURE 5.11

Layered text boxes and objects

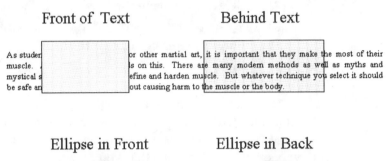

S E C R E T S

Frame Tips and Tricks

The frame around a picture is always rectangular, so you cannot have text follow an uneven contour. You can, however, make text appear to flow around an object drawn directly on the screen.

MYTHS AND METHODS OF MUSCLE REFINEMENT

The example shown here was created by placing a framed .WMF clipart picture in a drawn circle. The entire frame around the picture fit within the circle. The unframed circle was positioned in front of the text, then extra spaces inserted in the text so it appears to follow the contour of the circle.

You can use this technique to have text follow the contour of other inserted pictures or drawn objects. However, it is not very efficient. If you edit the text, you will have to insert or delete spaces to realign the text.

Word also provides a number of horizontal and vertical borders and dividers in the Clipart directory. In this example, a horizontal border picture was inserted into a text box, then set behind the text layer so the text would be displayed. Remember, any object in a text box can be placed beneath the text layer. An additional picture is used as a text divider.

You Are Cordially Invited
to attend

My Birthday Party
November 16, 1994
7 PM
at my house

To place the picture border around the whole page, create a text box and insert the border into it. Then, change the magnification to display the entire page, and enlarge the box to fill the page. Finally, place the text box behind the text layer.

To use the border on every page, change the top margin to –1, insert the border picture into the header, then enlarge it to fill the page.

 **Note**

A framed drawing object is considered to be part of the text layer, so it cannot be layered in relation to other objects. However, because it is in the text layer, you can move drawing objects to the back or front of the frame.

Grouping and Ungrouping Objects

Each object you draw is a separate entity. You can select each independently to change its position, size, color, or other aspect. However, suppose you use a number of objects to draw a picture. To change the position or color of the entire picture, you must group the individual objects. Grouping creates a new composite object consisting of the individual drawing elements.

To Group Objects

Click on the select objects button on the drawing toolbar, and then drag over the objects you want to group. You can also hold down the Shift key and click on each object. Then, click on the group button.

To Ungroup Objects

To return the group to individual objects, select it, and click on the Ungroup button.

 **Note**   **You cannot include one group in another. First ungroup any grouped objects.**

Flipping and Rotating

Use the flip horizontal button to mirror the object along an imaginary x-axis. The bottom of the object will now appear on top. Use the flip vertical button to mirror the object along an imaginary y-axis. What was on the left will now be on the right. Use the rotate button to rotate the object counter-clockwise in 90 degree increments.

 **Note**   **Text in text boxes will not flip or rotate, just the box itself. Use WordArt to create rotated text.**

S O L U T I O N S

Changing Drawing Object Formats

You can change the default formats applied to drawing objects by selecting Format ➤ Drawing Object to display the dialog box shown here.

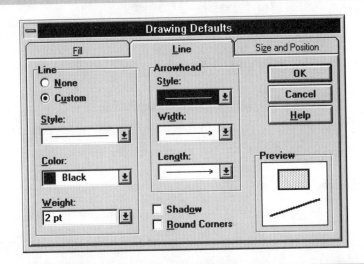

Use the Line tab to change the color, style, and thickness of lines, create shadow box and rounded corners, and to automatically add arrow heads to the end of lines.

Select the Fill tab to change the fill pattern and color. Select the Size and Position tab to change the size and position of a selected object, to adjust the internal margin of text boxes, and to anchor objects to text.

Use the Arrowhead section of the Line tab to automatically add arrow points to the ends of lines. The graphic shown here uses arrowheads on the end of callout lines. (See the previous section in this chapter on Adding Callout Lines.) Note that the arrows can be pointed to the callout text, the referenced object, or both. You can also change the width and the length of the arrowhead.

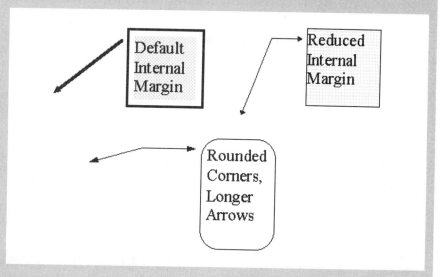

The callouts in this example also illustrate the effects of changing the internal margin width, the corner style to round, and the length of the arrow points.

Double-clicking on a unframed object displays the same dialog box, but labeled Drawing Object. You can only select options that apply to the selected object. For example, if the object is a rectangle, you cannot select arrowhead styles because they apply to lines. However, any changes you make in the dialog box will apply to the selected object as well as new objects that you draw.

Placing a frame around an object converts it into a picture. See the section on Creating and Editing Pictures later in this chapter.

Using Grid Lines

Underlying the screen is an invisible grid pattern. The grid consists of evenly-spaced horizontal and vertical lines 0.1 inch apart. When you draw an object, it automatically starts or ends on the nearest grid line.

Snap to Grid

The corners of every rectangle, and the starting and ending positions of all lines, for example, will always be placed on the intersection of a horizontal and vertical line, so every object is in some increment of .1 inches. This is called *snap to grid*. (The grid is useful when you need to align two objects, or draw two objects the same size.)

Dialog Box Options

To turn off snap to grid, and change the spacing of the grid pattern, click on the snap to grid button to display the dialog box shown in Figure 5.12.

FIGURE 5.12

Snap to Grid
dialog box

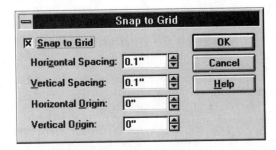

To turn the feature off, deselect the Snap to Grid checkbox. Change the spacing of the grid by entering new measurements in the Horizontal Spacing and Vertical Spacing boxes. (Entering different horizontal and vertical measurements may result in out of proportion objects, when snap to grid is on.)

Aligning Objects

You can also align an object relative to the page, or relative to other objects, by clicking on the align drawing objects button. The dialog box shown in Figure 5.13 will be displayed when one or more objects are selected.

If you only have one object selected, the Relative To Page button is on by default. Choose the horizontal and vertical position for the object, then select OK. For example, select Center in both the Horizontal and Vertical sections to place the object in the exact center of the page.

If you have more then one object selected, the Relative To Each Other button is on by default. Select the horizontal and vertical placement of the objects in relation to each other. Choosing both Center options, for instance, will center the two objects over each other.

FIGURE 5.13

Align dialog box

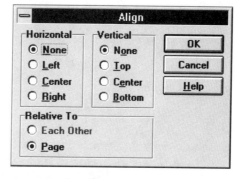

Creating and Editing Pictures

Make certain you understand the difference between a picture and a drawing object. A picture, either inserted from the disk or created in the picture window, is treated as a single unit in the text layer. Without a frame, you can only move the picture within existing text. You can only edit the picture, or its individual elements, in the picture window.

A drawing that you created in the document window is composed of individual elements. These can be placed in front of or below the text layer, and can be moved anywhere in the document. When you place a frame around a drawing in the document window, Word converts the drawing to a picture. You can then edit the drawing in the picture window, even if you later remove the frame.

S E C R E T S

Alignment Tips and Tricks

Rather than trying to draw objects in relation to each other, use the Align dialog box. For example, suppose you want to create the bullseye shown here.

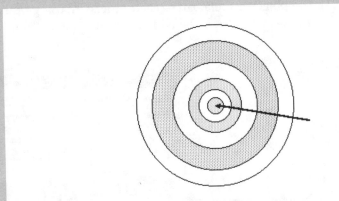

It would be difficult to drag smaller circles and fit them exactly in the center of larger ones. Instead, draw a series of circles, select them, then use the Align dialog box to center them horizontally and vertically.

If any circles do not appear, select the next larger circle, and choose the send to back tool on the drawing toolbar. Select and group all of the circles so you can move them as a single object.

The gray shades in the graphic shown here were created by using a fill pattern for alternate circles. The arrow was created as a line using an arrowhead line style.

Composing a Picture

To create a picture in a separate window, click on the create picture button in the drawing toolbar, or select Insert ➤ Microsoft Word 6.0 Picture. The drawing toolbar and an empty drawing area are displayed, as shown in Figure 5.14.

Create your drawing within the borders. To create a larger drawing, draw or drag an object outside of the displayed boundaries, then click on the reset boundary button, next to the close picture button in the Picture dialog box. When you are done, click on the close picture button. The drawing will appear in the position of the insertion point in the document.

FIGURE 5.14

Picture window
with drawing
toolbar

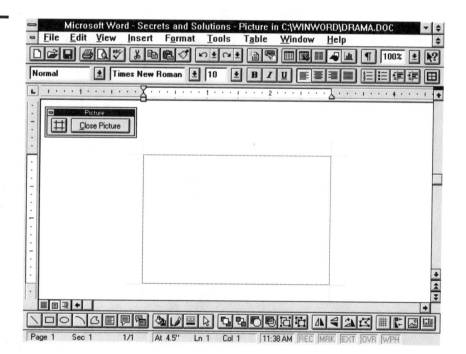

Note The drawing is inserted into the document as a picture, not as individual objects. That means that in the document, the picture is treated as a group—you cannot select the individual components that you draw in the picture window. You can change the size and position of the entire picture, just as you can a graphic added with the Insert ➤ Picture command.

Changing a Picture

To edit a picture created in the picture window, double-click on it. The picture window appears with the drawing ready to be edited. Make your changes to the drawing, then select Close. (You can also edit a selected picture by choosing Edit ➤ Picture Object ➤ Open, or Open Picture from the shortcut menu.)

You can also double-click to edit a WMF, WPG, TIF, or any other graphic added with the Insert ➤ Picture command. The graphic will appear in the drawing window.

Most WMF pictures are made up of individual objects. You can select, move, flip, rotate, and otherwise change the individual elements to create some unusual effects. For example, compare the original and the edited pictures in Figure 5.15.

FIGURE 5.15
Edited WMF
pictures

S O L U T I O N S

Creating Watermarks

A watermark is an object that appears in the background, behind the text on the page. To use a picture for a watermark, it must appear in a light shade of gray, or a light color, so the text can be read.

To include a watermark on every page, change the top margin to −1, select View ➤ Header and Footer, then insert the picture into the header pane. Double-click on the picture to display it in the drawing window.

You now need to change the solid black images to a lighter shade of gray. To change the entire drawing to one shade, click on the select drawing objects tool in the drawing toolbar, drag the mouse over the entire object, then click on the group button. Click on the fill button and select a shade.

Some drawings, however, will lose too much detail in one shade and will appear as a silhouette. If this occurs, select and change just larger black areas, or apply different shades to various portions of the object. Click on the close picture button, insert a frame around the picture, then drag it to the center of the page, or where you want it to appear.

In this example, the BUTTRFLY.WMF picture is applied twice as a watermark. The picture on the right is in one shade, the picture on the left is in several shades to retain some detail.

The Butterfly
by
Joshua Schneider

Fly Away
Fly Away
Fly Away
Butterfly

Fly Away
Fly Away
Fly Away
Fly

If you want a drawing to appear as a watermark on a single page, insert it into a text box set under the text layer. Create a text box, insert a picture into it, then change the shade. Click on the send behind text button so it appears in the background layer.

In Page Preview mode, a lightly-shaded watermark may not appear on the screen. Use Print Preview to see how the document will appear when printed.

Building Effective Charts and Graphs

Word's chart features let you create bar, line, pie, and other types of charts and insert them into your documents. You can enter chart data directly into the Chart application, or copy rows and columns from a Word table.

Using Microsoft Graph

Click on the insert chart button on the Word toolbar, or select Insert ➤ Object ➤ Microsoft Graph. The chart window will appear with a default sample chart and data, as shown in Figure 5.16.

FIGURE 5.16

The Microsoft Graph window

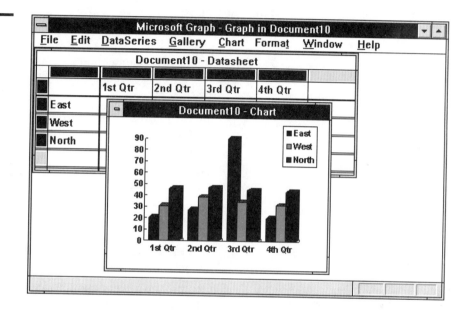

 **Tip** To chart data you've already typed in a table, select the rows and columns you want to chart, then click on the insert chart button on Word's toolbar, or select Insert ➤ Object ➤ Microsoft Graph. The Chart window will appear with the select data in a bar chart.

Entering Data

To enter your own chart data, click in the spreadsheet grid to bring it into the foreground, or select Window ➤ Datasheet. Select Edit ➤ Select All, Edit ➤ Cut, then click the mouse to deselect the table. Enter the rows and columns of data you want to chart. As you enter information in the table, the graph will appear in the background window.

Customizing Your Charts

Select options from the menu bar to customize your chart, then select File ➤ Exit and Return ➤ Yes to insert the graph into your document. Table 5.1 lists the functions of the menu bar options.

TABLE 5.1: Microsoft Graph menu options

MENU NAME	OPTIONS
File	Import a spreadsheet file, open an Excel chart, update the chart into Word, save the current chart as the default, and close and exit
Edit	Undo actions, insert and delete rows and columns; delete, cut, copy, select, and paste contents
DataSeries	Determine which data to use labels along the x-axis of a scatter chart, include or exclude rows and columns in the chart, change the x- and y-axis series, change between an overlay and the main chart when creating a combination chart
Gallery	Change the type of chart and select custom chart options (area, bar, column, line, pie, xy scatter, combination, 3-D area, 3-D bar, 3-D column, 3-D line, and 3-D pie)
Chart	Create and edit chart titles, data and axis labels; create and edit a legend, add callout arrows, and grid lines
Format	Add patterns, change the font, change the scale, column width, colors, and 3-D view
Window	Switch between the chart and datasheet, and change the displayed magnification

Working with Charts in Documents

Word inserts the chart into the document as a picture box without border lines. Add a frame, border, and change the size and shape of the box as you would any picture. To edit the chart itself, double-click on the chart to display the Graph application with the chart and its associated data displayed.

Tip

If you want to return to the document before finalizing the chart, minimize the chart window. You can then reopen the window by pressing Alt+Tab until you see a box labeled Microsoft Graph. This is faster than adding the incomplete chart, closing the application, then reopening it.

S E C R E T S

Chart Tips and Tricks

This chart illustrates the capabilities of Microsoft Graph. The chart includes titles, grid lines, a custom 3-D perspective, arrows and text.

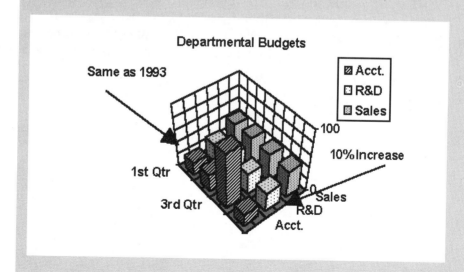

To add text, make certain no other text object is selected before you type. Don't worry if the text appears on top of some other section of the chart. When you are done typing, click on the text and drag it to another location.

Experiment with the Chart application on your own, referring to the online help system when you need assistance.

Other Drawing Options

Depending on your Windows environment, you may have other drawing options available. If you have the Paintbrush accessory installed, you can select Paintbrush Picture from the Insert Object dialog box. The Paintbrush application will run, you can create a drawing, then insert it into your document. If you later double-click on the drawing, the Paintbrush application will run so you can edit the displayed picture.

You may also see utilities from other Windows' applications. For example, if you have WordPerfect for Windows on your computer as well, the Object list will include TextArt (a WordArt-like application), WP Chart (a charting program), and WP Graphics (a drawing program). You can select any of these applications, create an object, and insert it into a Word document.

CHAPTER

6

Special Characters and Equations

A LONG WITH TEXT AND GRAPHICS, Word can print special characters and symbols, such as foreign-language characters and typo-
graphic symbols. You can also use Word's equation editor to create
equations that print as graphics. In this chapter, you will learn how to access and print special characters, create equations, and use these features
to create some interesting effects.

Working with Special Characters

Many fonts already contain accented characters needed to print documents in Spanish, French, and other languages. While these characters are
not shown on the keyboard, you can access them in a variety of ways. You
can also take advantage of other fonts to print Greek characters, mathematical, scientific, and graphical symbols.

Inserting a Special Character

To insert a special character or symbol, place the insertion point where
you want the character to appear, then select Insert ➤ Symbol to see the
dialog box shown in Figure 6.1.

Click on the Symbols tab, if necessary. By default, Word displays the
characters available in the font currently being used, listed as Normal Text
in the font box. If you see the character that you want to insert, double-
click on it, or highlight it and choose Insert. (When you click on a character, it appears enlarged.) Select Close to return to the document.

The character will appear at the position of the insertion point, in a
size to match that of the current font. You can change its size just as you
can for any text, by selecting the character and choosing another point
size from the toolbar or Font dialog box.

FIGURE 6.1

Symbol dialog box

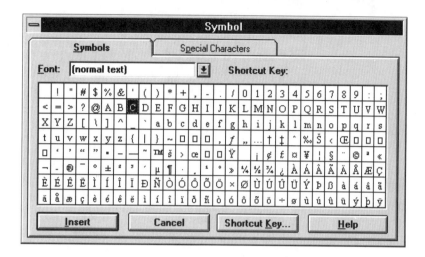

S E C R E T S

Keyboard Shortcuts

Many of the accented characters that you can insert from the normal text font can also be inserted by pressing shortcut key combinations. When you select the character in the Symbols dialog box, the key combination assigned to it will be shown next to the Shortcut Key prompt.

The keystrokes for entering the accented characters are shown here. Note that some of the key combinations require you to press Ctrl plus a punctuation mark that is in the upper section of a keyboard key. You must hold down the Shift key to access these characters. As a reminder, we've explicitly shown the Shift key in the key combination. For instance, Ctrl+Shift+^ indicates that you need to use the Shift key to enter the ^ character.

àèìòù ÀÈÌÒÙ	Ctrl`, then the letter
áéíóúý ÁÉÍÓÚÝ	Ctrl+', then the letter
âêîôû ÂÊÎÔÛ	Ctrl+Shift+^, then the letter
ãñõÃÑÕ	Ctrl+Shift+~, then the letter
äëïöüÿ ÄËÏÖÜŸ	Ctrl+:, then the letter
å Å	Ctrl+Shift+@, then a or A
æ Æ	Ctrl+Shift+&, then a or A
œ Œ	Ctrl+Shift+&, then o or O
ç Ç	Ctrl+comma, then c or C
ð Ð	Ctrl+', then d or D
ø Ø	Ctrl+/, then o or O
¿	Ctrl+Alt+Shift+?
¡	Ctrl+Alt+Shift+!
ß	Ctrl+Shift+&, then s
» «	Ctrl+`, then > or <

To enter an accented uppercase character, you must hold down the Shift key while pressing the character, you cannot use the Caps Lock key. However, you can use the Format ➤ Change Case command to covert the case of an accented character, from lowercase to uppercase.

You can also use special characters to enter dashes and special hyphens and spaces.

◆ Press Alt+Ctrl+ - on the numeric keypad for an m-dash.

◆ Press Ctrl+ - on the numeric keypad for an n-dash.

◆ Press Ctrl+_ (underline) for a non-breaking hyphen, to prevent wordwrap from dividing a hyphenated word between lines.

◆ Press Ctrl+ - (on the upper row of the keyboard) for an optional hyphen which only appears if Word must wrap the word between lines.

◆ **Press Ctrl+Shift+Space for a non-breaking space so two words are not divided between lines.**

In the Symbols dialog box, you can also insert an em-space and an en-space.

Selecting Another Font

If you do not see the character you want to insert, pull down the Font list and select another TrueType font. For example, select the Symbols font to display Greek characters and mathematical symbols. Select Wingdings to insert pictographs, circled numbers, and other special graphics included in this Windows font. Figure 6.2 shows the entire Wingdings character set. To return to the current font, select Normal Text in the font list.

FIGURE 6.2

Wingdings character set

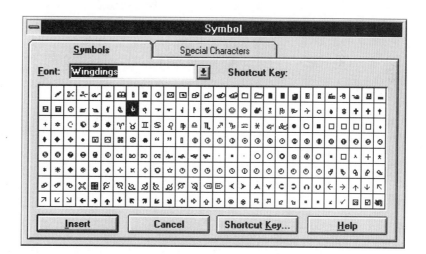

Tip

The font list may not include all of the TrueType fonts that you have installed in Windows. To use a font that is not listed, select the font from the toolbar or Font dialog box, then select Normal Text as the font in the Symbol dialog box.

S E C R E T S

Character Tips and Tricks

Suppose you want to search for a special character in your document. You cannot use the Symbols dialog box to enter a character in the Find What box of the Find dialog box. Instead, use the Alt key and the numeric keypad. Every character in the font is associated with a number, as shown here.

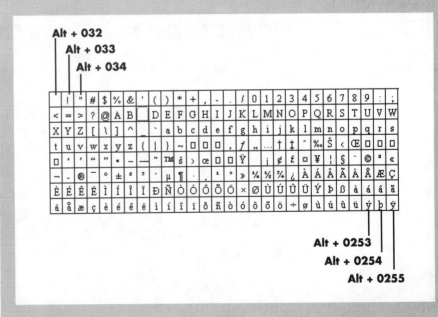

The first character, actually a space, is number 32, the next number 33, and so on. To enter the character, turn on the Num Lock key, hold down the Alt key, press 0, and then type the character's number. The character will appear when you release the Alt key. Remember to turn the Num Lock key off to use the insertion point functions.

You can also select the Wingdings font from the toolbar or Font dialog box. The font will be *mapped* to the keyboard. That is, many Wingdings characters can be entered by typing keys on the keyboard. The following illustration identifies each of the keyboard keys and its associated Wingdings character.

You can also determine how the characters are mapped by typing text in another font, selecting it, then choosing Wingdings from the toolbar or Font menu. Perform this in reverse to send a coded message or to create an exercise in deciphering. Select text in a normal font and change it to Wingdings, then see if someone can read your message.

To insert typographical characters, such as dashes and the copyright symbol, click on the Special Characters tab in the Symbols dialog box to display a list of characters. Double-click on the character you want to insert. The list also shows shortcut keys for adding these characters while you type.

For example, press Alt+Ctrl+C to insert the copyright symbol, press Alt+Ctrl+T for the trademark sign, press Alt+Ctrl+R for the registered mark, or press Alt+Ctrl+. for an ellipsis. Note that the ellipsis is treated as a single character and takes up less space than typing three consecutive periods.

Special characters are inserted the same size as the text. If you are using an 18-point font, for example, Word will scale the special characters to match that size. You can change the size of special characters by selecting them, then choosing another size from the toolbar or Font dialog box.

Assigning Shortcut Keys Step-by-Step

If you use symbols or characters from other fonts often, you can assign them to their own shortcut keys. For example, you may often use the Pi character from the Symbol font, or a graphic from the Wingdings font. Rather than use the Symbols dialog box, or have to change fonts to enter the character, assign it to a keystroke. The process is similar to assigning a style to the keyboard.

For example, suppose you want to number a series of steps using the reverse circled numbers in the Wingdings font, as shown in Figure 6.3.

Follow these steps:

1. Select Insert ➤ Symbol, then click on the Symbols tab, if necessary.
2. Pull down the Font list and select Wingdings.
3. Click on the reverse number 1, the character fourth from the right in the fourth row.
4. Select Shortcut key to display the Customize Keyboard dialog box.
5. In the Press New Shortcut Key box, press Alt+1.
6. Press Assign, then Close.
7. Click on the reverse number 2, select Shortcut key to press Alt+2, then choose Assign, then Close.
8. In the same manner, assign the remaining numbers 3 to 10 to the keystrokes Alt+3 through Alt+0.
9. Select Close to close the Symbols dialog box.
10. Type **Things To Do Today,** then press Enter twice.
11. Press Alt+1 to insert the first number.
12. Press Tab, type **Install Word for Windows,** then press Enter.
13. Press Alt+2 to insert the second number.
14. Press Tab, type **Buy Neibauer's book,** then press Enter.
15. Press Alt+3, press Tab, then type **Complete the budget proposal.**

FIGURE 6.3

Numbering with the Wingdings character set

Things To Do Today

❶   Install Word for Windows
❷   Buy Neibauer's book
❸   Complete the budget proposal

Using the Equation Editor

Word's equation editor provides tools for typing equations. It is used to format and print equations, not to perform the actual calculations. The equation is inserted into the document as a picture box. You can then manipulate the box using the mouse, by adding a frame, and by using the Format ➤ Picture command.

Accessing the Editor

To access the equation editor, select Insert ➤ Object, select the Create New tab, then double-click on Microsoft Equation 2.0. If you already created the equation, double-click on the equation box to return to the editor.

The equation editor has three main sections, as shown in Figure 6.4. The crosshatch picture box is where you type your equations. The small

FIGURE 6.4

Word's equation editor

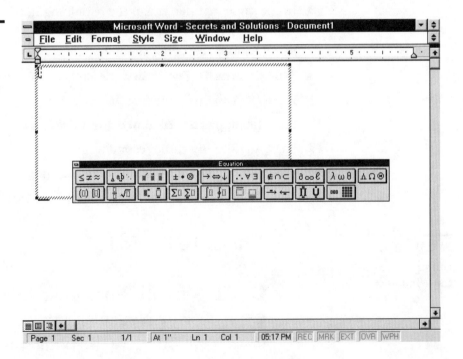

dotted rectangle in the box is called a slot, and it represents the position of an equation object. You can enter as much as you want in a slot, not just a single character or object. There is also an equation menu bar and toolbar.

Entering an Equation

You create an equation by entering letters, numbers, and punctuation marks from the keyboard, and by selecting options from the toolbar. The names of the buttons are shown in Figure 6.5. Clicking on a toolbar button displays a list of options. You then drag the mouse to select the option you want to insert in the equation. (The characters in the equation editor will appear in the same magnification that was active in the document.)

FIGURE 6.5

Equation toolbar buttons

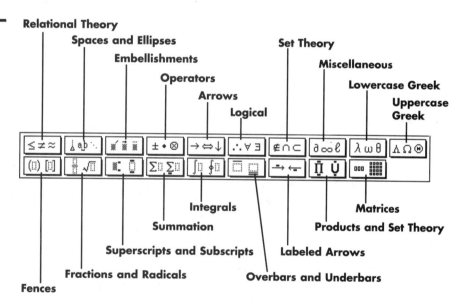

The toolbar is divided into two sections. Use the top row to select symbols —mathematical, Greek, logical, and other characters or spaces that you want to display. The button options are shown in Figure 6.6.

The buttons on the bottom of the toolbar select templates. A template represents the position of objects, often combined with an equation character, as shown in Figure 6.7.

189

FIGURE 6.6

Symbol toolbar
buttons

Relational Symbols

Spaces and Ellipses

Embellishments

Operators

Arrows

Logical Symbols

Set Theory Symbols

Miscellaneous Symbols

Lowercase Greek

Uppercase Greek

FIGURE 6.7

Templates toolbar
buttons

Fences

Fractions and Radicals

Superscripts and Subscripts

Summation

Integrals

Overbars and Underbars

Labeled Arrows

Products and Set Theory

Matrices

S E C R E T S

Template Tips and Tricks

The template shown here is used to display a fraction. The slots indicate the position of other elements in relation to the line. In this case, they show that the template requires two objects, one above and one below the line. You then enter the information in the slots to create the fraction.

$$\frac{\Box}{\Box}$$

Templates can also be nested. That is, you can insert one template within another. For example, consider this fraction:

$$\frac{X^{\Box}}{2}$$

The position of a superscripted number is determined by a template. After typing the character X into the slot above the line, the superscript template was chosen to create a slot for the superscripted number 2. If you nest templates, the slots in the outer template will disappear. To enter data, just click in the location or move the insertion point.

You can create your equation in any order. For example, you can select and position all of the templates, leaving the slots temporarily empty. When you are pleased with the overall design, you click in a slot, then enter the text or symbols required.

You can also enter the equation in a linear fashion, completing each section as you go along. If you make an entry, then realize it belongs in a template slot, select the entry, and then insert the template.

Equation Levels

Equations have various levels. When you are entering information, a horizontal line appears under the entry and an insertion point appears to its right. The line and the size of the insertion point indicate the current level.

Use the lines to keep track of your current level, so you do not enter information in the wrong position. Press the arrow keys to move between levels. For example, Figure 6.8 shows an equation with three levels, and how it will appear when you are entering text on each level.

The first level is on the same line as the characters X=Y. The second level is equal to the superscript Z. The third level is the super-superscript 2. When you are entering text on the first level, for example, the underline will appear under the complete equation and the insertion point will be equal to the maximum height of the text.

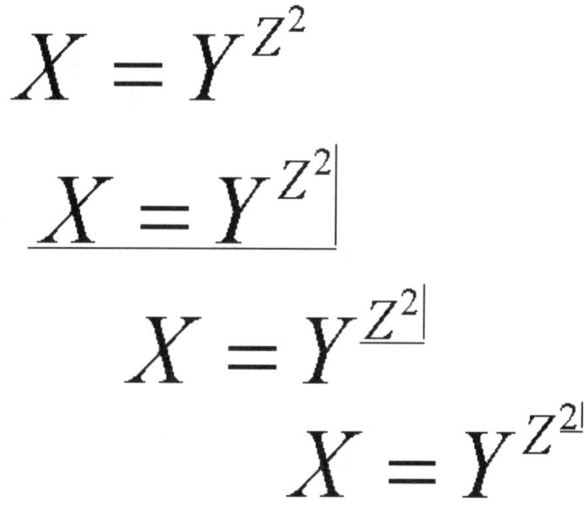

FIGURE 6.8
Levels in an
equation

$$X = Y^{Z^2}$$

$$\underline{X = Y^{Z^2}}$$

$$X = Y^{\underline{Z^2}}$$

$$X = Y^{Z^{\underline{2}}}$$

Equation Formatting

Word formats equation objects using a set of built-in styles. For instance, Word assumes that letters you type represent variables, and formats them in italics. It formats lower case Greek characters in italics, numbers in the regular font, and matrix vectors in bold.

Word automatically adds spaces around certain objects, such as the equal sign. By default, you cannot add spaces by pressing the spacebar. To add space between elements, use the options in the spaces and ellipses tool.

Entering Equations Step-by-Step

Now, let's practice by entering the equation shown in Figure 6.9.

1. Type **db.**

2. Press the spaces and ellipses button, and select the center option in the second row. This will enter a space between the two words treated as variables.

3. Type **loss=.** Word will automatically insert a space before and after the equal sign.

FIGURE 6.9

Completed
equation

$$db\ loss = 20 \log_{10}\left[\sqrt{\frac{Z_1}{Z_2}} + \sqrt{\frac{Z_1}{Z_2} - 1}\right]$$

4. Type **20,** then enter a space manually using the spaces and ellipses tool, as you did in the second step.

5. Type **log.** The word will not appear in italic because Word recognizes it as a function rather than a variable.

6. Pull down the subscript/superscript tool and select the second option in the first row, the subscript template. The insertion point will appear in the subscript slot.

7. Type **10.**

8. Press the → key to move the insertion point out of the subscript level.

9. Pull down the fences tool and select the brackets, the second option in the first row.

10. Pull down the fractions and radicals tool and select the radical symbol with a single slot—the first option in the fourth row.

11. Pull down the fractions and radicals tool and select the fraction template, the first option in the first row. Note that the brackets enlarge automatically to accommodate the objects within them.

12. Type **Z.**

13. Select the subscript template and type **1.**

14. Press the ↓ key to move to the slot below the fraction line.

15. Type **Z,** select the subscript template and type **2.**

 **Note**

> The next element, the + sign, must not fall within the division or under the radical. It must be placed on the same level as the equal sign. If you enter the plus sign at any other level, the equation would be incorrect.

16. Press the → key three times (once to leave the subscript level and enter the fraction level, again to leave the fraction level but remain under the radical, and again to leave the radical but remain within the brackets).

17. Press the + key.

18. From the fractions and radicals tool select the radical, and then the division operator.

19. Type **Z,** select the subscript template, type **1,** then press the ↓ key.

20. Type **Z,** select the subscript template and type **2.**

21. Press the → twice to leave the fraction level but remain under the radical, and then type **–1.**

Equation Printer Fonts

As long as you installed the equation editor when you installed Word, your equations should print without a problem. When Word installed the equation editor, it also installed a series of special fonts for printing fences and other special characters.

If you accidentally delete some of the fonts, or other files needed by the equation editor, your printouts will not appear correctly, if they print at all. If all of the fonts are installed, and your equations still do not appear correctly, make certain you are using TrueType fonts.

If you are not using a TrueType font, your printer must either be capable of scaling fonts on its own, or you'll need individual downloadable fonts. During the installation process, Word will install the necessary downloadable fonts for the printers installed in Windows. When all else fails, use the Word setup program to reinstall the equation editor.

S E C R E T S

Keyboard Shortcuts

While in the keyboard editor, you can enter a number of symbols and templates directly from the keyboard. To enter Greek characters, for instance, press Ctrl+G, then the English letter that would correspond to the Greek. Press Ctrl+I to enter an integral and Ctrl+R to enter a radical.

Other keyboard keys are shown here.

EMBELLISHMENTS

Overbar	Ctrl+Shift+-
Tilde	Ctrl+~
Arrow	Ctrl+Alt+-
Single prime	Ctrl+Alt+'
Double prime	Ctrl+"
Single dot	Ctrl+Alt+.

FENCES

Parentheses	Ctrl+9, Ctrl+0, Ctrl+T, (, or)
Brackets	Ctrl+[, Ctrl+], Ctrl+T, [, or]
Braces	Ctrl+{, Ctrl+}, Ctrl+T, {, or }

SUPERSCRIPT
AND SUBSCRIPT

Superscript	Ctrl+H
Subscript	Ctrl+L
Both	Ctrl+J

Moving Equation Characters

You can manually adjust the position of characters in an equation using a process called *nudging*. Select the characters you want to move, hold down the Ctrl key and press the arrow key representing the direction you want to move.

As you press the arrow keys, the selected character will move freely within the equation. Use nudging to create overstrikes and other special combinations of characters, including those from the Wingding font.

Equation Menu Options

You use the options on the menu bar to work with equations and to change the way equation objects are displayed. The File, Edit, Window, and Help menus contain the traditional Windows options.

Use the Format menu to align multiple equation lines, such as to center them or align several equations at the equal sign. Select Spacing from the Format menu to display the dialog box shown in Figure 6.10 for changing the default spacing. The preview window will illustrate the selected item.

FIGURE 6.10

Equation editor
Spacing dialog box

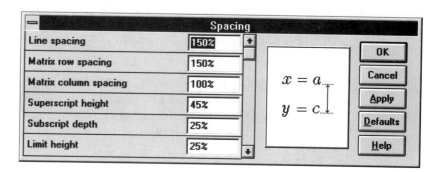

Spacing		
Line spacing	150%	OK
Matrix row spacing	150%	Cancel
Matrix column spacing	100%	Apply
Superscript height	45%	Defaults
Subscript depth	25%	Help
Limit height	25%	

$$x = a$$
$$y = c$$

Styles

While Word automatically applies styles to elements of the equation, you can manually apply styles or edit them. To select a new style, pull down the Style menu to select from these options:

◆ Math is the default style. Word will automatically apply styles to selected parts of the equation.

◆ Text is provided so you can enter text without Word applying other styles. Text appears in regular font, and you can use the spacebar to enter spaces between words. Use the text style to enter words that contain mathematical functions. For example, if you type **logical,** Word displays the characters **log** in the regular font assuming it is the log function, then the characters *ical* in italic font as a variable.

◆ Function is the style that Word applies to mathematical function names such as log and sin.

◆ Variable is the style applied to all letters not recognized as function names and not in text style.

◆ Greek displays lowercase Greek letters in italic, uppercase letters in Regular. The characters are taken from the Symbol font.

◆ Matrix-Vector is the style applied to characters that represent matrix or vector quantities. Bold is the default.

◆ Other lets you choose another font, and bold or italic, to format selected characters.

◆ Define displays the dialog box shown in Figure 6.11 to edit the style definition. For example, you should change the font to match the font of the text surrounding the equation.

Size

Word formats characters in default point sizes based on their position in the equation. For example, regular characters, at the first level, are 12 points and subscripts are 7 points. You can use the options in the Size menu to change the size of selected characters to match one of five preset options.

FIGURE 6.11

Equation editor
Styles dialog box

Style	Font	Character Format Bold	Italic	
Text	Times New Roman	☐	☐	OK
Function	Times New Roman	☐	☐	Cancel
Variable	Times New Roman	☐	☒	Help
L.C. Greek	Symbol	☐	☒	
U.C. Greek	Symbol	☐	☐	
Symbol	Symbol	☐	☐	
Matrix-Vector . . .	Times New Roman	☒	☐	
Number	Times New Roman	☐	☐	

Styles

Tip   Because the equation will appear in a picture box, you can always select the box and drag a handle to enlarge or reduce it.

◆ Full is the size applied to regular characters within most slots. The default is 12 points.

◆ Subscript is the size applied to subscripts and superscripts that are attached to full-size characters. The default is 7 points.

◆ Sub-Subscript is the size applied to subscripts and superscripts applied to characters smaller than full size, such as a subscript to a superscript. The default is 5 points.

◆ Symbol is the size applied to large symbols that are part of the integrals, summations, products, and other templates.

◆ Sub-Symbol is the size applied to symbols that appear in subscript and superscript slots.

◆ Select Other from the Size menu to choose a specific point size for selected characters.

◆ Select Define to display a dialog box in which you can change the automatic sizes applied to the preset elements.

S O L U T I O N S

Using the Equation Window

Depending on the speed of your computer system, it may take Word some time to start the equation editor. If you want to work on an equation while referring to text in the document, you'd have to exit the editor, and then restart it when you want to work on the equation.

As an alternative, before starting the equation editor, select Display as Icon in the Insert Object dialog box. When you start the equation editor it will be displayed in a separate window. The window will include a View menu in addition to the other equation menu options. If the toolbar does not appear, select View ➤ Toolbar. Other options on the View menu let you change the displayed magnification.

When you need to refer to the text, minimize the equation editor window, or press Alt+Tab to quickly display the Word document. To move back to the equation editor, press Alt+Tab again.

When you are done creating the equation, select File ➤ Exit and Return to close the equation editor. You can also select File ➤ Update, then minimize the editor in case you'll need it again later.

Microsoft
√α
Microsoft Equation
2.0

The equation will appear as an icon, but will print correctly. If you want to display the actual equation on screen, select it, then choose Edit ➤ Equation Object ➤ Convert. In the dialog box that appears, deselect the Display as Icon button and then select OK.

Creating Inline Equations

An inline equation is one that appears within a line of text, as shown in Figure 6.12. You can use the equation editor to create the equation, then frame the picture box and change its size to fit in the line. If you have a simple equation to enter, however, you can use the EQ form field.

FIGURE 6.12

Inline equations using the EQ field

The $\sqrt{25}$ equals 5.

What is the $\sqrt{\dfrac{1}{2}}$?

Note A form field is a command to Word to insert some information or object into the document. You can toggle between displaying the results and the instruction by selecting the field and pressing Shift+F9. For more information on form fields, see Chapter 14.

Inserting Form Fields

To insert the field, select Insert ➤ Field, select the Field Codes box, and delete the = sign. Type EQ, the codes and text that represent the equation, then select OK.

The equation appears in the line of text as a field, but it is treated as text. Characters in the equation appear in the same font and size that was in effect at the insertion point position. You can select the field (by itself or with other text) to change the font or size.

Editing Inline Equations

If you double-click on the equation, Word displays it in the equation editor so you can change it. However, when you exit the editor, the field will be converted to an equation object in a picture box. The characters in the box will now be displayed using the default fonts and sizes automatically applied to the style, no longer in the format of the text at the insertion point.

You can select and resize the equation picture box, but you can no longer format it as regular text. To change the text, use the Style menu in the equation editor.

Using Equation Code Switches

Equation codes consist of switches, which tell Word how to format objects or to insert special characters and text. Most of the switches also have options to further define the function you want to perform. The switches and options begin with the backslash (\) character.

One very useful switch is \x, which tells Word to create a box. Use it to simulate keyboard keys, as shown in Figure 6.13.

When the \x switch is not followed by options, the box is drawn with all four borders. Use one of the options illustrated in the figure to specify which borders to draw.

Use the \o switch to create an overstrike. The syntax is eq \o(X,Y). Word will superimpose character X on character Y, such as using eq \o (0,/) to display a slashed zero.

Here are some other EQ codes. Note that you can nest codes, such as using eq \r(\f(1,2)) to include a fraction under a radical.

◆ \a draws a matrix, as in eq \a \co3(1,2,3,4,5,6) to create:

123
456

Press Ctrl Alt Del to reboot your computer.

Draw a box { eq \x (box) }

Draw on the top { eq \x \to (top) }

Draw on the bottom { eq \x \bo (bottom) }

Draw on the left { eq \x \le (left) }

Draw on the right { eq \x \ri (right) }

Options include \al to align columns on the left; \ac to align columns in the center; \ar to align columns on the right; \coN to specify N number of columns; \vsN to specify the vertical spacing between lines as N points; and \hsN to specify the horizontal spacing between columns as N points.

◆ \b inserts a bracket around characters. The options specify the bracket to use. \lc\c inserts the left bracket indicated by c, either {, [, (, or <, as in \lc\{; \rc\c inserts the right bracket; \bc\c inserts both the left and right brackets. For example, eq \b \bc\{ (Secrets and Solutions) enclosed the specified words between left and right braces.

◆ \d moves the insertion point to position the next character. The options are \foN to move forward N points; \baN to move backward N points; and \li to draw a line from the end of the character to the beginning of the next character.

◆ \f inserts a fraction using the syntax:

`\f(numerator,denominator)`

◆ \i creates an integral, using the syntax:

`\1(lower limit, upper limit, integrand)`

Options are \su to use a capital sigma and a summation; \pr to use a capital Pi and a product; \in to use an inline format with the limits on the right; \fc\c to use a fixed-height character specified by c; \vc\c to use a variable-height character specified by c.

◆ \l inserts a list of values. The syntax is:

`\l (1,2,3,4,...)`

to display the values separated by commas.

◆ \r inserts a radical. When you use one parameter, as in eq \r(x), the parameter appears under the radical. When you use two, as in eq \r(x,y), the first parameter is above the radical, the second under it.

◆ \s creates a superscript or subscript, such as eq \s (x) to superscript the letter x. Options are \aiN to add N points of space above the baseline; \upN to superscript a character by n points; \diN top add n points of space below the baseline; and \doN to subscript a character n points.

SOLUTIONS

Custom Letter Spacing

You can also create interesting effects by spacing characters. You can condense characters to fit more on a line, expand them to take up additional spaces, and move characters up or down for custom subscripts and superscripts.

Select the characters you want to adjust, then choose Format ➤ Font ➤ Character Spacing to display the dialog box shown here.

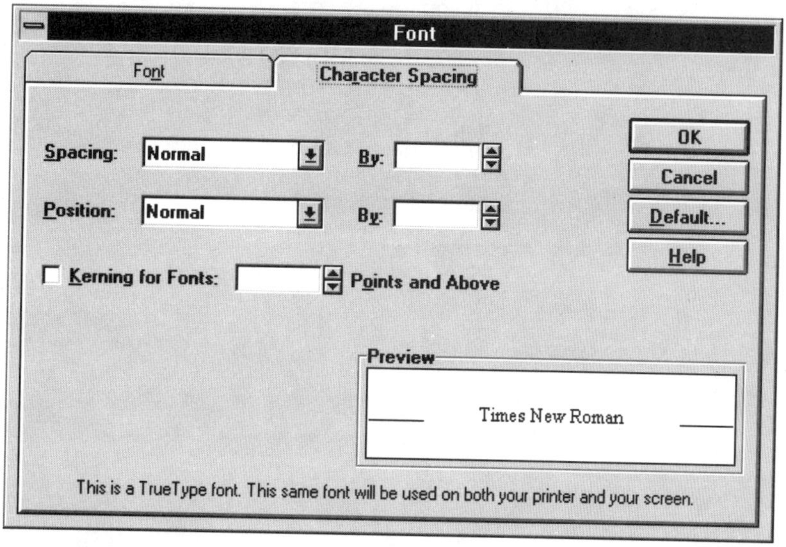

Spacing options are Normal, Expanded (extra space between characters), and Condense (less space). Position options are Normal, Raised (above the baseline), and Lower (below the baseline). As you enter size and position options, the text in the preview pane changes to reflect the settings.

Use the spacing and position options to make headlines fit across columns, or in other tight spaces, as shown here.

STRETCH A HEADLINE
STRETCH A HEADLINE
STRETCH A HEADLINE
STRETCH A HEADLINE

SHRINK A HEADLINE
SHRINK A HEADLINE
SHRINK A HEADLINE
SHRINK A HEADLINE

POSITION DO$_{OW_N}$

POSTION U^P U^P

CHAPTER
7

Columns and Tables

IF YOU PRODUCE NEWSLETTERS OR other multicolumn documents, you can take advantage of Word's column feature. To format tables, use the table feature. Tables are most often used to display statistical data, but they are also ideal for creating ruled forms of all types and a variety of special documents that would be difficult to create in any other way. In fact, the more you know about Word tables, the more uses you will find for them. (See Chapters 11 and 14 for more information.)

Working with Columns

Word can automatically format text in newspaper columns—text that flows from one column to the next across the page. When the far-right column is filled, the text moves to the left column on the next page. If you delete or insert text, Word will move the text from column to column or page to page as necessary to accommodate your changes.

You can type and edit your text in a single column, then format it in multiple columns when you're done. Or, you can create the column layout and then type your document. Either way, you can change the number of columns, and their size and spacing, until you get the layout you want.

Creating Columns

With a mouse, you can quickly create up to four equal-width columns. If you want to create columns of unequal width, use the Columns dialog box as explained later in this chapter.

The Column Format

The column format will affect all of the text in the current section. If your document is not divided into sections, all of its text will appear in the number of columns that you select. You can combine single and multiple column text on the same page, as shown in Figure 7.1.

FIGURE 7.1

Single and
multiple columns

MYTHS AND METHODS OF MUSCLE REFINEMENT

Place the insertion point where you want the columns to begin, then select Insert ➤ Break ➤ Continuous ➤ OK. Word will insert a section break that does not change pages.

Note   The number of columns specified will only affect text from the section break to the end of the document, or until the next section break is encountered.

Place the insertion point in the section you want to format as columns, then click on the column button in the toolbar to see a diagram of four columns. Select Cancel or click in the document window if you change your mind. Otherwise, click on the column in the diagram that represents the number of columns you want. You can also drag the mouse to the column, and then release the mouse.

For example, to create two columns, click on the second column in the diagram or drag to the second column and release the mouse button. All of the text in the current section will flow from column to column and from page to page. In Page Layout view, you'll see the columns side-by-side on the screen. In Normal view, the columns will appear under each other.

Ending a Column

To manually end a column, press Ctrl+Shift+Enter. The insertion point will move to the next column. If you press Ctrl+Shift+Enter at the right-most column, Word will insert a page break and begin the left column on the next page. If you insert a column break in existing text, the text following the insertion point will shift to the next column.

Changing Column Width

The ruler shows the width of each column, separated by *gutters*, the spaces between columns. Gutters are indicated by gray areas, as shown in Figure 7.2.

FIGURE 7.2
Column ruler
shows column
width and spacing

With equal width columns, the only way to change column width is to increase or decrease the gutter size. Dragging the left or right side of a gutter indicator increases or decreases the size of the gutters. However, all of the columns will adjust so they remain equal in width.

If you have two columns, for example, increasing the gutter by one inch will reduce each column by $1/2$ inch. Similarly, reducing the gutter by a half inch will increase each column by a quarter inch.

Tip

If you hold down the Alt key while you click or drag the mouse, Word will display the column width and gutter measurements in the ruler. Use the measurements to create columns or gutters of exact size.

If you have more than two columns, changing the size of one gutter automatically makes the other gutters the same size. As you increase or decrease one gutter, the other will change as well.

In Page Layout mode, you can drag the left or right margin indicators in the ruler to change the page margin. However, all of the columns will adjust equally to accommodate the new margin.

The Columns Dialog Box

If you want to create more than four columns, create unequal columns, or if you have trouble obtaining an exact measurement with the mouse, use the Columns dialog box. Select Format ➤ Column to display the dialog box shown in Figure 7.3.

FIGURE 7.3

Columns dialog box

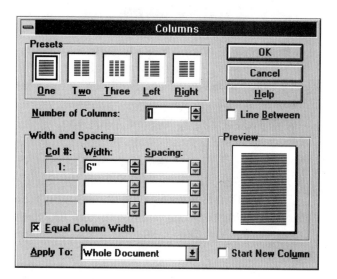

Equal Width Columns

To create columns of equal width, use the Two or Three preset options, or make sure the Equal Column Width checkbox is selected and enter a number in the Number of Columns box. The settings in the Width and Spacing section, and the graphic in the Preview pane, change to illustrate the column layout.

In the Width and Spacing section, only the first column will be active, the other columns will be dimmed. If you change the width of the first column, all of the columns will change to the same size, and the spacing will change accordingly to fit the columns on the page. You can increase the column width only until there is no spacing between them. If you change the spacing setting, the column widths will adjust automatically.

Tip   Select Line Between to display a vertical line between the columns—the line will extend only as far as the longest column on the page. Choose Start New Column to insert a column break.

Uneven Columns

To create two columns of unequal width, select the Left or Right preset options. With standard $8\frac{1}{2}$ inch-wide paper, the Left button creates a left column 1.67 inches wide and a right column 3.83 inches wide. The Right button places the narrow column on the right.

More than Two Columns

To create more than two columns, deselect the Equal Column Width checkbox, then enter the number in the Numbers of Columns box. Change the width of the columns or the spacing between them in the Width and Spacing section. Changing the width of one column, or the spacing between columns, will affect the size of the column to its right, while maintaining the same spacing.

Applying the Column Format

Before selecting OK in the Column dialog box, consider how you want the columns to be applied. Pull down the Apply To list for these options:

◆ **Whole Document:** The columns affect the entire document, even if it is already divided into sections.

◆ **This Point Forward:** Word adds a continuous section break at the location of the insertion point, creating columns from that point to the end of the document. Use this option to combine single and multiple columns on one page.

◆ **This Section:** The columns affect only the text in the current section, if the document is already divided into sections.

Creating Uneven Columns

When you create uneven columns, you can change the width of individual columns and the spacing between them using the mouse and the ruler. A small icon will appear in the center of the gutter indicator, as shown in Figure 7.4.

FIGURE 7.4

Gutter indicator icon

Drag the center of a gutter indicator to move the position of the gutter, changing the width of the columns on either side of the gutter, without changing the gutter size. Drag one of the sides of the gutter to change the gutter width and one column.

Tip

You can convert equal to unequal columns and back again. Display the Columns dialog box and select or deselect the Equal Column Width checkbox.

Single Column Format

To convert multiple columns to a single column, select one column from the column toolbar button or the One preset in the Column dialog box. Word will remove the columns but will retain the column breaks that you inserted by pressing Ctrl+Shift+Enter to manually end columns. The column breaks will serve as page breaks.

S E C R E T S

Column Tips and Tricks

The last text in a document, or section, may not be enough to fill all of the columns on a page. For example, you may have a page of three columns followed by a page with one, two, or three partial columns.

To balance the columns so the text is divided evenly across the page (as shown here), place the insertion point at the end of the text and select Insert ➤ Break ➤ Continuous ➤ OK.

You can also use the mouse to move and scale a picture so it appears within a column or across several columns. Insert the picture, surround it in a frame, then choose Format ➤ Frame.

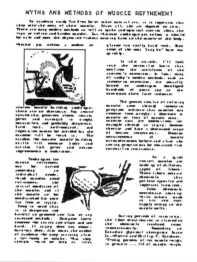

The Relative To option in the Horizontal section will be set at Column. In the Position option, select Left, Center, or Right to set the position of the picture within the column.

If you have two columns, center the picture in the page by selecting Center position, relative to the page or the margins. To center the picture between two of three columns drag it with the mouse.

Columns and Styles

If you use columns often, consider creating a template and styles to hold the definitions. Using the techniques covered in Chapter 2, for example, you could create a template and styles with all of the formats you need for a standard monthly newsletter.

Design the template with standard elements that you use with every edition:

◆ A masthead on the first page of the template

◆ A header or footer to display the date of publication, and the page number (alternated for odd and even pages)

Create styles for common formatted elements:

◆ A style for large multicolumn headings

◆ A style for smaller single column headings

◆ Styles for standard elements, such as an index of the contents or classified advertisements

Create empty frames that you can use as placeholders or text boxes:

◆ A frame for a single column figure box

◆ A frame for a two column figure box

◆ A frame for an index

When you need to create an edition of the newsletter, open the template and use the styles. Insert continuous section breaks and select columns when needed.

Creating Booklets with Columns

An easy way to create booklets is to use $8\frac{1}{2}$ by 11 inch paper in landscape orientation folded in half. The final booklet size is $5\frac{1}{2}$ by $8\frac{1}{2}$ inches.

Laying Out the Booklet

To create a booklet, select File ➤ Page Setup ➤ Paper Size, then select landscape orientation.

 **Tip** You should also change the margins, because the default margins will be too large for the smaller booklet page size. Select the Margin tab and change all four margins to .5 inch.

Next, pull down the Columns button and select two columns, or select the Two preset in the Columns dialog box. Widen the spacing between the column to one inch, so when folded there will be a .5 inch margin on all sides.

Now create a dummy (a sample layout) by folding full pages in half. Write the page number of each page, then unfold the sheet to see which pages are actually next to each other on the paper (see Figure 7.5). For example, if you're creating a four page booklet, which is one sheet folded in half, your pages will be in this order:

4 1
2 3

FIGURE 7.5

Folded booklet
page layout

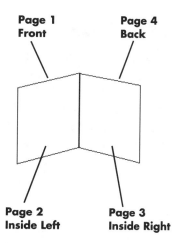

Page 1
Front

Page 4
Back

Page 2
Inside Left

Page 3
Inside Right

Entering the Text

Type the text of each page, pressing Ctrl+Shift+Enter after each. Enter the text in this order—4, 1, 2 and 3. If you want to create a booklet using existing text that already flows from page to page, you must rearrange the order of pages.

Open the document and set up the landscape page with two columns. Change to Page Layout view and zoom to display the whole page. Place the insertion point at the end of the first column on the right and press Ctrl+Shift+Enter to insert a column break, then Ctrl+Enter to insert a page break.

This moves the second booklet page to the left column of the next page, the third booklet page to the right column of the page, and the fourth booklet page to the third page.

Select and cut the text of the fourth page, place the insertion point after the column break that you entered, but before the page break, and paste the text.

 **Tip**   You can also number the booklet pages. Type the numbers manually or use the SEQ form field, as explained in Chapter 3.

Printing the Booklet

To print a booklet, select File ➤ Print, select Pages in the Page Range section, enter 1, then select OK. The first page will print with page 4 on the left and page 1 on the right. Turn the paper around and insert it into the printer. Reinsert it so the blank side will be printed. Do not rotate the page, but make sure that the top edge of the text is in the same direction. Then select File ➤ Print, enter 2 in the Pages section and select OK. Booklet pages 2 and 3 will print in the correct order.

Making Portrait and Landscape Brochures

Suppose that you need to create a brochure that includes a mailing address as shown in Figure 7.6. This is a common format that contains six panels of text when the page is folded in thirds. The format requires five panels of text in landscape orientation as well as one panel in portrait orientation.

We will create the brochure by printing the landscape text using a three column layout, then reinserting the page and printing the address panel in portrait orientation.

FIGURE 7.6

Brochure with landscape and portrait text

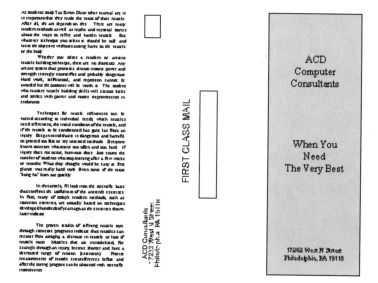

The Landscape Template

The landscape panels in both the inside and outside pages of the brochure use the same page size, orientation, and column layout. So rather than format the page twice, start by creating a template that you can use for both sides of the page. Use these steps:

1. Select File ➤ New ➤ Template, and then select OK.

2. Use File ➤ Page Setup to select landscape orientation and set the margins at .25 inches.

3. Format the page into three equal-sized columns.

4. Save the template as Broland, and close the window.

The Portrait Template

The address panel will be printed in portrait orientation. The page layout must be set up to position the panel between the two landscape panels on the same sheet of paper. Create a template for the panel using these steps:

1. Select File ➤ New ➤ Template.

2. Use File ➤ Page Setup and make sure the page is set at portrait orientation.

3. Set the left and right margins at .25, set the top margin at 3.9, and set the bottom margin at 4.

4. Save the template as Broport, and close the window.

Adding Landscape Text

All three of the inside panels use landscape orientation. To create the inside of the brochure, follow these steps:

1. Start a new document using the Broland template.

2. Type the text of the three inside panels. To end one page and start another, press Ctrl+Shift+Enter or let Word insert page breaks for you.

3. Print the page.

4. Save the document and close the window.

 **Note**

The outside panels of the brochure contain both landscape and portrait orientation. Because this part of the brochure will be folded, you must consider the order in which you enter the text.

5. Start a new document using the Broland template.

6. In the column on the left, type the text that you want to appear on page 5—the panel that will be folded inside.

7. Press Ctrl+Shift+Enter twice to reach the panel on the right, skipping over the center panel.

8. Type the text you want to appear on the cover. The cover in Figure 7.6 uses a shaded text box created with the drawing toolbar.

9. Insert the page that you just printed so the blank side will be printed, then print the document now on the screen.

10. Save the document on the screen, then close the window.

Creating the Address Panel

The address panel will print in portrait orientation in the blank space in the center of the outside panels.

1. Start a new document using the Broport template.

2. Enter the text of the panel including your return address. Make sure the text does not flow onto another page. In Figure 7.6, the boxes that represent the position of the stamp and mailing label were created with empty frames and borders.

3. Reinsert the page so the side with the two inside panels will be printed on.

4. Print the page.

Tip

As an alternative to printing the address panel in portrait orientation, use WordArt to rotate text and add it directly to the landscape page.

S E C R E T S

Brochure Tips and Tricks

You can have any number of variations in the layout of the inside pages of the brochure. As shown here, one alternative is to have two uneven columns, with the larger column spreading across two inside panels.

When You Need The Very Best in Computer Hardware...

We offer the very best hardware, software, and computer support. Just one call will get you everything you need. That's all there is to it.

Hardware

We have computers, printers, monitors, boards, disk drive, tape backup systems, and everything piece of computer hardware imaginable. If we do not have it in stock, we can still ship it out within 24 hours. If not, you get 10% off of your entire order.

Software

We have word processing, spreadsheet, database, utilities, programming, and game programs. We receive new software every day, so we have the latest versions. If you purchase a product from us, and a new version is released within 10 days, you get the update free, even if there is a charge from the manufacturer.

Service

Service should be our middle name! We give free services on a toll-free line, 24 hours, seven days each week. Just call. We will answer the call within five minutes, or you get a free gift.

Some Comments From Satisfied Customers

"They are the best"
William Watson, Philadelphia

"I would never order from anyone else"
Paul Smith, Margate

"If they go out of business, I will shoot myself"
J. Paul Jones, Denver

"My prices have never been lower"
Nancy Chesin, Alameda

"I buy everything from them"
Susan Smithson, Orem

To create the effect, start a document with the Broland template, then select the Left or Right preset in the Columns dialog box. Adjust the width of the columns, and their spacing as desired.

Working with Tables

You access Word's table feature using the toolbar or the Table pull-down menu. But before creating a table, you should decide how many rows and columns you will need. Although you can add or delete rows and columns, your table will be easier to work with if you start with the appropriate structure. With the default row height and one inch top and bottom margins, 54 rows will fit on an $8\frac{1}{2}$ inch by 11 inch page.

 **Note**   Word extends the table between the left and right margins, dividing the space into columns of equal size. If you create a two column table, for example, each column will be three inches wide. If you create a table in a newspaper column, the table extends between column margins. You can change the size of the table and the width of individual columns using the mouse or keyboard.

Creating a Spreadsheet

Word's table features are especially useful for designing and working with spreadsheets. We will start by creating the sample spreadsheet shown in Figure 7.7, which uses formulas and contains special formatting.

FIGURE 7.7
Sample spreadsheet

	Sun Manufacturing Company Comparative Analysis		
	1995	1996	1997
Sales	1246	1321	1282
Rentals	89	91	92
Total Income	1335	1412	1374
Salaries	543	552	522
Office	99	102	98
Total Expenses	642	654	620
Net	693	758	754
Net % of Sales	56%	57%	59%
All figures are in thousands of dollars			

Defining the Table Size

If you do not have a mouse, select Table ➤ Insert Table. In the dialog box that appears, type **7** for columns, press Tab, type **12** for rows, and then select OK. You can create a table of up to 31 columns and any number of rows.

Creating a Blank Table

To create a blank table with the mouse, follow these steps:

1. Select a 10 point type size.

2. Point to the table button in the toolbar and hold down the left mouse button. A miniature grid appears, representing the rows and columns of a table, as shown in Figure 7.8.

FIGURE 7.8

Table grid in the toolbar

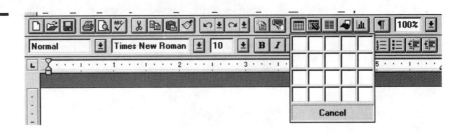

 **Note** You can use the toolbar to create a table of up to 10 columns and 16 rows. To create a table with up to 31 columns, use the Table ➤ Insert Table command.

3. Drag the mouse slightly down and to the right. As you drag the mouse, squares in the grid become selected. The cancel button at the bottom of the grid will change to reflect the number of rows and columns indicated by the selected squares.

4. Move the mouse until the cancel button says 12 x 7 Table, then release the mouse button. A blank table will appear at the top of the screen, as shown in Figure 7.9. (Notice that the ruler indicates the column width and the space between columns.)

FIGURE 7.9

Blank table

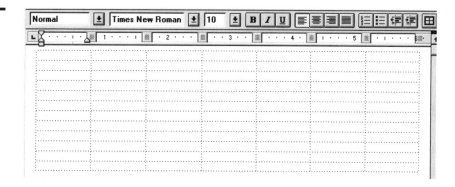

Navigating the Table

Each cell in the table is referenced by its row and column numbers. The top-left cell is A1. A four row by five column table would be referenced as follows:

	A	B	C	D	E
1	A1	B1	C1	D1	E1
2	A2	B2	C2	D2	E2
3	A3	B3	C3	D3	E3
4	A4	B4	C4	D4	E4

 **Note**

The gridlines around the cell are for your reference. They will not print. However, you can create printable gridlines using the Borders toolbar or dialog box. The gridlines can be toggled on or off by selecting Table ➤ Gridlines. If you create a table and its does not seem to appear on screen, then the display of gridlines has been turned off. Don't try to create the table again, just toggle on the gridline display.

The ruler will show the width of the columns. Note that between each column is a gray shaded spacing, or gutter, area. This represents a default .15 space that Word adds between the contents of the cells. The space is divided between the cells on either side, placing a 0.075 inch inside margin area around text. You will soon learn how you can change this spacing, and how it affects column width.

Entering Text and Data

To enter text in a cell, place the insertion point in the cell and type. To place the insertion point in a cell, click on the cell with the mouse, use the arrows, or the Tab key.

If you press Enter within a cell, or if word wrap takes effect in a long entry, the cell will increase its height by one line. If you press Enter by mistake, press Backspace to return the row to its original height.

Now we will enter some text and numbers in the blank table. Do not be concerned with alignment or cell size. We will format the table after it contains the data.

Type the following text in the cells in the first column. Remember, do not press Enter to move down to the next cell.

Cell A3: **Sales**

Cell A4: **Rentals**

Cell A5: **Total Income**

Cell A6: **Salaries**

Cell A7: **Office**

Cell A8: **Total Expenses**

Cell A9: **Net**

Cell A10: **Net % of Sales**

Enter the following figures in the columns. We won't be entering amounts in rows 5, 8, 9, and 10. These entries will later be calculated and inserted by Word. We'll enter the dates in columns B, D, and E after we adjust the width of the columns.

Cell C2: **1995**	Cell E2: **1996**	Cell G2: **1997**
Cell C3: **1246**	Cell E3: **1321**	Cell G3: **1282**
Cell C4: **89**	Cell E4: **91**	Cell G4: **92**
Cell C6: **543**	Cell E6: **552**	Cell G6: **522**
Cell C7: **99**	Cell E7: **102**	Cell G7: **98**

Selecting Cells

You must select cells in order to perform some table operations. You can select an entire cell, row, or column, or just the contents of cells. The way you select will affect the type of operation that you can perform.

To select entire cells, rows, or columns with the mouse, use one of these techniques:

◆ **Cells:** place the mouse pointer in the lower-left corner of the cell so it appears as a large arrow, pointing diagonally from the lower left to the upper right, then click. You can tell that a cell is selected, and not just its contents, when the selection highlight extends beyond the text of the cell to the cell border.

◆ **Rows:** place the mouse pointer in the left margin and click. You can also click twice when selecting a cell, or select Table ➤ Select Row. You can tell that the entire row is selected, not just its contents, when the selection extends one space beyond the right edge of the table. This selection includes the end of row marker, a special code you can display by clicking on the Show/Hide toolbar button.

◆ **Columns:** place the pointer on the top line of the column until it changes to a black arrow, and then click. You can also select Table ➤ Select Column.

◆ **Table:** select Table ➤ Select Table, or press Alt+5 (on the numeric keypad), or click three times when selecting a cell or a row.

◆ **Multiple Cells:** drag the mouse across cells, and click again to deselect the cells.

◆ **Cell Contents Only:** double-click on the contents, or drag over them with the mouse. You can also press F8 and use the arrow keys.

The contents are selected if the highlight only covers the contents, without extending beyond to the cell border.

 Note To select a cell with the keyboard, place the insertion point in the cell and press F8. To extend the selection, press the arrow keys.

S E C R E T S

Using the Show/Hide Button

If you click on the Show/Hide button in the toolbar, Word will display end-of-cell marks in each cell, and end-of-row marks at the end of each table row, as shown here.

When you select an entire cell or row, you also select the end-of-cell and end-of-row markers. That's how Word distinguishes between the selection of cells and just the contents of the cells.

Moving and Copying Cells

You can move or copy cells, or just the contents of the cells. When you copy a cell, Word inserts the contents and formats of the cell in another location, deleting the contents already there. When you move or copy a row or column, the other rows or columns shift over or down to make room. They are not deleted.

Using Drag and Drop

The easiest way to move a cell, row, or column is to drag and drop with the mouse. Select the cells you want to move, including the end-of-cell or end-of-row markers. Then, point to the selection so the mouse pointer appears as a large arrow pointing diagonally from the lower right to the upper left.

Hold down the mouse button, drag the mouse to the location where you want to insert the cells, then release the mouse button. To copy the cells, hold down the Ctrl key while you release the mouse button.

 **Tip**

> To move just the contents of a single cell, drag the mouse over the contents within the cell. Do not select the entire cell. When you move or copy just the contents, the data is added to any already in the cell, and the cell retains its own format.

Moving Entire Rows and Columns

When dragging an entire row, move the pointer to the first cell in a row, then release the mouse button. The row will be inserted, moving existing rows down. If you release the mouse button in another column of the row, the selected row will be inserted. This will push the existing cells to the left or right, outside of the rectangular area of the table.

When dragging an entire column, point to the first cell in another column before releasing the mouse. Otherwise, the column will push existing cells below the end of the table.

With the Keyboard

Using the keyboard, select the cells, then select Edit ➤ Cut or Edit ➤ Copy. Move the insertion point to where you want to insert the text and select Edit ➤ Paste Cells.

Changing Cell and Column Widths

You can change the width of an entire column, or of just selected cells. To change the column width, place the insertion point in any cell of the column, but make certain the cell is not selected. If you adjust the column width when a cell is selected, only the width of the cell will change, not that of the entire column.

Figure 7.10, for example, shows a three column table in which individual cells were selected, then the column width changed. (If you make any changes to your table that appear incorrect, just select Edit ➤ Undo.)

FIGURE 7.10

Changing cell and column widths

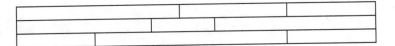

Using the Format Dialog Box

If you do not have a mouse, you must use the Format dialog box to change the width of columns. Place the insertion point in cell A3 of our sample table, then choose Table ➤ Cell Height and Width. Choose the Column tab to display the options shown in Figure 7.11.

FIGURE 7.11

Cell Height and Width dialog box

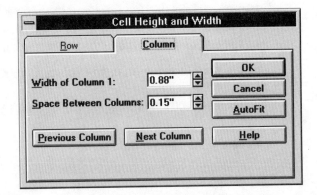

In the Width of Column 1 text box, type **1.14** and then select OK. Use the same procedure to change the widths of columns B, D, and F to .16. Change the width of columns C, E, and G to .92 inch.

 **N o t e** The column width you enter in the dialog box includes the .15 spacing. A column set at 1.14, for example, can only contain 0.99 inches of text. The AutoFit button adjusts all of the columns based on their contents.

Using the Mouse

With a mouse, you can change the width of columns by dragging. Follow these steps to change the width of columns in our table:

1. Point to a vertical line between column A and B, in any of the cells.

2. Move the pointer until it changes to a two-headed arrow.

3. Press and hold down the left mouse button. A dotted vertical line appears on the screen indicating the column border. It extends up to the ruler to aid in locating the proper position.

4. Hold down the Alt key and drag the mouse to the right until the column width says .99. The measurements in the ruler indicate the space for text in the column, after the .15 space. To enter this same width in the dialog box, you enter 1.14.

 **N o t e** Depending on the steadiness of your hand and the resolution of your mouse, you may not be able to get an exact setting using the mouse. Don't worry about it. Get as close as you can to the settings, then if necessary, set them exactly using the Cell Height and Width dialog box.

5. Drag the border line between column B and C to the left as far as it will go, to reduce the width of column B.

6. In the same way, reduce the widths of column D and F.

7. Drag the right edge of the table to the left to reduce column G to .77—or as close to .77 as you can.

8. Likewise, change columns C and E to .77 inches.

If necessary, use the Cell Height and Width dialog box to get the exact measurements. In the dialog box, row A should be set at 1.14; rows B, D, and F should be .16; and rows C, E, and G should be set at .92.

Formatting Tables

Through the Format menu and the toolbar, you can set the formats of individual or selected cells, columns, rows, or the entire table. For example, use Format ➤ Paragraph ➤ Alignment ➤ Center, or the Center toolbar button, to center text within a cell.

Let's use the following steps to format the text in the cells:

1. Select Cells C2 through G2.

2. Click on the Center button in the toolbar or select Format ➤ Paragraph ➤ Alignment ➤ Center.

3. Select cells C3 through G10.

4. Click on the Align Right button in the toolbar, or select Format ➤ Paragraph ➤ Alignment ➤ Right. (To align numbers on a decimal point, select the cells and set a decimal tab stop.)

Tip   The Table ➤ Headings option designates selected rows as *headers,* rows that automatically appear as the first row of the table if the table extends into another page.

S O L U T I O N S

Using AutoFormat

You can format an entire table in one step using the AutoFormat command. Place the insertion point in any cell of the table, then select Table ➤ Table AutoFormat to display the dialog box shown here. (You can also select AutoFormat from the Insert Table dialog box.)

Table AutoFormat

Formats:
- (none)
- Simple 1
- Simple 2
- Simple 3
- Classic 1
- Classic 2
- Classic 3
- Classic 4
- Colorful 1
- Colorful 2

Preview

	Jan	Feb	Mar	Total
East	7	7	5	19
West	6	4	7	17
South	8	7	9	24
Total	21	18	21	60

OK | Cancel | Help

Formats to Apply
- ☒ Borders ☒ Font ☒ AutoFit
- ☒ Shading ☐ Color

Apply Special Formats To
- ☒ Heading Rows ☐ Last Row
- ☒ First Column ☐ Last Column

The Format list contains over 30 preset styles that you can apply to the entire table. Choose a format and see how it looks in the Preview pane. To select a format, click on OK.

Each of the preset styles includes the settings for the formats shown in the Formats to Apply section. An X in a checkbox indicates that the format will be applied when you use the style. For

233

example, the X in the Borders checkbox means that the style will apply certain borders and shading to your table.

If you already applied a format that you want to retain, deselect the checkbox. Deselecting the Font box, for example, will prevent Word from changing the fonts that you've already applied to the table contents.

Some styles apply special formats to certain components of the table. These are indicated by selected boxes in the Apply Special Formats To section. Deselect any of the components that you do not want to change.

Merging Cells

When you merge cells in a row, the gridline separating the cells disappears and the area appears as one large cell. You cannot merge cells down a column.

We will merge several cells on the table and then enter some text. Merge cells when you want to enter more text than will fit in one line in a single column.

1. Select cells B1 through G1.

2. Select Tables ➤ Merge Cells.

3. Select cells A11 through G11, then select Tables ➤ Merge Cells.

4. In the same manner, merge cells A12 through G12.

5. To enter text in cell C1, click on the Center button, type **Sun Manufacturing Company,** press Enter, and type **Comparative Analysis.**

6. In cell A12, click on the Center button, and then type **All figures are in thousands of dollars.**

Note

> Once you merge cells, their column width measurement will not appear in the Cell Height and Width dialog box. To change the width of the column, select the cells first.

Adding and Deleting Rows and Columns

There are several ways to change the size of a table. To add a row to the end of the table, place the insertion point in the last cell of the table and press Tab. To add a column to the end of the table, place the insertion point just outside the right of the table (on the end-of-row marker), select Table ➤ Select Column, then click on the Insert Table button in the toolbar.

The Insert Table Button

The Insert Table button actually serves as a general purpose button when the insertion point is within the table. It works as follows:

◆ If you have no cells selected, clicking on the button will insert a new row above the row in which the insertion point is located.

◆ To insert a column, select a column and then click on the button. Word will insert a column to the left of the selected column.

◆ To insert several rows or columns, select an equal number of rows or columns and then click the button. For example, if you select two rows and click on the button, Word will insert two rows.

If you have a cell or several cells selected, clicking on the button will display the dialog box shown in Figure 7.12.

FIGURE 7.12
Insert Cells
dialog box

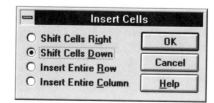

Select the action you want to perform, then select OK. Selecting to shift cells to the right will create a non-rectangular table, as shown in Figure 7.13.

FIGURE 7.13
Table after
inserted cells

The Delete Option

To delete a row or column, select it, then choose the Delete option from the Table menu. If you have a cell or several cells selected, you'll see the dialog box shown in Figure 7.14. Select an option, then OK.

FIGURE 7.14
Delete Cells
dialog box

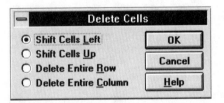

S O L U T I O N S

Instant Tables and Table Wizards

You can quickly convert tabular columns created with the tab key into a table. Select the text you want to convert, then select Table ➤ Insert Table. Word converts each Tab code to a cell boundary, and each hard carriage return to the end of a row.

To convert a table to text, select the entire table, then choose Table ➤ Convert Table to Text. A dialog box will appear asking how you want to treat the end of each cell. You can choose to separate the cell contents with paragraph marks (to make a list), tabs (to make a tabular format), commas, or another specific character.

You can also create a custom formatted table by using the Table Wizard. Select Table ➤ Insert Table, then select Wizard from the dialog box. Follow the prompts and dialog boxes that appear on the screen. You will be asked to select an overall layout, alignment of text and numbers in cells, and either portrait or landscape orientation. The Table Wizard box shown here, for example, allows you to automatically add dates or numbers as column headings.

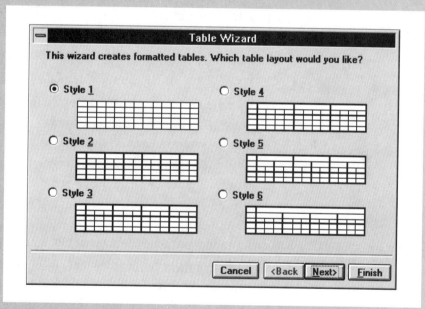

A similar dialog box will appear for selecting row headings. The Table AutoFormat dialog box will appear when you complete the Table Wizard. Select a format, then OK to display the completely formatted table.

 **Tip**
Don't forget that you can also use the shortcut menu when working with tables. Point to a cell in the table and click the right mouse button.

Table Lines and Shading

To add printable lines in and around a table, use the Borders toolbar or dialog box. You can also add shading to make cells stand out. Let's add borders and shading using the following steps:

1. Display the Borders toolbar.
2. Select Table ➤ Select Table to select the entire table, then click on the Outside Border button.

 **Note**
If you want to convert all gridlines to printable borders, click on the Outside Border and Inside Border buttons. In this case, however, we will be adding a few selected borders. If your table will contain most of the inside borders, it may be faster to click on the Inside Border button, then remove the individual border lines not needed.

3. Click the mouse to deselect the table.
4. Place the insertion point in cell A1, then click on the Bottom and Right Border buttons.

 **N o t e**   You do not have to select a cell to add a border to it. If you do select the cell, however, make sure the entire cell is selected, not just its contents. If you only select the contents, the border may not extend the full height or width of the cell.

5. Select cell A2 (Sun Manufacturing Company) and click on the border button.

6. Select Cell C2 and click on the bottom border button.

7. In the same way, add a bottom border to the following cells:

> cell E2
>
> cell G2
>
> cell C5
>
> cell E5
>
> cell G5
>
> cell C8
>
> cell E8
>
> cell G8

8. Select row 11, then click on the top and bottom border button.

9. With row 11 still selected, pull down the Shading list in the borders toolbar and select Solid (100%).

10. Select cells B2 through B10, then apply a 20% shading.

11. In the same way, add a shading to cells D2 through D10, and F2 through F10.

12. To change the height of a row to make it appear as a thick line, select row 11. Because it is formatted in a solid black shade, it will appear clear when selected. If you do not select a row, the options you choose in the Cell Height and Width dialog box will affect the entire table.

13. Select Table ➤ Cell Height and Width.

14. Click on the Row tab.

15. Pull down the list under Height of Row 11, and select Exactly.

16. In the At box, enter 6, then select OK.

17. Select the entire table, or make certain that no cells are selected, then select Table ➤ Cell Height and Width, choose Center in the Alignment Section, then select OK. This centers the table between the left and right margins of the page.

 **Note** You can set the row height at Auto, Exactly, or At Least. Under Auto (the default), the row height will expand to accommodate the size of the font. If you select Exactly, you can enter a specific height of the row. The row will remain that size no matter what point size font you are using. If the font is too large to fit in the row, not all the characters will appear. When set at At Least, the row will expand to fit the text, but you cannot reduce the height smaller than the set amount. Make sure you reset the height to Auto before continuing.

Adding Graphics

You can add a graphic image to a table in the same way you insert one in a document, using the Insert ➤ Picture command. Our sample table has a picture in its top-left corner.

1. Place the insertion point in cell A1.

2. Select Insert ➤ Picture.

3. Scroll the list and double-click on Computer.WMF.

4. Adjust the size of the picture to about half the size.

Performing Math in Tables

You could use a calculator to compute the results and type them in yourself, but inserting table formulas is much more efficient. By using formulas, you can change any of the numbers and have Word recalculate the formula for you.

Using Formulas

A formula can include mathematical operators, numeric values, and cell references. You reference a cell by its location in the table. For example, entering =B2-B3 in cell B4 will calculate and display the difference between cells B2 and B3 in cell B4.

1. Place the insertion point in cell C5.

2. Select Table ➤ Formula to display the dialog box shown in Figure 7.15. Word will display a default formula =SUM(Above) or =SUM(Left) depending on the content of surrounding cells. You cannot use the SUM(Above) function here because it would count the year 1995 as a number and add it to the total.

FIGURE 7.15

Formula dialog box

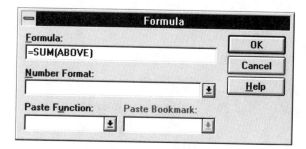

3. Delete the contents in the formula box except for the equal sign (=), then type C3+C4. It should appear as =C3+C4.

4. Pull down the Number Format list and select 0. This prevents Word from inserting decimal places in the calculated result.

5. Select OK.

6. Now in the same way, enter these formulas in the following cells, selecting the 0 number format for each:

Cell	Formula
E5	E3+E4
G5	G3+G4
C8	C6+C7
E8	E6+E7
G8	G6+G7
C9	C5-C8
E9	E5-E8
G9	G5-G8

7. In cell C10, type **(C9/C3)*100** and select the 0% number format.

8. Similarly, type the formulas **(E9/E3)*100** in cell E10 and **(G9/G3)*100** in cell G10.

If you later change the value in a cell referenced in the formula, you must calculate the results again. Select the results in the cell—it will appear in a shade of gray rather than a black background indicating you have selected a field—then press F9.

Tip   To update every formula in the table, select Edit ➤ Select All, then press F9. The formulas are actually field codes. To display the formulas in the table, select the fields, and press Shift+F9. Press Alt+F9 to display all the formulas in the table.

To print a reference copy of the table showing the formulas, select File ➤ Print ➤ Options, then select Fields Codes in the Include With Document section.

Using Functions

Word provides the following functions for performing math and logic operations in tables. You can type the function in the Formula text box yourself, or select it from the Paste Function list.

ABS

AND

AVERAGE

COUNT

DEFINED

FALSE

IF

INT

MAX

MIN

MOD

NOT

OR

PRODUCT

ROUND

SIGN

SUM

TRUE

All of the functions require at least one parameter. The average function, for example, computes and displays the average of a series or range of cells or a series of numbers. To indicate a range of cells, separate the first cell and the last cell in the range with a colon.

For instance, the function: AVERAGE(A1:A6) calculates the average of the values in the six cells from cell A1 to cell A6. To specify a number of non-consecutive cells, separate them with commas. The command: SUM(A1,C5,G6) computes the total of the values in just those three cells.

The functions AVERAGE( ), COUNT( ), MAX( ), MIN( ), PRODUCT( ), SUM( ) can also accept the parameters Above, Below, Left, and Right. The function: =AVERAGE(Below) computes the average of the cells below the current cell.

Tip

You can also perform math in a cell using a field code and cell references. Select Insert ➤ Field, select the Field Codes box and enter the formula, such as =A1+B2.

S O L U T I O N S

Handy Math

There may be times when you need to perform math in text, rather than in a table. For example, suppose you are typing a document that contains the sentence:

```
You ordered 25 units at $12.25 each for a total of $
```

To insert the total of the order, press Ctrl+F9 to display the field brackets {} then type = 25 * 12.25. The sentence will look like this:

```
You ordered 25 units at $12.25 each for a total of ${= 25 *
12.25}.
```

If you press F9 when the field is selected, Word will calculate the total but not display it. Pressing Ctrl+F9 changes to the display of field codes. To see the calculated result, press Alt+F9, or select Tools ➤ Options ➤ View ➤ Field Codes ➤ OK. (You can also insert the formula in the Field Code box of the Insert Field dialog box.)

Word gives precedence to multiplication and division. For example, it will calculate the formula {= 90 + 95 + 85 /3} as 213.33 by first dividing 85 by 3, then adding 90 and 95 to the result. If you want the average of the three numbers—90—enter the code as {=(90 + 95 + 85)/3}. Word performs the math within parentheses first, then divides the results by 3.

The only problem with performing math using this technique, is that you would need to edit the field code if you change one of the numbers. A better alternative is to use bookmarks. With bookmarks, you give names to the numbers used in the formula, much like referring to a cell reference or using the name of a variable in an equation.

Select Tools ➤ Options ➤ View ➤ Bookmarks ➤ OK. Bookmarks will appear as square brackets, []. To create a bookmark, select the number you want to use in a formula, then select Edit ➤ Bookmark to display the dialog box shown here.

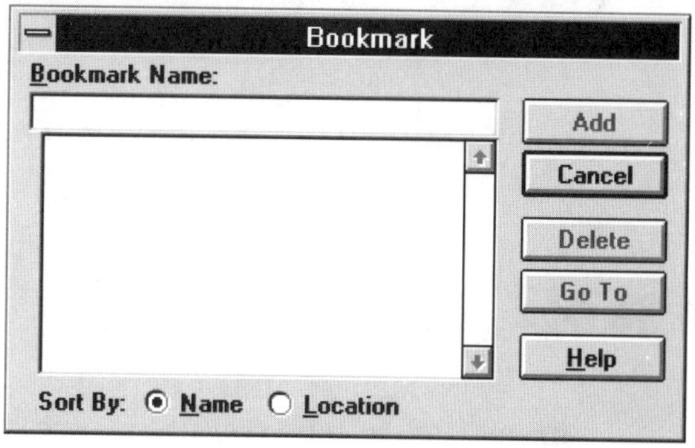

Type a name for the bookmark, then select Add. When you create the formula, use the bookmark name, instead of the actual values. The following example shows a sentence with bookmarks and a field code using them, as well as how the sentence will appear when printed. The bookmarks are named Income and Expenses. If you include the dollar sign in the bookmarks, it will automatically appear in the calculated result.

Our income was $156,000.00, and our expenses were $123,767.00, resulting in a net profit of { = income - expenses * MERGEFORMAT }

Our income was $156,000.00, and our expenses were $123,767.00, resulting in a net profit of $32,233.00

You can change the value in the bookmark and update the calculation by selecting it and pressing F9. To change the value, make certain bookmarks are displayed, then place the insertion point within the brackets surrounding the number. If you have a single number in the bookmark, type the new number first, then delete the old number. Deleting the only character in a bookmark may delete the bookmark itself. Select the field code containing the formula, then press F9.

Special Table Applications

Word's table feature can be used to create a wide variety of useful forms, such as invoices, attendance sheets, questionnaires, and calendars. You can also design graphics as tables. In Part 5 of this book, you will learn how to create interactive forms. In this chapter, we'll consider some other uses for tables.

Designing a Calculating Invoice

With the Word table feature, you can create an invoice template that automatically adds the sales tax and calculates the total amount due for a number of items. Using the table shown in Figure 7.16, you enter only the item number, description, and quantity of each item. Then, you select the entire table and press F9 to update the fields. You can modify the form to add shipping charges or any other extra items.

FIGURE 7.16

Calculating invoice

Watson Computers
1783 West Street
Philadelphia, PA 19117
215-555-5067

The best source for all of your computer needs

Sold To:

Date:

Item #	Description	Quantity	Cost	Total
		0	0	0
		0	0	0
		0	0	0
		0	0	0
		0	0	0
		0	0	0
		0	0	0
		0	0	0
		0	0	0
		0	0	0
		0	0	0
		0	0	0
		0	0	0
		0	0	0
Thanks for the order!		Item Total	0	
		Sales Tax	0.0	
		Total	0.0	

> **Note**
>
> We will use the invoice form in later chapters to illustrate how to automate operations using macros, merge, and form commands. Even if you do not produce invoices, create this table so that you can see how the other techniques work.

Creating the Table

To create the table portion of the invoice, use the following steps:

1. Create a table with 20 rows and 5 columns.

2. Widen the second column to about 2.9 inches.

3. Select the entire table and add inside and outside border lines.

4. Remove the border lines to create the format shown. For example, to delete the line after the column head Item #, place the insertion point in the cell and click on the right border button.

5. Select cells C2 through C17, then click on the align right tool.

6. Select cell D2 through D17, then use the Tab dialog box to set a decimal align tab at position .35. In a table, the tab stops are referenced from the cell gridline.

7. Select cell E2 through E20, then use the Tab dialog box to set a decimal align tab at position .35.

8. Select the entire table and set the row height at Exactly 12 points. This prevents cells from being accidentally expanded, pushing rows to the next page.

9. Select the first row and select the Center tool.

10. Merge cells C18 and D18, C19 and D19, C20 and D20.

11. Select cells C18 through D20 and click on the Center tool.

12. Insert a 0 value in the Quantity and Cost columns. If you do not insert the value, the formulas will display error messages.

Entering the Formulas

The total columns in the table contain the formulas shown in Figure 7.17. Because you merged several cells at the bottom of the table, the last cells in rows 18, 19, and 20 are considered to be in column D, not in column E. You cannot use the SUM(Above) function in the Item Total cell. The cell is considered to be D18, and the formula would total column D, not the individual item totals in column E.

FIGURE 7.17

Formulas used in
the invoice

Total
{ =c2*d2 }
{ =c3*d3 }
{ =c4*d4 }
{ =c5*d5 }
{ =c6*c6 }
{ =c7*d7 }
{ =c8*c8 }
{ =c9*d9 }
{ =c10*d10 }
{ =c11*d11 }
{ =c12*d12 }
{ =c13*d13 }
{ =c14*d14 }
{ =c15*d15 }
{ =c16*d16 }
{ =c17*d17 }
{ =SUM(E2:E17)
{ =D18*0.06 }
{ =D18+D19 }

Instead of displaying the Formula dialog box to enter each formula, use the field code. Place the insertion point in each cell, press Ctrl+F9, type the formula and press F9. To see the results, turn off the display of field codes.

Creating Questionnaires

Designing questionnaires is as much a science as it is an art. The questionnaire must be written and structured to encourage response and to insure valid interpretation of the results. The design usually requires boxes that can be checked off, or lines in which to write a response. You can create this type of format as a table, as shown in Figure 7.18.

The large boxes in the sample are table cells. The pointing hand, the small check boxes, and the checkmark were created using characters from the Wingdings font in 18-point. The box with the checkmark in it was formatted as an overstrike using the EQ field code and the \o switch.

To insert the Wingdings character in the EQ field code, create an overstrike using any two characters, such as:

```
EQ \o (a,b)
```

FIGURE 7.18

Sample
questionnaire

Annual Alumni Survey				
Please answer all questions. Thank you.				
Graduation Year ☞ Please check one	Prior to 1970	1970 to 1979	1980 to 1989	1990 to 1995

☑ Please check one item for each of the following groups:

Alumni Giving   Academic Quality
☐ I give every year   ☐ Excellent courses
☐ I sometimes give   ☐ Average courses
☐ I never give   ☐ Fair courses

School Spirit
☐   I strongly recommend the school to others
☐   I sometimes recommend the school to others
☐   I would never recommend the school to others

Display the field code, delete the characters a and b, then use the Insert ➤ Symbol command to replace them with the Wingdings characters.

The Calendar Wizard

Use the Calendar Wizard to quickly create an attractive calendar. You can select from three calendar styles and either portrait or landscape orientation. You can select the months and years for the calendar, so you can create a calendar for just one month, one year, or several years.

The Wizard will also ask if you want to leave room for a picture. If you select Yes, Word will insert a sample picture as a placeholder, as shown in Figure 7.19. You can delete the picture and replace it with your own.

Customized Calendars

You can also create your own calendars using a table of 7 columns and 6 rows. If you want to include graphics or other information on top of the calendar, as shown in Figure 7.20, use portrait orientation. Select a landscape paper size, forgo the graphics, and set the margins to zero to make the date blocks as large as possible.

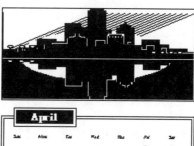

In the first row, enter the abbreviated days of the week. Shade the row and customize the lines as desired. Select the last five rows and set a fixed row height of at least one inch. You can make the rows even larger depending on the other elements on the page.

Save the blank calendar table as a template, then add the dates for specific months. Place the insertion point in the first day of the month, type **1,** press Tab, type **2,** press Tab, then continue to the end of the month.

Join any cells that are not used for days at the beginning or end of the month.

Add the month and year, along with any graphics or other messages, above the calendar. Finally, add reminders, messages, and graphics to mark events in the date blocks.

SOLUTIONS

Parallel Columns and Resumes

Parallel columns are columns in which text does not flow freely from one to the next. Material in a paragraph on the right relates directly to text on the left, and they should always be kept side by side. If you are creating a resume, as shown here, you could enter a previous job title on the left and a description of the job on the right. You would not want later editing to separate the related items.

With Word, create parallel columns using tables. For two parallel columns, for example, create a two column table. Change the width of the columns based on your design. You can even use border lines to set off certain sections of text.

For a variety of easy resume ideas, try out the Resume Wizard.

Landscape Labels

A label form is really nothing more than a table for which Word calculates the column width and row height. You can confirm this by creating a label document, then selecting Table ➤ Cell Height and Width.

Now suppose you want to print on a label using landscape orientation. You cannot do this using the built-in label feature because it always sets up the page in portrait orientation. The solution is to first create the portrait labels, and then write down the margin settings in the Page Setup dialog box and the label measurements in the Cell Height and Width Box.

Next, start a new document and select landscape orientation and set the margins. You have to remember, however, that the orientation of the page is different. The measurement that was the top margin for the portrait orientation is now the left margin in landscape, as shown here:

	Portrait	**Landscape**
Top	.5	.16
Bottom	0	.16
Left	.16	.5
Right	.16	0

A dialog box may appear warning you that the margins are incorrect—just select Ignore.

Now, create a table, but reverse the numbers of rows and columns. If the portrait labels have two columns and five rows, the landscape labels have five columns and two rows. Finally, use the Cell Height and Width dialog box to set the label size.

Select the entire table, set the column width to the original cell height, and the row height to the original column width. If you used a 2 inch high by 4 inch wide label in portrait, make the columns 2 inches wide and the rows exactly 4 inches high in landscape. The landscape labels are shown in Figure 7.21.

FIGURE 7.21

Landscape labels

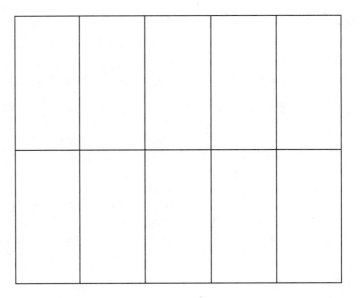

Once you create the basic landscape label, you can always drag the table gridlines to customize the form.

PART
three

The Word on Macros

8

Macros and Customized
Menus

9

WordBasic Programming

10

Advanced WordBasic

CHAPTER
8

Macros and
Customized Menus

A MACRO IS A SERIES of keystrokes or command selections stored in a template. You can repeat the keystrokes or commands automatically by playing the macro. Macros can repeat text, such as your company's name, or execute complex formatting commands, such as changing the paper size and inserting a header or footer. This chapter describes how to record, edit, and write macros. It also explains how to create custom toolbars and menus that include your macros. More advanced macro functions are discussed in Chapters 9 and 10.

Basic Macro Recording

The simplest way to create a macro is to record the keystrokes and mouse selections that perform the tasks you want to accomplish. After you have recorded the actions, you can play them back.

Naming a Macro

Double-click on the dimmed characters REC in the status bar, or select Tools ➤ Macro ➤ Record, to display the dialog box shown in Figure 8.1. In this dialog box, you assign a name to your macro.

Word will suggest Macro1 for the first macro you record, Macro2 for the second, and so on. While you can accept the suggested macro name, it is a good idea to name the macro yourself. Use a name that clearly describes the macro's purpose. You can also enter a description of the macro in the Description box.

FIGURE 8.1

Record Macro
dialog box

Tip

The macro name and description will help you identify macros when you want to run them. A year from now, you probably won't remember what MACRO10 does, but you would remember the macro called PrintPage.

Macro names must start with a letter and cannot contain any punctuation marks. If you enter an invalid name, the OK button in the Record Macro dialog box will be dimmed. Use lowercase and uppercase letters to indicate words, such as SaveMyDocument. Do not use words that are already associated with commands, such as bold and underline. See the section on Changing a Command Function later in this chapter.

Recording a Macro

Select OK to begin recording. When you are recording, the mouse can only be used to select menu and dialog box options. You must select text and move the insertion point with the keyboard. The mouse pointer will include an icon of a cassette tape when it is in the text area of the screen.

A small toolbar with two buttons appears on the screen. Select the button on the left when you want to stop recording the macro. You can also stop recording by double-clicking on the REC characters in the status bar, or by selecting Tools ➤ Macro ➤ Stop Recording.

 **N o t e**
Select the button on the right to pause recording. Pausing allows you to temporarily stop recording so you can perform some functions that you do not want as part of the macro. Click on the Pause button again when you are ready to continue recording.

Saving a Macro

The setting All Documents(Normal.dot) in the Make Macro Available To box indicates that the macro will be saved in the normal template. This means that your macros will be *global,* available for use with every document.

If you are using a template other than normal, you can select to store the macro in that template instead. Pull down the Make Macro Available To list. You'll see an option labeled Document Based on, followed by the name of the attached template, such as: Documents Based on Broland.dot. Select the template where you want to save the macro.

 **N o t e**
If you store a macro in a custom template, it will not automatically be available to other documents. To access the macro, attach the template to a document, or make it global. In addition, you can use the Organizer dialog box discussed in Chapter 2, to move and copy macros from one template to another. You will find out how to display the Organizer from the Macro dialog box later in this chapter.

S O L U T I O N S

Recording Dialog Box Selections

If you open a dialog box and select OK, Word records all the current settings in the dialog box as part of the macro. You can use this feature to create macros that quickly return settings to their default values. For example, to create a macro that restores the default page setup options, start a new document that uses the defaults, then record a macro with the commands File ➤ Page Setup ➤ OK. You can later run this macro to change a document to the default values.

Word does not record any dialog box operations if you select Cancel to remove the box. Word does not record the actual keystrokes or mouse clicks you make in a dialog box, but the state of the dialog box when you select OK. This ensures that no matter what actions you performed to select the dialog box settings, your macro only performs the end result.

Recording a Macro Step-by-Step

The first macro we will create will insert the text and formatting to produce a letterhead. Start Word (or open a new document) and follow these steps:

1. Select Tools ➤ Macro ➤ Record.
2. Type **Letterhead** and select OK.

 **Note**   If you try to create a macro with the same name as an existing macro, a dialog box will appear asking if you want to replace it. Select Yes to replace the macro, or No to try another name.

3. Press Ctrl+E to center the insertion point, type your name and press Enter. (If you make a typing error, just correct it as usual.)

4. Type your street address and press Enter.

5. Type your city, state, and zip code, then press Enter twice to insert a blank line between the address and the date.

6. Select Insert ➤ Date and Time.

7. If the Insert As Field box is not selected, select it now.

8. Select the fourth date format, then click on OK.

9. Press Enter, then press Ctrl+L for left justification.

10. Click on the Stop icon, or Select Tools ➤ Macro ➤ Stop Recording ➤ Close, to end keystroke recording.

11. Close the document without saving it.

 **Note**   Macros are stored independently of the document you used to record the keystrokes. Closing the document without saving it will not affect macros already saved in the template. When you exit Word, the normal template will be saved automatically.

Running a Macro

You can run your macro by selecting it in the Macro dialog box. Select Tools ➤ Macro to display the dialog box shown in Figure 8.2. The dialog box lists all of the macros available in the active templates. This includes the normal template, the attached template, and any global templates.

FIGURE 8.2

Macro dialog box

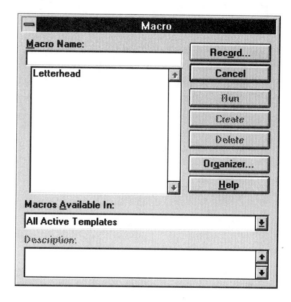

To run a macro, double-click on its name in the list box, or highlight its name and select Run.

 **Tip**

> To list macros only in the normal, attached, or global template, pull down the Macros Available In list, and select the template. (You'll learn about the Word Commands option soon.)

Assigning Macros

If you use a macro often, you may want to add it to a shortcut key, a menu, or a toolbar. That way, you can run the macro by pressing a keystroke combination, or by clicking on a screen object. You can assign a macro to an object as you record it, or after it's been created.

To Shortcut Keys

When you are recording a macro, you can assign it to a keyboard combination in much the same way you learned to assign styles in Chapter 2. In the Record Macro dialog box, type the name and description of the macro, then click on the keyboard icon in the Assign Macro To section. Word will display the Customize Keyboard dialog box.

Press the key combination you want to assign the macro, then select Assign, and then Close. Record the keystrokes or selections of the macro, then click on the Stop Recording button.

If you already created the macro and want to assign it to a keystroke, select Tools ➤ Customize ➤ Keyboard. Scroll the Categories list and select Macros. In the Macros list, choose the macro you want to assign to a keystroke. Select the Press New Shortcut Key text box, and press the key you want to assign to the macro, select Assign and then Close.

 **Note**   If you select the Keyboard icon before naming the macro, you can still change its name in the Organizer dialog box.

To the Toolbar

Assigning a macro to a toolbar lets you run the macro with a single click on the mouse. First, make sure the toolbar that you want to assign the macro to is displayed. If it is not, select View ➤ Toolbars, click on the name of the toolbar, then select OK. You can also right-click on any toolbar, then select the name of the toolbar from the shortcut menu.

Selecting the Toolbar

When you are recording a macro in the Record Macro dialog box, type the name and description of the macro, then click on the toolbars icon in the Assign Macro To section. Word will display the Toolbars tab of the Customize dialog box with the name of the macro highlighted, as shown in Figure 8.3.

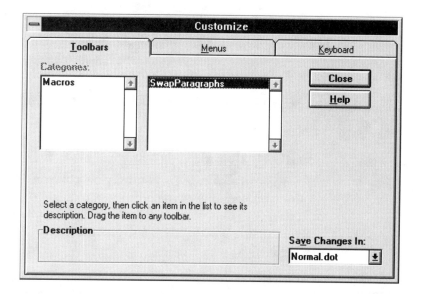

Point to the name of the macro and hold down the mouse button. You'll see an icon of a blank toolbar button. Drag the mouse to the position where you want the button to appear on the toolbar.

Choosing the Button

When you release the mouse button, you'll see the Custom Button dialog box (Figure 8.4). You can select to have a text button that contains the name of the macro or some other text, or an icon button.

◆ For a text button, the default setting, enter the text you want on the button face in the Text Button Name box. It will automatically contain the name of the macro. Then, select Assign.

FIGURE 8.4

Custom Button
dialog box

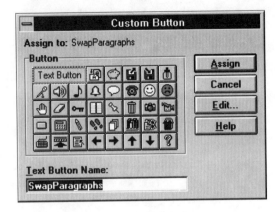

◆ For an icon button, click on one of the sample icons shown, then
select Assign.

Editing the Button

You can also create an entirely new button, or edit one of the sample
buttons. Select one of the buttons you'd like to edit, or select Text Button
to start with a blank button face. Then, select Edit to display the Button
Editor dialog box. Figure 8.5 shows the Button Editor with one of the suggested icons.

FIGURE 8.5

Button Editor
dialog box

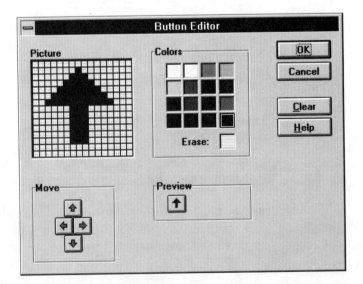

The Picture section is divided into a grid, each square representing another pixel (dot) of the icon drawing. Clicking on a blank square will insert a pixel.

In the Colors section, select the color of the pixel you want to insert. You can also select a color already in the Picture area by clicking on it with the right mouse button.

Erase a pixel by clicking on it again when using the same color. If you changed colors, click on the Erase box in the Colors section. With Erase selected, clicking on any color pixel erases it. Use the arrows in the Move section to shift the entire drawing up, down, left, or right one column or row at a time. You cannot use them to shift an individual pixel.

As you draw, a sample of the button will appear in the Preview pane. Select Clear to erase the entire drawing and start over.

Doing It Step-by-Step

Now, let's create a macro to switch the position of two paragraphs and add it to the standard toolbar.

1. Type **This is paragraph one,** press Enter, type **This is paragraph two,** and press Enter.

2. Place the insertion point anywhere in the second paragraph.

3. Select Tools ➤ Macro ➤ Record, type **SwapParagraphs.**

4. Click on the Toolbars icon in the Assign Macro To section.

5. Point to the name SwapParagraphs and hold down the mouse button.

6. Drag the mouse to the standard toolbar, where you want to insert the button, then release the mouse. The Custom Button dialog box appears.

7. Click on one of the icons, then select Assign. Now record the macro.

8. Press Ctrl+↑, then press Ctrl+Shift+↓ to select the paragraph.

9. Select Edit ➤ Cut (or press Ctrl+X) to delete the paragraph and place it into the Clipboard.

10. Press Ctrl+↑, then press Ctrl+V to paste the paragraph.

11. Click on the Stop Recording tool.

S E C R E T S

Toolbar Tips and Tricks

Here are some other tips for working with toolbars:

◆ When the Customize Toolbars dialog box is displayed, delete a button from a toolbar by dragging it off the toolbar into the document window.

◆ Change a button's position by dragging it to a new location, or to a different toolbar.

◆ Hold down the Ctrl key and drag the button to make a copy of it.

◆ To delete, move, or copy a button from a toolbar when the Customize dialog box is not displayed, hold down the Alt key while you drag.

◆ To restore a toolbar to its default condition, if you delete a function accidentally, for example, select View ➤ Toolbars, click on the toolbar you want to restore, select Reset, then OK.

◆ To add a macro or other item to a toolbar at any time, select Tools ➤ Customize ➤ Toolbars.

◆ Word has buttons for many functions that are not already on a toolbar. Select the category of the function in the Categories list to display predefined tools in the Button panel. Click on a button, and read its function in the description panel. Drag the button to the position on a toolbar.

◆ If you selected to add a macro, font, AutoText entry, or style, you can select a text button or icon, as when assigning a macro.

◆ To create a new toolbar, select View ➤ Toolbars ➤ New, type a name for the toolbar, and then select OK.

◆ You can also drag a button from the Customize box to the text window.

To a Menu

A toolbar can only display a limited number of buttons. As an alternative, you can add your macros to Word's menus, or even create a new menu to store your macros.

Adding to an Existing Menu

When you are recording a macro, in the Record Macro dialog box, type the name and description of the macro, then click on the menus icon in the Assign Macro To section. Word will display the Customize dialog box with the name of the macro highlighted in the Commands list, as shown in Figure 8.6.

FIGURE 8.6

Menus tab of the Customize dialog box

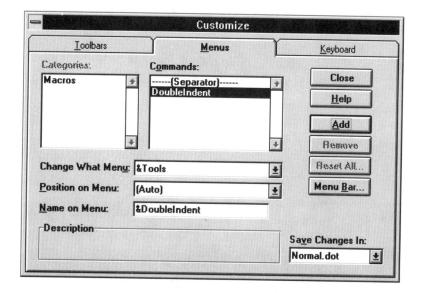

1. Pull down the Change What Menu list and select the menu you'd like to add the macro to.

2. Pull down the Position on Menu list and select a position. The default setting, Auto, will place the macro at the end of the menu. You can also select At Top, At Bottom, or the existing menu item that you'd like your macro to follow in the menu.

3. In the Name on Menu box, enter the name you want to appear on the menu. Use the ampersand to indicate the underlined selection letter, such as MyM&acro.

4. Select Add, or Add Below if you selected a specific position, then select Close.

Tip

Choose the Separator option in the Commands list to place a horizontal line in a menu. Use the separator, for example, to separate the names of your own macros from Word's built-in commands. Select the option, then choose the menu and position, just as if you were inserting a macro.

Creating a New Menu

You can also create a new menu to hold your macros and other custom commands. In the Customize menu dialog box, select Menu Bar to display the dialog box shown in Figure 8.7. Type the name for the menu, select a position in the list, then select Add or Add After. You can then add your own macros to the menu.

FIGURE 8.7

Menu Bar
dialog box

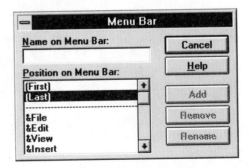

Tip

To later delete an item from the menu, you do not have to display the Customize dialog box. Press Alt+Ctrl+- to change the mouse pointer to a large hyphen character. Pull down the menu containing the item you want to delete and click on the item.

Doing It Step-by-Step

Let's create a macro for indenting text on both the left and right, and add it to the Format menu.

1. Select Tools ➤ Macro ➤ Record, and type **DoubleIndent.**
2. Click on the Menus icon in the Assign Macro To section.
3. Pull down the Change What Menu list and select F&ormat.
4. Select Add, then Close.
5. To record a macro, select Format ➤ Paragraph.
6. Select Left in the indentation, type .5, press Tab, type .5, and select OK.
7. Click on the Stop Recording button.

S E C R E T S

Menu Tips and Tricks

You can use similar techniques to add commands to any menu, or to create new menus. Select Tools ➤ Customize ➤ Menus. The dialog box will appear. The categories box will contain a list of the major classifications of Word commands, as well as the Macros, Fonts, AutoText, and Styles options. The Commands box lists the functions in the selected category.

Choose the category of the function you want to add to a menu, then select the function in the Command list. Select the menu, position, and menu text, then select Add or Add Below.

To delete a menu item, select it in the Position on Menu list, and click on Remove. Select Reset All to return all of the Word menus to their default values.

Putting Macros to Work

You can run any macro by selecting its name in the Macros dialog box. This is useful if you forgot the shortcut key you assigned to a macro, or the toolbar containing a macro button is not displayed. You can also run a macro on startup or automatically run a macro by linking it to an event.

Creating a New Document

Let's use our recorded macros to create a new document.

1. Start a new document.
2. Select Tools ➤ Macros, then double-click on the Letterhead macro.
3. Place the insertion point after your letterhead, then type the following:

```
Re: Case #1023
Common Pleas Court
```

4. Press Enter.
5. To switch the position of two sentences by running the macro you assigned to the toolbar, place the insertion point anywhere in the last sentence.
6. Click on the toolbar icon that you assigned to the SwapParagraphs macro to exchange the two lines of text.

7. Select Format ➤ DoubleIndent to run the indentation macro. Notice that the left and right indentation markers adjust.

8. Close the document without saving it.

Running a Macro on Startup

You can start Word and automatically run one of your macros located in the normal or in a global template. In the Program Manager, select File ➤ Run. Type **winword /m** followed by the macro name as in: **winword/mLetterhead.** The macro named on the command line will be executed as soon as the program is loaded.

To run a macro every time you start Word, change the command line that executes when you select the Word icon in the Program Manager. In the Program Manager, highlight the Winword icon, then select File ➤ Properties.

You'll see a dialog box with a text box labeled Command Line containing an entry like this:

```
C:\WINWORD\WINWORD.EXE
```

Edit the command line to include the /M switch and the name of the macro:

```
C:\WINWORD\WINWORD.EXE /mLetterhead
```

Be sure to have a space after the EXE extension. Select OK to close the dialog box. The macro will be played whenever you start Word by selecting the icon. When you no longer want the macro to run, delete the switch and macro name from the command line.

Automatic Macros

By using a special macro name, you can also automatically run a macro by linking it to a Word event.

Special Macro Names

Here are some examples:

◆ **AutoExec:** runs whenever you start Word. The AutoExec macro is useful for such tasks as automatically opening a default document or template, running a Wizard, or changing to a specific directory which contains your documents.

◆ **AutoNew:** runs a macro when you start a new document by selecting File ➤ New or by clicking on the New button in the toolbar. For example, use an AutoNew macro to create a standard header or footer for every new document, or to apply a series of default format settings.

◆ **AutoOpen:** runs whenever you open a document. For example, use the AutoOpen macro to automatically move the insertion point to its position when you last saved the document—record the Shift+F5 keystroke or write the GoBack command.

◆ **AutoClose:** runs when you close a document. You can use it to make a backup copy of the document or remind the user to record the name of the file in a log or journal.

◆ **AutoExit:** runs when you exit Word. The macro is useful to reset the screen display, for example, so the default toolbars and view will be used when you next start Word.

 **Note** The AutoExec and AutoExit macros must be stored in the normal template. The other macros can be stored in either the normal template or a global template.

Disabling Automatic Macros

To disable the automatic macros, use the DisableAutoMacros command. (You'll learn about editing macros in the next section.) For example, to run a macro that includes the FileNew command without it triggering the AutoNew macro, add the command:

```
DisableAutoMacros 1
```

before the FileNew instruction. Omitting the argument 1 also disables automatic macros.

 **Note**

> The Disable Auto Macros command only affects the AutoOpen, AutoClose, AutoNew, and AutoExit macros. It remains in effect during the current Word session, or until you use the DisableAutoMacros 0 command.

To disable the AutoExec macro, hold down the SHIFT key when you start Word, or start Word by specifying the DisableAutoMacros statement in the command line:

```
winword.exe /mDisableAutoMacros
```

Editing Macros

Editing a macro allows you to correct any mistakes you made when recording the macro without repeating the entire procedure. While it is easy to correct typographical errors or add text to a macro, making more complex changes requires knowledge of Word's macro language. In this and later chapters, you'll learn Word macro commands and some fundamentals of programming.

Opening a Macro File

To edit a macro, you must display the commands of the macro on the screen. If the macro is stored in a template other than normal.dot, you must first start a new document that uses the template or choose it as a global or attached template.

Select Tools ➤ Macro. Click on the macro name, and then select Edit to display the text of the macro on screen along with the macro toolbar, as shown in Figure 8.8.

FIGURE 8.8

Macro text and toolbar

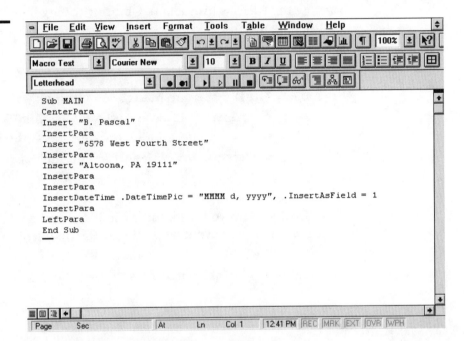

```
Sub MAIN
CenterPara
Insert "B. Pascal"
InsertPara
Insert "6578 West Fourth Street"
InsertPara
Insert "Altoona, PA 19111"
InsertPara
InsertPara
InsertDateTime .DateTimePic = "MMMM d, yyyy", .InsertAsField = 1
InsertPara
LeftPara
End Sub
```

 **Note**   The macro appears according to a style named Macro Text Style. You can edit the style if you want to display macro text in another font or size. See Chapter 2 for additional information on styles.

The names of the toolbar buttons are shown in Figure 8.9. You'll learn more about the toolbar later in this chapter.

FIGURE 8.9

Macro toolbar
buttons

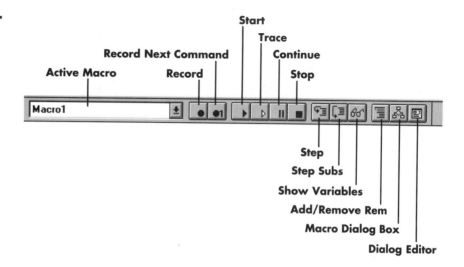

Start
Trace
Record Next Command
Continue
Active Macro
Record
Stop

Macro1

Step
Step Subs
Show Variables
Add/Remove Rem
Macro Dialog Box
Dialog Editor

SOLUTIONS

Understanding Macro Commands

Each of the functions and commands in the displayed macro
are listed in WordBasic, Word's macro language (see Chapters 9
and 10). This is an extensive programming language that can
be used to write complete applications built around Word for
Windows.

Here's what the codes of the Letterhead macro represent:

◆ *Sub MAIN*—Every macro you record begins with this command, which marks the beginning of the macro instructions. The word MAIN signifies that this is the principal
subroutine or section, of the macro. You'll learn in later
chapters how to create other subroutines to build complex
macros in sections.

◆ *CenterPara*—Centers the insertion point, just like clicking on the Center button, or pressing Ctrl+E, or selecting Format ➤ Paragraph ➤ Alignment ➤ Center

◆ *Insert "Name"*—Inserts the text enclosed in quotation marks into the document.

◆ *InsertPara*—Inserts a carriage return (like pressing Enter)

◆ *InsertDateTime .DateTimePic = "d MMMM, yyyy", .InsertAsField = 1*—Inserts the date code as a field. The .DateTimePic option described the format of the inserted date. When the InsertAsField option is equal to 1, the date will be inserted as a field code.

◆ *LeftPara*—Performs the Ctrl+L command to align the text with the left margin.

◆ *End Sub*—Ends the macro.

Editing Macro Text

If you want to change the text that a macro generates, just edit any of the text within the quotation marks of an Insert command. To insert new text you have to add an Insert command.

Let's use this method to change the letterhead macro to include your telephone number.

1. With the text of the macro on the screen, move the insertion point to the end of the line containing the city, state, and zip code Insert command.

2. Press Enter. This performs a carriage return, inserting a blank line, but it will not insert a carriage return in the document when the macro is run.

3. Type **InsertPara** and press Enter.

4. Type **Insert** " then your telephone number, then a quotation mark. It should appear something like: Insert "555-1212". (Notice that when editing a macro, AutoCorrect does not change quotation marks to smart quotes.)

5. Select File ➤ Save Template ➤ Yes. This saves the macro and the normal template. (You can now run the macro from the Macro menu.)

 **Tip**

> Select File ➤ Save Copy As to save a copy of the macro as a text file. You can later retrieve and copy the macro instructions into another macro. The text file itself is not a runable macro.

Writing Macros

Macros created by recording keystrokes are useful, but they only touch upon the power of Word's macro language. By writing a macro, you can create entire applications much like a computer programmer can create using C, BASIC, or another computer language. You can type an entire macro, or you can add your own commands to one that you've already recorded.

Starting a New Macro

To start a new macro, select Tools ➤ Macro. Type the name for your macro in the Macro Name text box, then select Create. A new window will open with the macro bar, and the Sub Main and End Sub commands. (You add your instructions between these two commands.)

Tip Use the Rem command, or the ' mark, as the first characters on the line to create a remark. Word will ignore any other instructions on the line. Use remarks to write brief explanations about the macro, to explain how an instruction works, or why you added the instruction into the macro.

There are three general categories of WordBasic instructions.

◆ **Statements:** carry out a command, such as selecting an option from a menu or a dialog box.

◆ **Functions:** acquire information, such as the name of the active document, or some status condition. You would use a function, for example, to determine if the Overtype mode is on or off before inserting some text into a document. Some function macros, such as ParaDown( ), also carry out a command.

◆ **Programming commands:** control the flow of a macro, make decisions, and perform complex operations.

You'll learn about functions and programming commands in later chapters.

S O L U T I O N S

Adding Recorded Instructions

Some macro commands can be quite complex. If your macro will perform tasks that can be recorded, it may be more efficient to record the instructions, then display them on screen so you can edit them. You can add your own commands, or copy and paste the macro instructions to a macro in another window.

You can also record instructions directly into a macro that you are editing or creating. The names of all open macros will be available in the list box on the macros toolbar.

To record instructions directly into a macro being created or edited, place the insertion point in the macro where you want the new instructions to appear. Then, change to a window that does not contain a macro, pull down the list in the macro toolbar, and select the macro you want to edit. Next, click on the Record Next Command button (the second toolbar button on the left with the circle around the number 1), then perform the action you want to record.

When you are done performing one action—selecting from one dialog box, menu, or typing one paragraph—the button will pop up. When you return to the window containing the macro, the recorded instruction will be there.

You can also use the Macro toolbar to run an open macro. Select the macro name in the list box, then click on the Start button, the third button from the left. The macro toolbar will only be available when there is an open macro. You'll learn more about the toolbar in Chapter 9.

Using Macro Commands

Word has a macro statement for every action that you can take. For example, if you want to save the current document, the statement is: File-Save. If the document does not yet have a name, the Save As dialog box will appear. Otherwise, the document will be saved immediately.

 **Note**   The FileSave command performs the same function as selecting File ➤ Save, or clicking on the Save button in the toolbar.

Dialog Box Commands

There is a statement for every dialog box that you can display. The statement name usually reflects the keystrokes required to display the box, such as FilePageSetup, FormatStyle, and TableSort. Using the statement name by itself does not display the dialog box, rather it performs the same function as if you selected the box then immediately selected OK.

Using Arguments

If you want to change the settings in the dialog box, you must use arguments. Arguments specify what options of the dialog box you want to change. The syntax for these commands is:

```
Statement-Name .argument1 = setting, .argument2 = setting ....
```

An argument specifies a dialog box option that will be affected by the macro. Notice that the arguments begin with a period, and are separated from each other with a comma. A setting specifies the exact measurement applied to the option, or the state of a checkbox or button, or the selection from a list box.

For example, to change the top margin you can use the command:

```
FilePageSetup .TopMargin = "2"
```

When this macro is run, it will change the top margin to two inches, just as if you entered from the keyboard.

 **Note**   The setting in this command is surrounded by quotation marks. For more information, see the section on Units of Measurement later in this chapter.

S E C R E T S

Macro Command Tips and Tricks

The order you enter the arguments does not matter, and when you want to include more than one argument, separate them with a comma, as in:

```
FilePageSetup .TopMargin = "2", .BottomMargin = "4"
```

You could obtain the same macro command by recording the keystrokes. Writing them, however, is useful when you want to use a variable to specify the parameter value. You will learn how to input values into variables in Chapter 9.

Don't worry about the spacing between commands, arguments and punctuation marks. For instance, you can enter the FilePage-Setup command without any spaces, such as:

```
FilePageSetup.TopMargin="2",.BottomMargin="4"
```

Word uses the punctuation marks as delimiters, so it knows when the command ends and the argument begins. In fact, when you save the template, or run the macro, Word will automatically add spaces between the various elements.

You cannot delete the space in the Sub Main and End Sub commands, however, and you cannot add extra spaces between words of commands, unless the spaces are part of the syntax. For example, the command File Page Setup would result in an error message because the command must be entered as one word. The command On Error Resume Next, however, must have spaces between the words.

Most dialog box command macros have a number of arguments, but in most cases, they are optional. If you include some arguments, but not others, only those values specified will be changed. The following example shows the complete syntax of the FilePageSetup statement, with all its possible arguments. When writing the command, you need only include those you want to change.

```
FilePageSetup .Tab = "0", .PaperSize = "0", .TopMargin = "1" + Chr$(34),
.BottomMargin = "1" + Chr$(34), .LeftMargin = "1.25" + Chr$(34),
.RightMargin = "1.25" + Chr$(34), .Gutter = "0" + Chr$(34), .PageWidth =
"8.5" + Chr$(34), .PageHeight = "11" + Chr$(34), .Orientation = 0,
.FirstPage = 0, .OtherPages = 0, .VertAlign = 0, .ApplyPropsTo = 4,
.FacingPages = 0, .HeaderDistance = "0.5" + Chr$(34), .FooterDistance =
"0.5" + Chr$(34), .SectionStart = 2, .OddAndEvenPages = 0,
.DifferentFirstPage = 0, .Endnotes = 0, .LineNum = 0, .StartingNum = "",
.FromText = "", .CountBy = "0", .NumMode = -1
```

When you are typing long commands, let Word wrap the arguments from line to line. If you want to space the arguments in several lines yourself, end each line with the \ character before pressing Enter, as in:

```
FormatFont .Points = "10", .Underline = 0, .Color = 0,\
.Strikethrough = 0, .Superscript = 0, .Subscript = 0
```

You must still use a comma to separate arguments. You can place the \ character between elements, such as:

```
FormatFont .Points \
= "10", .Underline =\
0, .Color = 0
```

but not within a set of quotation marks.

Other macro commands have one or more required arguments, along with several optional ones. The EditAutoText macro, for example, requires the Name argument, listing the name of the autotext entry you want to edit. If you do not include any of the optional arguments, Word inserts the named entry into the document. You would use the optional arguments to create an entry or delete one from the autotext list.

Entering Settings for Arguments

How you enter the settings for arguments depends on the argument itself. Options controlled by checkboxes, for example, are turned on (selected) by assigning the argument the value 1, and turned off (deselected) by assigning the value 0. Do not surround the value in quotation marks.

Choosing Options by Number

Where there are several options available, each is assigned a number. For example, the Alignment argument for the FormatParagraph command sets paragraph alignment to the left, center, right, or justified. Each of these conditions is represented by a number:

FormatParagraph .Alignment = 0	**Left**
FormatParagraph .Alignment = 1	**Centered**
FormatParagraph .Alignment = 2	**Right**
FormatParagraph .Alignment = 3	**Justified**

Units of Measurement

Settings that are measurements require a little more thought. When you record the command to change the top margin, it will appear like this:

```
FilePageSetup .TopMargin = "1.5" + Chr$(34)
```

The notation chr$(34) represents the quotation mark symbol used to indicate a measurement in inches. Word inserts the notation because it reserves the quotation marks to surround the margin settings.

The measurements are considered to be strings, representing key-strokes that you enter on the keyboard. In most programming, strings are always surrounded by quotation marks.

 **Note**

The plus sign between the measurement and the chr$(34) code is called a concatenation. This tells Word to connect two strings together. When you run the macro, Word will first insert the characters 1.5 in the dialog box, then it will insert the characters represented by the chr$(34) notation. In effect, this is the same as typing 1.5".

Designating Default Measurements

Inches is the default unit of measurement for margins. That is, if you select File ➤ Page Setup ➤ Margins and then type 2 in the Top Margin box, Word will assume you mean two inches.

Because inches is the default, you don't have to worry about typing the chr$(34) notation when you write FilePageSetup instructions. When Word runs the command:

```
FilePageSetup .TopMargin = "2"
```

it will automatically assign the unit as inches.

The options in other dialog boxes, however, may use points as the default unit. If you use the command:

```
FormatParagraph .After = "20"
```

Word will automatically assume the measurement is in points—the default unit for the Spacing After option in the Format Paragraph dialog box.

 **Tip**

If you are not sure what the default unit of measurement is for an option, enter it with the setting. Instead of using the chr$(34) notation, use *in* to represent inches, as in "2 in". Use *pt* to represent points, as in "32 pt." You cannot use the " character to indicate inches.

If you enter a number not surrounded by quotation marks, Word assumes you mean points. So, the command:

```
FilePageSetup .TopMargin = 2
```

will create a top margin of just two points, which Word will convert to 0.03 inches.

WordBasic Command Syntax

To become proficient in writing macros, you need to know the syntax of WordBasic commands. The following sections tell you more about the commands used in this book and how to obtain additional information.

Using Word's Help System

Select Help ➤ Contents ➤ Programming With Microsoft Word, then work your way through the extensive help system. You can even copy sections of macros from the help system, and paste them into your own macros.

With the Help system, you can select a command from an alphabetical list, or by function. Word classifies the commands into the categories shown in the following list:

Application Control	Definitions and Declarations
AutoCorrect	Dialog Box Definition and Control
AutoText	Disk Access and Management
Basic File Input/Output	Documents, Templates, and Add-Ins
Bookmarks	Drawing
Borders and Frames	Dynamic Data Exchange (DDE)
Branching and Control	Editing
Bullets and Numbering	Environment
Character Formatting	Fields
Customization	Finding and Replacing
Date and Time	Footnotes, Endnotes, and Annotations

Forms	Proofing
Help	Section and Document Formatting
Macros	Strings and Numbers
Mail Merge	Style Formatting
Moving the Insertion Point and Selecting	Tables
	Tools
Object Linking and Embedding	View
Outlining and Master Documents	Windows
Paragraph Formatting	

 **Note**

If you receive a message that the WordBasic help system is not installed, you have to add the Help system from the floppy disks. Run the Word Setup program from the Program Manager, and select the Add/Remove button. Select the option named Online Help, Examples, and Demos, then click on Change Option. Select WordBasic Help in the dialog box that appears, then select OK and then Continue. Follow the prompts that appear on the screen.

You can also get specific information on a macro's commands as follows:

◆ Type the macro command into a macro and press the F1 key for online help.

◆ Record a macro that performs the functions you want you to write, then edit it to look at the code.

◆ Call Microsoft and order the Microsoft Word Developer's Kit. The kit includes some utility programs and detailed documentation on all macro commands.

Other Macro Commands

Other commands do not involve dialog boxes but duplicate keystroke entries or menu choices. They include commands for moving the insertion point. For example, the command CharLeft moves the insertion point one character to the right.

Moving the Insertion Point and Selecting Text You can also specify the number of characters you want to move the insertion point. The command:

```
CharLeft 5
```

moves the insertion point five characters to the left. To select the characters as you move the insertion point, use this command:

```
CharLeft 5,1
```

The number 1 following the comma tells Word to select characters. Most of the insertion movement macro commands use the same arguments.

Here are some other macro commands for moving the insertion point and selecting text:

CharLeft	GoToPreviousItem
CharRight	LineDown
ColumnSelect	LineUp
EndOfColumn	NextCell
EndOfDocument	NextField
EndOfLine	NextObject
EndOfRow	NextPage
EndOfWindow	NextWindow
ExtendSelection	OtherPane
GoBack	PageDown
GoToAnnotationScope	PageUP
GoToHeaderFooter	ParaDown
GoToNextItem	ParaUp

PrevCell   StartOfColumn

PrevField   StartOfDocument

PrevObject   StarOfLine

PrevPage   StartOfRow

PrevWindow   StartOfWindow

SelectCurWord   WordLeft

SentLeft   WordRight

SentRight

Commands to Perform Menu Selections There are also commands that perform menu selections. The command FileList 1, for instance, opens the
document listed next to the number 1 in the File menu. So, you can use a
macro with the FileList 1 command, for example, to quickly open the last
document that you opened or edited.

Check out these other commands for working with files:

CopyFile   FileRoutingSlip

DocClose   FileSave

FileClose   FileSaveAll

FileCloseAll   FileSaveAs

FileFind   FileSendMail

FileNew   FileSummaryInfo

FileNewDefault   FileTemplates

FileNumber   InsertFile

FileOpen   Kill

FilePageSetup   LockDocument

FilePrint   Name

FilePrintDefault   SaveTemplate

FilePrintSetup   SetAttr

Changing the Document View There are many commands for changing the state of Word. The commands ViewNormal and ViewPage, for instance, change the view of the current document. They use no arguments and cannot be used as toggles. If the view is already in Normal, the command ViewNormal has no effect.

Here are some other commands for changing the display:

FilePrintPreview	ViewFootnotes
FilePrintPreviewFullScreen	ViewFootnoteSeparator
FilePrintPreviewPages	ViewHeader
Magnifier	ViewMasterDocument
ShowAll	ViewNormal
ViewAnnotations	ViewOutline
ViewBorderToolbar	ViewPage
ViewDraft	ViewRibbon
ViewDrawingToolbar	ViewRuler
ViewEndnoteArea	ViewStatusBar
ViewEndnoteContNotice	ViewToggleMasterDocument
ViewEndnoteContSeparator	ViewToolbars
ViewEndnoteSeparator	ViewZoom
ViewFieldCodes	ViewZoom100
ViewFooter	ViewZoom200
ViewFootnoteArea	ViewZoom75
ViewFootnoteContNotice	ViewZoomPageWidth
ViewFootnoteContSeparator	ViewZoomWholePage

Commands with Optional Arguments Other commands have optional arguments. For example, the command Overtype, without an argument, toggles between overtype and insert mode. If you want to ensure that Word is in a specific mode, use an argument—enter Overtype 1 to turn the mode on; Overtype 0 to turn it off.

Using the buttons in the toolbar bar acts like a toggle, so using the related macro command without an argument also toggles the state. The command to toggle the bold button on or off, for instance, is simply Bold. Use an argument, however, when you want to set a specific state, such as Bold 1 to turn bold on, Bold 0 to turn it off. Most character formatting commands will serve as toggles when you do not include an argument.

Character Formatting Commands You can also control character formatting with the Font dialog box. The command to turn bold on from the dialog box is:

```
FormatFont .Bold = 1
```

The command to turn bold off is:

```
FormatFont .Bold = 0
```

If you do not include a parameter, it will always turn bold on, not toggle between the two states.

Here are some useful macro commands for formatting characters and selected fonts and font sizes:

AllCaps	NormalFontPosition
Bold	NormalFontSpacing
CharColor	ShrinkFont
CopyFormat	ShrinkFontOnePoint
DottedUnderline	SmallCaps
DoubleUnderline	Strikethrough
Font	Subscript
GrowFont	Superscript
GrowFontOnePoint	SymbolFont
Hidden	Underline
Italic	WordUnderline

Text Command Macros

As explained earlier in this chapter, you use the Insert command to have a macro insert text into a document. This command can include either text or a string variable as a parameter. A string variable is a variable that contains text, not a numeric value. You'll learn about variables in Chapter 9.

You cannot press Enter within a text string. If you want to print part of the text on another line, use two Insert commands, separated by an InsertPara command. You can, however, press the Tab key to separate text within the quotation marks. When you save the template, or run the macro, Word will replace the tab with the Chr$(9) code, and concatenate it, so it would appear like:

```
Insert "column 1" + Chr$(9) + "Column 2"
```

When you run the macro, Word will insert a Tab space between the two parts of the inserted string.

Font and Character Formats

Font changes and character format codes in the parameter will be ignored. In fact, when you are editing a macro, selecting bold, italic, and underline buttons have no effect, and all of the options in the Format menu, except Change Case, will be dimmed.

To format text, you must include the appropriate commands. For example, to insert this text in a document:

This is in **bold** and this is <u>underlined</u>

you would use the commands:

```
Insert "This is in "
Bold 1
Insert "bold"
Bold
Insert " and this is "
Underline 1
Insert "underlined"
Underline
```

 **Note**   You need the argument that turns bold on before inserting the bold characters. That's because you will not know the status of the bold setting when you run the macro. You do not need to include the argument to turn it off, since you know the macro already turned bold on. However, it is always safer to specify arguments, just in case the user unexpectedly presses a key combination while the macro is running.

Text Alignment Commands

To center text and then return to left alignment, use the following commands:

```
Sub MAIN
CenterPara
Insert "This is centered"
InsertPara
LeftPara
Insert "This is not centered"
End Sub
```

You could also use the FormatParagragh command with the Alignment argument:

```
Sub MAIN
FormatParagraph .Alignment = 1
Insert "This is centered"
InsertPara
FormatParagraph .Alignment = 0
Insert "This is not centered"
End Sub
```

Other Paragraph Formatting Commands

Check out these other paragraph formatting macro commands:

CenterPara	ParaPageBreakBefore
CloseUpPara	ParaWidowOrphanControl
HangingIndent	PasteFormat
Indent	ResetPara
InsertPara	RightPara
JustifyPara	SpacePara1
LeftPara	SpacePara15
OpenUpPara	SpacePara2
ParaKeepLinesTogether	UnHang
ParaKeepWithNext	UnIndent

Changing a Command Function

You can also perform every Word command using the macro dialog box. Select Tools ➤ Macro, pull down the Macros Available In list and select Word Commands. A list of all Word commands will appear. Scroll the list and double-click on the command you want to perform.

You can change the function performed by a command, such as changing the action Word takes when you click on a button in the toolbar, press a built-in shortcut key, or select a menu item. You do this by either writing or recording a macro with the same name as the Word command. To return the function to its default setting, select Tools ➤ Macro, select the macro name, and then click on Delete.

For example, suppose you are preparing a report using the 12 point Courier New font. However, you feel that characters in bold just do not

stand out enough. You can redefine the function of the bold toolbar button, and the Ctrl+B keystroke, to display characters in 13-point Courier
New bold.

Locating the Word Command

Select Tools ➤ Macros, then type the name of the Word command you
want to change. If you do not know the name of the command, select
Word Commands from the Macros Available In option, scroll the list, and
click on the name of the command.

Creating a New Macro

To record a macro for the function, select Record, and then record the
keystrokes that you want to perform with the command.

To redefine the function by writing a macro, make sure the Macros
Available In option is set at either All Active Templates or Normal.dot,
then choose Create. (The Create option will be dimmed if the Macros
Available In option is set at Word Commands.) Word will begin a new
macro, inserting the command between the Sub Main and End sub
commands.

Editing the Macro

You can delete the statement and enter your own instructions. Or, you
can add additional instructions. For example, if you create a macro from
the FileSave command, Word will display:

```
Sub MAIN
FileSave
End Sub
```

If you want to automatically close a document and open a new one
on saving, edit the macro like this:

```
Sub MAIN
FileSave
FileClose
FileNew
End Sub
```

Tip

To prevent a user from closing any documents, create a macro called FileClose that contains only the commands Sub Main and End Sub. Nothing will occur when the user selects File ➤ Close, although pressing Alt+F4 will still exit Word.

S O L U T I O N S

Word's Sample Macros

Word provides a number of sample macros to perform some very useful tasks. These macros will be installed in four templates in the Macros subdirectory of your hard disk. The templates are:

◆ *Tables*—exports tables to Microsoft Access format, automatically fills in table rows or columns, presents information about your table, builds formulas, performs math operations, and numbers rows or columns.

◆ *Convert*—batch converts a number of files between various formats, edits conversion options, converts outlines to Microsoft PowerPoint format.

◆ *Layout*—performs common layout and formatting operations, arranges windows, adjusts font size, letter and line spacing; and manages multiple sections.

◆ *Macros*—runs a Wizard for completing a mailing address and label, creates and manages custom tips of the day, saves and prints selected text, performs calculations on dates, turns automatic backup of files on and off, finds and replaces special characters and symbols, generates a sample of fonts, creates organizational charts, plays a mind bender game, runs Wizards, and presents detailed document statistics.

To use the macros, select File ➤ Templates ➤ Add, select the Macros subdirectory, and double-click on the template name. Close the Templates and Add-Ins dialog box, then select the template and macro in the macro dialog box.

CHAPTER

9

WordBasic Programming

Y OU CAN WRITE SOPHISTICATED MACRO programs to automate a
variety of tasks using Word's programming commands. These commands control the flow of a macro, make decisions, and perform complex operations. This chapter introduces WordBasic programming commands and
the purposes they can serve in your macros. Later chapters describe how the
techniques here can be expanded to create fully automated applications.

Programming Command Basics

Word's programming commands are similar to commands found in
most other programming languages. In fact, if you already know how to
program in a language like C, BASIC or Pascal, you'll be able to program
easily in Word.

 **Note** If you are not familiar with the logic and structure of some
programming language, you should gain more program-
ming experience before using Word's more advanced macro
commands. This chapter also presents examples of macro
code to illustrate the commands discussed. Although the
examples perform a complete function, some of them are
not complete macros because they do not include the Sub
Main and End Sub commands.

Command Formatting Conventions

The macro programs in this and remaining chapters follow these formatting conventions:

◆ *Var*—represents a user-defined variable.

◆ *Value*—represents whatever value you have assigned to the variable.

◆ Words or commands that you just replace with your own selections are shown in italics, as in Bold *ON*. Note that the word *On* is in italic, meaning that you should replace it with the proper argument.

◆ Variable names and commands are shown in mixed uppercase and lowercase letters, such as NetIncomeTax. However, variable names are not case sensitive; the variables NetIncomeTax, NETINCOMETAX, and netincometax are considered the same.

◆ The contents of string variables are case sensitive. For example, two string variables are not equal unless their values match letter by letter in the same case.

◆ Quotation marks indicate that the parameter must be surrounded by quotation marks. For example, the syntax:

```
MsgBox "Message"
```

indicates you must insert your own text for the message

```
MsgBox "Sample Message Box"
```

Macro Variables

In Word macros, variables must be one word of up to 40 characters. They must start with a letter, although they can contain numbers and the underline character. Variables can contain either numeric values or strings.

The names of string variables must end with the dollar sign, as in Name$. The value assigned to a string variable can be up to 65,280 characters, including letters, numbers, and punctuation marks. Strings that contain all numbers are not treated as numeric values and they cannot be used in math operations unless they are converted to numbers. The string "123" is simply the combination of the three characters, not the value one hundred and twenty three.

 **Tip**   If you receive a Type Mismatch error when working with a string variable, check for the $ symbol at the end of the variable name.

Assigning Values to Variables

To assign a value to a variable in the macro, use the operator =, with the syntax:

```
VAR = value
```

For example, the command to assign the value 35 to the variable Years is:

```
Years = 35
```

The command:

```
Int = 1245*.05
```

assigns the result of the calculation to the variable Int.

You can also use the optional keyword Let, as in:

```
Let X = 5
```

The command:

```
Name$ = "Ted"
```

means that the variable Name$ will be the string Ted.

 **Note**

Text you are assigning to the string must be within quotation marks. You can also concatenate string literals (the characters in quotation marks) and other string variables, as in: CompletePath$ = "C:\Winword" + NameOfFile$ + ".DOC".

Line Breaks, Tabs, and Punctuation

You cannot press Enter when defining a string, so let Word wrap long strings between lines for you. However, you can press Tab within the quotes to create tabular strings. When you run the macro, Word will substitute the tab character with the Chr$(9) command. To insert a quotation mark, use chr$(34), as in:

```
Quote$ = "Her name is " + Chr$(34) + "Sam" + Chr$(34)
```

to create the string:

```
Her name is "Sam"
```

Displaying Numeric Values

Assigning a value to a variable does not insert it in the document. To display the value, you must use the Insert command. However, remember that Insert can only display a string literal in quotation marks, or a string variable ending with the dollar sign. You can use the command:

```
Insert Name$
```

but you cannot display a numeric variable. The commands:

```
Cost = 34.45
Insert Cost
```

would result in an error message.

303

To display numeric variable, you must convert the number to a string using the command:

```
Str$(VAR)
```

as in:

```
Cost = 34.45
Insert Str$(Cost)
```

Note The Str$() function converts a numeric value to its character equivalent. For instance, the number 34.45 will be converted to a string of five characters. Note that the function does not alter the contents of the variable named Cost. It continues to store the numeric value 34.45.

Programming for User Input

Using Word's programming commands, you can write macros that allow the user to make entries or selections while the macro is running. You can also write macros with variables and use programming commands to assign values to those variables.

Displaying Prompts for Input

The Input command allows the user to enter a string or a numeric value into a variable as the macro is running. It displays a prompt in the status bar telling the user what to enter. As the user enters characters, they appear in the status bar until the user presses Enter.

The syntax for the command is:

```
Input "Prompt", Var
Input "Prompt", Var$
```

For example, the command:

```
Input "Enter the amount of the loan", Principle
```

displays the status bar shown in Figure 9.1. The number that you enter will be assigned to the variable Principle. Use a string variable if you want to enter a string value.

FIGURE 9.1

Status bar prompt of the Input command

You can input more than one item on a line by separating the variable named with commas, as in:

```
Input Name$, Address$, Age
```

The user must enter the items separated by commas, as in:

```
Alan, Market Street, 56
```

 **Tip** The command by itself does not display the value in the document. If you wanted to display the entry you must use the Insert command.

 **Tip** If you want to enter text that includes a comma, use the Line Input command. This accepts only a single string variable, considering any commas as part of the string.

Inputting with a Dialog Box

The Inputbox$( ) function displays a dialog box containing the OK and Cancel buttons, along with a text box for entering data. The command pauses the macro until the user selects OK or Cancel. Because the command is a string function (ending in a dollar sign), it can only be used to accept a string variable. Use the command by assigning it to a variable, with the syntax:

```
Var$= InputBox$("Prompt","Box-Title","Default")
```

 **Note**   If you omit the title, Word uses "Microsoft Word." The default string, up to 255 characters, is text that appears selected when the box appears. If the user selects OK without typing anything, the default text is assigned to the string.

The command:

```
Var$= InputBox$("Enter your name","Membership", \
     "Your Name")
```

will display the dialog box shown in Figure 9.2. The user can enter as many lines of text as desired, even pressing Enter between lines. Otherwise, Word will wrap lines at the right edge of the dialog box.

The assignment is performed when the user selects OK. Selecting Cancel will result in an error condition.

FIGURE 9.2

Dialog box from the InputBox$() functions

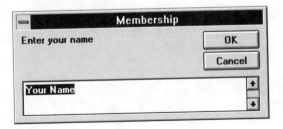

Input Tips and Tricks

If you have a number of InputBox$ commands in a macro, you can use variables to save retyping the same prompt or title, such as:

```
MyTitle$ = "Membership List"
Var$= InputBox$("Enter your name", MyTitle$,"Your Name")
```

For example, if you type the same title in 20 InputBox$( ) commands, then decide to change the title, you'd have to edit all 20 instructions. If you used a variable, you'd only have to edit the title once in the command that assigned it to the string variable.

To convert a string to a number, use the Val( ) function. This enables you to input a number in a dialog box using the InputBox$( ) function, then convert the string to a numeric value for use in math operations. Here's a sample:

```
Var$ = InputBox$("Enter your the cost",\
    "Invoice", "0000")
Cost = Val(var$)
Total = Cost * 1.06
Insert "The total including sales tax is " + Str$(Total)
```

You can enter a number using a thousands separator.

Message Boxes

The MsgBox command can be used as a statement or as a function. When used as a statement, it displays a message box that pauses the macro until the user selects a button.

The syntax is:

```
MsgBox Message$, Title$, Type
```

The Message$ string, up to 255 characters, will appear in the box. The optional title$ string appears in the box's title bar. If you omit the title, Word uses Microsoft Word.

Icon and Button Types

The type determines what icons and buttons appear in the box. If you omit the type, Word displays just the OK button with no icon. To determine the type, you select an option from one or more of the groups shown in Table 9.1, then add the three numbers together.

TABLE 9.1: Message box type options

OPTION	TYPE
Buttons	
0	OK
1	OK, Cancel
2	Abort, Retry, Ignore
3	Yes, No, Cancel
4	Yes, No
5	Retry, Cancel
Icons	
0	None
16	Stop sign
32	Question mark
48	Attention symbol
64	Information symbol
Default Button	
0	First button
256	Second button
512	Third button

For example, the dialog box shown in Figure 9.3 was created with the command:

```
MsgBox "Do you want to continue", "Error", 18
```

The type 18 was created by adding 2 from the buttons group with 16 from the icon group.

FIGURE 9.3

Message box

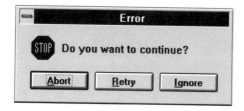

 **Tip**   You can also use MsgBox to display a prompt in the status line. Use type –1 to display the message until another replaces it, or use –2 or –8 to display the message until you move the mouse or press a key.

The syntax of the MsgBox() function is similar but it returns a value based on the command button the user selects. The syntax is:

```
Var = MsgBox(Message$, Title$, Type)
```

Values and Variables

The function returns a numeric value and must be assigned to a numeric variable. Table 9.2 shows which value is returned. For example, if you select Retry when using type 2, the variable will be assigned the value 0.

TABLE 9.2: Return values from the MsgBox() function

TYPE	VALUE RETURNED		
	−1	0	1
1	OK	Cancel	
2	Abort	Retry	Ignore
3	Yes	No	Cancel
4	Yes	No	
5	Retry	Cancel	

Note   If you use a negative type number, the message appears in the status bar and the returned value is always 0.

S O L U T I O N S

Using the Print Command

The print command displays a message in the status line, while the macro is running. It does not stop the macro, nor does it allows for any input. It is most often used to let the user know what is happening.

The syntax is:

```
Print expression
```

The expression can be a string or numeric variable, or a literal value, as in:

```
Print "Please wait while the document is printing"
Print Title$
Print Principle
Print 1001
```

You can combine elements by separating them with semicolons as in:

```
Print "This macro is for "; Name$ ; "Age :" ; Age
```

You can also concatenate strings and string variables with the plus sign. Separating strings by a comma inserts a tab. Print automatically inserts a space before positive numbers.

Variables and Dialog Boxes

You can use the name of a variable wherever you can use a literal value. For example, suppose you want to create a macro that lets you quickly change the left indentation of paragraphs. The command to change the margin to $1/2$ inch is this:

```
FormatParagraph .LeftIndent = "0.5"
```

You'd like to the use one macro, however, no matter how far you want to indent the paragraph. So rather than type a literal value into the argument, use a string variable, like this:

```
Input "Enter the enter", A$
FormatParagraph .LeftIndent = A$
```

Because a string variable is being used, you can enter a number and a unit of measurement. For example, if you enter 1, 1", 1 in, or 72 pt, Word will set the left indentation at one inch. When you do not enter a unit, Word uses the default unit of measurement for the option.

If you do not want to enter a unit but ensure that the measurement is set in inches, use the Chr$(34) code, as in:

```
FormatParagraph .LeftIndent = A$ + Chr$(34)
```

However, with Chr$(34) in the argument, you will get an error if you do enter a unit as well as a number. Entering 1″ to the Input prompt, for example, would enter 1″″ into the dialog box, an invalid entry.

If you use a numeric variable, as in:

```
Input "Enter the enter", A
FormatParagraph .LeftIndent = A
```

Word will automatically assume the value was in points.

 **Note** If you use a numeric variable, you cannot concatenate the Chr$(34) code or enter a unit of measurement. You cannot mix variable types.

Programming for Decision Making

The If command is called a conditional because it makes a determination regarding which instructions are to be executed while the macro is running.

Using the If Command

To perform one instruction when the condition is true, the syntax is:

```
If condition Then instruction
```

This structure means "If the condition is true, then perform the following instruction. If the condition is not true, skip the instruction."

The condition can include any one of these operators:

= equals

< less than

> greater than

<> not equal to

>= greater than or equal to

<= less than or equal to

String Variables

If you use string variables in an If condition, values must be enclosed in quotation marks, as in:

```
If Company$="SYBEX"
```

**Note**   The value of the variable must match the case exactly. For example, if Company has been assigned the value Sybex, the If condition would be false.

AND and OR Operators

The condition can also include AND and OR logic operators. For example:

```
If Company$="SYBEX" AND Program$="WINWORD"
```

will be considered true only when both conditions are true. Note that you do not repeat the If command with each condition. An OR condition is true when either of the conditions are true. The command:

```
If Company$="SYBEX" OR Program$="WINWORD"
```

is true as long as at least one of the conditions is met.

Performing Conditional Instructions

To perform a series of instructions when the condition is true, the syntax is:

```
If condition Then
     instructions
EndIf
```

This structure means "If the condition is true, then perform the following instructions. If the condition is not true, skip the instruction up to the EndIf command."

Note that in both cases, the instructions following the command are always performed. However, suppose you want to perform an instruction only then the condition were false. Use this syntax:

```
If condition Then instruction Else instruction
```

Or

```
If condition Then
    instructions
Else
    instructions
Endif
```

This structure means "If the condition is true, then perform the instructions up to the Else command. If the condition is not true, perform the instructions between the Else and EndIf commands."

Nesting Conditions

You can even nest conditions:

```
If condition1 Then
    instructions1
ElseIf condition2 Then
    instructions2
Else
    instructions3
Endif
```

The second condition is tested only when the first condition is false. So, the second set of instructions are performed only when the first condition is false and the second is true. The third set of instructions are performed only when both conditions are false. The Else instruction is optional, depending on the logic you want to perform. (You can have multiple ElseIf commands in the same If structure.)

Performing Several Instructions

It is possible to perform several instructions using the If condition Then syntax. Separate each instruction with a colon, as in:

```
Choice = MsgBox("Do you want to start a new document",\
    "Save Options" , 4)
If Choice = - 1 Then FileSave: FileClose
```

S O L U T I O N S

Message Box Selection Macro

The If command is useful for programming responses to a message or dialog box. For example, here is a macro that displays a message box and executes a task depending on the user's selection from that box:

```
Sub Main
Choice = MsgBox("Do you want to start a new document",\
    "Save Options" , 3)
If Choice = - 1 Then
    FileSave
    FileClose
    FileNew
ElseIf Choice = 0 Then
    FileSave
EndIf
End Sub
```

The Yes, No, and Cancel Options

This program displays a dialog box with the options Yes, No, and Cancel. If the user selects the Yes button (which places the value –1 in the variable Choice) Word saves the document, displays the Save As dialog box if necessary, closes the window, and then starts a new document.

If the user selects No from the message box, the document is saved but not closed. If the user selects Cancel, the macro ends without performing any operation because no instructions are given for when the Choice is 1.

The Select Case Command

Select Case is another conditional command that let's you perform an action based on a test value. A typical structure looks like this:

```
Input "name", FirstName$
Fname$ = UCase$(FirstName$)
Select Case Fname$
Case "JOHN"
     Insert "Lennon"
     InsertPara
     Insert "The Beatles"
Case "RINGO"
     Insert "Starr"
     InsertPara
     Insert "The Beatles"
Case "BILL", "HILLARY"
     Insert "Clinton"
     InsertPara
     Insert "President and Spouse"
Case Else
     Insert "Unknown"
End Select
```

The structure begins with the command words Select Case followed by the name of the variable being tested. Each Case command tests specific values of the variable. If none of the conditions are met, Word performs the statements in the Case Else section.

In this example, the user is asked to enter a name into the variable FirstName$. The next line uses Word's Ucase$ function to convert the name to all uppercase characters in the variable Fname$. The case statements will be comparing the name against specific string literals. For a match to occur, the case of the characters must also be the same. Creating a new variable of all uppercase letters assures finding a match for a name no matter what case the user entered it.

The Select Case Fname$ command sets up the structure by identifying the name of the variable to be compared. The first comparison compares the variable with the literal "JOHN." If the value of Fname$ is JOHN, Word performs the instructions up to the next Case statement, in this case printing:

```
Lennon
The Beatles
```

Word would then skip the remainder of the structure, performing the instruction following the End Select command.

If the comparison is false, Fname$ is not JOHN, then the second condition is tested—Fname$ equal to RINGO. Each condition in the structure is tested in the same way. If none of the conditions are true, Word performs the instructions at the Case Else command.

Comparing More than One Value

Note that the condition can compare with more than one value. The instruction:

```
Case "BILL", "HILLARY"
```

compares the variable Fname$ with two values using an Or condition. If either values match, the condition is true and the statements are performed.

Building Relational Conditions

In addition for testing for an exact match, you can use the Is keyword to build relational conditions, as in:

```
Input "Age", Age
Select Case Age
Case Is < 18
```

Here, the case condition is testing whether the variable Age is less than 18. You must use the Is keyword with any relational operator.

The To keyword can be used to determine if a value is within a range, as in:

```
Case 19 to 25
```

Here, the condition is true if the variable is greater than or equal to 19 and less than or equal to 25.

Determining Word's Status

In many cases, the decisions your macro has to make will depend on the current status of your document or Word. You may not want to run a macro, for example, if the screen is blank, or if a specific document in not displayed.

Using Functions

You use functions to determine a Word condition. There are functions that match every statement for an on or off condition. For example, while the Bold 1 statement turns bold on, the Bold() function determines whether selected character are bold or not.

Returning a Value

Like MsgBox(), you use functions to return a value to an assigned variable. Some functions return numbers. For example, the command:

```
IsBold = Bold( )
```

assigns a numeric value to the variable named IsBold. It returns 0 if the selected text is not bold, −1 if part of the selection is bold, and 1 if all of the selected text is bold.

Returning Text

Other functions return text and must be assigned to a string variable. For example, the command:

```
name$ =Selection$( )
```

places the selected text into the variable name$.

The function:

```
FileName$( )
```

returns the complete path and name of the current document. Still other variables can return a number of possible values. The FileNameInfo$() function, for example, uses arguments to return one of six values, using the syntax:

```
Var$ = FileNameInfo$(FileName$, Type)
```

The types, and what they return to the variable, are shown in Table 9.3.

TABLE 9.3: FileNameInfo$ types

TYPE	VALUE RETURNED
1	The full path and name of the file (if FileName$ does not include path, function makes up path from current directory)
2	The name and extension of the file when the file is in the current directory (if in another directory, complete path returned)
3	The name and extension of the file without the path
4	The name of the file without its extension
5	The path of the file without its name
6	The network path and name of the file

FileName$ is a string variable or literal containing all or part of the file's path and name. Use the FileName$() function to determine information about the active document, as in:

```
If FileNameInfo$(FileName$(), 3) <> "INVOICE.DOC" Then
    FileOpen("INVOICE.DOC")
```

This macro opens the document named Invoice if it is not already the active document. The function FileName$() returns the path and name of the active document. The function FileNameInfo$() using type 3 returns just the name and extension, not the path.

 **Note**

Word always returns the document name in all uppercase letters, so it must be in uppercase in the If condition. However, the parameter in the FileOpen command is not case sensitive.

Getting System Information

You can also obtain detailed information about the status of Windows and the Word application. The MicrosoftSystemInfo command, for example, displays the dialog box shown in Figure 9.4.

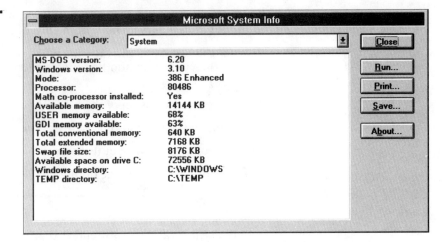

Categories of information include System, Printing, System DLL's, Fonts, Proofing, Graphic Filters, Text Converters, Display, Applications Running, and OLE Registration. Select the Print button to print a report of your system configuration, or click on Save to save the report in the file MSINFO.TXT.

For specific information, use the AppInfo$() or GetSystemInfo$() functions. Each returns information based on the value of the parameter. The parameters, and the information returned, are shown in Tables 9.4 and 9.5.

In addition, the SelInfo() function returns a numeric value based on a selected portion of text. If no text is selected, the value refers to the insertion point location. Table 9.6 lists the arguments. Note that arguments 13 through 18 return a −1 if the selection is not in a table.

TABLE 9.4: AppInfo$ () parameters

TYPE	VALUE RETURNED
1	Windows version number
2	Word version number
3	Returns –1 when in a special mode such as CopyText or MoveText
4	Number of points between the left edge of the screen and the Word window
5	Number of points between the top of the screen and the Word window
6	Width of the workspace
7	Height of the workspace
8	Returns –1 when maximized, 0 if not maximized
9	Total kilobytes of conventional memory
10	Kilobytes of available conventional memory
11	Total kilobytes of expanded memory
12	Kilobytes of available expanded memory
13	Returns 0 if no math coprocessor is installed, –1 if installed
14	Returns 0 if no mouse is installed, –1 if installed
15	Kilobytes of available disk space
16	Language version of Word
17	List separator setting in WIN.INI
18	Decimal setting in WIN.INI
19	Thousand separator in WIN.INI
20	Currency symbol in WIN.INI
21	Clock format in WIN.INI
22	A.M. string in WIN.INI

TABLE 9.4: AppInfo$ () parameters (continued)

TYPE	VALUE RETURNED
23	P.M. string in WIN.INI
24	Time separator in WIN.INI
25	Date separator in WIN.INI

TABLE 9.5: GetSystemInfo$() parameters

TYPE	VALUE RETURNED
1—20	Reserved for the Macintosh version of Word
21	Environment (Windows or Windows NT, for example)
22	Central processing unit type
23	DOS version number
24	Windows version number
25	Percent of available system resources
26	Bytes of available disk space
27	Windows mode: "Standard" or "386-Enhanced"
28	"Yes" or "No" whether a math coprocessor is installed
29	Country setting in WIN.INI
30	Language setting in WIN.INI
31	Vertical display resolution
32	Horizontal display resolution

TABLE 9.6: SelInfo() arguments

TYPE	VALUE RETURNED
1	The page number that would print on the page containing the end of the selection
2	The section number
3	The number of the page containing the end of the selection, counting consecutively from the first page and ignoring any new page number commands
4	Total number of pages in the document
5	The distance of the selection from the left edge of the page in "twips"—there are 20 twips in a point, or 1440 twips to an inch—valid only in Page Layout view
6	The distance of the selection from the top of the page, in twips—valid only if background pagination is on, and Draft Font is off
7	The distance of the selection to the left edge of the text surrounding the selection, in twips
8	The distance of the selection to the top edge of the text surrounding the selection, in twips
9	The position of the first selected character, as would appear after Col in the status bar
10	The line number of the first selected character
11	Returns −1 if an entire frame is selected, 0 if any part of the selection is outside of the frame
12	Returns −1 if the selection in within a table, 0 if not
13	The row number of the start of a selection in a table
14	The row number of the end of a selection in a table
15	The number of rows in the table
16	The column number of the start of a selection in a table
17	The column number of the end of a selection in a table

TABLE 9.6: SelInfo() arguments (continued)

TYPE	VALUE RETURNED
18	The largest number of columns in any selected rows
19	The zoom magnification
20	The selection mode: 0 for normal, 1 for extended (Ext), 2 for column (Col)
21	Returns −1 if Caps Lock is on, 0 if off
22	Returns −1 if Num Lock is on, 0 if off
23	Returns −1 if Overtype is on, 0 if off
24	Returns −1 if revision marking is on, 0 if off
25	Returns −1 if the selection is in a footnote or endnote pane, 0 if not
26	Returns −1 if the selection is in an annotation pane, 0 if not
27	Returns −1 if the selection is in a macro editing window, 0 if not
28	Returns −1 if the selection is in a header or footer pane, 0 if not
29	The bookmark number enclosing the start of the selection
30	The bookmark number enclosing the start of the selection, however, if more than one bookmark contains the starting point, returns the number of the last bookmark containing it
31	Returns −1 if the insertion point is on an end-of-row marker of a table.
32	Returns a value based on the selection of a footnote, endnote, or annotation reference: −1 if the selection includes more than the reference number, 0 if it does not include the reference, 1 if it is a footnote reference, 2 for an endnote reference, and 3 for an annotation reference

Using Screen Updating Commands

If you create a macro that arranges windows or changes the display, you'll see the changes as they occur. This may cause some macros to run slowly and can be quite distracting.

To prevent the display changes from appearing, use the ScreenUpdating 0 command. This will not affect the display of prompts, message, input, and dialog boxes. Use the ScreenRefresh command to update the screen without turning updating back on.

Screen updating is returned to normal when the macro ends, or when the ScreenUpdating 1 command is encountered. Using the command without a parameter toggles screen updating on or off.

The ScreenUpdating() function returns 0 if updating is off, and 1 if it is on.

Repeating Macro Commands

A loop is a series of commands that are repeated. When programming loops, you must make sure to include some way of stopping the repetition. Otherwise, you may be caught in an endless loop in which the macro continuously repeats until you press ESC to stop the macro or turn off your computer.

Repeating in Steps

The For command is used to perform a loop a specific number of times. The syntax is:

```
For Var = Start To End Step Increment
    instructions
Next Var
```

The command performs the repetition in sequence, counting from the starting value to the ending value. The values can be numbers, numeric variables, or mathematical expressions. The loop continues until the value of the assigned variable is greater than the ending value.

Step represents the amount by which to increment the variable. If you omit the step, Word increments by 1 with each repetition. For example, these commands print the numbers 1 to 50 down the left of the page:

```
Sub MAIN
StartOfLine
For Count = 1 To 50
    Insert Str$(Count)
    InsertPara
Next Count
End Sub
```

The StartofLine command moves the insertion point to the left margin. The command:

```
For Count = 1 To 50
```

starts the For loop using the variable Count, initializes Count at 1 (the starting value), sets the condition so the loop will repeat as long as the variable Count is less than or equal to 50.

 **Note** Since no step value is given, the value of Count is incremented by 1 with each repetition. The loop will stop when Count is greater than 50.

The command Insert Str$(Count) converts the numeric variable into a string and inserts it in the document, then InsertPara performs a carriage return.

If you wanted to print all odd numbers, from 1 to 49, enter the For instruction:

```
For Count = 1 To 50 Step 2
```

To count down, start with a larger initial value and use a negative step value as in:

```
For Count = 50 To 10 Step -1
```

S O L U T I O N S

Nested Multiple For Loop Macro

You can also nest multiple For loops to create some interesting effects. For example, this macro includes nested For commands:

```
Sub MAIN
StartOfLine
For row = 1 To 10
For Col = 1 To Row
Insert "*"
Next col
InsertPara
Next row
End Sub
```

It creates this design:

```
*
**
***
****
*****
******
*******
********
*********
**********
```

The Loop Commands

The first For loop sets up 10 rows of lines. For each of these lines, the second For loop prints as many asterisks as the row number, using the variable Row to determine the ending value of the loop. The InsertPara command between the Next commands causes each row of asterisks to print on a separate line.

Next Commands

You must have a Next command for each For command in the program. The Next commands must be placed so one entire For-Next loop is contained within the other, as in this general structure:

```
For A
     For B
           For C
           Next C
     Next B
Next A
```

Rearranging Items

A For loop can also be used to rearrange items, as in the following example (the lines are numbered just for reference; do not enter the line numbers as part of the macro):

```
1 Name$ = InputBox$("Please enter your name", \
  "Backwards Printing")
2 Times = Len(Name$)
3 For Char = Times To 1 Step - 1
4 Letter$ = Mid$(Name$, Char, 1)
5 Insert Letter$
6 Next Char
```

This program accepts a name, then prints it backwards. The commands work as follows:

◆ Line 1: The InputBox$ functions displays a dialog box to accept the entry of a name.

◆ Line 2: The Len (length) command assigns the number of characters in the name to the variable Times.

◆ Line 3: Begins the For loop, assigning the variable Char the initial value of the length of the name. The condition will repeat the loop as long as the variable Char is greater than 0, while the step reduces the value by one for each repetition.

◆ Line 4: The MidStr function assigns a number of characters of the Name$ variable, starting at the specified position, to the Char variable. It uses the syntax:

```
Var$=MidStr$(String-variable;Position;Number-of-Characters)
```

 **Note**

> When the loop starts, the position is set at the number of characters in the string. So the variable is assigned 1 character of the name starting at the last character. The next time the loop repeats, Char has been reduced by 1, so the starting position is the next to the last character. The loop repeats taking the next character to the left with each repetition.

◆ Line 5: Inserts each character returned by line 4 into the document.

◆ Line 6: Repeats the loop until the condition is no longer true.

Numbering Items

Another use for loops is to number items. For example, this macro allows you to specify the number of paragraphs you want to number in a document:

```
1 Input "Number of paragraphs to number", times
2 Overtype 0
3 StartOfDocument
4 For Count = 1 To times
5 Insert Str$(count) + Chr$(9)
6 ParaDown
7 Next count
```

Here is a description of each line:

◆ Line 1: Requests the number of lines you want to number.

◆ Line 2: Ensures that Insert is on by turning off the Overtype mode. If overtype were on, the line numbers would replace the first letter in each line.

◆ Line 3: Moves the insertion point to the start of the document.

◆ Line 4: Begins the For loop.

◆ Line 5: Converts the variable count into a string, enters the number, and inserts a tab.

◆ Line 6: Moves the insertion point to the next paragraph.

◆ Line 7: ends the loop when the condition is no longer true.

 **Tip** A routine like this could be used to automatically number a macro program so you could print a reference copy with each command numbered. However, the While command provides a more efficient way to perform the same function.

Conditional Repeating

The While command performs a series of statements as long as a condition is true. The loop ends when the condition is false. The syntax is:

```
While Condition1
     instructions
Wend
```

The structure means "While the condition is true, repeat all the following instructions up to the Wend command." You must make sure that the instruction inside the loop will eventually make the text condition false to end the repetition. If the test is false to begin with, the instructions will not be performed at all.

One Way to Number Paragraphs

As an example, the following program inserts line numbers in front of each paragraph in a document:

```
1 StartOfDocument
2 Overtype 0
3 count = 1
4 While AtEndOfDocument() <> - 1
5 Insert Str$(count) + Chr$(9)
```

```
6 ParaDown
7 Count = count + 1
8 Wend
```

Here's how it works:

- ◆ Line 1: Moves the insertion point to the start of the document.
- ◆ Line 2: Ensures that Overtype is off.
- ◆ Line 3: Assigns the variable Count the value 1.
- ◆ Line 4: Sets the While loop to continue as long as the insertion point is not at the end of the document. When the insertion point is at the end, the function:

```
AtEndOfDocument()
```

  returns the value -1. You could also enter the command using the Not operator:

```
While Not(AtEndOfDocument())
```

- ◆ Line 5: Converts the variable count into a string, enters the number, and inserts a tab.
- ◆ Line 6: Moves the insertion point to the beginning of the next paragraph.
- ◆ Line 7: Increments the value of Count by one. (This wasn't needed with the For loop example because the loop itself increments the value.)
- ◆ Line 8: Continues the loop as long as the condition is met.

Another Paragraph Numbering Macro

There are usually several ways to perform the same task. For example, here is another macro for numbering paragraphs:

```
StartOfDocument
count = 1
Overtype 0
Insert Str$(count) + Chr$(9)
While ParaDown()
Count = count + 1
Insert Str$(count) + Chr$(9)
Wend
EditUndo
```

In this macro, the condition is repeated using the ParaDown() function. This function moves the insertion point down but returns a false condition (the value 0) if the insertion point is at the end of the document. The condition:

```
While ParaDown()
```

can be substituted for either of these statements:

```
While ParaDown() <> 0
While ParaDown() = -1
```

Word logic assigns the value 0 when a function is false, and –1 when the function is true.

When the loop ends using the ParaDown() command, the insertion point will be at the end of the document, where the macro will insert a final number. Since the number will appear at the end of a paragraph, or at the start of a blank line, the number is deleted with the EditUndo.

S O L U T I O N S

Determining if a Window Is Blank

Use the AtEndOfDocument() function to determine if the current document window is blank. For example, suppose you have a macro that searches for text in a document. You wouldn't want to run the macro if the document window contains no text. Use this technique:

```
StartOfDocument
If AtEndOfDocument() = - 1 Then Stop(-1)
```

The instructions move the insertion point to the start of the document, then test to determine if the insertion point is at the end. When the insertion point is at both the start and end, the document is blank. When the condition is true, the Stop(–1) command stops the macro. Without the –1 argument, Word would display a message box reporting that the macro has been interrupted.

Programming with Subroutines

A subroutine is a series of instructions that can be performed as a unit. Picture a subroutine as a program within the program. Whenever you want to perform the instructions in the subroutine, no matter where you are in the macro, you branch (move to) to the subroutine.

Word allows two types of subroutines. An internal subroutine is a series of instructions within the macro itself. You use the Goto command to move to the routine to perform its instructions. An external subroutine is outside of the routine that branches to it, and it can even be in another macro entirely.

Using Internal Subroutines

You designate a subroutine by a label name. The syntax is:

```
subroutine-name:
```

The label, followed by a colon, must be the first text on a line, with no preceding spaces or tab characters. The name must begin with a letter and can contain up to 40 characters.

The GoTo Command

When you want to perform the instructions in the subroutine, use the Goto command, followed by the subroutine name, but without the colon. The syntax is:

```
Goto subroutine-name
```

When the macro encounters this command, it moves to the routine indicated by the subroutine name. After performing the routine, it continues from that point on, without returning to the original location. (You cannot use a Goto command within a Select Case structure.)

Sample Internal Subroutines

For instance, a macro could have this structure:

```
instructions...
Goto Report
instructions...
```

```
Report:
     instructions
End Sub
```

The instructions at the start of the macro are performed, then the Goto command sends the macro to the subroutine called Report. The instructions following the subroutine name are performed then the macro ends. Note that the instructions between the Goto and the subroutine are never executed.

Here is a slight modification of the same menu structure:

```
instructions...
Goto Report
instructions...
Report:
     instructions
Invoice:
     instructions
End Sub
```

In this case, three sets of instructions will be performed. After the program completes the instructions in Report, it continues with the instructions in Invoice. The instructions following the Goto Report command are never performed.

A Sequence that Won't Work

You could modify the macro to perform either Report or Invoice but not both, but this sequence would not work:

```
instructions...
If Condition Then
Goto Report
Else
Goto Invoice
EndIf
instructions...
Report:
     instructions
Invoice:
     instructions
End Sub
```

When the If command sends the program to Report, its instructions are executed. But the program then continues through the Invoice subroutine as well.

Correcting the Problem

To correct the problem, you could use this structure:

```
instructions...
If Condition Then
Goto Report
Else
Goto Invoice
EndIf
instructions...
Report:
     instructions
Goto End
Invoice:
     instructions
End:
End Sub
```

With this structure, after completing the Report subroutine, the program would branch to the End subroutine and stop. The End subroutine does not need any instructions.

Using External Subroutines

Sometimes you want to perform the instructions in a subroutine, then return to the original location in the macro. To branch to, then return from a subroutine, use an external subroutine.

An external subroutine follows the End Sub command of the Main routine, like this:

```
Sub Main
     instructions
End Sub

Sub MyOwnRoutine
     instructions
End Sub
```

The Call Command

To move to the subroutine, just uses the routine's name, or use the Call command, with the syntax:

```
Call subroutine-name
```

When the program encounters the end of the subroutine, the program returns to the line following the call to the command.

Sample External Subroutine

Here is an example of a macro structure using an external subroutine:

```
Sub Main
instructions...
Report
instructions...
End Sub

Sub Report
     instructions
End Sub
```

This macro performs the instructions at the start of the main routine, then performs those in the Report subroutine. At the end of Report subroutine, the macro returns to the Main routine, and continues at the instruction following the call to Report. The macro ends when it reaches the End Sub command for the Main routine.

 **Note**   You can have as many external subroutines as you need. Each must be contained, however, within its own set of Sub and End Sub commands.

You can also call one subroutine from another, as in:

```
Sub Main
instructions...
Report
instructions...
End Sub
```

```
Sub Report
     instructions
     Invoice
     instructions
End Sub

Sub Invoice
     instructions
End Sub
```

 **Note**

When a subroutine ends, the macro always returns to the last position. So, for example, after the Invoice routine ends, the macro will return to the Report routine. Then, when Report ends, the macro returns to the Main routine.

Calling a Subroutine in Another Macro

You can also call a subroutine in another macro stored in the normal or a global template, with the syntax:

```
Call MacroName.SubName
```

The keyword Call is optional. Word will run the macro indicated, then branch to the specified subroutine name.

Variables in Subroutines

Variables that you use in a subroutine are local. That means that the variable will only retain its value in the routine in which it is assigned. If you want to use a variable in more than one routine, define it using the DIM SHARED command before the main routine, like this:

```
DIM SHARED COST
Sub Main
```

You could now refer to and use the variable named COST in any subroutine in the macro.

 **Tip**

> If you use the DIM command without the keyword SHARED to declare a variable, the variable will be local to the first subroutine in which it is assigned a value. Use this technique if you want to be able to trace the value of a variable using the macro toolbar. Refer to the section on Testing Your Macro later in this chapter.

Passing Variables to Other Routines

You can also pass variables from one routine to the next using an argument list, as in this macro:

```
Sub Main
Cost = 45
AddTax Cost
End Sub

Sub AddTax(Price)
    Total = Price * 1.06
    Insert "Total cost is " + Str$(Total)
End Sub
```

Here, the value of the variable Cost is copied to the variable named Price that is used in the AddTax subroutine. The variable Cost cannot be used in the AddTax routine, and the variable Total cannot be used in the Main routine.

Passing by Reference

Passing a variable this way is called "passing by reference." If you change the value of Price, the value of Cost would change as well. For example, consider this macro:

```
Sub Main
Cost = 45
AddTax Cost
Insert Str$(Cost)
End Sub
```

```
Sub AddTax(Price)
    Price = Price * 1.06
    Insert "Total cost is " + Str$(Price)
End Sub
```

The change made to the variable Price will also affect the Cost variable in Main. At the end of the macro, both variables will contain the value 47.70.

Passing by Value

You can also pass a variable by value. You must call the subroutine with its name only, not use the Call command, and you must enclose the variable being passed in parentheses, as in:

```
Sub Main
Cost = 45
AddTax (Cost)
Insert Str$(Cost)
End Sub
```

 **Note**   Any changes made to the variable Price in the AddTax subroutine will not affect Cost.

S O L U T I O N S

Creating Your Own Functions

A function is similar to an external subroutine, except it is designed to return a single numeric or string value. Functions have the general structure:

```
Function FunctionName
    instructions
    FunctionName = value-to-be-returned
End Function
```

339

CHAPTER 9 WordBasic Programming

Note that the name of the function is used twice, once in the function heading, then again to assign the value to be returned. To return a string value, make the function name a string variable by ending it with a dollar sign.

If you pass an argument to the function, it must be passed by value, within parentheses. You use a function just as you use those provided by Word. For example, consider this macro which calculates the number of days between two dates:

```
Sub Main
MeetingDate$ = InputBox$("When is the meeting")
Insert "You have " + Str$(Daysleft(MeetingDate$)) \
    + " days to prepare"
End Sub

Function DaysLeft(Deadline$)
TargetDate = DateValue(Deadline$)
DaysLeft = TargetDate – Today()
End Function
```

The user is asked to enter the date when a meeting will occur. (Enter the date in MM/DD/YY format.) The Insert command enters the words "You have" in the text, followed by a space. Then, before the results of the Str$() function are displayed, the date, in string variable named MeetingDate$, is passed to the variable Deadline$ in the function DaysLeft.

In DaysLeft, the built-in function DateValue() converts the date into a serial number (TargetDate), then the function name is assigned the difference between TargetDate and the result of the built-in function Today(), which represents the serial number of the current day.

When the function ends, it's name represents the number of days between the current day and the day of the meeting. This number is converted to a string, with the Str$() function, and inserted into the document, with the remainder of the Insert command.

Trapping Errors

Errors can occur no matter how careful you are. For example, suppose the FileSave statement displays the Save As dialog box. If you select Cancel from the dialog box, Word stops the macro and displays an error message. All macro instructions past that point will not be performed. Rather than prematurely end a macro on an error, you should detect when an error occurs so you can take some alternate action, or ignore the error and continue the macro.

The On Error Command

This is called error trapping, because it traps the error before Word can end your macro. The On Error command is used to set an error trap, and it can be used in several ways. (You must include the spaces between the words of these commands.)

◆ **On Error Goto label**—tells Word to go to an internal subroutine when an error is encountered.

◆ **On Error Resume Next**—continues the macro following the line that caused the error.

◆ **On Error Goto 0**—turns off the error trap.

For example, an error will be generated if the user selects cancel from an Input box. To avoid this problems, use an error trap such as this:

```
On Error Resume Next
Var$ = InputBox$("Enter your Name")
On Error Goto 0
```

If the user selects cancel in the Input box, Word will not report an error but continue with the line following the InputBox$() command. The On Error Goto 0 command turns off the error trap in case some other error occurs that you do not want to ignore.

SECRETS

Error Trap Limitations

Word can only trap one error at a time. When the error occurs, Word assigns a value to the built-in variable Err, indicating the type of error. When Word encounters the On Error Resume Next or the On Error Goto 0 command, it resets the value in Err to 0, indicating that no error condition currently exists, so you can continue the macro.

Word does not reset the variable when you branch to a routine by using the On Error Goto command. If another error is detected in the routine, or elsewhere in the program, the error trap will not work and the macro will stop. For example, without the command Err=0, if the user selects Cancel a second time, an error message will appear and the macro will be halted. With the command, the routine will repeat.

If the user selects Cancel in the dialog box, the error trap branches back to the AskForIt label and again displays the box. This will continue as long as the user selects Cancel.

Taking Corrective Action

You may not want to ignore the error but take some corrective action. For example, in this macro, the InputBox is repeated until the user selects OK. (Remember, a label name must start at the beginning of a line.)

```
Sub Main
    On Error Goto AskForIt
AskForIt
    Err = 0
    meetingdate$ = InputBox$("When is the meeting",\
        "11/12/94")
```

```
On Error Goto 0
Insert "You have " + Str$(Daysleft(MeetingDate$)) \
     + " days to prepare"

End Sub
```

This macro creates an error trap that branches to the AskForIt internal subroutine when an error occurs. The macro then assigns the value 0 to the variable Err.

Testing Your Macros

Use the macro toolbar to thoroughly test a macro while it is open. Write or edit the macro, then switch to or open another document window. Make certain the macro name appears in the macro bar list box. If not, pull down the list and select the name of the macro you want to test. Then, click on the Run button.

Working with Error Messages

If an error occurs, Word will display an error message. Select OK, then return to the macro window. The line which caused the error will appear highlighted. Click the mouse to deselect the text—Word will display the line in red reminding you where the error occurred. Correct the problem, then switch windows and try running the macro again. When the macro runs without an error, select File ➤ Save Template.

Macro Toolbar Options

Other buttons in the macro toolbar can also help find and correct errors. For best results, use the Window ➤ Arrange All command to display both the macro and the window where you are testing the macro. You can then move between windows with a click on the mouse.

◆ **Trace:** Highlights each command as it is performed, but does not stop after each command. The highlight will move quickly through the macro.

◆ **Step:** Each time you click on the step button, Word performs one macro command, highlights the command in the macro, then pauses.

Repeatedly click on the button to see how each line performs. Click on the Continue button to run the macro without stepping from that point on, or click on the Stop button to stop running the macro.

◆ **Step Subs:** Steps through macro, but performs called external sub-routines without stepping through them.

◆ **Show Variables:** When you pause a macro, or step through it, click this button to display a dialog box showing the values of declared variables—those defined with the DIM command.

◆ **Add/Remove Rem:** Adds or removes the Rem command from the start of the current line, or from selected lines. Use this to quickly convert instructions to remarks, to see the effects of running the macro without the instructions. To reinsert the instructions, select them and click the button again to remove the Rem commands.

CHAPTER 10

Advanced WordBasic

ONCE YOU'RE FAMILIAR WITH WORD'S macro language, you can write macros that streamline tasks of all types, such as filling out and merging forms, and printing raffle tickets. This chapter teaches you to create macros for automating all kinds of operations and applications using advanced WordBasic programming techniques.

Creating Customized Macros

Word has built-in features for all word processing tasks, but you may want to customize an operation to suit the way you like to work. Perhaps you don't like the way a function operates, or you want to create a macro that makes a function even easier to use for a less experienced Word user.

Confirmed Search and Replace Operations

The macro in the following sidebar, for example, performs a confirmed search and replace operation. It is similar to Word's built-in Replace command but it doesn't require the user to deal with the Replace dialog box. More importantly, it ensures that the user does not accidentally replace text by not entering a replacement string.

S O L U T I O N S

Custom Find and Replace Macro

This is a good macro to study if you are just learning how to program. It incorporates a number of basic programming elements—message boxes, input boxes, decision making, loops, and subroutines.

```
Sub MAIN
RCount = 0
SCount = 0
On Error Goto Endmacro
FIND$ = InputBox$("Enter the text to find")
Replace$ = InputBox$("Enter the text to insert")
If Len(Replace$) = 0 Then
MsgBox "Sorry, you must enter a replacement string"
Stop(- 1)
EndIf
StartOfDocument
ToolsOptionsEdit .SmartCutPaste = 0
EditFindClearFormatting
EditFind .Find = Find$, .Direction = 0, .MatchCase = 0,\
.WholeWord = 0, .PatternMatch = 0, .SoundsLike = 0,\
.Format = 0, .Wrap = 1
While EditFindFound() <> 0
Choice = MsgBox("Replace this string?", \
    "Options", 3)
If Choice = - 1 Then
    EditCut
    Insert Replace$
    Rcount = Rcount + 1
ElseIf Choice = 0 Then
    Scount = Scount + 1
Else
    Goto ReportEnd
EndIf
```

```
RepeatFind
Wend
ReportEnd:
      If Rcount = 0 And SCount = 0 Then
      MsgBox "The text was not found"
      Else
      MsgBox "You deleted " + Str$(RCount) +\
      " and you skipped " +      Str$(SCount)
      EndIf
ToolsOptionsEdit .SmartCutPaste = 1
EndMacro:
End Sub
```

Controlling the Replacement Process

The macro gives you control over the replacement process. It begins by setting the variables RCount and SCount to 0. These will be used to count the number of replacements made, and the number of matching strings that you choose not to replace. The macro then sets up an error trap. (The macro will end without an error message if you select Cancel from one of the input boxes.)

The macro then accepts search and replacement strings assigning them to the variables Find$ and Replace$. If you do not enter a replacement string, the macro stops because of this structure:

```
If Len(Replace$) = 0 Then
    MsgBox "Sorry, you must enter a replacement string"
    Stop(- 1)
EndIf
```

Moving the Insertion Point

The macro moves the insertion point to the start of the document, then turns off a feature called Smart Cut and Paste, available in the Tools ➤ Options ➤ Edit dialog box.

 **Note** With this feature on, Word will automatically delete the space following a deleted word. If this occurs, when the macro deletes a word and replaces it with another, there will be no space between it and the next word.

The EditFind Command

The EditFindClearFormatting command removes any formatting specification that may have been selected previously, then the EditFind command searches for the first occurrence of the text.

The While Loop

The macro then begins a While loop that will continue until a matching text string is not found. This is accomplished by testing the value of the function EditFindFound(), which returns a 0 when Word cannot locate the specified text.

The loop is only begun when a matching string has been located—the string is selected in the document window. Its first task is to display a message box asking if you want to replace the string. If you select Yes, the value of Choice will be –1, and the macro deletes the selected text, inserts the replacement setting, and increments the Rcount variable.

If you select No, the value of Choice is 0 and the macro only increments the Scount variable without deleting and replacing the text. If you select Cancel, the macro jumps to the ReportEnd label. If you select either Yes or No, the RepeatFind command searches for the next occurrence of the string.

The ReportEnd Subroutine

When you select Cancel from the message box, or if the search string cannot be found, the ReportEnd subroutine is executed. This selects one of two message boxes. One box appears when the search text has not been located in the document, the other reports the number of replacements made and those that were skipped. The Smart Cut and Paste option is then turned back On and the macro ends.

Automating Data Entry

When you use a table to set up a form that requires calculations, you can automate the entry of totals and other formula results (See Chapter 7). By using macros, you can take the automation even further.

S O L U T I O N S

Automated Invoice Form Macro

Here is a macro that completes the invoice form described in Chapter 7. The macro prompts you for the client name and address information, then inserts the date. It then accepts the details for each order until all 16 lines have been completed, or until you select Cancel or press ESC.

```
Sub MAIN
DisableInput
Startit:
     FileOpen("C:\Winword\INVOICE.DOC")
StartOfDocument
ToolsOptionsView .FieldCodes = 0
For l = 1 To 8
     ParaDown
Next
EndOfLine
Input "Enter the Client's Name", Name$
Insert Name$
LineDown
Line Input "Enter the Client's Name", Name2$
EndOfLine
Insert Name2$
LineDown
Line Input "Enter the Address", Address1$
EndOfLine
Insert Address1$
LineDown
Line Input "Enter the Address", Address2$
EndOfLine
```

```
Insert Address2$
LineDown
Line Input "Enter the Address", Address3$
EndOfLine
Insert Address3$
LineDown
Line Input "Enter the Address", Address4$
EndOfLine
Insert Address4$
LineDown
LineDown
LineDown
LineDown
EndOfLine
InsertDateTime .DateTimePic = "MMMM d, yyyy",\
.InsertAsField = 0
EditGoTo .Destination = "t"
LineDown
x = 1
Input "Enter Item Number", A$
While A$ <> "" And X < 17
Insert A$
NextCell
Input "Enter the description", A$
Insert A$
NextCell
Input "Enter the quantity", A$
Insert A$
NextCell
Input "Enter the cost", A$
Insert A$
NextCell
NextCell
x = x + 1
If X < 17 Then Input "Enter the item number ", A$
Wend
```

```
Complete:
EditSelectAll
UpdateFields
Cancel
LineDown
PrintNow = MsgBox("Print the Invoice Now?", "Invoice", 4)
If PrintNow = - 1 Then FilePrint
Another = MsgBox("Another Invoice ?", "Invoice", 4)
If Another = O Then
  Goto EndMacro
  Else
  On Error Goto EndMacro
GetName:
  InName$ = InputBox$("Enter a file name for this invoice")
  If InName$ = "" Then Goto GetName
  FileSaveAs .Name = InName$
  FileClose
EndIf
Goto StartIt
EndMacro:
End Sub
```

Starting the Macro

The DisableInput command prevents you from interrupting the macro by pressing Esc. The StartIt label serves as a branching point if you later select to prepare another invoice.

The StartOfDocument Command

The macro then opens the invoice document and ensures that the insertion point is at the very start. Always include the full path and name of the document in a FileOpen command. Edit the command shown in the macro for the location of your document.

 **Note**

When Word opens a document, it automatically places the insertion point at its start. If the document is already open, however, Word just switches to the document. The insertion point may be at some other position. The StartOfDocument command moves the insertion point to the beginning of the document. You'll learn more about this in Chapter 13.

Field Codes and For Loops

The next line turns the display of field codes off. If the display were on, you would not see the results of the table calculations when the macro ends, although they will be printed correctly.

The series of ParaDown commands in the For loop, position the text on the form. If you use this macro, you may have to adjust the number of ParaDown repetitions to match the spacing of your invoice.

Line Input Commands

A series of Line Input commands display prompts in the status bar and input the name and address information. Line Input is used particularly for address information that may include commas, such as between the city and state names.

 **Note**

String variables are used for all of the entries, even quantity and cost. This will not prevent Word from calculating the table. The calculations for the totals are performed using formula fields on the table cells. Word performs the math using the values of the cell entries. Word can perform the math as long as the user enters numeric characters.

Programming for User Input

The macro uses Line Input and Input commands for all of the information, rather than InputBox$() commands. The Input commands display the prompts in the status bar, so the user's view of the invoice-in-progress is not obscured with dialog boxes. In addition, the user can type each entry and press Enter without the need to move the mouse and select the OK button in an input box. This is important in a busy office where a number of invoices need to be processed.

Finally, the user can only enter one line of text in the status bar. If the macro had used input boxes, the user could accidentally press Enter to insert a line break in the entry, affecting the spacing of the invoice.

The Line Down commands move the insertion point to the appropriate line, then the EndofLine command moves the insertion point to the proper position on the line. On the sample invoice, Tab spaces have been inserted so the address information will align evenly on the page.

Inserting the Date

The macro then inserts the date as text, not as a field. This way, you'll have a record of the invoice date. If you used a field, the date would change if you later retrieved the invoice from the disk file.

Placing the Insertion Point

The insertion point must be placed in the first cell of the invoice table where you want the user to enter an item number. You could use Line-Down or ParaDown commands to position the insertion point in the table. Instead, the command:

```
EditGoTo .Destination = "t"
```

causes Word to search the document, placing the insertion point in cell A1 of the first table it encounters. Other destination codes are shown in Table 10.1.

TABLE 10.1: Destination codes for the EditGoTo command

CODE	DESTINATION
p	page, such as "p3"
s	next section
l	line from the current location, such as "l+10"
a	annotation text, as in "a'Adam Chesin'"
f	next footnote, use "f-" for the previous footnote
e	specified endnote reference, as in "e3"
d	specified field, as in "d'TIME'"
t	next table
g	specified graphic, as in "g3"
q	next equation, use "q-" for the previous equation
0	object, as in "o'WordArt'"

Since the first row of the table contains column labels, the LineDown command moves the insertion point to the first detail row, then the variable X is set at 1. The variable will be incremented for each row you enter—keeping track of the number of rows—so you must stop when all 16 detail lines have been completed.

Entering Item Numbers

An input command requests the first item number, then a While loop is begun that repeats as long as you enter an item number, or until all 16 lines of the invoice have been completed.

Note

> You can stop the loop by pressing Enter before typing an item number. This places a null value in the string variable ItemNum$ causing the While condition to be false.

Updating the Fields

When there are no more invoice items, the document is selected and the fields updated, calculating the item totals, sales tax, and grand total. The Cancel and LineDown commands ensure that the invoice is deselected.

Printing and Repeating the Invoice

You are then asked if you want to print a copy of the invoice. If you select Yes, the invoice is printed. A message box is then displayed asking if you want to prepare another invoice. If you select No, the macro ends. If you select yes, an input box appears asking for the file name.

Note

> The On Error Goto EndMacro command ends the macro and prevents an error message from appearing if you select Cancel in the input box. The GetName label and the If, which tests the contents of the InName$ variable, ensure that you enter a file name.

Creating Numbered Documents

When you create numbered tickets or other small documents using a label, you must copy the ticket from label to label, as explained in Chapter 3.

S O L U T I O N S

Copying and Numbering Macro

The macro shown here will automate the process for you. Select the ticket format, create the first ticket with the text centered and the SEQ field for inserting the number, then run the macro. It requests how many tickets you want to print.

```
Dim NumOfTick
Sub MAIN
ScreenUpdating 0
StartOfDocument
Input "Number of Tickets", NumOfTick
NextCell
PrevCell
EditCopy
Cancel
For Tickets = 1 To NumOfTick - 1
NextCell
EditPaste
Cancel
Next
EditSelectAll
UpdateFields
Cancel
LineDown
End Sub
```

Copying and Pasting the Contents of Cells

The NextCell and PrevCell commands move the insertion to the next or previous cell and select its contents. The commands here select the contents of the first cell, copy it into the clipboard, and then deselect the text. A For loop then moves from cell to cell, pasting the contents of the ticket. When the loop ends, the entire document is selected and the fields are updated to increment the ticket numbers.

 **Note**

Screen updating was turned off at the start of the macro to help speed the process along. The hourglass icon will appear as the macro runs reminding you to be patient—the process can take some time.

Changing the Appearance of the Mouse Pointer

If you want your macro to change the appearance of the mouse pointer, use the WaitCursor or Magnifier commands. The WaitCursor command changes between the standard pointer and the hourglass. Use:

```
WaitCursor 1
```

to change to the hourglass. (Use the 0 argument to change to the standard pointer.)

To change the pointer to a magnifying glass, use the command:

```
Magnifier 1
```

A 0 parameter changes to the standard pointer, while no parameter toggles between the two settings. The Magnifier () function returns −1 if the pointer is a magnifying glass, 0 if it is the standard pointer.

Performing Math with Macros

While Word tables can perform math with formulas and functions, you may need to perform a series of calculations that cannot be entered into one cell. Rather than use several cells to store intermediate results, you can perform the math in a macro, then use the STR$ and Insert commands to insert the results into a table cell.

For example, the table in Figure 10.1 requires the input of a loan amount, interest rate, and length of the mortgage.

FIGURE 10.1

Table that requires
complex math

Mortgage Payment Calculator

Prepared for:	
Amount of principle:	
Interest rate:	
Length of mortgage in years:	
Your monthly mortgage payment:	

S O L U T I O N S

Exponential Math Macro

The formula for calculating the mortgage payments in our sample table requires exponential math. In order to calculate and insert the mortgage amount, the form was automated by the macro shown here.

```
Sub MAIN
StartOfDocument
EditGoTo .Destination = "t"
Client$ = InputBox$("Enter Client Name")
NextCell
Insert Client$
NextCell
NextCell
NextCell
NextCell
GetPrin:
Input "Enter Principle", Principle
  If Principle <= 0 Then Goto GetPrin
Insert Str$(Principle)
NextCell
NextCell
GetRate:
Input "Enter Rate", Rate
If Rate < 0 Then Goto GetRate
If Rate < 1 Then Rate = Rate * 100
```

```
Insert Str$(Rate)
NextCell
NextCell

GetYears:
Input "Enter Years", Years
If Years <= 0 Then Goto GetYears
Insert Str$(Years)
J = 0
Rate = Rate / 1200
N = Years * 12
Inc = 1 + Rate
X = Inc
For Var = 1 To N
     X = X * Inc
Next
Temp = (Rate / (1  (1 / X)))
Payment = Temp * (Principle + J + 2000)
NextCell
NextCell
Payment = Int(Payment * 100) / 100
Insert Str$(Payment)
End Sub
```

Using If Commands to Validate Entries

The IF commands in the routines GetPrin, GetRate, and GetYears ensure that a valid entry has been made. If not, the routine is performed again. Another If command checks if the interest rate has been entered as a whole number or as a decimal (such as .07 for seven percent). If it is entered as a decimal, it is converted to a whole number for use later in the macro.

Taking Values to the Nth Power

The task of taking a value to the Nth power is performed in a FOR loop. Initial values are set before the loop, then the amount multiplied with each repetition.

360

 **Note**

The macro does not assume that the table is the first element in the document. That is, you can have a letterhead or other text in the document before the table. The EditGoTo command places the insertion point in the table, then the NextCell commands move the insertion point to the proper cells for entry.

Working with Programming Arrays

If you are familiar with any programming language, you should know about arrays. An array is a special type of variable that contains a series of elements. You can visualize an array as a list of items. The array name is the name you'd give to the list. Each item in the list is another array element. Array elements are actually separate variables that can be referred to the same array name.

Declaring an Array

To use an array, you must first declare it. You declare an array by giving its name and maximum number of elements in each dimension:

```
DIM Var (size, size)
```

Note that the array subscripts are enclosed in parentheses. Word array elements begin with 0, so the size actually indicates the last element number. That is, an array declared as:

```
Dim Clients$(10)
```

can hold 11 elements, numbers 0 through 10. Once you declare the array, you access the elements using a subscript number. The first array element is Clients$(0), the second Clients$(1), and so on.

A two-dimensional array of 21 elements in each dimension would be declared:

```
DIM Var(20,20)
```

Arrays can occupy quite a bit of memory space. If you will be using several arrays in a macro, but not at the same time, you can reuse the same array space. The Redim command empties the entire contents of an array, so its elements can be used again. The syntax is:

```
Redim Var(Size, Size)
```

Sorting an Array

The values of array elements do not have to correspond to an element's position in the array. Element 0, for example, does not necessarily have to be greater or lesser in value than element 1. If you want the array elements to be in order, use the SortArray command. The command rearranges the elements so their values are either in ascending or descending order.

The syntax of the command is:

```
SortArray Var() Order, From, To, SortType, SortKey
```

The arguments are optional. Without the arguments, Word sorts all of the array elements in ascending order. Word can only sort one- and two-dimensional arrays.

Here are the arguments:

- ◆ **Order:** specifies 0 for an ascending sort, 1 for a descending sort.
- ◆ **From:** specifies the first element you want to sort.
- ◆ **To:** specifies the last element you want to sort.
- ◆ **SortType:** for two-dimensional arrays only, specify 0 to sort by rows, 1 to sort by columns.
- ◆ **SortKey:** for two-dimensional arrays only, specify the row or column to use as the key—0 is the first row or column, 1 the second, and so on. If the sort type is by rows, the key is the column, and visa versa.

Let's look at two examples of sorting that also illustrate the ways to enter and manipulate arrays.

S O L U T I O N S

String Array Input and Sort Macro

A macro that inputs a string array, and displays them sorted and unsorted, is shown here.

```
Sub MAIN
Dim Clients$(9)
For x = 0 To 9
   Clients$(x) = InputBox$("Enter name")
Next
For x = 0 To 9
   Insert Clients$(x)
   InsertPara
Next
InsertPara
SortArray Clients$()
For x = 0 To 9
   Insert Clients$(x)
   InsertPara
Next
End Sub
```

Input and Comparison For Loops

The first For loop inputs a series of 10 strings, each into another element of the array. The next For loop displays the array elements so you can compare them with the sorted list. Notice that the InsertPara command enters a carriage return to place each element on a separate line.

The SortArray Command

The entire array is then sorted with the command SortArray Clients$() command. This rearranges the elements in ascending order. The final For loop displays the array in its sorted order.

S O L U T I O N S

Two-Dimensional Array Sorting Macro

Here is a similar macro that enters, sorts, and displays a two-dimensional numeric array.

```
Sub MAIN
Dim COST(5, 5)
For row = 0 To 3
  For col = 0 To 3
  Input "Enter Number", Cost(Row, Col)
Next
Next
For row = 0 To 3
  For col = 0 To 3
  Insert Str$(Cost(Row, Col)) + Chr$(9)
Next
InsertPara
Next
InsertPara
SortArray Cost(), 1, 0, 15, 0, 2
For row = 0 To 3
  For col = 0 To 3
  Insert Str$(Cost(Row, Col)) + Chr$(9)
Next
InsertPara
Next
End Sub
```

Using Nested For Loops

Because the array has two dimensions, two nested For loops are needed. Each loop increments a dimension. If you visualize the array as a table, the first loop increments the rows, the second loop increments the columns. In the first repetition of the outer loop (rows), the user enters the values for the first row. Each repetition of the inner loop accepts another column in the row.

The sort is performed with the command:

```
SortArray Cost(), 1, 0, 15, 0, 2
```

It sorts all 16 elements (numbered 0 through 15) by rows using the third column as the key.

Working with Word's Dialog Boxes

When you use a dialog box macro command, Word changes the settings in the dialog box, but does not display the box on the screen. When you want the user to specify a value when the macro is running, you can have them input a value into a variable, then assign the value to a dialog box setting.

As an alternative, you can display the dialog box on the screen, then pause the macro so the user can enter measurements or select options directly in the box. The process requires a number of steps.

Dialog Box Settings

Word deals with dialog box settings as a record. Picture the record as a sheet of paper listing all of the dialog box settings. The record for the Format Font dialog box, for example, would list these settings:

.Points

.Underline

.Color

.Strikethrough

.Superscript

.Subscript

.Hidden

.SmallCaps

.AllCaps

.Spacing

.Position

.Kerning

.KerningMin

.Default

.Tab

.Font

.Bold

.Italic

Each setting is a field in the record. In order to access the dialog box, you must declare a record variable—a variable that can store all of the box fields. Use the syntax:

```
Dim Dialog-Var As Dialog-Box
```

For example, to create a record to store the Font dialog box settings, use the command:

```
Dim FontFields As FormatFont
```

 **Note**   You can use any variable name you want, but you must include the words DIM and AS, and you must use the correct dialog box name. The dialog box names are the same as the macro commands that set the box settings.

The next step is to assign the values in the dialog box to the record, using the syntax:

```
GetCurValues Dialog-Var
```

as in:

```
Dim FontFields As FormatFont
GetCurValues FontFields
```

 **Note** | This step is optional. It is only required if you want to display or change individual dialog box settings using macro commands.

Displaying the Dialog Box

You can now display the box itself. You can do this two ways, using the Dialog() function or the Dialog statement. Use the function with this syntax:

```
Var = Dialog(Dialog-Var)
```

The assigned variable will store a value based on the command button the user selects in the dialog box—0 if the user selects Cancel, –1 if the user selects OK. This series of commands, for example, displays the Font dialog box:

```
Dim FontFields As FormatFont
GetCurValues FontFields
Choice = Dialog(FontFields)
```

 **Note** | The instructions will display the dialog box until the user selects OK or Cancel. Changes made in the box will be stored in the dialog record, but they will not take effect in the document, even when the user selects OK. Displaying the dialog box does not actually perform the dialog box function.

Applying Dialog Box Settings

If you make changes in the Font dialog box, select OK, then select Format ➤ Font, your changes will not appear. To perform the dialog box function with your changes, you must use a command with this syntax:

Dialog-Box Dialog-Var

as in:

```
FormatFont FontFields
```

This performs the FormatFont command applying all of the settings in the FontFields dialog record. The complete macro is:

```
Dim FontFields As FormatFont
GetCurValues FontFields
Choice = Dialog(FontFields)
FormatFont FontFields
```

Unfortunately, Word will apply some dialog settings even when the user selects Cancel. With the Font dialog box, for example, Word will apply the font style selected, but not the font name or other options. So if the user runs the macro, chooses italic, and then selects Cancel, the italic format will still be applied.

Similarly, if your macro displays the File Open dialog box, the selected file will be opened even if the user selects Cancel. To avoid this situation, use an If command to perform the dialog box command, as in:

```
Dim OpenFile As FileOpen
GetCurValues FontFields
Choice = Dialog(OpenFile)
If choice = -1 then FileOpen OpenFile
```

Avoiding Dialog Box Errors

You can also display a dialog box using the Dialog statement, as in:

```
Dialog FontFields
```

When you use the statement, however, Word will display an error message if the user selects the dialog box's Cancel button. To avoid the error message, use the On Error command, as in:

```
Dim FontFields As FormatFont
GetCurValues FontFields
On Error Resume Next
Choice = Dialog(FontFields)
FormatFont FontFields
```

You can also trap the error to display your own message or take some alternate action.

Accessing Individual Settings

You can access the individual settings of the dialog box without displaying the box itself. You refer to settings using the dialog variable and the setting name, as in:

```
FontFields.Bold
FontFields.Font
```

Inserting the Current Font Name

This macro, for instance, inserts the name of the current font in the document:

```
Dim FontFields As FormatFont
GetCurValues FontFields
Insert FontFields.Font
```

 **Note**   FontFields.Font is treated as a string and inserted into the document with the Insert command, even though it does not end in a dollar sign.

Displaying without Inserting

If you want to display a setting but not actually insert it into the document, use the MsgBox command. For example, the box shown in Figure 10.2 was created with this command:

```
MsgBox "The font is " + FontFields.Font + " " + FontFields.Points
```

FIGURE 10.2

Dialog box created
with MsgBox
command

 **Tip**

To learn which fields are available in a dialog box, consult
the on-line help system, or record a macro that selects
options from the dialog box and edit the macro to display it
on the screen.

Changing a Setting

To change a setting, you need to assign it a new value, and then assign
the record to the dialog box, as in:

```
Dim Var As FormatFont
GetCurValues Var
Var.Bold = 1
FormatFont Var
```

A record (Var) is created for the Font dialog box, then the current settings in the dialog box are placed into the record. The Bold setting of the
record is then assigned the value 1, then the edited record is inserted into
the dialog box. You do not need to display the box to access or change its
settings.

 **Tip**

Using a dialog box record to merely display or change a
setting is not really very efficient. You can turn on bold, for
example, with one statement: FormatFont .Bold = 1

S O L U T I O N S

File Preview Macro

The real usefulness of the dialog box record is to change a setting before you display the box. For example, suppose you want to use the File ➤ Find command to display previews of your document files. Here's a macro that does just that.

```
Sub MAIN
Loop:
  Input "Enter the file extension", Ext$
  If Len(Ext$) > 3 Then Goto Loop
Loop1:
  Input "Enter the path", Pth$
  If Pth$ = "" Then Goto Loop1
Fname$ = "*." + Ext$
Dim FView As FileFind
Fview.SearchPath = Pth$
Fview.Name = Fname$
Fview.View = 1
Choice = Dialog(FView)
End Sub
```

File Extension and Path Inputs

The macro inputs a file extension and a file path. The extension must be three characters or less, and a path must be entered. The extension is then concatenated into a search string, the FileFind dialog box is dimensioned, and the path and filenames of the file search are set. The View parameter determines how the files are displayed in the File Find box—use 0 for file information, 1 for a thumbnail preview, or 2 for summary information.

Listing Files

When the dialog box is opened with the Dialog() function, it will list files with the specified extension, as shown in Figure 10.3.

FIGURE 10.3

Find File dialog box

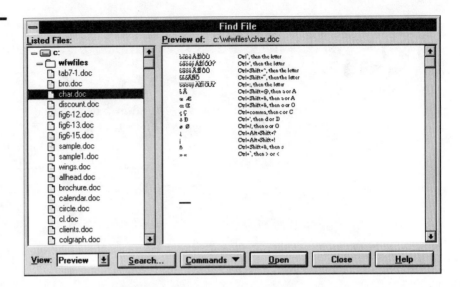

 **Tip**

See Chapter 14 for more information on the Find File command, and on how to manage your files.

Creating Custom Dialog Boxes

In addition to using Word's built-in dialog boxes, you can create your own—complete with check boxes, radio buttons, list boxes, and other standard dialog box features. Constructing a dialog box using macro commands requires a number of steps and some careful planning, but the results can greatly enhance the look and efficiency of your automated application.

You create and use a dialog box in the following sequence:

◆ Design the dialog box and its controls

◆ Insert information into list boxes

◆ Display the dialog box on the screen

◆ Act upon dialog box entries and selections

 **Tip**

Because of the number of steps involved in creating a dialog box, and the intricacy of the macro commands, it is best if you refer to the macros shown later in this chapter as you read this discussion.

Defining a Dialog Box

When you define a dialog box, you specify its size and position on the screen, and you designate its contents. Items that you place in a dialog box are called controls. They include:

◆ Command buttons (such as OK, Cancel, and your own custom push buttons)

◆ Option buttons (exclusive radio buttons in groups)

◆ Checkboxes

◆ Text (for use on labels or notes)

◆ Text boxes (for user entry)

◆ List boxes (for selection from multiple options)

◆ Drop-down list boxes

◆ Combo boxes (for selection or entry)

◆ Picture boxes (to display graphics)

◆ File Preview window (to display the active document or a document on the disk)

A dialog box illustrating all of the options is shown in Figure 10.4.

FIGURE 10.4

Custom dialog box
options

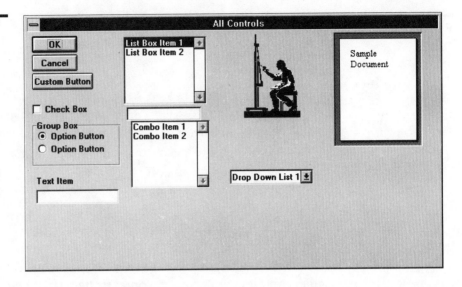

You can define the box manually, using the syntax of the various commands. However, you can more quickly create the box using the dialog editor. With the editor, you graphically insert, move, and adjust the size of the box and its contents. You then save the definition to the clipboard and paste the completed commands into the macro.

 **Note**   The dialog editor only creates the appearance of the box and its controls. It does not add items to a list or create commands for acting on dialog box selections.

Using the Dialog Editor

To start the dialog editor from the Program Manager, double-click on the Word Dialog Editor icon in the window where you installed Word. You can also click on the Dialog Editor button in the Macro toolbar. If you are already in Word, select Program Manager from the Task List. The dialog editor window will appear with an empty dialog box, as in Figure 10.5.

FIGURE 10.5

Dialog Editor

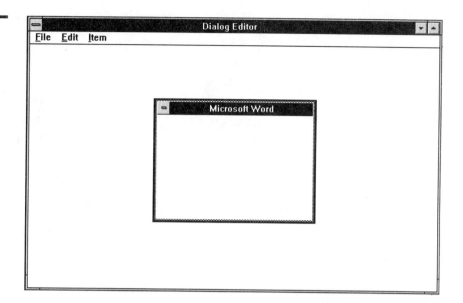

 **Tip**

If the dialog editor is not available, run the Word Setup program. In the Setup dialog box, Select Add/Remove ➤ Tools ➤ Change Options ➤ Macro Tools ➤ OK ➤ Continue. Follow the prompts that appear on the screen.

Moving and Sizing the Box

You can move the position of the dialog box and change its size by dragging the mouse. To add an item, select an option from the Item pull-down menu, move it to the desired position, and then change its size. (Hold down the Shift key to move or size an item only in a horizontal or vertical direction.)

 **Note**   When you run the dialog box, the first item inserted will have focus. That is, it will be selected and ready for your action. When you press Tab to move from item to item, Word will follow the order you inserted the items, not their position within the dialog box. You can later change the order when you paste the dialog definition into the macro.

Inserting and Deleting Items

When you insert an item it will appear selected, surrounded by a dotted selection box. If the item contains a default label, such as Option Button, type a new label while it is selected. (You cannot change the text of the OK and Cancel buttons, and you cannot type in a text box.)

To add another item of the same type, leave the item selected and press Enter. The next item will appear aligned under the previous item. (You must insert at least one command button in every dialog box.)

To delete an item, select it and press Del. To remove all of the items, select Edit ➤ Clear ➤ Yes.

Using the Keyboard

To move the item with the keyboard, select it and press the arrow keys. To change its size, hold down the Shift key and use the arrow keys. Each time you press an arrow the item changes by four units. To move in one-unit increments, hold down Ctrl and Shift while you press the arrow keys.

Saving Your Dialog Box to the Clipboard

When done arranging the dialog box, select Edit ➤ Select Dialog, then Edit ➤ Copy, then exit the dialog editor. You can also select File ➤ Exit, then select Yes to save the box in the clipboard. In Word, place the insertion point in the macro where you want the box definition to appear, then select Edit ➤ Paste.

Saving the Dialog Box as a Text File

The dialog editor does not have an option to save the design as a separate file on disk. To save the design so you can continue working in it at a later time, select Edit ➤ Select Dialog, then Edit ➤ Copy, then exit the dialog editor. Run the Notepad accessory and select Edit ➤ Paste to display the dialog box definition, then save the text file.

When you want to continue designing the box, open the text file into Notepad, Word, or another Window's word processing program, then select and copy the definition instructions. Run the dialog editor and select Edit ➤ Paste to display the dialog box design.

Dialog Box Control Options

Now let's look at some of dialog box control options in detail.

Adding Buttons

To add a command button, option button, or check box, select Item ➤ Button to display the list shown in Figure 10.6.

Select the item you want to add, then select OK. The item will appear selected in the dialog box. Change the size or position, and enter new label text. Press Enter to insert another button or box.

You can only have one OK or Cancel button. When you press Enter to create another button, Word will display one of the buttons not already in the box. You must have more than one option button. If you only have one button, it will always be selected and you will not be able to deselect

FIGURE 10.6

New Button options

it. (If you have an individual option that you want to turn off or on, use a checkbox.)

When you add option buttons, Word automatically assigns them to the same group, no matter where they are on the screen. If you want to group a specific set of buttons together, first select Item ➤ Group Box to insert a group box.

When the Group Box is selected, press Enter for each option button that you want inserted. The first button that you insert in a group will be selected by default when the dialog box is displayed. (To create a box surrounding text or controls other than option buttons, create a group box and delete its label)

List Boxes

To insert a list box, select Item ➤ List Box to display the options shown in Figure 10.7.

A standard list box is one that displays as many items as possible, with a scroll bar to bring additional items into view. You must select an option from the list, you cannot type your setting.

A Combo box is a list box with an associated text box. You can either select from the list or type an entry in the text box. A drop-down list displays a single item until you pull down the list.

The dialog editor only creates the box, you must add the items to the lists by editing the macro in Word.

FIGURE 10.7

New List Box
options

Text Boxes

A text box is a rectangular area where the user enters data from the keyboard. In the dialog editor, the text box will contain the dimmed words Edit Text, but they will not appear when you run the macro.

The box itself has no label so the user will not know what type of item to enter. Add a text item just above the box to identify its purpose. (Use text items to also add subtitles and other notes to the dialog box.)

If you insert the text item first, then the text box, the two items will be linked. You will be able to select and move the text item and the box at the same time.

Picture Boxes

A picture box can display the contents of a graphics file. When you select Picture from the Item list, you can choose the source of the contents. The options are a file on disk, an AutoText entry, a bookmark associated with a graphic in the active document, and the contents of the clipboard.

 **Tip** You cannot insert a preview box using the dialog editor. To create a preview box, insert a picture box as its placeholder, then edit the macro in Word. To create a preview box, see the section on Dynamic Dialog Boxes later in this chapter.

Using the Info Box

You can customize a dialog box item by selecting it, then choosing Edit ➤ Info to display the dialog box shown in Figure 10.8.

FIGURE 10.8

Check Button
Information
dialog box

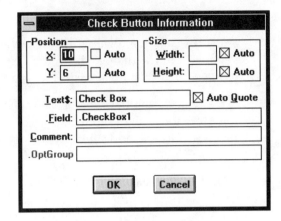

Setting an Item's Size and Position

Set the position and size of the item, or choose the Auto options to prevent you from manually changing the size or position. If you adjust an item and then select Auto, Word returns the item to its original size and position.

 **Tip** To link a text item with a text box, select the box and choose Auto to position the items in the Information box. When you move the text item that is above the box, the box will move with it.

Other Info Box Options

Now let's look at the other Info box options.

◆ **Text$:** Contains the label that will appear with the item, if any, or the text of a text item. (A text box has no label.) Use an ampersand to indicate a selection character for choosing a button item. The character to the right of the ampersand will appear underlined, and the item can be selected by pressing Alt and the character.

**Note** For a list box, this option contains the name of a string array that will contain the list items. You can change the name of the array, if desired, but it must be a string array.

◆ **Auto Quote:** When selected, Word inserts the label into the dialog box definition as a quoted string. Deselect the box if you want to use the label as a variable name that you can assign in the macro.

◆ **Field:** Contains the control identifier that you use to return a value from the box. It is a dialog box field and must start with a period. Word assigns standard field names designating the type of item, along with a number. For example, the first checkbox is .CheckBox1, the next is .CheckBox2, and so on. If you insert then delete an item, Word will not reuse its number.

**Note** You can change the field names, as long as they are unique and start with a period. You will be using the field names in your macro, so enter labels that identify the purpose of the item. For example, change a text box that will store a client's name from .TextBox1 to .Client. You can include an optional dollar sign to clearly identify the contents as a string.

◆ **Comment:** Adds a comment that will appear as a Rem line in the macro.

◆ **OptGroup:** The group with which an option button is associated. You can change the group, or create a new one, to associate option buttons that are not in a group box.

Dialog Definition Commands

You paste the dialog box definition into a macro, somewhere following the Sub MAIN command. The definition appears as a series of commands within the Begin Dialog UserDialog and End Dialog statements.

S O L U T I O N S

Dialog Box Definition Macro

Here is the definition used to create the dialog box shown previously in Figure 10.4, but without the commands for the file preview window. (File previews will be discussed later.)

```
Sub MAIN
Dim ListBox2$(1)
Dim ComboBox1$(1)
Dim DropListBox1$(1)
ListBox2$(0) = "List Box Item 1"
ListBox2$(1) = "List Box Item 2"
ComboBox1$(0) = "Combo Item 1"
ComboBox1$(1) = "Combo Item 2"
DropListBox1$(0) = "Drop Down List 1"
DropListBox1$(1) = "Drop Down List 2"
Begin Dialog UserDialog 798, 308, "All Controls"
  OKButton 10, 6, 88, 21
  CancelButton 10, 30, 88, 21
  PushButton 10, 54, 118, 21, "Custom Button", .Push1
  CheckBox 10, 93, 111, 16, "Check Box", .CheckBox1
  GroupBox 10, 115, 172, 60, "Group Box"
  OptionGroup .OptionGroup2
  OptionButton 20, 127, 133, 16, "Option Button",\
  .OptionButton2
  OptionButton 20, 144, 133, 16, "Option Button",\
  .OptionButton3
  Text 15, 187, 72, 13, "Text Item", .Text2
  TextBox 15, 205, 160, 18, .TextBox2
```

```
    ListBox 187, 7, 160, 84, ListBox2$(), .ListBox2
    ComboBox 193, 99, 160, 108, ComboBox1$(), .ComboBox1
    DropListBox 391, 182, 160, 108, DropListBox1$(),\
    .DropListBox1
    Picture 372, 6, 204, 108, "C:\WINWORD\CLIPART/ARTIST.WMF",\
    0, .Picture1
End Dialog

Dim sdlg As UserDialog
SHOWIT = Dialog(sDlg)
End Sub
```

The Begin Dialog Command

The syntax of the command is:

```
Begin Dialog UserDialog Horizontal, Vertical, Width, Height, Title

End Dialog
```

Here's each of the parameters in more detail:

◆ **Horizontal:** Determines the position of the dialog box in relation to the left side of the window. The measurement is in dialog units, eight units are equal to the size of an average character in the system font.

◆ **Vertical:** Determines the position of the dialog box in relation to the top of the window. The measurement is in dialog units, 12 units are equal to the size of an average character in the system font.

◆ **Width:** Selects the width of the box, in dialog units.

◆ **Height:** Selects the height of the box in dialog units.

◆ **Title:** Determines the text that appears on the title bar.

 **Tip**

If you omit the horizontal and vertical measurements, Word centers the box on the screen. You do not need placeholders for the omitted arguments. If Word detects only two numbers in the command, it assumes they are the width and height settings.

Dialog Box Controls

Each of the controls is described in a command. While the format of each control varies, however, they all start with these elements:

```
Control-type Horizontal, Vertical, Width, Height
```

Table 10.2 shows the syntax of the control commands.

TABLE 10.2: Dialog box control commands

CONTROL COMMAND SYNTAX
OKButton Horizontal, Vertical, Width, Height, .ID
CancelButton Horizontal, Vertical, Width, Height, .ID
PushButton Horizontal, Vertical, Width, Height, Label, .ID
CheckBox Horizontal, Vertical, Width, Height, Label, .ID
Text Horizontal, Vertical, Width, Height, Label, .ID
OptionButton Horizontal, Vertical, Width, Height, Label, .ID
GroupBox Horizontal, Vertical, Width, Height, Label
OptionGroup, .ID
TextBox Horizontal, Vertical, Width, Height, .ID, MultiLine
ComboBox Horizontal, Vertical, Width, Height, Array, .ID
ListBox Horizontal, Vertical, Width, Height, Array, .ID
DropListBox Horizontal, Vertical, Width, Height, Array, .ID
PictureBox Horizontal, Vertical; Width, Height, Contents, Type, .ID

Other Command Elements

In addition to the position and size settings, a command may include these elements:

◆ **Label:** the text label that appears on the item—a string variable or literal

◆ **Array:** the string array that stores list items

◆ **Contents:** the string variable or literal specifying the name of the picture file, AutoText entry, or bookmark—ignored for a clipboard graphic

◆ **Type:** the source of a picture image: 0 from a file, 1 from an AutoText entry, 2 from a bookmark, 3 from the clipboard

 **Note**

If Word cannot locate the graphic file indicated by the picture command, it will display the notation "missing picture" in the box. If you want to generate and trap an error when the picture is not found, use the types 16, 17, 18, and 19, rather than 0, 1, 2, and 3.

◆ **.ID:** the control field used to return dialog box selections

◆ **MultiLine:** for text boxes use 0 (or omit the option), for one-line boxes use 1 to accept multiple lines, for multiple-line boxes press Enter or Shift+Enter to begin a new line

Using .ID Fields

The .ID fields of the OK and Cancel buttons are optional, and they are not inserted by the dialog editor. The .ID field of text items and option buttons are inserted by the editor, but they are only used with dialog functions, discussed later.

The Option Group command specifies the field that will return a value indicating which button in the group is selected. The field of a picture item is optional. You can use the field with a dialog function to change the picture being displayed.

 **Tip** If desired, change the order of the commands to determine their Tab sequence. You can also change any of the labels or field names.

Adding List Items

When you create a list box you have to specify the items that are displayed in the list for selection. This is performed by dimensioning the array and adding elements before the dialog box definition.

Dimension the array using the array name given in the list item's dialog box commands. For example, suppose a list box is defined with this command:

```
ListBox 187, 7, 160, 84, ListBox1$(), .ListBox1
```

Use a DIM command to specify the last element numbers, then add strings to each of the elements, as:

```
Dim ListBox1$(3)
ListBox1$(0) = "Apple Raisin"
ListBox1$(1) = "Chocolate"
ListBox1$(2) = "Rocky Road"
ListBox1$(3) = "Vanilla"
```

When you display the dialog box, the array items will appear in the list.

Adding Default Text and Checkbox Selections

Text boxes, including those associated with a combo box, will be blank when the macro is first displayed. However, you can add default text that will appear in a text box, and that will be applied if the user does not enter text or select another combo box option. You can also choose to have a checkbox already selected when the macro starts.

After the DIM command that creates the dialog variable, but before the command to display the box, assign the text box field a value. Refer to the item by the dialog variable and field name:

```
Dim MyBox AS UserDialog
MyBox.TextBox1 = "Blueberry"
MyBox.Client = "Sam Smith"
MyBox.CheckBox1 = 1
```

When the dialog box is displayed, for example, the text box identified with TextBox1 will contain the word Blueberry.

 **Note**

> Because the identifiers are field names, you do not need to use the dollar sign as you would with string variables. Assigning a 1 to a checkbox will display it already selected.

Displaying a Dialog Box

To display a dialog box on the screen, create a dialog variable using the Dim command, then use the variable name in the Dialog statement or Dialog function. These commands must appear after the End Dialog statement.

The commands will look like this:

```
Dim MyBox AS UserDialog
Choice = Dialog(MyBox)
```

The Dialog statement and Dialog() function can accept two additional arguments:

```
Dialog Dialog-Var, Default, Time
Var = Dialog(Dialog-Var, Default, Time)
```

The Default argument specifies which command button is activated when the user presses Enter. Use –2 to have no default button, –1 for the OK button, 0 for the Cancel button, and numbers above 0 for any custom push buttons—in the order of their statements in the macro.

The third argument sets the number of milliseconds the dialog box remains displayed. When the argument is omitted, the box remains on the screen until the user selects a command button. (You can use the arguments when displaying Word's built-in dialog boxes. However, the default button argument is ignored.)

 **Tip**

> When you specify a time, the box will be removed from display when the time is up. Keep in mind that there are 1000 milliseconds in a second, so make sure you give the user enough time.

Acting on Dialog Box Selections

When you select a pushbutton from a dialog box, the box is removed from display. (Double-clicking on a list box item or an option button also selects the item and closes the dialog box.) You can use the values assigned to the dialog box control ID to perform some action based on your selections.

Accessing Return Values

Your macro can perform alternate actions based on the values returned from the dialog controls. Except for the OK and Cancel buttons, all the values are returned in the control ID, as listed in Table 10.2. The following list will help you determine which values will be returned:

◆ The OK and Cancel buttons return the values –1 and 0, as described for using built-in dialog boxes.

◆ The ID of a push button will return a –1 if the button was pushed, 0 if it was not pushed.

◆ The ID of a checkbox will be 1 if the box is selected, 0 if the box is not selected.

◆ The contents of a text box and the selection from a combo box can be inserted using the Insert command and the control identifier, as in:

```
Insert MyBox.TextBox1
Insert MyBox.ComboBox1
```

Word recognizes the field as a string.

◆ The ID of a list box and drop-down list box is assigned the position of the selected item in the list, starting with 0. MyBox.ListBox1, for example, will be 0 if the user selects the first item in the list, 1 if the user selects the second item, and so on.

◆ The ID of an option group is assigned a number corresponding to the position of the selected button. The position refers to the order of the OptionButton commands in the macro, not their position on screen or within the group box. If the user selects the button listed first under the OptionGroup command, for example, then MyBox.Option-Group1 is assigned a 0.

S O L U T I O N S

Multiple Dialog Box Macro

You can only display one custom dialog box at a time but you can use more than one in a macro. Define a second dialog box after the commands that display and act on the first, as shown here.

```
Sub MAIN
Begin Dialog UserDialog 298, 108, "Box One"
  OKButton 10, 6, 88, 21
  CancelButton 10, 30, 88, 21
  PushButton 10, 54, 118, 21, "Custom Button", .Push1
End Dialog
Dim BOX1 As UserDialog
SHOWIT = Dialog(BOX1)

Begin Dialog UserDialog 298, 208, "Box Two"
  OKButton 10, 6, 88, 21
```

```
    CancelButton 10, 30, 88, 21
    CheckBox 10, 93, 111, 16, "Check Box", .CheckBox1
    GroupBox 10, 115, 172, 60, "Group Box"
    OptionGroup .OptionGroup2
    OptionButton 20, 127, 133, 16, "Option Button",\
    .OptionButton2
    OptionButton 20, 144, 133, 16, "Option Button",\
    .OptionButton3
End Dialog
Dim BOX2 As UserDialog
SHOWIT = Dialog(BOX2)
End Sub
```

A Dialog Box Example

Let's take a look at how a custom dialog box can be used to streamline word processing, as shown in Figure 10.9. The user can select to insert a date, choose the recipient, and a standard closing. A custom push button exists for addressing a letter to a particular individual who the user corresponds with frequently. The option button group allows the user to select plain or letterhead paper.

FIGURE 10.9

Custom letter
writing dialog box

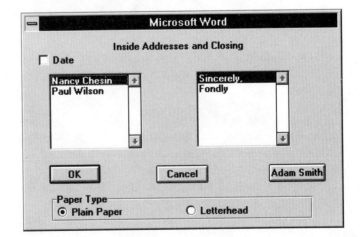

Letter Writing Macro

To keep the macro listing short, the list boxes were created with only two items each. You could include as many as you want by increasing the value in the array declaration.

```
Sub MAIN
Dim ListBox1$(1)
Dim ListBox2$(1)
ListBox1$(0) = "Nancy Chesin"
ListBox1$(1) = "Paul Wilson"
ListBox2$(0) = "Sincerely,"
ListBox2$(1) = "Fondly"
Begin Dialog UserDialog 538, 226, "My Letters"
  ListBox 41, 50, 160, 84, ListBox1$(), .ListBox1
  ListBox 294, 48, 160, 84, ListBox2$(), .ListBox2
  OKButton 40, 155, 88, 21
  CancelButton 224, 156, 88, 21
  PushButton 415, 156, 98, 21, "Adam Smith", .Push1
  Text 152, 12, 223, 13, "Inside Addresses and Closing",\
  .Text1
  GroupBox 43, 188, 447, 33, "Paper Type"
  OptionGroup .OptionGroup1
    OptionButton 53, 201, 116, 16, "Plain Paper",\
    .OptionButton1
    OptionButton 274, 201, 111, 16, "Letterhead",\
    .OptionButton2
  CheckBox 23, 25, 65, 16, "Date", .CheckBox1
End Dialog

Dim MyBox As UserDialog
Choice = Dialog(MyBox)
If Choice = 0 Then Goto EndMac
If Mybox.OptionGroup1 = 0 Then
  FilePageSetup .TopMargin = "1" + Chr$(34)
```

```
Else
  FilePageSetup .TopMargin = "3" + Chr$(34)
EndIf
If MyBox.CheckBox1 = 1 Then
InsertDateTime .DateTimePic = "MMMM d, yyyy",\
  .InsertAsField = 0
  InsertPara
  InsertPara
EndIf
If MyBox.Push1 = -1 Then
  Insert "Adam Smith"
  InsertPara
  Insert "567 Paul Street "
  InsertPara
  Insert "West Palm Beach, FL 98223"
  InsertPara
  InsertPara
  Insert "Dear Adam:"
  InsertPara
  InsertPara
  Insert "Sincerely Yours,"
  Line Up
  Line Up
  Goto Endmac
EndIf

Select Case MyBox.ListBox1
  Case 0
     Insert "Nancy Chesin"
     InsertPara
     Insert "1726 West Fifth Street"
     InsertPara
     Insert "West Palm Beach, FL 98223"
     InsertPara
     InsertPara
     Insert "Dear Nancy:"
     InsertPara
     InsertPara
```

```
    Case 1
        Insert "Paul Wilson"
        InsertPara
        Insert "26 Market Street"
        InsertPara
        Insert "Philadelphia, PA 19100"
        InsertPara
        InsertPara
        Insert "Dear Paul:"
        InsertPara
        InsertPara
    Case Else
        Stop
End Select

Select Case MyBox.ListBox2
    Case 0
        Insert "Sincerely Yours,"
    Case 1
        Insert "Fondly"
    Case Else
        Stop
End Select
Line Up
Line Up
Endmac:
End Sub
```

Actions Based on Selections

After the dialog box is displayed with the command:

```
Choice = Dialog(myBox)
```

a series of If commands determines what actions should be taken based on selections from the box, by checking the status of the control identifiers.

The first condition ends the macro if the user selects Cancel, by transferring control to the Endmac label immediately above the End Sub command.

The next conditions determine which option button was selected. The two option buttons are in OptionGroup1. If the user selects the first button, the value of MyBox.OptionGroup1 will be 0. This indicates a letter on plain paper so the top margin is set at one inch. If the user selects the Letterhead button, the margin is set at three inches to place the text below the printed letterhead.

Date, Address, and Closing

The macro then determines if the user selects to insert a date. If the check box was selected, the InsertDateTime command is executed, then a blank line inserted.

When the user clicks on the push button, the value of MyBox.Push1 will be –1. The macro inserts the inside address of the most popular correspondent, adds the Sincerely closing, then moves to the EndMac label and stops.

Otherwise, a Select command determines which name in the first list box was selected, and inserts the appropriate inside address. The second Select command inserts the selected closing.

Dynamic Dialog Boxes

A dynamic dialog box is one that can change as the user selects options. Some examples are:

◆ A dialog box that uses tabs to change the panel of options

◆ A series of options that are enabled or disabled based on another selection in the box

◆ A file or graphic preview panel that displays the file selected in a list box

Creating a Dynamic Dialog Box

You can create a dynamic dialog box from one of your custom boxes by adding a dialog function.

Note

When you write a regular macro function, the function is only called when you use the function name in a command. A dialog function, on the other hand, is called automatically. Word calls the function when the dialog box is first displayed (initialized), every time you take an action in the dialog box, and at regular intervals when the dialog box is idle, not being used. By calling the function continuously, you could create a dialog box that contains a running clock or timer, very much like the Window's Clock application.

Calling Dialog Functions

When you first display the dialog box, the function is called to see if there are any commands that you want to perform at that time. For instance, you can dim some options by default by using the DlgEnable command, or hide options entirely with the DlgVisible command.

Tip

Word calls the function each time you act on the dialog box. So, you can have the function make a dimmed option active, or display hidden options, once the user clicks a specific option.

You must first declare the dialog function at the end of the Begin Dialog UserDialog command, like this:

```
Begin Dialog UserDialog 784, 322, "File Preview", .DlgFun
```

You can use your own name for the function.

Creating the Dialog Function

Next, you create the function itself. The overall structure is:

```
Function DlgFun(identifier$, action, suppvalue)
     instructions
End Function
```

You must use the same function name that you included on the dialog box definition, and you must include the argument names exactly as shown.

 **Note**

> The identifier$ will receive the identifier of the dialog box control which caused the function to be called. For example, suppose a dialog box has a check box identified as .CheckBox1. When the user clicks on the check box, or makes it the focus, the string "CheckBox1" will be passed to the function and received by the identifier$ argument.

Action Arguments

The Action argument will contain a number indicating the type of action performed. The possible values are listed in Table 10.3.

TABLE 10.3: Action argument values

ACTION	OPERATION
1	The dialog box was opened (initialized)
2	A command button, option button, or checkbox, was selected or the value of a dialog box control was changed. When action has a value of 2, Identifier$ contains the identifiers of the control. Clicking in a combo box also sends this action, but not typing in a text or combo box.

TABLE 10.3: Action argument values (continued)

ACTION	OPERATION
3	A change has occurred in a text or combo box, and the user moved to another control. The identifier$ will contain the identifier of the box.
4	The control focus has been changed. The identifier$ will contain the ID of the control receiving the focus.
5	The dialog box is idle. The identifier$ will be empty ("").
6	The user moved the position of the dialog box. The identifier$ will be empty ("").

The SuppValue will contain a number indicating some additional information about the action. The value depends on the type of control effected, as listed in Table 10.4.

TABLE 10.4: SuppValue control values

CONTROL	ACTION
List Boxes	Suppvalue will contain the number of the item selected in a list, drop-down, or combo box. The numbers begin with 0 for the first item, 1 for the second, and so on.
Check box	Suppvalue will be 1 if the box is selected, 0 if it is cleared.
Option button	Suppvalue will be the number of the option button selected.
Text box	Suppvalue will contain the number of characters in the text box.
Combo box	When the value of Action is 3, Suppvalue will contain the number of characters in the combo box.
Command button	Suppvalue will contain the number of the button selected.

 **Note**   When a control gains focus (action 4), the Suppvalue will contain the number of the control that lost the focus. When the box is idle, Suppvalue will contain the number of times Action 5 has been passed to the function. Suppvalue will be 0 when the user moves the dialog box (Action 6).

Writing Action Commands

Within the function, you write the commands that decide what action to take. (The DLG commands discussed here can only be used within a dialog function.)

For example, suppose you want to dim ListBox1 until the user selects Checkbox1. Use this dialog function:

```
Function DlgFun(identifier$, action, suppvalue)
If action = 1 Then
     DlgEnable "ListBox1", 0
Else
If action = 2 Then
         If identifier$ = "Checkbox1" Then
               DlgEnable "ListBox1", SuppValue
         End If
     End If
EndIf
End Function
```

The function first checks to determine if the dialog box has just been initialized. If it was just initialized, the Action value will be 1. If so, the list box is dimmed. This is performed with the commands:

```
If action = 1 Then
     DlgEnable "ListBox1", 0
Else
```

The DlgEnable command uses the syntax:

```
DlgEnable "Identifier", value
```

If the value is 1, the control is activated, if it is 0 it is dimmed.

If the box was not just opened, the function checks to see if it was called because a command button, option button, or checkbox was just selected.

```
If action = 2 Then
```

If this was the case, the macro determines if the control changed was the checkbox.

```
If identifier$ = "Checkbox1" Then
```

When it is the checkbox, it either activates or dims the list box.

```
DlgEnable "ListBox1", SuppValue
```

 **Note**

> The control to dim or activate is ListBox1. The second argument is taken from the value of SuppValue. If the user selects the checkbox, SuppValue 1, the listbox is activated. If the user deselects the checkbox, SuppValue 0, the list box is dimmed. There is also a DlgEnable(Identifier) function that returns −1 if the control is enabled, 0 if the control is disabled (dimmed).

A Dynamic Example

As an example of a dynamic dialog box, let's look at a macro that displays a preview of graphic files you can insert in a document (see Figure 10.10).

The dialog box displays a listing of all picture files, sorted alphabetically, based on the extension and path the user specifies. If no files are found in the directory, the list box contains the string "NO FILES" and the Open button is dimmed. If there are files listed, the user can select a file to display its preview, and then click on the Open button to insert the picture in the document.

FIGURE 10.10

Art Preview
dialog box

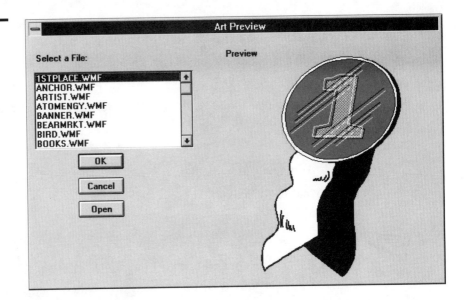

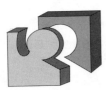

S O L U T I O N S

Art Preview Macro

Here's the macro to create an Art Preview dialog box.

```
Dim Shared previewfilename$
Dim Shared FoundFiles
Sub MAIN
Loop:
  Input "Enter the file extension", Ext$
  Ext$ = UCase$(Ext$)
  Pos = InStr("BMPPCXTIFWMFWPG", Ext$)
  If Len(Ext$) > 3 Or Pos = 0 Then Goto Loop
Loop1:
  Input "Enter the path", Pth$
  If Pth$ = "" Then Goto Loop1
Fname$ = "*." + Ext$
```

```
FileFind .SearchPath = Pth$, .Name = Fname$
NumFiles = CountFoundFiles() - 1
If NumFiles > - 1 Then
Dim ListBox1$(NumFiles)
For x = 0 To NumFiles
  ListBox1$(x) = FileNameInfo$(FoundFileName$(x + 1), 3)
Next
OldDir$ = DefaultDir$(0)
ChDir Pth$
SortArray ListBox1$()
FoundFiles = 1
Else
FoundFiles = 0
Dim ListBox1$(0)
ListBox1$(0) = "NO FILES"
End If

Begin Dialog UserDialog 784, 322, "Art Preview", .DlgFun
  ListBox 10, 46, 303, 96, ListBox1$(), .ListBox1
  Text 14, 23, 101, 13, "Select a File:", .Text1
  Text 375, 19, 61, 13, "Preview", .Text2
  If FoundFiles = 1 Then
    Picture 375, 31, 396, 284, ListBox1$(0), 0, .Picture1
  End If
  OKButton 92, 152, 88, 21
  CancelButton 92, 183, 88, 21
  PushButton 92, 213, 88, 21, "Open", .Push1
End Dialog
Dim MyFile As UserDialog
ShowFile = Dialog(MyFile)
If ShowFile = 1 Then InsertPicture .Name = previewfilename$
If FoundFiles = 1 Then ChDir OldDir$
End Sub
```

```
Function DlgFun(identifier$, action, suppvalue)
If FoundFiles = 0 Then DlgEnable "Push1", 0
If FoundFiles = 1 Then
  If action = 1 Then
     previewfilename$ = DlgText$("ListBox1")
     ElseIf action = 2 Then
         If identifier$ = "ListBox1" Then
         previewfilename$ = DlgText$("ListBox1")
         DlgSetPicture "Picture1", previewfilename$, 0
     EndIf
     EndIf
EndIf
End Function
```

DIM Command Variables

The DIM commands create variables that can be used in both the main subroutine and the function. The variable previewfilename$ will contain the name of the file to be previewed and inserted. The variable FoundFiles will be used to indicate whether or not the directory contains any files of the specified type.

The command:

```
Pos = InStr("BMPPCXTIFWMFWPG", Ext$)
```

ensures that the extension entered is a valid extension for supported picture files. The InStr() function returns the position of one string in another, using the syntax:

```
InStr(String1$, String2$)
```

 **Note**   If String2$ is located in String1$, the function returns its starting position in the string. For example, if the user enters the extension WMF, the function returns the number 10. If the string is not located, the function returns 0, and the loop repeats.

The FileFind Command

The FileFind command then searches the path looking for files that match the specification. The number of matching files is returned in the built-in function CountFoundFiles(). Because the number will be used to dimension the list box array, one is subtracted from it (array subscripts start with 0) and it is assigned the variable NumFiles.

The List Box Array

If any files were found, their names are inserted into the list box array, in these lines:

```
If NumFiles > - 1 Then
Dim ListBox1$(NumFiles)
For x = 0 To NumFiles
 ListBox1$(x) = FileNameInfo$(FoundFileName$(x + 1), 3)
Next
```

The ListBox1$() array is dimensioned using the value of NumFiles, then the name of each file inserted into individual array elements. The function:

```
FoundFileName$()
```

returns the names of the files located by the previous FileFind command. The first file name is FoundFileName$(1), the second is FoundFile-Name$(2), and so on.

 **Note**

The parameter used is x (the value of the For loop) plus 1. While array subscripts start with 0, FoundFileName$() arguments start with 1. The FileNameInfo$() function changes the assignment to the name only. You can use the full names, including the path, but you'll have to widen the list box. However, when you use just the file names in the list box, Word will not know where to locate a picture file that you select to open.

The command:

```
OldDir$ = DefaultDir$(0)
```

stores the current directory in the variable OldDir$, then the macro changes to the path the user entered with the command:

```
ChDir Pth$
```

The array is then sorted and the FoundFiles variable set at 1 indicating that at least one matching file was located.

 **Note**

We are using FoundFiles to prevent errors from occurring. The macro could use an On Error Goto command to end itself if no files were found. Using the variable, however, will help demonstrate other dialog box concepts.

The Else Structure

The Else structure performs several commands when no matching files are located in the directory. It assigns FoundFiles the value of 0, dimensions the array with a single element, and assigns the NO FILES string to the element.

The Picture Box Controls

The custom dialog box is then created with a dialog function. Notice that the picture box control is only defined when matching files were located in the directory:

```
If FoundFiles = 1 Then
     Picture 375, 31, 396, 284, ListBox1$(0), 0, .Picture1
End If
```

The Picture control command displays the first file in the list, the picture whose name is in the array element ListBox1$(0). The dialog variable is then dimensioned, and the box displayed.

 **Tip**

> You can use IF commands within the dialog box definition to customize the box when the macro runs. For example, you can display some controls only when a specific document, or type of document is displayed.

When the box is closed, the value of ShowFile is tested. If the Open (Push1) button was clicked, the InsertPicture command is performed using the name of the file selected in the list box. Then, the macro returns the user to the original directory when it has been changed because matching files were located.

Finding Files to Open

The name of the file to open is determined in the dialog function:

```
Function DlgFun(identifier$, action, suppvalue)
```

The first command in the function dims the Open button if no DOC files were located in the directory. This is done because the list box contains the words NO FILES (not any files that can actually be inserted).

If matching files were located, the macro determines if the dialog was just initiated. If it was, the command:

```
previewfilename$ = DlgText$("ListBox1")
```

assigns the name of the file selected in the list box to the variable preview-filename$, in case the user decides to insert the first picture listed. The command DlgText$() returns the name of the item in the box specified by the identifier.

Displaying the File in the Picture Box

The function then determines if it was called by an action on a control. If it was, it tests to determine if the action affected the list box. If it did, it assigns the name of the selected file to the variable previewfilename$. Then, the command:

```
DlgSetPicture "Picture1", previewfilename$, 0
```

displays the file in the picture box. The syntax is:

```
DlgSetPicture Identifier, filename$, type
```

It inserts the named file into the picture box referenced by the identifier. Use type 0 for a file on disk; 1 for an AutoText entry; 2 for a bookmark; or 3 for a clipboard picture.

 **Tip** You can also use the DlgText command to change the contents of a text box, the selected item in a list, or a control label. The syntax is: DlgText Identifier$, Text$.

File Preview Boxes

A file preview box displays a thumbnail sketch of a selected file. While you can display file previews using the FileFind command, you can also create custom previews with dynamic dialog boxes.

Creating a File Preview Box

You cannot add a preview box in the Dialog Editor. Instead, use the dialog editor to insert a picture box in the position and size you want the preview box, then edit the command in Word, so it appears as:

```
FilePreview 375, 31, 396, 284, .Fileprev
```

If you want to display the current document (in the window from which you run the macro), you simply use an empty function, like this:

```
Function DlgFun(identifier$, action, suppvalue)
End Function
```

If you want to specify another file, you must specify a file name using the DlgFilePreview$ command, as in:

```
Function DlgFun(identifier$, action, suppvalue)
    DlgFilePreview$ "C:\winword\clients.doc"
End Function
```

Modifying the Picture Preview Macro

To modify the picture preview macro to display a preview of a document file, use this function:

```
Function DlgFun(identifier$, action, suppvalue)
If FoundFiles = 0 Then DlgEnable "Push1", 0
If FoundFiles = 1 Then
If action = 1 Then
    previewfilename$ = DlgText$("ListBox1")
    DlgFilePreview$ previewfilename$
ElseIf action = 2 Then
    If identifier$ = "ListBox1" Then
        previewfilename$ = DlgText$("ListBox1")
        DlgFilePreview$ previewfilename$
    End If
End If
End If
End Function
```

In the dialog definition, create the file preview control like this:

```
If FoundFiles = 1 Then
    FilePreview 375, 31, 396, 284, .Fileprev
End If
```

Then after the dialog box is displayed, open the document:

```
If ShowFile = 1 Then FileOpen .Name = previewfilename$
```

 **Note** There is also a DlgFilePreview$(Identifier) function that returns the path and name of the document being displayed. If the active file is being displayed and it does not have a name, the function returns the name of the window.

Table 10.5 lists other dynamic dialog box functions.

TABLE 10.5: Dynamic dialog box functions

COMMAND	ACTION
DlgControlId(Identifier$)	Returns the numeric identifier of the control (the number, starting with 0, representing the order of controls in the dialog box definition—seen in place of the string identifier in dynamic dialog box commands)
DlgFocus Identifier	Sets the focus to the named identifier
DlgFocus$(	Returns the identifier of the control that has the focus
DlgListBoxArray Identifier, Array$()	Fills the identified list box, combo box, or drop-down list, with the contents of the array
DlgListBoxArray(Identifier, Array$())	Fills the array with the contents of the identified list box, combo box, or drop-down list
DlgUpdateFilePreview Identifier	Updates the displayed file preview picture to reflect changes made to the document format from within the dialog box (Identifier is optional)
DlgValue Identifier, Value	Selects or deselects the identified check box, combo box, drop-down list box, or option button (1 selects the control, 0 deselects it)

TABLE 10.5: Dynamic dialog box functions (continued)

COMMAND	ACTION
DlgValue(Identifier)	Returns the state of the identifier (1 if selected, 0 if deselected, −1 if filled with gray)
DlgVisible Identifier, On	Makes the identifier control visible or invisible (1 to make the control visible, 0 to make it invisible, or omit the second parameter to toggle the control)
DlgVisible(Identifier)	Returns the state of the control (0 if invisible, −1 if visible)

PART
four

The Merging Word

11

Form Documents and
Databases

12

Database Management

Form Documents and Databases

I N ADDITION TO THE TYPICAL uses of form documents—advertisements, account statements, invoices, and announcements—there are many other applications, such as project bids, requests for proposals, and contracts. This chapter shows you how to produce a variety of form documents, and also how to create databases for the information you want to merge with them.

Creating a Database

In Word, the database is called a *data source*. A data source contains the pertinent information about a group of items. It could be the name, address, and other information about clients or employees. It could be the company's inventory or price list.

Picture the data source as an electronic version of an index card file. Every card, called a *record,* contains all the data about one item. Each record has several pieces of information, such as the name of the item, quantity on hand, supplier, and price. Each piece of information is called a *field.* To create a data source, you first need to determine which fields are needed.

Planning Fields

In this and later chapters, we will be developing a client invoicing system using mail merge and macro techniques. The data source for the system must contain the information needed for form letters as well as for tracking order information, so we will use the following fields:

FIELD NAME	FIELD CONTENTS
Company	Company name
Title	Contact person's form of address
FirstName	Contact person's first name
LastName	Contact person's last name
JobTitle	Contact person's title
Address	Street address
Location	Post office box, suite, or other location
City	City
State	State
Zip	Zip code
Telephone	Telephone number
Credit	Credit limit
Due	Amount due
LastAmount	Amount of the last order
LastDate	Date of the last order

Building the Data Source

The data source can either be in a table or paragraph format, as shown in Figure 11.1.

Using a table, the first row—called the header record—contains the names of the fields, each field in a separate column. There cannot be any text or blank lines above the table. Each record is then contained in another row.

In paragraph format, each record is contained in a paragraph, with fields separated by a tab or by a comma. Because a Word table can have a maximum of 31 columns, you'll need to set up a data source as a paragraph if it contains more than 31 fields.

FIGURE 11.1

Data source as a table and paragraph

FirstName	LastName	HomePhone	WorkPhone
Adam	Chesin	555-4983	467-3745
Sandra	Kaufman	875-3973	312-2742
Mike	Stack	763-3978	312-3987

FirstName → LastName → HomePhone → WorkPhone¶
Adam → Chesin → 555-4983 → 467-3745¶
Sandra → Kaufman → 875-3973 → 312-2742¶
Mike → Stack → 763-3978 → 312-3987¶

Using the Mail Merge Helper

If you want to use a table format, you can create it yourself, as explained in Chapter 7, or have Word create it for you using Mail Merge Helper. Select Tools ➤ Mail Merge to display the dialog box shown in Figure 11.2.

FIGURE 11.2

Mail Merge Helper

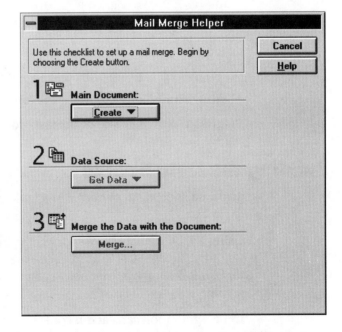

The options are:

◆ **Main Document:** creates form letters, envelopes, labels, and catalogs (lists).

◆ **Data Source:** opens or creates a data source.

◆ **Merge:** selects merge options and merges the main document and the data sources.

Data Source Step-by-Step

Follow these steps to build a data source:

1. Select Tools ➤ Mail Merge ➤ Create to display the options Form Letters, Mailing Labels, Envelopes, Catalog, and Restore to Normal Word Document.

2. Select Form Letters to display the options shown in Figure 11.3. You would select Active Window if the current window is blank or if it contains text that you want to use as the basis for the document.

FIGURE 11.3
Window options

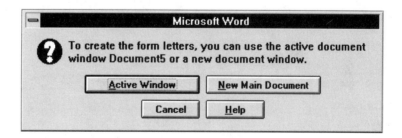

3. Select New Main Document. Word opens a new document window and redisplays the Mail Merge Helper dialog box. There is now an Edit button next to Create, and Word lists the type and name of main document.

Note You could write the main document now by selecting the Edit button. But you should create or open a data source first. This links the data source with the main document so its fields are available.

4. Select Get Data to display the options Create Data Source, Open Data Source, and Header Options. You would use the Open Data Source option to link an existing data source.

Note The Header options are used when you have a header record that is separate from the data as explained in the section on Using A Separate Header Record later in this chapter.

5. Select Create Data Source to display the dialog box shown in Figure 11.4.

FIGURE 11.4

Create Data Source
dialog box

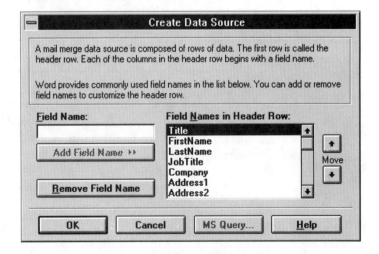

 **Tip**

The Field Names in Header Row box lists a set of field names used commonly when creating mailing lists and form letters. You can use all of the suggested fields by simply selecting OK. You can also delete some fields, add others, and change the order of the fields in the list. To change the order of a field, select it in the list, then click on the up or down arrows to move its position. While we will be using some fields with the same names as those already listed, it is really just as easy to delete all of the suggested names and start over.

6. Click on the Remove Field Name button 13 times. Each time you click, Word deletes one of the suggested field names. When you are done, the name of the last field deleted appears selected in the Field Name text box.

7. Type **Company,** and then press Enter, or select the Add Field Name button. The Company field is added to the list box.

8. Type **Title,** then press Enter.

9. Type **FirstName,** then press Enter.

10. In the same way, enter the remaining 12 fields for the database, as listed at the beginning of this section.

11. Select OK when you have entered the last field. The Save Data Source dialog box appears.

12. Type **Clients,** and then select OK. Word displays the options Edit Data Source and Edit Main Document options. You could select to edit the main document now, then add the data records later.

13. Select Edit Data Source to display the Data Form shown in Figure 11.5.

FIGURE 11.5

Data Form
dialog box

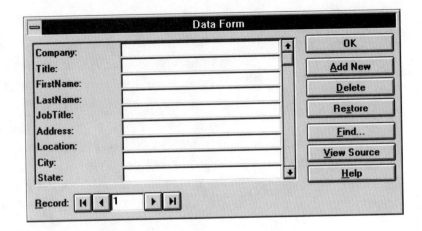

Entering Records in the Data Form

The Data Form is a convenient way to enter field information. The insertion point is in the text box for the first field in the record. Let's enter four records into the data source.

1. Type **Comhype Computers,** then press Enter. The insertion point moves to the next text box. You can also press Tab to move forward through the fields, Shift+Tab to move backward.

2. Type **Miss.** and then press Enter.

3. Type the following text in the fields, pressing Enter after each field.

```
Elaine
Cunningham
President
431 Broad Street
Suite 120
Margate
NJ
08712
609-555-1765
1500
550.50
245.98
94/12/01
```

 **Note**

When you press Enter after the last field, Word adds the record to the data source, clears the text boxes, and moves the insertion point to the first text box to accept another record. We are entering the date in the format Year/Month/Day, padded with zeroes to two characters, so we can later sort the file by date.

4. In the same manner, enter the following information for the next three records. (The blank line between fields in two of the records indicate records that do not have a second address line. To enter a blank field, simply press Enter when the insertion point moves to text box.)

```
DupliCopy Company
Mr.
Jackson
Montgomery
President
42 East Broad Street

Reynoldstown
PA
19011
215-295-0983
1500
635.25
552.34
94/11/16

Chandler Scientific
Mr.
Adam
Chandler
President
Osage and Wilson Avenues
```

```
Dallas
TX
31223
346-845-1987
1500
612.10
150
94/06/12

Computers-R-Us
Ms
Wilamini
Boyle
Vice President
401 Ocean Avenue
Box 12
Northfield
NJ
01652
609-567-0893
1000
235.76
267.50
94/02/01
```

5. When you have entered all of the records, click on the OK button to close the dialog box and to display the main document.

6. Select File ➤ Close. A dialog box appears warning you that you have not yet saved the database with the added records.

7. Select Yes to save the data source.

Data Form Options

The Data Form serves as a convenient platform for working with the records in your database. The options in the dialog box are:

◆ **Record:** displays a record. The number of the record appears in the text box. The buttons are (left to right) First Record, Previous Record, Next Record, Last Record.

◆ **Add New:** stores the record currently displayed, and displays a blank record.

◆ **Delete:** deletes the displayed record.

- ◆ **Restore:** cancels changes you made to a record while it is still displayed on the screen. This does not undelete a deleted record.
- ◆ **Find:** locates a record. Word displays a dialog box where you can enter the text you are looking for and select a field to locate it.
- ◆ **View Source:** displays the data source in table format.

Creating a Main Document

Now that you have a data source, you can create the main document, which is the document that contains the form letter. When you come to a place where you want the variable information to appear, you have to enter a merge field giving the name of the field that you want inserted at that location. Word will insert variable information during the merge process.

When you create a main document, you can link it with a specific data source. This means that you can access the list of fields while you are writing the letter. When you later merge the form letter, Word will automatically know which data source to use for the field information.

 **Tip**

If you do not link the main document with a data source when you create it, you can select the data source at a later time. You can even change the link if you want to obtain information from another data source that contains the same field names.

Now we will create a main document for all of the clients in the database. The inside address will include a second line if it is available. However, if the address does not include a second line, a blank line will not appear in the merged document.

1. Select Tools ➤ Mail Merge ➤ Create ➤ Form Letters ➤ New Main Document.

2. Select Get Data ➤ Open Data Source.

3. Select CLIENTS.DOC, then select OK. Word displays a dialog box with the options Edit Main Document, Cancel, and Help.

 **Note** This dialog will not appear if you selected the Active Document option previously, and the document already contained merge codes. Instead, the Mail Merge Helper dialog box will appear. To edit the main document, pull down the Edit button in the Main Document section and select the name of the document file.

4. Select Edit Main Document. Word displays the document window with the Mail Merge toolbar. The toolbar options are shown in Table 11.1.

5. Enter your address and the date. You can use the Letterhead macro that you created in Chapter 8.

6. Click on the Insert Merge Field button in the toolbar to display the lists the fields in the associated data source.

7. Click on the Title field to insert the field code into the document.

TABLE 11.1: Mail Merge toolbar

ICON	NAME
Insert Merge Field	Insert Merge Field
Insert Word Field	Insert Word Field
« » ABC	View Merged Data

TABLE 11.1: Mail Merge toolbar (continued)

ICON	NAME
⏮	First Record
◀	Previous Record
`1`	Record #
▶	Next Record
⏭	Last Record
	Mail Merge Helper
	Check for Errors
	Merge to New Document
	Merge to Printer
	Mail Merge
	Find Record
	Edit Data Source

In most cases, the name of the field appears in chevrons (<<Title>>) to represent the value in the Title field. The code may also appear as a merge field , like this:

{MERGEFIELD Title}

This means that the display of merge fields is turned on. Press Alt+F9, or select Tools ➤ Options ➤ View ➤ Field Codes ➤ OK.

8. Press the spacebar to insert a space.

9. Now in the same way, insert the FirstName field, then press the spacebar.

10. Insert the LastName field, then press Enter to move the insertion point to the next line in the document.

11. Insert the JobTitle field, and then press Enter.

12. Insert the Company field, and press Enter.

13. Insert the Address field, and press Enter.

14. Insert the Location field, and press Enter.

15. Insert the City field.

16. Type a comma, and then press the spacebar.

17. Insert the State field.

18. Press the spacebar twice.

19. Insert the Zip field. The line will appear like this:

```
<<City>>, <<STATE>> <<ZIP>>
```

20. Press Enter twice to insert a blank line between the inside address and the salutation.

21. Type **Dear** then press the spacebar.

22. Insert the Title field, then press the spacebar.

23. Insert the LastName field.

24. Type a colon (:), and then press Enter twice before typing the body of the letter.

25. Type the beginning of the first sentences (do not press Enter):

```
    It has been ten years since we first opened for business
and we want to celebrate our anniversary with a special offer
to one of our most valued customers.
```

26. Press the spacebar, then insert the Company field.

27. Press the period (.) to close the sentence, and then press Enter to start a new paragraph.

28. Type the remainder of the letter. The completed form letter is shown in Figure 11.6.

> Please deduct 15% from the merchandise total of your next order. Sorry, we cannot offer a discount on shipping and handling charges. If you have any questions about this offer, contact your sales representative.
>
> We appreciate your support, and we pledge to provide the best in quality and service.
>
> Sincerely,
>
> Alvin A. Aardvark
> President

29. Select File ➤ Save, type **discount,** and select OK.

30. Select File ➤ Close to clear the screen.

FIGURE 11.6

Completed form letter

Aardvark Computers
111 Albany Avenue
Altoona AL 11111

December 16, 1994

«Title» «FirstName» «LastName»
«JobTitle»
«Company»
«Address»
«Location»
«City», «State» «Zip»

Dear «Title» «LastName»:

It has been ten years since we first opened for business and we want to celebrate our anniversary with a special offer to one of our most valued customers, «Company».
Please deduct 15% from the merchandise total of your next order. Sorry, we cannot offer a discount on shipping and handling charges. If you have any questions about this offer, contact your sales representative.
We appreciate your support, and we pledge to provide the best in quality and service.

Sincerely,

Alvin A. Aardvark
President

—

 **Tip** If you do not link a form file when you first create it, you can define the link later. Open the main document, click on the Mail Merge Helper button, then pull down Get Data. Select either Create Data Source to create a new data source for the document, or select Open Data Source to link the document with an existing data file. Use the same technique to change the data source linked with a main document.

Merging Form Documents and Databases

After you have created the form document and the data source, you can merge them to produce the final documents. You can merge the documents to a new window, or directly to the printer.

Merging Form Letters

To merge form letters, open the main document. To merge a specific record, click on the View Merged Data button, click on the next or previous buttons until the data appears, then select File ➤ Print. To merge all of the records, click on the Merge to New Document or Merge to Printer button.

By default, Word will not print a blank line in an address if the only field in the line is empty.

Controlling the Merge Process

You can control the merge process by clicking on the Mail Merge button, or by selecting Tools ➤ Mail Merge ➤ Merge, to display the dialog box shown in Figure 11.7.

Pull down the Merge To list and select either New Document or Printer. The Setup option will be dimmed unless you have a Fax system or Microsoft Mail installed.

FIGURE 11.7

Merge dialog box

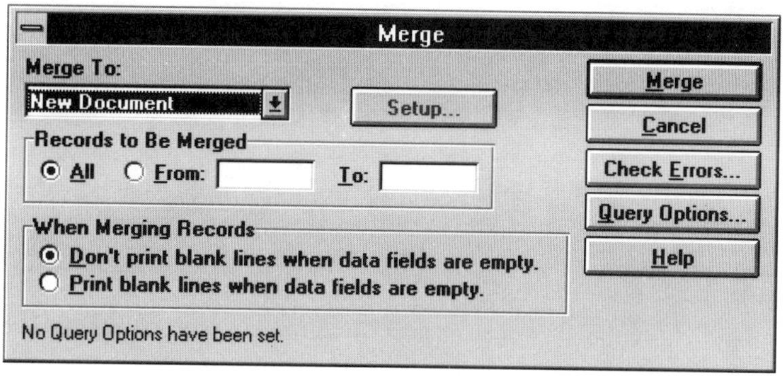

Use the Records To Be Merged option to print all of the records, or a range of them. For example, to merge just the first three records, enter 1 in the From text box, and enter 3 in the To text box.

The When Merging Records option determines how blank records are treated in addresses. The default setting will not print blank lines when a field is empty.

Use Check Errors to test the integrity of the mail merge. (You can also check for errors by clicking on the Check Error button in the mail merge toolbar.)

The options are:

◆ Simulate the merge and report errors in a new document

◆ Complete the merge, pausing to report each error as it occurs

◆ Complete the merge without pausing, and report errors in a new document

Invalid Merge Fields

Select Merge to begin the merge. If you attempt to insert a merge field that does not exist in the data source, Word will display the dialog box shown in Figure 11.8. You can select either to remove the field from the main document, or replace it with one of the fields from the data source.

FIGURE 11.8

Invalid Merge Field
dialog box

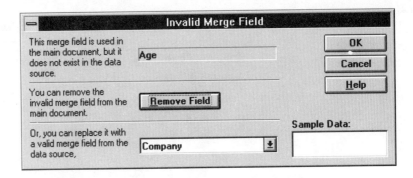

 **Tip** Query Options let you sort the database on up to three fields, and select records based on up to six conditions. We will discuss Query Options in detail in Chapter 12.

Changing the Merge Type

You can easily change the type of merge operation, from a form letter to a catalog, for example. Open the main document, click on the Mail Merge Helper button, then select to create the desired merge type. In the dialog box that appears, select Change Document Type.

 **Note** The Restore To Normal Word Document option converts the main document to a normal document. This unlinks any association with a data source, and when you open the file, the mail merge toolbar will not appear. To restore the document as a main document, open it, select Tools ➤ Mail Merge ➤ Create, select one of the options, then choose Active Window. You will then have to reselect the data source to restore the link.

Working with Data Sources

Since the database is merely a Word table, you can use all of the editing commands to maintain the information. It's easy to search for specific records, edit the text, move and copy data between records, and delete records. You can also perform data management tasks using the Data Form dialog box or the database toolbar.

Editing the Data Source

To work with the data source, open the main document, click on the Edit Data Source button to display the Data Form. (You can also select Edit from the Data Source section of Mail Merge Helper.) From the data form, you can add, edit, delete, and find records. For additional capabilities, select View Data Source to display the data source in table format along with the database toolbar, shown in Figure 11.9. Table 11.2 shows the names of the toolbar buttons.

FIGURE 11.9

Data source
displayed as a table

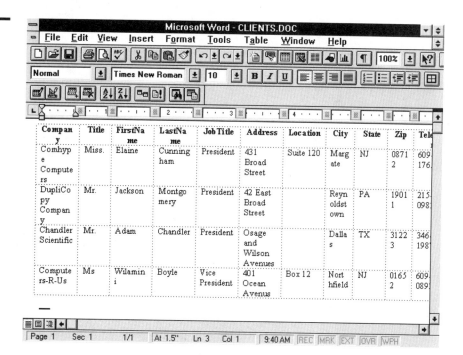

Company	Title	FirstName	LastName	Job Title	Address	Location	City	State	Zip	Tele
Comhype Computers	Miss.	Elaine	Cunningham	President	431 Broad Street	Suite 120	Margate	NJ	08712	609 176
DupliCopy Company	Mr.	Jackson	Montgomery	President	42 East Broad Street		Reynoldstown	PA	19011	215 098
Chandler Scientific	Mr.	Adam	Chandler	President	Osage and Wilson Avenues		Dallas	TX	31223	346 198
Computers-R-Us	Ms	Wilamini	Boyle	Vice President	401 Ocean Avenus	Box 12	Northfield	NJ	01652	609 089

TABLE 11.2: The Database toolbar

ICON	NAME	FUNCTION
	Data Form	Display the data form
	Manage Fields	Add, remove, or rename fields
	Add New Record	Insert a new row at the bottom of the table
	Delete record	Delete the record containing the insertion point
	Sort Ascending	Sort the rows of the table in ascending order, using the field in which the insertion point is placed (does not sort the first row containing the header)
	Sort Descending	Sort the rows in descending order
	Insert Database	Insert records from another data source
	Update Fields	Update any Word fields that are selected on the data sources
	Find Record	Locate records
	Mail Merge Main Document	Display the main document

Data Source Tips and Tricks

Until you select to view the data source as a table, the data source document will not be listed in the Window menu. You can only display the data by selecting to edit the data source from the main document window. You can then return to the main document by selecting OK in the data form.

Changes you make to the data source on the form will not automatically be saved on your disk. If you do make changes, Word will display a dialog box when you attempt to close the main document. Select Yes if you want to save the modified data source.

Once you display the data source as a table, however, its document name will be added to the Window menu, and you can select it as you do any open document. When you close the main document, no warning message will appear asking if you want to save the data source. You must manually save the data source from its own window, just as you would save any other document. Closing the data source window will not affect the main document and the data form.

Use the database toolbar, or any of the table editing techniques that you learned in Chapter 7 to work with the data source data.

Changing Data Source Fields

To change the data source fields, select the Manage Fields button in the database toolbar. Word displays the dialog box shown in Figure 11.10.

FIGURE 11.10

Manage Fields
dialog box

- ◆ To add a field to the data source, enter the name in the Field Name text box, then select Add.

- ◆ To delete a field, select the name in the list box, select Remove, then Yes. Deleting a field also deletes all of the information for that field in the data source, just as deleting a column from a table.

- ◆ To change the name of a field, select it in the list box, choose Rename, type the new name, then select OK.

S E C R E T S

Database Toolbar Tips and Tricks

You can also open the data source table by selecting it's name in the File Open dialog box. Word will display the table on screen, but it will not display the database toolbar. To display the toolbar, select View ➤ ToolBars ➤ Database.

You can use all of the toolbar buttons except Mail Merge Main Document. In fact, when you point to that button, a message appears in the status bar reporting that the table is not a valid mail merge main or data file. To link the data source with a main document, you must access it through the main document's window.

Word will treat the first row of the table as column headings. So if you select the Data Form button, the data form appears with the items in the first row as field names. Blank cells in the row will be given the names AutoMergeField, AutoMergeField1, AutomergeField2, and so on.

Using a Separate Header Record

In most cases, the first row of your data source table will contain the field names. However, you can also use an external header record. This can be a file that contains just a header record, or the name of another data source that contains its own header record.

Creating Two Header Records

Sometimes, long field names makes it difficult to align text, or to visualize the final spacing of the merged documents. The solution is to create two separate header records, one with full field names, another with single letters, such as A, B, and C.

Use the header record with full names for most form letters, and the header record with single letters when you want to control the spacing. (You may also need an external header record if you are importing data from other sources, or using an existing table that does not contain column headings.)

Using Mail Merge Helper

To create a header record using Mail Merge Helper, select Tools ➤ Mail Merge ➤ Create, specify the type of main document, then select New Main Document. Next, select Get Data ➤ Header Options. Choose Create to display the Create Header Source dialog box. The box has the same options as the Create Data Source box. Enter or select the field names, select OK, then give the header source a file name.

Creating a Data Source with Headers

To immediately create a data source that uses the header record, select Get Data ➤ Create Data Source. Enter a name for the data source, then select OK. The Data Form dialog box appears with the field names from the header record.

To later create the data source, select Get Data ➤ Header Options ➤ Open, then select the file name of the header record.

You can also use the header record of an existing data source. For example, suppose you want to create a second data source contain all of the same fields that you entered for CLIENTS. Instead of entering the fields again, open the CLIENTS file as the header source, create a new data source, or open an existing one that does not have its own header record. Word will use the fields of CLIENTS but ignore the records for the new data sources.

Merging the Documents

When you want to merge the documents, open the header source and the data source. If the data source for which you are using a separate header already has its own header record, it will be ignored. However, Word will treat the header record as a normal data record. The field names (column headings) in the data source will be merged into the first merge document.

Merging Envelopes and Labels

You can merge addresses directly onto envelopes using the same data source you create for form letters. This is useful if you need a set of envelopes for a mass mailing that does not include a form letter.

Setting Up the Envelope

In the Mail Merge Helper, select Create ➤ Envelopes ➤ New Main Document, create or open a data source, then choose Setup Main Document. Word will display the Envelope Options dialog box. (Refer to Chapter 3 if you need to refresh your memory on creating envelopes.)

Select the options from the box, then select OK to display the Envelope Address box shown in Figure 11.11. Place the insertion point in the Sample Envelope Address box, then use the Insert Merge Field to create the form for the mailing address.

FIGURE 11.11

Envelope Address
dialog box

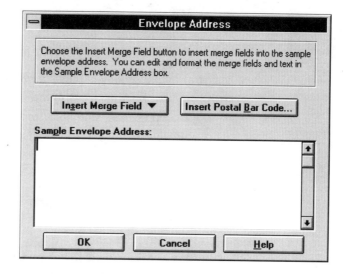

Including a Postal Bar Code

To include a bar code on the envelopes, click on Insert Postal Bar Code to display the dialog bow shown in Figure 11.12. Select the field that contains the zip code, then the field that contain the street address. You can also select to include a FIM-A courtesy reply code.

FIGURE 11.12

Insert Postal Bar
Code dialog box

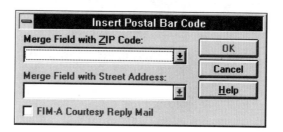

Select OK and close the mail merge helper, or select Edit, and then the name of the envelope form. The merge codes for the address will appear in a frame. Word uses the frame to position the address on the envelope.

S E C R E T S

Envelope Tips and Tricks

If you are preparing form letters, you can create the envelopes at the same time as you merge the letters. Each envelope will be inserted or printed before its associated letter, so this is not really efficient if you do not have separate paper trays for the envelopes and paper.

If you have separate trays, you can set Word to feed the envelope from one tray, then the letter that matches it from the other tray. If you only have one tray, you'll have to set the envelope to print from the manual feed and the paper from the tray. You can then start the print process and stand by the printer, feeding envelopes as they are needed.

Create the envelopes using the same techniques as you learned in Chapter 3. Open the main document and select the field codes that make up the address. Select Tools ➤ Envelopes and Labels, then check the mailing address and other envelope settings.

Click on the Feed button, or select Options, to display the Printing Options dialog box, then select the paper source in the Feed From list. Exit the dialog box, then select Add to Document to insert the envelope form before the main document. Finally, perform the merge, either to a document window or to the printer.

Creating Mailing Labels

You can merge data onto mailing labels as easily as envelopes. Select Create ► Mailing Labels from Mail Merge Helper, create or open the data source, then select Setup Main Document. The Label Options dialog box appears. Use the techniques you learned in Chapter 3 to select the appropriate label form, or to design a custom form.

When you exit the dialog box, the Create Labels dialog box appears. This is similar to the Create Envelopes box. Use the Insert Merge Field list to design the format of the text on the label, and insert a postal code if desired.

When you exit the Mail Merge Helper, the merge codes will be duplicated in each of the labels. Select the View Merged Data to see how the labels will appear. (To print a hardcopy record of your mailing list, create a mail merge label but print it on plain paper.) Figure 11.13 shows mail merge labels.

FIGURE 11.13

Mail merge labels

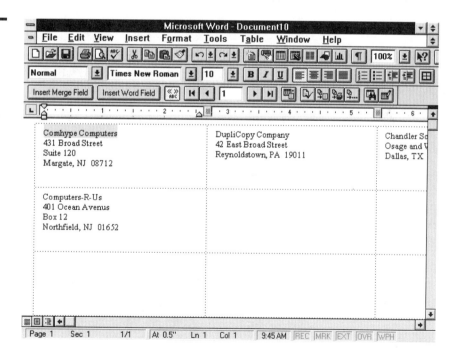

Creating Reports

Select the catalog option in Mail Merge Helper to create lists. When you merge a catalog, Word does not insert a section break between each record. Instead, the items in the main document appear on the same page. Word only inserts a page break when each page is filled. Use the catalog feature to create informative reports, such as price lists, student records, and sales reports.

 **Tip**   Word will merge the catalog to a new document. If you want page titles or column headings, add them after the records are merged.

Aligning Data in Columns

To align data in columns, set custom tab stops in the main document. As long as you press Enter after the line containing the field codes, the tab stops will be applied to the resulting document. In fact, you must press enter after the field codes. Otherwise, Word will begin the next record immediately after the previous one, instead of inserting each on a separate line.

For example, Figure 11.14 shows a client contact list that was created by mail merge. Tab stops were set at the 2.5 inch and 5 inch positions. The report title, page number, date, and column headings were entered after the merge.

FIGURE 11.14

Client contact list

Client Contact List
February 23, 1994

Company	Contact	Phone Number
Comhype Computers	Miss Elaine Cunningham	609-555-1765
DupliCopy Company	Mr. Jackson Montgomery	215-295-0983
Chandler Scientific	Mr. Adam Chandler	346-845-1987
Computers-R-Us	Ms Wilamini Boyle	609-567-0893

Entering the Text Codes

The text of the document uses the following codes. When entering the commands, press Tab after the Company and LastName fields, and press Enter after the Telephone field.

```
<<Company>> <<Title>><<FirstName>><<LastName>> <<Telephone>>
```

 **N o t e** Create the catalog main document and save it under the name Contacts. We'll be using it in later chapters.

Creating a Sales Order Report

You can use similar techniques to produce other database reports. To print a sales order report, create the following form file:

```
<<Company>>        <<LastDate>>        <<LastAmount>>
```

Save the document under the name orders, then close the document. (You cannot merge a catalog directly to the printer. Merge it to a new document, then select File ➤ Print to print a copy.)

Next, create a main document to print a client contact sheet:

```
Client: <<Company>>
Name: <<Title>> <<FirstName>> <<LastName>>
Address: <<Address>> <<Location>>
        <<City>>, <<STATE>> <<ZIP>>
Telephone: <<Telephone>>
Amount Due: <<DUE>>
Last order: <<LastDate>> for <<LastAmount>>
```

To prevent Word from dividing a client record between pages, press Shift+Enter (instead of just Enter) after each line except the last—press Enter after that. Then select all of the lines, choose Format ➤ Paragraph ➤ Text Flow ➤ Keep Lines Together ➤ OK. Word will move an entire record to the next page if there is not enough room for it on the current page.

Save the document under the name Leads, then close the document window.

Controlling a Merge with Fields

You can also control and customize how documents are merged using fields. When you use the Insert Word Field menu in the mail merge toolbar, Word will prompt you for the required arguments. You can also use the Insert ➤ Field command.

 **Tip**

If you insert a Word field but it does not appear on the screen, turn on the display of field codes. To see the results of the field operation, turn off the display of field codes. Toggle the display by pressing Alt+F9, or selecting Field Codes from the Tools ➤ Options ➤ View dialog box.

S E C R E T S

Field Tips and Tricks

How field codes appear in your main document depends on the Field Codes setting in the Options View dialog box.

If the display of codes are turned off, the names of merge fields from the data source will appear in chevrons. (To see the actual data in the merge fields, click on the View Merged Data button.) However, you will see the results of Word fields, not the fields themselves.

IF Then Else and Formula fields will be calculated using the contents of the current record—the record whose number is shown in the toolbar. Fields that do not show results, such as Set and Ask, will not be displayed at all. When you move to another record using the toolbar, the results of the fields will automatically be updated.

When you select to display fields, merge fields will appear like this:

{MERGEFIELD Client}

You will see the actual Word fields. Clicking on the View Merged Data button will have no affect.

You can move, copy, and delete merge fields just like any other text. If two fields are next to each other, however, you may have difficulty selecting just one. To select one field, first add a space between the fields, then drag over the field with the mouse.

Inserting Conditional Data

The IfThenElse command is useful for inserting information based on the contents of a field. For example, in a form letter, you may want to include a friendly thank you to clients who have no outstanding debts, and a subtle reminder to clients who owe money.

To use the field, place the insertion point where you want the message to appear, select Insert Word Fields, and then select IfThenElse to display the dialog box shown in Figure 11.15.

FIGURE 11.15

Insert Word Field: If dialog box

```
┌─────────────────────────────────────────────────────────────┐
│ ─            Insert Word Field: IF                            │
│ ┌─IF────────────────────────────────────────┐   ┌─────────┐  │
│ │ Field Name:      Comparison:   Compare To: │   │   OK    │  │
│ │ [Company    ±]  [Equal to  ±]  [         ] │   ├─────────┤  │
│ │                                            │   │ Cancel  │  │
│ │ Insert this Text:                          │   ├─────────┤  │
│ │ ┌────────────────────────────────────┐    │   │  Help   │  │
│ │ │                                  ±│    │   └─────────┘  │
│ │ │                                  ±│    │                │
│ │ └────────────────────────────────────┘    │                │
│ │ Otherwise Insert this Text:                │                │
│ │ ┌────────────────────────────────────┐    │                │
│ │ │                                  ±│    │                │
│ │ │                                  ±│    │                │
│ │ └────────────────────────────────────┘    │                │
│ └────────────────────────────────────────────┘                │
└─────────────────────────────────────────────────────────────┘
```

443

Comparison Options

Pull down the Field Name list and select the field to use for the condition. Pull down the comparison list and select the condition desired. The options are:

Equal To

Not Equal To

Less Than

Greater Than

Less Than or Equal

Greater Than or Equal

Is Blank

Is Not Blank

Then, select the Compare To box and enter the value you want to compare with the field. For our sample, to reach clients with no outstanding debts, the options would appear like this:

FIELD NAME	COMPARISON	COMPARE TO
Due	Equal To	0

Inserting Text

In the Insert This Text box, type the text that you want to appear when the condition is true:

We sincerely appreciate your prompt payments.

In the Otherwise Insert This Text box, type the text that you want to appear when the condition is false:

We would appreciate prompt payment of your outstanding debt.

When you select OK, the field will appear like the following one, if field codes are displayed. (If the display of field codes is turned off, you will see the text that relates to the current record.)

```
{IF {MERGEFIELD Due } = O "We sincerely appreciate your prompt pay-
ments." "We would appreciate prompt payment of your outstanding
debt."}
```

Including a Merge Field

To include a merge field in the text, you must display the field codes and insert the field manually. For example, suppose you want to print this sentence:

```
We would appreciate prompt payment of your outstanding debt, $800.
```

The amount of the debt is contained in the Due field and the final instruction will appear like this:

```
{IF {MERGEFIELD Due } = O "We sincerely appreciate your prompt pay-
ments." "We would appreciate prompt payment of your outstanding
debt of {MERGEFIELD Due}."}
```

Create as much of the command as you can using the Insert Word Field button, then insert the merge field manually. Place the insertion point where you want the merge field to appear—between the end of the text and its closing quotation marks—then pull down the Insert Merge Field list and select the field.

 **Note**

Check your work carefully to ensure that the merge codes, quotation marks, and braces are in the proper locations.

Inserting the If Code

You can also insert the If command by selecting Insert ➤ Field, then typing the field into the Field Codes text box. Use the Options and Help button to learn more about the code.

The basic structure of the command is:

```
{IF expression1 operation "comparison" "text when true" "text when
false"}
```

You only need to surround the text in quotation marks when it is more than one word, so this is valid statement:

```
{IF {Mergefield Due} = 0 Thanks Deadbeat}
```

The text to print when the condition is false is optional. (If you want a carriage return to print only when the condition is met, press Enter within the true text or false text quotation marks.)

Handling Blank Fields

The IF command is useful for dealing with empty fields. Even though Word will not print a blank line if a field is empty in an address, empty fields can still create problems. For example, our sample database has a field called Location which is empty in several records.

Using the IfThenElse Command

Suppose you use a sentence such as this in your main document:

```
We will personally deliver the package to <<Location>>.
```

When the field is blank, the sentence will end abruptly. Instead, use the IfThenElse command, like this:

```
{IF {MERGEFIELD Location } = "" "your office" "{MERGEFIELD Loca-
tion}." }
```

Note that the location merge field is included in the quotation marks used to indicate the false text.

If the field is blank (there is no location), the sentence will appear merged like this:

```
We will personally deliver the package to your office when it
arrives.
```

When the field is not blank, the location merge field will be inserted.

An Alternative Method

As with all programming languages, there are usually several ways to perform the same task in WordBasic. For example, you could handle the blank location field just as well using this structure:

```
We will personally deliver the package to {MERGEFIELD Location}{IF
{MERGEFIELD field}="" "your office" ""}.
```

Here, the location merge field will always print. Of course, if the field is empty, nothing will appear. The words "your office" will also print when the field is empty.

Compound Conditions

You can use the IfThenElse command to create compound conditions using AND or OR logic. To create an AND condition, use a second IF field in the area where the true text would appear.

Using an AND Condition

For example, this command displays a message only when the client is located in New Jersey and owes more than $100:

```
{ IF { MERGEFIELD STATE } = "NJ" "{ IF { MERGEFIELD Due}>
100 "New Jersey Deadbeat" ""}" "" }
```

Because the second condition is in the true text, it is tested only when the first condition is true. The true text is printed when the second condition is true, making it an AND condition—both IF conditions must be true.

Using an OR Condition

You can also structure the statement to create an OR condition, testing when any one of a number of conditions are met. To do this, place the second IF statement in the false text of the first. This command displays a message for clients in either New Jersey, Pennsylvania, or Delaware:

```
{ IF { MERGEFIELD STATE } = "NJ" "We welcome our East Coast cli-
ent." "{ IF { MERGEFIELD STATE } = "PA" "We welcome our East Coast
client." "{ IF { MERGEFIELD STATE } = "DE" "We welcome our East
Coast client." ""}"}"}
```

Using the COMPARE Field

Another way to create compound conditions is to use the COMPARE field. This field returns 1 if two values are the same, 0 if they are different. The syntax is:

```
{COMPARE Expression Operator Expression}
```

The expressions can be merge fields, bookmarks, strings, numbers, or formulas. For example, this command prints the word Yes if the client's title is President:

```
{ IF { COMPARE { MERGEFIELD Title }=President"} = 1 "YES" "NO"}
```

Creating Compound Conditionals

Because compare is a function that returns a value, it can used in formula fields. By combining it with the AND or OR functions, you can create compound conditionals. For example, this function returns a 1 if either comparison is true—either the client's title is President or they are located in New Jersey:

```
{= OR({ COMPARE { MERGEFIELD Title }="President"},{ COMPARE
{ MERGEFIELD State }="NJ"})}
```

If you used the AND operator, the function returns 1 only when both conditions are true.

Place the function in an IF field like this:

```
{ IF {= OR({ COMPARE { MERGEFIELD Title }="President"},{ COMPARE {
MERGEFIELD State }="NJ"} )}= 1 "The client is either a president or
located in New Jersey" "The client is neither a president nor lo-
cated in New Jersey" )
```

Tip
You can use wildcard characters in the second expression when the compare operator is either = or <>. Use a question mark as a substitute for any one character, or use an asterisks for a number of characters.

Performing Math in Fields

Another typical use of fields it to perform math operations. In an earlier chapter, you learned how to use the formula field to perform math using bookmarks. You can do the same with the contents of merge fields.

Calculating a Discount

Suppose, to encourage sales, you want to give clients a 2 percent discount based on their line of credit. The sentence will appear something like:

```
Please deduct $45 from your next order.
```

The amount of the discount is calculated by multiplying the Credit field times 0.02. The field would appear like this:

```
Please deduct ${={MERGEFIELD Credit} * 0.02} from your next order.
```

To create the line, press Ctrl+F9 to insert the field braces, then type the equal sign. Pull down the Insert Merge Field list and click on the Credit field. Then, type the remainder of the equation. Make sure that you type the equation within the formula fields braces, not in the merge field braces. When you merge the documents, Word updates the field automatically.

Calculating a Derived Column

Calculations are also used in listings (catalog merges) to create a derived column. A derived column is one that contains information that is not in the data source but calculated from it.

For example, suppose you want to print a report listing the balance of available credit for each client. The balance is derived by subtracting the amount due from the credit limit. The following main document will create the report:

```
{MERGEFIELD Company} {={MERGEFIELD Credit}-{MERGEFIELD Due}}
```

For each record, the contents of the Company field will be inserted, then the formula field will calculate and display the difference between the Credit and the Due fields.

Repeating the Calculated Amount

If you want to use calculated amount in several locations on the form document, you could repeat the formula field or assign the results to a bookmark using the Set command, like this:

```
{SET net {={MERGEFIELD Credit}-{MERGEFIELD Due}}} {COMMENTS
}{MERGEFIELD Company} {net}
```

For each record, the Set command assigns to the bookmark the difference between the credit limit and the amount due, and then prints a line in the report.

The Set field assigns a value to a bookmark, using the syntax:

```
{Set Bookmark value-or-expression}
```

You can assign a literal value such as:

```
{Set Shipping 5.50}
```

or you can use merge fields. To enter merge fields, insert the Set command using the Insert Word Field button or the Insert ➤ Field dialog box, then insert the fields manually.

 **Tip**   To print the contents of a bookmark, press Ctrl+F9, then type the bookmark name. You can insert the bookmark more than once in the same document.

Subtracting the Fields

In the merge file, the expression:

```
{={MERGEFIELD Credit}-{MERGEFIELD Due}}
```

subtracts the fields. Notice that the complete command has three closing parentheses at the end:

```
{SET net {={MERGEFIELD Credit}-{MERGEFIELD Due}}}
```

One parentheses ends the MERGEFIELD code after the field named Due. Another parentheses ends the formula field. A third parentheses ends the entire SET command. You must always have the same number of opening and closing parentheses in an expression.

Using the Comment Command

The Comment command can be used to insert notes to yourself, such as:

```
COMMENT{This merge file prints the credit remaining}
```

Anything within the parentheses is ignored during the merge operations.

Line Spacing and Carriage Returns

The Comment command is also useful for spacing the merge program onto several lines, making codes easier to read and understand. You cannot just press Enter to end lines of code in the form file. When the file is merged, Word will insert the carriage return into the final documents. Let Word wrap the lines for you, or use the COMMENT command at the end of the line, and press Enter when the insertion point is within the braces.

Word will ignore the carriage return because it is part of the comment parameter. Remember, however, to press Enter after the line of merge codes when creating a catalog.

Preventing Extra Lines

For example, this form file was entered without the Comment command:

```
{SET net {={MERGEFIELD Credit}-{MERGEFIELD Due}}}
{MERGEFIELD Company} {net}
```

After the SET command is executed, Word inserts a carriage return into the document. Then the line containing the field and the bookmark prints, and another carriage return is added to move to the next line.

This sequence would be repeated for every record, so the report would appear double spaced. With the Comment command and its opening parentheses at the end of one line, and its closing parentheses at the beginning of the next line, the carriage return would be ignored.

Tip Another way to prevent extra lines from appearing, is to click the show/hide button and format the paragraph marks at the end of the extra lines as hidden text. When you print the document, turn off the display of hidden text to prevent the extra lines from printing.

Selecting Records with Field Codes

In Chapter 12, you will learn how to use query options to select and sort records to be merged. You can also select records using field codes. For example, you may want to contact clients who have exceeded their credit limit.

You can do this using the SKIPIF command like this:

```
{SET net {={MERGEFIELD Credit}-{MERGEFIELD Due}}}
{SKIPIF {net}<800}
```

If the condition is true, Word will ignore the record and move into the next. Add the code using the Insert Merge Field button in the mail merge toolbar, or the Insert ➤ Field dialog box.

Note The position of the code is not important, it will effect the current record no matter where it is placed in the main document. That's because Word evaluates all of the fields before producing the document. If you use the code in a form letter, for instance, you can place it at the beginning, end, or at any other location in the main document.

Programming for User Input

You can combine information from a database with information that you enter at the time of merging. You can also create a form file that doesn't use a database at all, but obtains all of its information directly from the user. Forms will be discussed in Chapter 15.

To enter data at the time of a merge use the ASK or Fill-In merge fields.

Note You must place the ASK or SET fields before you use the bookmark in a document. Word will display an error message if it encounters the bookmark before it is assigned a value. This will only affect the first merged document and only when the merge is first run.

The Fill-In Field

The Fill-In command allows the user to enter information into the resulting merged document at the location of the command. The command displays a dialog box with your prompt, and optional default text that will be inserted if you select OK without entering text, as shown in Figure 11.16.

FIGURE 11.16

Fill-In command
dialog box

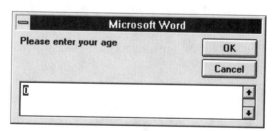

Pull down the Insert Word Field list and select Fill-in to display the dialog box shown in Figure 11.17. In the Prompt box, enter the text that you want to appear in the message box, prompting the user what to enter during the merge. In the Default Fill-In Text box, enter any text that you want to use by default in the merged documents.

FIGURE 11.17

Insert Word Field:
Fill-In dialog box

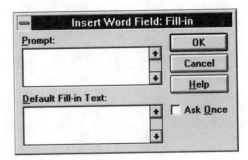

 **Tip**   By default, the prompt will appear with each copy of the merged document. This means, you can change the fill-in text for each copy. Select the Ask Once checkbox if you only want the box to appear when you first start the merge. The entry in that box will appear in every copy of the merged document.

When you select OK, Word will display a sample fill-in box. Select OK or Cancel to remove the box. The field is inserted in the document using this structure:

```
{ FILLIN "prompt" \d "default" \o }
```

 **Note**   The \d switch indicates that the text that follows is the default text. The \o switch indicates that the box will appear once, only when the first document is merged.

By combining keyboard commands with other merge codes, you can mass produce form documents while customizing them at the time they are created. For example, this portion of a form file lets you personalize letters by entering a suitable salutation depending on the recipient and tone of the letter:

```
{MERGEFIELD Title} {MERGEFIELD FirstName} {MERGEFIELD LastName}
{MERGEFIELD Company}
{MERGEFIELD Address}
{MERGEFIELD Location}
{MERGEFIELD City}, {MERGEFIELD State}{MERGEFIELD Zip}

Dear {FILLIN "Enter the salutation and click OK" \d "Friend"}
```

When you merge the main document, Word will pause at the location of the command and display the dialog box. Enter the data and select OK.

The Ask Command and Bookmark Fields

The ASK command also pauses the merge and displays a dialog box. However, text you enter is inserted into a bookmark instead of into the document itself. You must insert the bookmark field to display the value in the document. You can place the text in several locations by repeating the bookmark field. As with the Fill-In field, you enter a prompt and default text, and select to display the box only once.

The syntax is:

```
{ ASK var "prompt" \d "default" \o }
```

For instance, start a main document this way to merge records of clients in a specific city:

```
{ ASK AREA "Please enter the city" \o }
{ SKIPIF {MERGEFIELD City} <> {AREA} }
```

A bookmark is treated as a string or number depending on the operation. These commands allow you to selectively increase the credit limit for a special mailing. (Notice that the Company field is included in the ASK prompt. This way, the name of the company will appear when Word is merging its record.)

```
{ ASK More "Addition Credit for {MERGEFIELD Company}"}
{SET new {={MERGEFIELD Credit} +{More}}}
Your new credit limit is now {New}
```

 **Note**

If you select to display the box only once, the value of the bookmark you enter for the first record will be carried into the remaining merges.

S E C R E T S

Ask and Fill-In Tips and Tricks

If you specify default text in the Insert Word Field dialog box, it will appear in each of the Ask or Fill-In dialog boxes that appear during a merge operation. Entering other text in the box affects only the current record—the default text will appear the next time the box is displayed.

However, if you do not enter default text for the Fill-In and Ask fields, the default becomes the last entry you make in the Ask or Fill-In dialog box.

For example, if you enter text in the sample dialog that appears immediately after closing the Insert Word Field box, that text will appear for the first merge document. It will continue to appear in the Ask or Fill-In dialog box until you make another entry. That entry will then appear in the next box until you type something else. The last entry will be stored with the main document when you save it, so it will appear at the start of its next merge operation.

If you do not want the text to be repeated from one record to the next—that is, have no default text—use the \d switch followed by empty quotation marks, like this:

```
{ ASK var "prompt" \d ""}
{ FILLIN "prompt" \d ""}
```

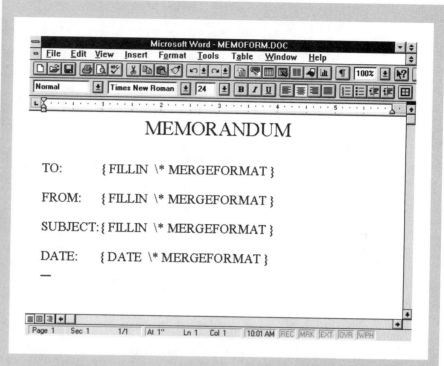

You can use the ASK and FILLIN fields in a non-merge document as well. The dialog boxes will be displayed when you update the fields. For example, the document shown here serves as a blank memo form.

When you need to fill out a memo, select the entire document and press F9. Word will display the Ask and Fill-In dialog boxes as it encounters them in the document. (In Chapter 15, you'll learn other ways to create forms.)

The Next field tells Word to get the data from the next record without inserting a section break. You use it to include data from more than one record on a page or label.

In previous versions of Word, the Next field was used to create lists and labels. This is now performed automatically when you select to create labels or a catalog. In fact, Word uses the command automatically when it creates mail merge labels, as shown on the label form here with the fields displayed.

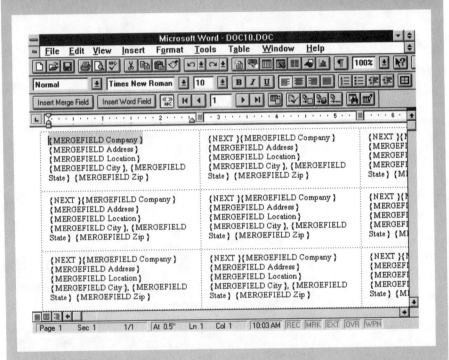

Use the Next Record If command to create lists or labels of selected records.

Use the Merge Record # and Merge Sequence # commands to number records. When you do not use Query Options to select records, the Merge Record # command inserts the row number of the record in the data source. The syntax is:

`{MERGEREC}`

For example, use it in a catalog merge to print reference numbers at the start of each line. You can also use it in the footer of a form letter to print a reference, or in a formula field to create invoice numbers, as in:

`{= {MERGEREC} + 2000}`

When you use Query Options to select records, as discussed in Chapter 12, Merge Record # functions the same as Merge Sequence #. The Merge Sequence # command inserts the number of the record in the set of those being merged. The syntax is:

`{MERGESEQ}`

For example, if a query selects just the records in rows 25 and 30 of a large data source, they would be numbered 1 and 2 by the Merge Sequence # command.

Using the SKIPIF command to select records, or the From and To options in the Merge dialog box, will not affect the Merge Record # order—the number will still reflect the row number in the data source table.

Remember, sorting the data source will change the record (row) numbers.

Database
Management

I T'S POSSIBLE TO MANAGE THE databases you create in Word with standard text-editing techniques and the mail merge toolbar, but you can also customize your database management efforts by combining macros and mail merge features. This chapter shows you how to automate many standard tasks, such as adding and deleting records, and creating invoices. You'll also learn to create some useful macros for interactive sorting, record selection, and error prevention.

Automated Database Management

By combining macro and merge commands, you can automate common database-management functions. The following sections describe how to streamline adding records, deleting records, and locating duplicated records.

 **N o t e** The macros shown in this chapter assume your files are stored in the default locations, or that you change to the directory where these files are stored before running the application. When writing your macros, always use the complete path and filename when specifying the names of files you want to open or save. You'll learn more about opening files later in this chapter.

New Record Entry

The Mail Merge Helper and Data Form are certainly convenient but they do not provide any means of checking the data entered. For example, suppose that your office policy allows only three credit levels—$500, $1000, and $1500. When you enter the credit amount in the Data Form, there is nothing to prevent you from accidentally typing 15000 instead of 1500.

S O L U T I O N S

Automated Record Entry Macro

For greater control, create a macro, such as the one shown here to automate the addition of new records to the data source.

```
Sub MAIN

Begin Dialog UserDialog 766, 352, "Client Data Source"
     Text 46, 21, 80, 13, "Company: ", .Text1
     Text 47, 43, 67, 13, "Address:", .Text2
     Text 47, 65, 72, 13, "Location:", .Text3
     Text 78, 88, 35, 13, "City:", .Text4
     Text 423, 89, 47, 13, "State:", .Text5
     Text 562, 89, 31, 13, "Zip:", .Text6
     Text 31, 111, 87, 13, "Telephone:", .Text7
     Text 420, 212, 93, 13, "Amount Due", .text8
     Text 377, 235, 136, 13, "Last Order Amount", .Text9
     Text 392, 259, 121, 13, "Last Order Date", .Text10
     TextBox 130, 18, 263, 18, .Company
     TextBox 130, 41, 263, 18, .Address
     TextBox 130, 63, 263, 18, .Location
     TextBox 130, 86, 263, 18, .City
     TextBox 479, 86, 55, 18, .State
     TextBox 605, 86, 142, 18, .Zipcode
     TextBox 130, 108, 160, 18, .Telephone
     GroupBox 133, 132, 232, 101, ""
     Text 73, 144, 40, 13, "Title:", .Text11
     Text 33, 167, 87, 13, "First Name:", .Text12
     Text 35, 186, 87, 13, "Last Name:", .Text13
     Text 44, 208, 72, 13, "Job Title:", .Text14
```

```
      TextBox 141, 141, 160, 18, .Title
      TextBox 141, 162, 160, 18, .FirstName
      TextBox 141, 183, 160, 18, .LastName
      TextBox 141, 204, 160, 18, .JobTitle
      GroupBox 92, 286, 547, 45, "Credit Limit"
      OptionGroup .Credit
          OptionButton 131, 305, 67, 16, "$500", \
              .Credit500
          OptionButton 301, 305, 76, 16, "$1000", \
              .Credit1000
          OptionButton 489, 306, 76, 16, "$1500", \
              .Credit1500
      GroupBox 525, 199, 196, 80, ""
      TextBox 536, 209, 160, 18, .Due
      TextBox 536, 231, 160, 18, .LastAmount
      TextBox 536, 254, 160, 18, .LastDate
      OKButton 654, 7, 88, 21
      CancelButton 654, 31, 88, 21
End Dialog

Dim MyBox As UserDialog
FileOpen .Name = "c:Clients.doc"
Choice = - 1
While Choice = - 1
Choice = Dialog(Mybox)
If Choice = - 1 Then
ToolsAddRecordDefault
Insert MyBox.Company
NextCell
Insert MyBox.Title
NextCell
Insert MyBox.FirstName
NextCell
Insert MyBox.LastName
NextCell
Insert MyBox.JobTitle
NextCell
Insert MyBox.Address
NextCell
Insert MyBox.Location
```

```
NextCell
Insert MyBox.City
NextCell
Insert MyBox.State
NextCell
Insert MyBox.Zipcode
NextCell
Insert MyBox.Telephone
NextCell
Select Case MyBox.Credit
     Case 0
       Insert "500"
     Case 1
       Insert "1000"
     Case 2
       Insert "1500"
End Select
NextCell
Insert MyBox.Due
NextCell
Insert MyBox.LastAmount
NextCell
Insert MyBox.LastDate
MyBox.Company = ""
MyBox.Title = ""
MyBox.FirstName = ""
MyBox.LastName = ""
MyBox.JobTitle = ""
MyBox.Address = ""
MyBox.Location = ""
MyBox.City = ""
MyBox.State = ""
MyBox.Zipcode = ""
MyBox.Telephone = ""
MyBox.Due = ""
MyBox.LastAmount = ""
MyBox.LastDate = ""
EndIf
Wend
End Sub
```

The User Input Dialog Box

The macro displays a dialog box, shown in Figure 12.1, that allows the user to enter the necessary field information. Notice that the allowable credit limits are selected in an option group, so the user cannot enter an incorrect amount.

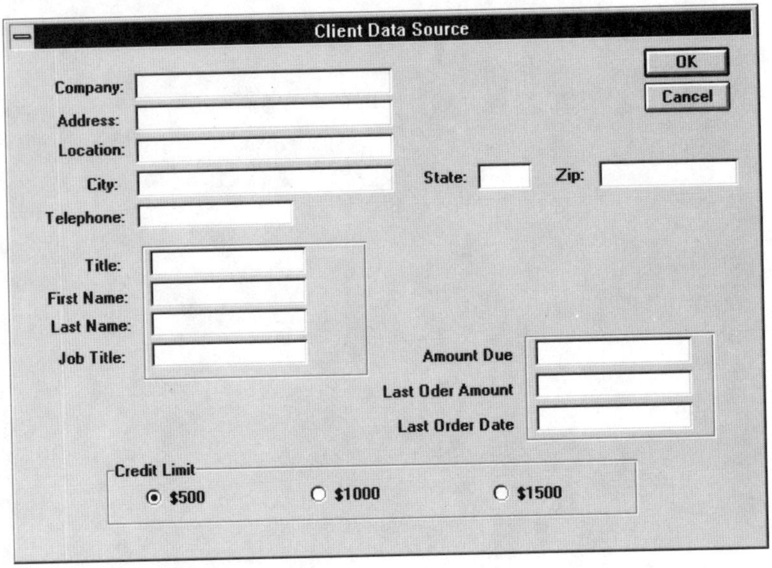

FIGURE 12.1

Client Data Source
dialog box

After defining the dialog box, the macro opens the data source with the command:

```
FileOpen .Name = "c:Clients.doc"
```

(In your own macro, be sure to use the full path and name of the data source.)

The macro then sets the value of the variable Choice to −1. The variable will be used to determine when the user has no more clients to enter, since the While loop will repeat as long as the variable is set at that value. In the loop, the macro displays the custom dialog box, where the user can enter client information.

Note   If the user selects Cancel, even after filling out the dialog box, the macro will end without adding the record to the data source. The Dialog() function will return 0 to the variable Choice. The instructions to insert the information into the table will be ignored and the loop will end because the While condition will be false.

Adding a Record to the Data Source

When the user selects OK, the Dialog() function returns −1 to the variable Choice and the If condition will be true:

```
If Choice = - 1 Then
```

The macro adds a blank record (table row) to the end of the data source with the command:

```
ToolsAddRecordDefault
```

Tip   You can use this command to add a row to the bottom of any Word table, and to add a blank line at the end of a data source in paragraph format.

Inserting Data in Fields

A series of Insert and NextCell commands then add the contents of the dialog box to the table cells. For example, after inserting the contents of Company into the first cell in the row, the macro uses the Next Cell command to move to the next cell, and then inserts the Title field.

The credit field can have one of three values, so it is inserted using a select structure:

```
Select Case MyBox.Credit
     Case 0
       Insert "500"
     Case 1
       Insert "1000"
     Case 2
       Insert "1500"
End Select
```

 **Note**

Three option buttons are contained in the Credit group. The number of the button selected (starting with 0) is returned in the identifier of the group, which is .Credit. You must refer to the identifier using the dialog box variable name, MyBox.Credit. The macro inserts the amount of credit based on which button in the group is selected. For instance, if the user selects the first option button, the value of the control, represented by MyBox.Credit, is 0. The select structure then inserts the number 500. Using option buttons and a select command ensures that only valid entries can be inserted in the cell.

Resetting the Indentifiers

After all of the values have been inserted in the record, the values of all of the identifiers, except the credit groups, are set to empty. This prevents the same values from appearing in the text boxes when the dialog box is displayed for the next record. The last selection of the credit limit is not changed, to make it easier to enter consecutive clients with the same limit, and ensure that a credit limit is actually selected.

Selecting the OK Button

If the user selects the OK button, the dialog box reappears for another record. Note that the command which displays the dialog box:

```
Choice = Dialog(Mybox)
```

is within the While loop. However, the instructions that defined the custom dialog box and dimension it are outside of the loop. Since you are only using one dialog box, you do not have to repeat these instructions each time you want to display the box on the screen. (In Chapter 13 you will learn how to use two custom dialog boxes in the same program.)

Saving the Data Source

This macro does not automatically save the data source when the macro ends. This provides the user with an opportunity to review the new records. If you want to save the file, add the command FileSave just before the end of the macro.

Record Deletion

Another common database task is deleting records. Fortunately, Word provides several ways to streamline this operation—you do not have to scroll through the table to locate the record you want to delete. You can open the data source, then use the Find Record and Delete Record buttons in the Database toolbar, or you can use the Find and Delete Buttons in the data form. (These methods, however, require user skill with these resources.)

Setting the Variable Count

The macro begins by setting the variable count to 0. The variable will be used to count and report the number of deleted records. It then sets up an error trap and opens the data source.

Entering the Search Text

The InputBox$ function inputs the name of the client to delete. Actually, as long as the Find options are not set at Whole Word, the macro will locate any occurrence of the characters entered into the variable Deleteit$.

469

S O L U T I O N S

Automated Record Deletion Macro

Use a macro such as the one shown here to automate the deletion of records. Type the macro and save it under the name Del.

```
Sub MAIN
count = 0
On Error Goto Endmacro
FileOpen .Name = "c:Clients.doc"
StartOfDocument
Deleteit$ = InputBox$("Enter the client to delete", \
        "Delete Clients")
EditFind .Find = Deleteit$
While EditFindFound() <> 0
    Erase = MsgBox("Delete this record?",\
        "Delete Clients", 3)
    If Erase = - 1 Then
        ToolsRemoveRecordDefault
        Count = Count + 1
        RepeatFind
    ElseIf Erase = 0 Then
        RepeatFind
    ElseIf Erase = 1 Then
        Goto Endmacro
    EndIf

Wend
Endmacro:
    MsgBox "You have deleted " + Str$(count)\
        + " records."
    LineDown
End Sub
```

The user can enter part of the company name, the contact's name or information in any of the fields. This way, you can delete multiple records that have some field in common.

For instance, to delete several clients in Philadelphia, enter Philadelphia as the search text. However, be sure to enter enough search text information so that Word doesn't stop too often.

 **Tip**

> Using the InputBox$() function displays a nice dialog box on the screen, but it is not the most effective way to input data. If the user accidentally presses Enter before clicking on OK, the carriage return will be considered part of the string and the client will not be located—Chandler with a carriage return will not be matched with Chandler by itself in a table cell. If this becomes a problem, use the Input command instead.

Entering the Search Criteria

The first occurrence of the text is then located with the command:

```
EditFind .Find = Deleteit$
```

The full syntax of the EditFind command is:

```
EditFind .Find = text$, .Direction = 0, .MatchCase = 0, .WholeWord
= 0, .PatternMatch = 0, .SoundsLike = 0, .Format = 0, .Wrap = 1
```

The arguments represent the various setting in the Find dialog box. If you do not specify any options other than .Find, the EditFind command will use the settings last entered in the Find dialog box during the current Word session. When you want specific find options to be used, add the necessary arguments to the EditFind command. For example, set Whole Word to 1 if you want to limit the search to whole words. In the macro, the contents of the variable Deleteit$ represents the characters to locate.

 **Note**

When .Wrap is set at 1, Word will search the entire document even if begins somewhere other that the start. When set at 2, Word will stop and display a message asking if you want to continue when it reaches the end of the document. When set at 0, the search ends at the end of the document.

Error Traps and Loops

The error trap will end the macro if the text is not located. Otherwise, a loop is begun that repeats as long as a matching record is found. This is performed with the condition:

```
While EditFindFound() <> 0
```

(When a find operation is unsuccessful, the function EditFindFound() returns a 0.)

Deleting a Record

The find command moves the insertion point and selects the matching text. A message box, with the Yes, No, and Cancel command buttons, is then displayed asking the user if they want to delete the record.

If the user selects the OK button, placing −1 in the variable Erase, the row is deleted, the counter is incremented, and the find operation is repeated:

```
If Erase = - 1 Then
    ToolsRemoveRecordDefault
    Count = Count + 1
    RepeatFind
```

Repeating the Search

The RepeatFind command repeats the previous find operation, searching for the text specified last, and using the previous find options.

 **Tip**

You can also repeat the previous find operation by using the EditFind command itself without any arguments. However, do not use either method in a macro without first including an EditFind command that specifies the search text in a .Find argument.

If the user selects the No button, the find operation is repeated without deleting the record. (Since the data source is just a Word table, you can also delete the row using the command: TableDeleteCells .ShiftCells = 2.)

Ending the Search

When the user selects Cancel, or the find operation does not locate matching text, a dialog box appears reporting the number of records deleted. When the user selects OK from the dialog box, the LineDown command ensures that any selected text is deselected and the macro ends.

S E C R E T S

Using the StartOfDocument Command

When you first open a document, the insertion point is automatically at its start. So, why do most of the macros we've been working with follow the File Open command with StartOfDocument?

When Word encounters a file open command, it determines if the document is already open. If the file is already open, Word just switches to the window in which the document appears. The insertion point will be in the same position it was when the user switched away from the window.

Changing to an already open document, rather than opening it, can create a problem. Many macros are designed to begin operating at the start of the document. The macro to delete records, for example, performs a find operation to locate matching text. If the insertion point is not at the start of the data source, some matching records may not be located.

The StartofDocument command ensures that the insertion point is at a known location, whether or not the document was actually opened by the macro, or just made active.

This feature of Word makes it even more necessary to always use the complete path and filename of files in your macro commands. When you do not specify the path of the document, just its name, Word assumes you want to open a file in the current directory. If you already opened a file with that name from a different directory, Word will not switch to its window unless you specify the path. Instead, Word will display an error message if the file is not in the current directory.

For example, suppose you open the clients.doc document, then change the directory in the File Open dialog box. If you run a macro that opens the clients database by only specifying its name, Word will look for the file in the current directory rather than switching to the open file.

For more information about opening files, see the section on Changing Windows later in this chapter.

Finding Duplicate Records

Have you ever received two of the same magazines or advertisements? Duplicated records in a database can be an expensive proposition. Before sending out a mailing, you want to make sure that no client is listed twice.

SOLUTIONS

Duplicate Deletion Macro

The macro shown here scans the data source and strikes out possible duplicate records. A duplicate record is defined as one that has the same company name as another record in the data source. The macro does not save the file, but leaves it on the screen so the user can confirm that the records are duplicates before deleting them from the file. Type the macro and save it under the name dup.wcm.

```
Sub MAIN
count = 0
FileOpen .Name = "c:Clients.doc"
StartOfDocument
TableSortAToZ
StartOfDocument
NumRows = SelInfo(15) - 2
LineDown 1
NextCell
PrevCell
Selected$ = Selection$()
For Rows = 1 To NumRows
LineDown 1
NextCell
PrevCell
Match$ = Selection$()
If Match$ = Selected$ Then
    Count = Count + 1
    TableSelectRow
    FormatFont .Strikethrough = 1
EndIf
Selected$ = Match$
Next
MsgBox "You have " + Str$(count)\
    + " possible duplicates."
LineDown
End Sub
```

Opening and Sorting the Database

The macro starts by initializing the value of count to 0, then turning off screen updating. If you want to watch as the macro operators, leave out the ScreenUpdating command.

The macro then opens the clients database, uses the StartOfDocument command to ensure that the insertion point is in the first cell, and then sorts the rows in ascending order with the commands:

```
StartOfDocument
TableSortAToZ
```

Sorting the data source when the insertion point is in the first column, places company's with the same name consecutively in the table. (Use the TableSortZToA command to sort a table in descending order.)

Determining the Extent of the Search

The macro then uses the SelInfo(15) function to determine the number of rows the macro will have to move through to complete the process. With an argument of 15, the SelInfo() function returns the total number of rows in a table.

 **N o t e**

Because the first table row contains the header record, and the second table row will be used as the basis for the first comparison, two rows are subtracted from the total to compute the number of repetitions needed to look at each client.

Finding and Deleting Records

The macro moves into the first data row, selects the contents of the first cell, and assigns the contents of the cell to the variable Selected$.

It then begins a loop to move through each of the table rows. The loop moves to the next row, selects the company name of the record and inserts it into the variable Match$.

The If command compares Selected$ (the previous record) with Match$ (the current record). If they are the same, it counts it as a possible duplicate, then strikes out the entire row.

```
If Match$ = Selected$ Then
     Count = Count + 1
     TableSelectRow
     FormatFont .Strikethrough = 1
EndIf
```

Before the subroutine is repeated for the next record, the command:

```
Selected$ = Match$
```

assigns the name of the current record to the variable Selected$. When the next record is read, its name is assigned to Match$.

This process continues until the end of the data source. When the entire data source has been searched, screen updating is turned back on, and a dialog box reports the number of possible duplicates.

Designing an Invoice Entry System

In Chapter 7, you learned how to create an invoice form as a table. Chapter 10 presented a macro for filling out the invoice. Using this system, the user still must type the client's name and address, even though it is already in the data source. You can create a more efficient system by combining macro and merge techniques.

Creating the Merge Invoice

The main document for the invoice system is shown in Figure 12.2. It is the same invoice used in Chapter 7, but converted into a main document. Merge fields have been added to automatically insert the name and address of the client.

To create the document, open the invoice, then select Tools ➤ Mail Merge ➤ Create ➤ Form Letters ➤ Active Window. Then, select Get Data ➤ Open Data Source, and select the Clients data source. Edit the main document by inserting the merge codes, and then save it under the name Mvoice.doc.

FIGURE 12.2

Merge commands
for an automated
invoice table

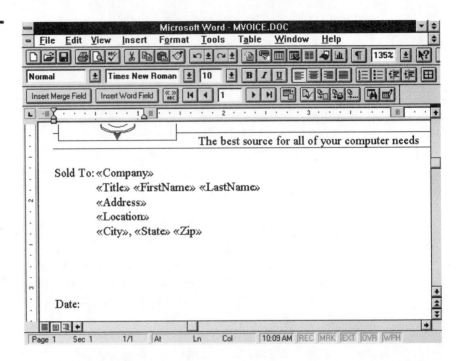

S O L U T I O N S

The Invoice Merge Macro

The macro shown in here locates the record of the client placing the order. It then begins the merge specifying a single record in the data source so the user does not have to enter the name and address information manually.

Write the macro and save it with the name Inmerge.

```
Sub MAIN
NoMerge = 0
On Error Goto Endmacro
Loop:
FileOpen .Name = "c:Clients.doc"
StartOfDocument
```

```
Mergeit$ = InputBox$("Enter the client to invoice", \
     "Invoice A Client")
EditFind .Find = Mergeit$
While EditFindFound() <> 0
     InvoiceIt = MsgBox("Invoice this record?",\
          "Invoice Clients", 3)
     If InvoiceIt = - 1 Then
          NoMerge = 1
          mergewith = SelInfo(14)
          mergewith = mergewith - 1
          client$ = Str$(mergewith)
          FileOpen .Name = "C:Mvoice.DOC"
          MailMerge .Destination = 0, .MergeRecords = 1, \
          .From = client$, .To = client$, .MailMerge
          ToolsMacro .Name = "Mergeinv", .Run
          FileClose
          Goto Donemacro
          ElseIf InvoiceIt = 0 Then
          RepeatFind
     ElseIf Invoiceit = 1 Then
          Goto Endmacro
     EndIf

Wend
Endmacro:
     MsgBox "You Did Not Complete An Invoice."
     LineDown
Donemacro:
AnotherNow = MsgBox("Another Invoice Now?", "Invoice", 4)
If AnotherNow = - 1 Then
     Goto Loop
EndIf
If NoMerge = 1 Then
     FileClose 2
EndIf
     FileClose 2
End Sub
```

Setting Up the Process

The macro starts by initializing the variable NoMerge at 0. The variable will be used to determine how many open documents will need to be closed when the macro ends. It sets up an error trap, and designates a label with the name Loop. The label will be used to repeat the entire process if the user selects to complete more than one invoice.

Selecting a Client to Invoice

The data source is opened, the user enters the name of the client to be invoiced, and the first occurrence of the string is located with the EditFind command. When a match is found, a message box appears asking if the user wants to invoice that client. If the users selects No, the EditFind is repeated looking for the next occurrence of the string.

If the user selects Cancel, the macro moves to the Endmacro label, where a message appears reporting that no invoice has been completed. Any highlighting is removed from the data source, then the user is asked if they want to try again to complete another invoice.

Preparing the Client Record

When the user selects Yes in the message box after a client record is found, the macro sets the variable NoMerge to 1, then obtains the client's record number with these commands:

```
mergewith = SelInfo(14)
mergewith = mergewith - 1
client$ = Str$(mergewith)
```

The SelInfo(14) function returns the row number of a table in which the insertion point is located. A mail merge operation, however, does not count the header row as the first data record—the first client record is in row 2.

Note The macro subtracts 1 from the actual table row number to obtain the client's record—so row 3, for example, becomes client record 2. The record number is then converted to a string to be used in the command which performs the merge.

Merging the Main Document and the Client Record

Next, the main document is opened and merged with the selected record:

```
FileOpen .Name = "C:Mvoice.DOC"
MailMerge .Destination = 0, .MergeRecords = 1, \
          .From = client$, .To = client$, .MailMerge
```

Note When the MergeRecords parameter is 1, Word will only merge the main document with the records specified in the From and To parameters. The .MailMerge parameter actually performs the merge.

Inserting the Date and Invoice Items

When the merge is complete, the invoice contains the name and address information of the selected record. The next step is to insert the date and complete the items of the invoice. This is done by running the Merge-inv macro:

```
ToolsMacro .Name = "Mergeinv", .Run
```

Ending or Repeating the Process

When that macro is complete, Word returns to InMerge. The FileClose command will close the just completed invoice.

If the user selected to cancel the File Save As dialog box, rather than selecting OK to save the document, a warning box will appear. The user can select to save the file or close it without saving. The macro then jumps to the Donemacro label. The user is asked if they want to complete another invoice. If they select Yes, the macro jumps back to the Loop label. If they select no, whatever document is on the screen is closed.

The command:

```
FileClose 2
```

closes the active document without displaying a prompt asking if the user wants to save it. The number of documents that have been opened by the macro, however, depends on whether or not the user actually completed an invoice.

If the user started the macro then selected Cancel, for example, only the clients data source will have been opened. In this case, only one file must be closed. If the user completed an invoice, the Mvoice main merge document will also be open, and two documents must be closed. The correct number of documents are closed by testing the value of the variable NoMerge:

```
If NoMerge = 1 Then
     FileClose 2
EndIf
     FileClose 2
End Sub
```

When NoMerge is set at 1, two files are closed, one within the If condition and one outside of it.

 **Tip**

Closing the correct windows can be a major headache when working with complicated macros, especially if you use the FileClose 2 command. Having one more command than necessary could accidentally close a document that you have edited and not saved. As a safeguard, use the FileSave command without an argument. This way, a prompt will appear if the macro tries to close a document that you have not yet saved. You could alternatively switch to the window you know you want to close before using the command. You'll learn more about switching windows later in this chapter.

Completing the Invoice

The MergeInv macro, shown here, completes the invoice.

```
Sub MAIN
DisableInput
StartOfDocument
ToolsOptionsView .FieldCodes = 0
EditGoTo .Destination = "t"
For l = 1 To 4
     ParaUp
Next
EndOfLine
InsertDateTime .DateTimePic = "MMMM d, yyyy",\
 .InsertAsField = 0
EditGoTo .Destination = "t"
LineDown
x = 1
Input "Enter Item Number", A$
While A$ <> "" And X < 17
Insert A$
NextCell
Input "Enter the description", A$
Insert A$
NextCell
Input "Enter the quantity", A$
Insert A$
```

```
NextCell
Input "Enter the cost", A$
Insert A$
NextCell
NextCell
x = x + 1
If X < 17 Then Input "Enter the item number ", A$
Wend
Complete:
EditSelectAll
UpdateFields
LineDown
ToolsOptionsView .FieldCodes = 0
PrintNow = MsgBox("Print the Invoice Now?",\
 "Invoice", 3)
If PrintNow = - 1 Then FilePrint
On Error Goto GetName
GetName:

    Dim FS As FileSaveAs
    NameIt = Dialog(FS)
    If NameIt = - 1 Then
        FileSaveAs FS
    EndIf

EndMacro:
End Sub
```

The macro uses many of the same commands as the Invoice macro shown in Chapter 10. If you entered the macro in that chapter, edit it as shown here. Create a new macro called MergeInv, then edit the Invoice macro to display it on the screen. Select and copy the entire macro, then paste it to the MergeInv macro window. Don't forget to delete the duplicate Sub Main and End Sub commands.

Inserting the Date

When this macro is run, the invoice form has already been opened and merged with the client record. The macro turns off the display of field codes, then moves to the proper line to insert the date.

One way to move to the date line is to go to the start of the document then perform the correct number of LineDown commands. This will not work in the merge document, however. The number of lines between the top of the page and the date will vary based on whether or not the address contained any empty fields. The invoice for a client without a second address line in the location field, for instance, will have one less line before the date than a client with a location.

The solution it to move to the table, then go up to the date line. The distance from the table to the date will not change from client to client. The command:

```
EditGoTo .Destination = "t"
```

places the insertion point in the first cell of the table. The For loop then moves up four lines, then to the end of the line containing the Date prompt:

```
For l = 1 To 4
    ParaUp
Next
EndOfLine
```

Accepting the Order Information

The date is inserted, then the insertion point moves to the first item line in the table and the macro accepts the order information. When the invoice is complete, the formulas are updated and the user is asked if they want to print the invoice.

 **Note**

The invoicing macro in Chapter 10 used InputBox$() and FileSaveAs commands to name and save the document. The technique, however, can lead to several problems.

Saving the Invoice

When you save a document with a command such as:

```
FileSaveAs .Name = InName$
```

Word will overwrite an existing file with the name you entered. It will not display a warning box asking if you actually want to replace the file. In addition, you can easily enter an invalid file name—a file name that is too long, or uses invalid characters—resulting in an error condition when Word attempts to save the file.

You can set up an If condition to test the length of the file name to ensure it is eight characters or less, but you cannot trap an invalid filename error.

As a solution, this macro dimensions a dialog record for the FileSaveAs dialog box, then displays the box with the Dialog() function:

```
Dim FS As FileSaveAs
NameIt = Dialog(FS)
```

When the user selects OK, the command is performed using the name and options selected in the dialog box:

```
If NameIt = - 1 Then
     FileSaveAs FS
EndIf
```

 **Note** If the user selects Cancel, and thus does not save the invoice, the warning message will be displayed when the FileClose command is encountered in the InMerge macro.

Working with Separate Data Sources

Sometimes, you might want to create a subset of a data source—a separate file containing selected records. You can do this easily by opening a separate window, then copying the header record and selected data records to it. You can then merge a main document to the newly created data source.

S O L U T I O N S

Separate Data Source Macro

Here is a modified section of the InMerge macro that creates a separate data source with one selected client record.

```
FileOpen .Name = "c:Clients.doc"
CWindow = Window()
TableSelectRow
EditCopy
FileNewDefault
HeadWin = Window()
EditPaste
WindowList CWindow
StartOfDocument
Mergeit$ = InputBox$("Enter the client to invoice",\
     "Invoice A Client")
EditFind .Find = Mergeit$
While EditFindFound() <> 0
     InvoiceIt = MsgBox("Invoice this record?",\
      "Invoice Clients", 3)
     If InvoiceIt = - 1 Then
     TableSelectRow
     EditCopy
     WindowList HeadWin
     EditPaste
     FileSaveAs .Name = "c:\Temp.DOC"
     FileClose
     WindowList CWindow
     FileClose
     FileOpen .Name = "C:Mvoice.DOC"
     MailMergeOpenDataSource .Name = /
     "c:Temp.DOC "
     MailMergeToDoc
```

Inserting the Header into a New Window

The Window() command returns the number that would appear next to the clients.doc document in the Window menu. The header record is then copied, a new document opened, and the header inserted into the new window with the commands.

The number of the new window is stored in the HeadWin variable, then the macro returns to the clients data source using the WindowList command. The syntax is:

```
WindowList number
```

Copying the Record to the Window

The macro then locates the client record to be merged, and copies the record to the window containing the header record. When Word pastes the record, it will be inserted as the second table row.

Merging the Main Document

The data source is then saved, and both data sources are closed. The main document is opened, and then merged with the temporary data source containing the single record:

```
FileOpen .Name = "C:Mvoice.DOC"
MailMergeOpenDataSource .Name = "c:Temp.DOC "
MailMergeToDoc
```

 **Note**

The MailMergeOpenDataSource links the displayed main document with a data source. It is your responsibility, however, to ensure that the data source contains the fields used in the main document. If you use the command when a normal document is displayed, the document will be converted to a main document.

Changing Windows

The Window() function is a convenient way to keep track of windows, but it has a major drawback. Word places documents in the Window menu in alphabetical order. If you use the function to store a window number in a variable, then open another document, the window numbers may change. For example, a document originally opened into window 1, may later be listed in some other window.

In the invoicing macro shown in this chapter, we first opened a file called Clients.doc, then started a new document whose title begins with the word Document. The order of the two files will remain unchanged, so their window numbers will not change. If you are writing a macro that is not so well planned, however, using the WindowList command can lead to disastrous results.

There are, fortunately, several alternate methods. If all of the windows you want to use contained named documents, use the File Open command. Word will change to the window rather than opening the file again.

S O L U T I O N S

Document Name Search Macro

Another alternative is to create a macro to search all of the open windows to determine if the file is already open. If the file is open, the macro should change to its window, otherwise it should open the file. The macro shown here does just that by using the FileNameFromWindow$() function to return the name of the document in a window.

```
Dim Shared numwin
Sub MAIN
finddoc$ = InputBox$("Enter the file path and name", \
    "Open File")
REM Filename match with uppercase only!
REM So change the name to all uppercase
finddoc$ = UCase$(finddoc$)
numwin = CountWindows()
```

```
it = FindWindow(finddoc$)
If it > numwin Then
    FileOpen .Name = finddoc$
    Else
    WindowList it
    EndIf
End Sub

Function FindWindow(docfind$)
Foundit = numwin + 1
x = 1
While x <= numwin
    docname$ = FileNameFromWindow$(x)
    If docname$ = docfind$ Then
        Foundit = x
        x = numwin + 1
        Else
        x = x + 1
    EndIf
Wend
FindWindow = Foundit
End Function
```

Opening a Document by Window Number

A user-defined function returns the number of the window containing the open document. When the number is larger then the count of open windows, it means that the document is not yet opened—the macro opens the document using the File Open command. When the number is within the range of open windows, it uses the WindowList command to change to the window.

 **Note**

The File Open command cannot open a window that contains an unnamed document. When the document has not yet been saved, the window name is Document1, or Document2, and so on. The command: File Open .Name = "Document2" will result in an error condition.

Returning a Window's Title

The FileNameFromWindow$() function will return an empty string if it is used with a window containing an unnamed document. To return the window's title—whatever appears next to the words Microsoft Word in the title bar, including titles such as Document1—use this command:

```
WindowName$(window-number)
```

Returning the Full Path and Name

However, the WindowName$() function will only return the file name of a named document, not its path. So to be safe, use a macro like this one that returns the full path and name of all open files, and the title of windows containing unnamed documents:

```
Sub MAIN
numwin = CountWindows()
For x = 1 To numwin
    WindowList X
    If FileName$()=FromWindow$(x) = "" Then
        Insert WindowName$(x)
    Else
    Insert FileNameFromWindow$(x)
    EndIf
    InsertPara
Next
End Sub
```

Saving a Window's Title after It's Open

There are several alternatives if you are creating a macro that opens a new window, and you must later switch to it. One method is to use the FileName$() function to save the title of the window after you open it:

```
WTitle$=FileName$()
```

The function returns the path and name of the document, or the title of an unnamed document, in the active window. When you need to switch back to the window, switch to each open window and check for a matching title:

```
numwin = CountWindows()
x = 1
Loop:
    WindowList X
    If FileName$() <> Wtitle$ And X <= numwin Then
        X = X + 1
        Goto Loop
    EndIf
End Sub
```

Saving a Window's Contents to Give It a Name

Another method is to first save the contents of the newly opened window so it has a file name:

```
FileSaveAs .Name="C:\winword\temp.doc"
```

Then, use the FileOpen command when you need to return to the window:

```
FileOpen .Name="C:\winword\temp.doc"
```

Merging Selected Records

If you want to merge the main document with a specific record, you can use the View Merged Data button, or specify the number in the From and To options of the Mail Merge dialog box. In many cases, however, you may want to merge the main document with records based on the content of selected fields.

Displaying the Filter Options Dialog Box

For example, you may want to send collection letters to all clients who owe you over a certain amount, or a thank you letter to those who have purchased in the last several weeks. To select records for a merge, choose Query Options from the Mail Merge dialog box, or from Mail Merge Helper, then click on the Filter Records tab to display the dialog box shown in Figure 12.3.

FIGURE 12.3

Filter Records tab of the Query Options dialog box

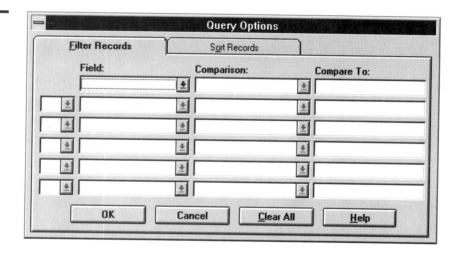

Each of the six rows in the dialog box represent a condition that you can use to select records.

 **Note**

Setting filter options to select records does not change the actual data source. It only tells Word which records to use for the merge operation.

Using the Field List

In the first row of the dialog box, pull down the Field list and select one of the data source fields that you want to use as a condition. For instance, if you want to send letters to clients based on the amount of their credit, select the Credit field.

Choosing an Operator

Next, pull down the Comparison list and select the operator that you want to use for the condition. The options are:

Equal To

Not Equal To

Less Than

Greater Than

Less Than

Less Than or Equal

Greater Than or Equal

Is Blank

Is Not Blank

Entering a Value

Then, enter the value you want to use for the condition in the Compare To box. For instance, to send letters to all clients with a $1500 credit limit, fill out the first row of the dialog box like this:

FIELD	COMPARISON	COMPARE TO
Credit	Equal To	1500

Setting AND or OR Conditions

Use the other rows in the dialog box to add additional conditions. Pull down the first box in the row and select either AND or OR. Use an AND condition when you want a record to meet more than one condition. For example, to send letters to clients in California who owe more than $500, set the dialog box like this:

	FIELD	COMPARISON	COMPARE TO
	State	Equal To	CA
And	Due	Greater Than	500

Use the Or condition to sort records that meet one criteria or another, but not necessarily both.

 **Tip**   Word will save the most recent Query settings with the main document. If you do not want to use the filter for other merges, display the Filter Records dialog box and click on the Clear All button before saving the main document.

Sorting Your Records

For some applications, you may also want to sort the records in your data source before merging them with the form file. Here are some reasons for sorting records:

◆ You are planning a mass mailing. You can take advantage of lower postage rates by printing mailing labels sorted by zip code.

◆ Your cash flow is slowing down. You can print a report of clients sorted by the amount they owe, and then contact those at the top of the list.

Sorting while Merging

To sort the records at the time of a merge, choose Query Options from the Mail Merge dialog box, or from Mail Merge Helper, then click on the Sort Records tab to display the dialog box shown in Figure 12.4.

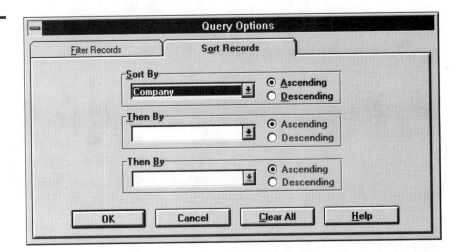

FIGURE 12.4

Sort Records tab of the Query Options dialog box

Select up to three fields, and either an ascending or descending order for each, to use for the sort. When you select OK, Word will sort the records using the field in the Sort By box as the primary key, and the Then By fields as the second and third keys.

For example, if you select to sort by the state, then by city, and then by amount due, all of the clients will first be grouped by the state. Within each state group, the clients will be in order of their city name. Within each city, they will be in order of the amount due.

Click on the Merge button to merge the main document with the sorted records.

 **Note**

The records in the data source will be sorted even if you select Cancel from the Mail Merge dialog box and do not perform the merge. Sorting the records actually changes their order in the data source table. When you use the Query Options to sort the records, you cannot undo the sort using the Edit ➤ Undo option, or the Undo button in the toolbar. If you want to sort the records temporarily for a specific merge operation, save the data source table before sorting.

Sorting without Merging

You can also sort the database table as it is displayed on the screen, separate from a merge operation. To quickly sort the records when the data source table is displayed, click on the Sort Ascending or Sort Descending buttons in the database toolbar.

 **Tip**

The Sort Ascending and Sort Descending buttons can sort numeric and text information. They will not sort by date, however, if the date is entered in MM/DD/YY format, such as 11/11/93. To use the keys to sort by date, enter the date in the format we've used with the clients database, YY/MM/DD.

Sorting on Multiple Keys

To sort on multiple keys or other date formats, place the insertion point in the table, then select Table ➤ Sort to display the dialog box shown in Figure 12.5.

FIGURE 12.5

Sort dialog box

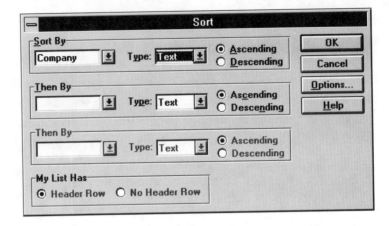

You can sort the table on up to three fields. Pull down the Sort By list and select the field to use as the primary key. In the Type box, select Text, Number, or Date. Select an ascending or a descending sort order. To sort on additional fields, select the field, type, and order in the Then By sections.

After sorting the records, either save the table or perform a merge operation.

Date Formats

When you sort by date using the Table Sort feature, Word recognizes the following formats:

Nov 16

Nov-16

Nov. 16, 1994

November 16, 1994

11/16/94

11 16 94

11-16-94

16-Nov-94

11/16/94 5:45 PM

Note
The options in the My List Has section, will be set for you, depending on whether or not the data source contains its own header record.

Sorting Non-Data Source Tables

If the table is not a data source, you can sort it by any of its columns. Options in the Sort By and Then By lists will be Column 1, Column 2, and Column 3. You will also be able to select the options in the My List Has section. Select Header Row to sort all of the rows except the column headings; select No Header Row to sort every row of the table.

Tip
If the insertion point is not in a table, the option appears as Sort Text in the Table menu. Use this option to sort lists or paragraphs.

Interactive Sorting and Selection

If you want users to sort or select without teaching them how to use the sort or query dialog boxes, create your own macro. The macro command for setting query options is MailMergeQueryOptions.

Interactive Sorting

The general syntax of the command to sort records is

```
MailMergeQueryOptions .SQLStatement = "SELECT * FROM C:CLIENTS.DOC
ORDER BY FIELD-NAME1, FIELD-NAME2, FIELD-NAME3"
```

An ascending sort is used for default. To sort the clients database by company in descending order, then by last name, and then by the job title, use the command:

```
MailMergeQueryOptions .SQLStatement = "SELECT * FROM C:CLIENTS.DOC
ORDER BY Company DESC, LastName, JobTitle"
```

The DESC notation tells Word to sort the preceding field in descending order.

S O L U T I O N S

Sorting and Merge Macro

The macro shown here streamlines the sort process by using a custom dialog box. It sorts the Clients data source and performs a merge using the main document displayed in the active window. Create it and save it under the name Sort. The macro creates the dialog box shown here.

```
┌─────────────────────────────────────┐
│ ▬           Client Sorting           │
│                                       │
│   Select up to three fields to        │
│   sort by for this merge operation    │
│                                       │
│   ☐ Company          ┌────────┐       │
│   ☐ First Name       │   OK   │       │
│   ☐ Last Name        └────────┘       │
│   ☐ Job Title        ┌────────┐       │
│   ☐ City             │ Cancel │       │
│   ☐ State            └────────┘       │
│   ☐ Zipcode                           │
│   ☐ Credit                            │
│   ☐ Amount Due                        │
│   ☐ Last Order Amount                 │
│   ☐ Last Order Date                   │
│                                       │
└─────────────────────────────────────┘
```

```
Sub MAIN
Begin Dialog UserDialog 334, 294, "Client Sorting"
OKButton 216, 59, 88, 21
     CancelButton 216, 83, 88, 21
     CheckBox 64, 59, 111, 16, "Company", .Company
     CheckBox 64, 76, 111, 16, "First Name", .FirstName
     CheckBox 64, 93, 111, 16, "Last Name", .LastName
     CheckBox 64, 110, 111, 16, "Job Title", .JobTitle
     CheckBox 64, 127, 111, 16, "City", .City
     CheckBox 64, 144, 111, 16, "State", .State
     CheckBox 64, 161, 111, 16, "Zipcode", .Zip
     CheckBox 64, 178, 111, 16, "Credit", .Credit
     CheckBox 64, 195, 121, 16, "Amount Due", .Due
     CheckBox 64, 212, 171, 16, "Last Order Amount", \
          .LastAmount
     CheckBox 64, 229, 151, 16, "Last Order Date",\
          .LastDate
     Text 56, 17, 203, 13, "Select up to three fields to", \
          .Text1
Text 56, 36, 236, 13, "sort by for this merge operation",
/.Text2
End Dialog
Dim Mine As UserDialog
Choice = Dialog(Mine)
If Choice = - 1 Then

Total = Mine.Company + Mine.FirstName + Mine.LastName +
Mine.JobTitle + Mine.City + Mine.State + Mine.Zip +
Mine.Credit + Mine.Due + Mine.LastAmount + Mine.LastDate

If Total > 3 Then Goto TooMany
If Total = 0 Then
     SString$ = ""
Else
     SString$ = "ORDER BY "

If Mine.Company = 1 Then SString$ = SString$ + " Company,"
If Mine.FirstName = 1 Then SString$ = SString$ + \
     " FirstNAme,"
If Mine.LastName = 1 Then SString$ = SString$ + " LastName,"
If Mine.JobTitle = 1 Then SString$ = SString$ + " JobTitle,"
```

```
If Mine.City = 1 Then SString$ = SString$ + " City,"
If Mine.State = 1 Then SString$ = SString$ + " State,"
If Mine.Zip = 1 Then SString$ = SString$ + " Zip,"
If Mine.Credit = 1 Then SString$ = SString$ + " Credit,"
If Mine.Due = 1 Then SString$ = SString$ + " Due,"
If Mine.LastAmount = 1 Then SString$ = SString$ +\
     " LastAmount,"
If Mine.LastDate = 1 Then SString$ = SString$ + " LastDate,"
x = (Len(SString$) - 1)
SString$ = Left$(SString$, X)
EndIf
MailMergeQueryOptions .SQLStatement = "SELECT * FROM C:CLI-
ENTS.DOC " + SString$
MailMerge .CheckErrors = 1, .Destination = 0, .MergeRecords =
0, .From = "", .To = "", .Suppression = 0, .MailMerge, .Mail-
Subject = "", .MailAsAttachment = 0, .MailAddress = ""
Goto EndMacro
TooMany:
MsgBox "You Selected Too Many Fields. Only 3 are allowed"
EndMacro:
EndIf
End Sub
```

Setting Up the Merge

If the user selects Cancel, the Macro ends and the merge operation is not performed. Otherwise, the macro checks the number of fields that were selected for the sort by adding the values of the checkboxes. (Remember, a selected checkbox has a value of 1, a deselected checkbox a value of 0.)

If the user selects more than three fields, the macro displays a message, then stops. If the user selects no checkboxes, the variable SString$ is set at an empty field and the merge is performed without sorting.

Selecting 1, 2, or 3 Fields

When the user selects 1, 2, or 3 fields, the macro creates a string to insert in the MailMergeQueryOptions command. It starts by assigning the string the words ORDER BY. It then uses a series of IF commands to add the names of the fields selected in the dialog box.

For example, if the user selected the Company field, the command:

```
If Mine.Company = 1 Then SString$ = SString$ + " Company,"
```

will result in the string:

```
ORDER BY Company,
```

 **Note**

Because fields must be separated by a comma, the comma is included after each field name. However, when all of the selected fields have been added, the comma after the last field name must be deleted.

The command:

```
x = (Len(SString$) - 1)
```

returns the number of characters in the string minus one.

Then the command:

```
SString$ = Left$(SString$, X)
```

returns the string without the last character, the extra comma.

The final string containing the order specification is then added to the MailMergeQuestOptions command and the merge is performed.

Interactive Selection

The syntax for selecting records from a data source is shown here:

```
MailMergeQueryOptions .SQLStatement = "SELECT * FROM C:CLIENTS.DOC
WHERE ((Company = 'Computer') And (Title = 'President')) Or ((City
= 'Margate'))"
```

(Notice that matching text is enclosed in single quotes because double quote marks are used to surround the entire Select string.)

SOLUTIONS

Sorting and Selection Macro

Creating a macro to both select and sort records would be quite long, since you can select on up to six fields. The macro shown here, however, illustrates how the process would be performed by allowing the user to choose one select field and one sort field from six of the fields in the clients data source. The macro displays the dialog box shown here.

```
Select and Sort

Select A Field
● Credit Limit
○ Amount Due
○ Amount of Last Order
○ Last Order Date
○ State
○ Zipcode

Operator
● =
○ <>
○ <
○ >
○ <=
○ >=

Compare With:
[                    ]

☐ Merge All          [ OK ]
☐ No Sort            [ Cancel ]

Sort By
● Credit Limit
○ Amount Due
○ Amount of Last Order
○ Last Order Date
○ State
○ Zipcode

1. In the Select A Field box, choose a field to
   select records.
2. Choose an Operator to use for the
   comparison.
3. Enter the text or number to compare the
   field to.
4. Select a sort  field.
```

```
Sub MAIN
Begin Dialog UserDialog 654, 276, "Select and Sort"
GroupBox 24, 8, 204, 120, "Group Box"
GroupBox 24, 8, 204, 120, "Select A Field"
OptionGroup .SelectGroup
OptionButton 34, 20, 113, 16, "Credit Limit",\
     .SelectCredit
OptionButton 34, 37, 121, 16, "Amount Due", .SelectDue
```

```
OptionButton 34, 54, 189, 16, "Amount of Last Order", /
    .SelectLastAmount
OptionButton 34, 71, 149, 16, "Last Order Date",\
      .SelectDate
OptionButton 34, 88, 69, 16, "State", .SelectState
OptionButton 34, 105, 91, 16, "Zipcode", .SelectZip
GroupBox 27, 144, 204, 120, "Sort By"
    OptionGroup .SortGroup
    OptionButton 37, 156, 113, 16, "Credit Limit", \
        .SortCredit
    OptionButton 37, 173, 121, 16, "Amount Due",\
        .SortDue
    OptionButton 37, 190, 189, 16, "Amount of Last Order",\
        .SortLastAmount
    OptionButton 37, 207, 149, 16, "Last Order Date", \
        .SortDate
    OptionButton 37, 224, 69, 16, "State", .SortState
    OptionButton 37, 241, 91, 16, "Zipcode", .SortZip
    GroupBox 275, 16, 78, 121, "Operator"
    OptionGroup .Operator
    OptionButton 285, 30, 39, 16, "=", .Equal
    OptionButton 285, 47, 48, 16, "<>", .NotEqual
    OptionButton 285, 64, 39, 16, "<", .LessThan
    OptionButton 285, 81, 39, 16, ">", .GreaterThan
    OptionButton 285, 98, 48, 16, "<=", .LessOrEqual
    OptionButton 285, 115, 48, 16, ">=", .GreaterOrEqual
    Text 422, 21, 112, 13, "Compare With:", .Text1
    Text 422, 40, 35, 13, "Text", .Text2
    TextBox 422, 37, 160, 18, .CompareText
    OKButton 534, 79, 88, 21
    CancelButton 536, 107, 88, 21
    GroupBox 275, 147, 368, 108, ""
    Text 285, 159, 35, 13, "Text", .Text13
    Text 280, 238, 165, 13, "4. Select a sort field.", \
        .Text14
    Text 280, 159, 345, 13, "1. In the Select A Field box,
choose a field to", .Text6
    Text 300, 172, 113, 13, "select records.", .Text7
```

```
    Text 280, 186, 279, 13, "2. Choose an Operator to use
for the", .Text8
    Text 300, 198, 92, 13, "comparison.", .Text9
    Text 280, 210, 323, 13, "3. Enter the text or number to
compare the", .Text11
    Text 300, 223, 59, 13, "field to.", .Text12
    CheckBox 383, 81, 100, 16, "Merge All", .MergeAll
    CheckBox 383, 98, 87, 16, "No Sort", .NoSort
End Dialog

Dim Mine As UserDialog
Choice = Dialog(Mine)
If Choice = 0 Then Goto EndMacro
If Mine.MergeAll = 1 Then
    SelString$ = ""
    Goto TrySort
EndIf
If Mine.CompareText = "" Then Goto MustCompare
If Mine.SelectGroup = 0 Then SString$ = "Credit"
If Mine.SelectGroup = 1 Then SString$ = "Due"
If Mine.SelectGroup = 2 Then SString$ = "LastAmount"
If Mine.SelectGroup = 3 Then SString$ = "LastDate"
If Mine.SelectGroup = 4 Then SString$ = "State"
If Mine.SelectGroup = 5 Then SString$ = "Zip"
If Mine.Operator = 0 Then OString$ = " = "
If Mine.Operator = 1 Then OString$ = " <> "
If Mine.Operator = 2 Then OString$ = " < "
If Mine.Operator = 3 Then OString$ = " > "
If Mine.Operator = 4 Then OString$ = " <= "
If Mine.Operator = 5 Then OString$ = " >= "
SelString$ = "Where ((" + SString$ + OString$ + "'" +
Mine.CompareText + "' ))"

TrySort:
If Mine.NoSort = 1 Then
    SortString$ = ""
    Goto MergeIt
EndIf
```

```
If Mine.SortGroup = 0 Then SrtString$ = "Credit"
If Mine.SortGroup = 1 Then SrtString$ = "Due"
If Mine.SortGroup = 2 Then SrtString$ = "LastAmount"
If Mine.SortGroup = 3 Then SrtString$ = "LastDate"
If Mine.SortGroup = 4 Then SrtString$ = "State"
If Mine.SortGroup = 5 Then SrtString$ = "Zip"
SortString$ = "ORDER BY " + SrtString$
MergeIt:
MailMergeQueryOptions .SQLStatement = "SELECT * FROM C:CLI-
ENTS.DOC " + SelString$ + SortString$
MailMerge .CheckErrors = 1, .Destination = 0, .MergeRecords =
0, .From = "", .To = "", .Suppression = 0, .MailMerge, .Mail-
Subject = "", .MailAsAttachment = 0, .MailAddress = ""

Goto EndMacro
MustCompare:
     MsgBox "Sorry. You must enter comparison text or number."
EndMacro:
End Sub
```

Setting Up the Sort

When the user selects OK in the dialog box, the macro first checks if the user clicked on the check box labeled Merge All. This indicates that the user does not want to select specific records. The macro sets the string SelString$ to null, then jumps to the TrySort routine.

Determining Selection Criteria

If the user did not select the Merge All box, the macro checks the text in the CompareText text box. This should contain a value that will be used for the comparison when selecting records. If the user did not enter a comparison string, the macro jumps to the MustCompare label, displays a message box, then ends.

Otherwise, a series of If commands determine which field was chosen for the selection condition, assigning the field name to SString$. Another series of If commands assign the selected comparison operator to Ostring$.

The selection criteria is then concatenated into the proper syntax for the MailMergeQueryOptions command:

```
SelString$ = "Where ((" + SString$ + OString$ + "'" + Mine.Com-
pareText + "' ))"
```

 **Note**

> For example, suppose the user clicked on the Credit and < option buttons, and entered 500 in the text box. The resulting select string will be: Where ((Credit<'500'))

The No Sort Button

The macro then checks if the user clicked on the No Sort button, indicating that the data source should be used in its current record order. If the box is selected, the macro assigns a null value to the variable Sort-String$, then it jumps to the label MergeIt to perform the merge.

If the user did not click on the No Sort box, the macro determines which field was selected for sorting, then concatenates the sort string:

```
SortString$ = "ORDER BY " + SrtString$
```

Specifying Query Options

The select and sort strings are then used to specify the query options:

```
MailMergeQueryOptions .SQLStatement = "SELECT * FROM C:CLIENTS.DOC
WHERE " + SelString$ + SortString$
```

Note that when you type the complete query statement yourself, it must be surrounded in quotation marks:

```
"SELECT * FROM C:CLIENTS.DOC WHERE ((Company = 'Computer') ORDER BY
City"
```

**Note** | The quote marks indicate the start and end of a string literal. When you concatenate a string literal with string variables, the quotation marks only surround the literal, as in the MailMergeQueryOptions command used in the macro.

Enhancing Select, Sort, and Merge Macros

Depending on how much time you want to spend writing your macros, there are a number of enhancements you can make to macros that select, sort, and merge records.

Clearing and Resetting Specifications

For example, to clear all filter and sort specifications from a main document, use the command:

```
MailMergeQueryOptions .SQLStatement = "SELECT * FROM C:CLIENTS.DOC"
```

Add the command to the end of a macro that selects or sorts records to reset the Query dialog box. Otherwise, the same criteria will be applied to the next merge you perform with the main document, even if you do not select Query Options.

To reset all settings in the Mail Merge dialog box, use the command:

```
MailMerge .CheckErrors = 1, .Destination = 0, .MergeRecords = 0,
.From = "", .To = "", .Suppression = 0, .MailSubject = "",
.MailAsAttachment = 0, .MailAddress = ""
```

**Note** | Do not include the .MailMerge parameter. Without the parameter, Word changes the settings in the box without actually performing the merge.

Opening and Merging Main Documents

The macros shown in this chapter merge the main document that is already displayed on the screen. You must open the main document before running the macro. As an alternative, you can input the name of the main document, like this:

```
main$ = InputBox$("Enter the main document name", "merge")
FileOpen .Name = main$
```

When you perform the merge, Word will display an error message if the data source named in the MailMergeQueryOptions command is not the one linked to the main document. To prevent this from occurring, check to ensure that the displayed main document is linked with the specified data source, like this:

```
If MailMergeDataSource$(0) <> "C:CLIENTS.DOC" Then
MsgBox("Error! Invalid main document","Merge",0)
Stop
EndIf
```

In this case, the macro will stop if the main document is not linked with the clients data source.

If the main document is linked to the wrong data source, you can change the link using the MailMergeOpenDataSource command, as in:

```
If MailMergeDataSource$(0) <> "C:CLIENTS.DOC" Then
MailMergeOpenDataSource .Name = "C:CLIENTS.DOC"
```

Returning Data Source Information

The MailMergeDataSource$() function returns information about the data source. Type 0 returns the path and name of the data source, type 1 returns the path and name of the header. Type 2 returns a text value indicating the source of the data:

0	from a Word data source or file converter
1	from Microsoft Access using Dynamic Data Exchange (DDE)
2	Microsoft Excel using DDE

0	from a Word data source or file converter
3	Microsoft Query using DDE
4	through an Open Database Connectivity driver

Type 3 returns a similar value indicating the source of the header. Type 4 returns a connecting string used when merging with external data sources, and type 5 returns the SQL query statement used to select and sort records.

Other Merge Commands

Table 12.1 lists other merge commands. Refer to later chapters, or to Word's on line help system, for additional information.

TABLE 12.1: Other mail merge macro commands

COMMAND	ACTION
CountMergeFields()	Returns the number of merge fields in the header record
GetMergeField$()	Returns the value in a merge field
InsertMergeField	Inserts a merge field in a main document
MailMergeCheck	Checks the main document for errors
MailMergeCreateDataSource	Creates a data source with an optional header record
MailMergeCreateHeaderSource	Creates a header record
MailMergeDataForm	Displays the data form
MailMergeEditDataSource	Opens the data source for editing, from a main document
MailMergeEditHeaderSource	Opens the header record from a main document
MailMergeEditMainDocument	Opens the main document from a header source

TABLE 12.1: Other mail merge macro commands (continued)

COMMAND	ACTION
MailMergeFindRecord	Locates the first record that matches a specified value
MailMergeFirstRecord	When the view merged data option is active, displays the value for the first record in the data source
MailMergeFoundRecord()	Reports if the MailMergeFindRecord command was successful in locating a record
MailMergeGotoRecord	When the view merged data option is active, displays a specified record
MailMergeGotoRecord()	Returns the number of the displayed record
MailMergeHelper	Opens the mail merge helper dialog box
MailMergeInsertAsk	Inserts an ask field
MailMergeInsertFillIn	Inserts a fillin field
MailMergeInsertIf	Inserts an if field
MailMergeInsertMergeRec	Inserts a merge record # field
MailMergeInsertMergeSeq	Inserts a merge sequence # field
MailMergeInsertNext	Inserts a next record field
MailMergeInsertNextIf	Inserts a next record if field
MailMergeInsertSet	Inserts a set bookmark field
MailMergeInsertSkipIf	Inserts a skipif field
MailMergeLastRecord	When the view merged data option is active, displays the value for the last record in the data source

TABLE 12.1: Other mail merge macro commands (continued)

COMMAND	ACTION
MailMergeMainDocumentType	Makes the active window a main document of the type specified: 0 for form letters, 1 for labels, 2 for envelopes, 3 for catalog
MailMergeMainDocumentType()	Returns the type of the main document
MailMergeNextRecord	Inserts a next record field
MailMergeOpenHeaderSource	Attaches a header source to the main document
MailMergePrevRecord	When the view merged data option is active, displays the value for the previous record in the data source
MailMergeReset	Converts a main document to a normal Word document
MailMergeState()	Returns a value indicating the current setup of mail merge: Type 1 returns information about the main document, type 2 about mail merge options, type 3 the mail merge destination
MailMergeToDoc	Merges the main document to a new document
MailMergeToPrinter	Merges the main document to the printer
MailMergeViewData	Toggles the view merged data options
MailMergeViewData()	Returns the setting of the view merged data option
MergeFieldName$()	Returns the name of the field in the specified column
ToolsAddRecordDefault	Inserts a new blank record
ToolsRemoveRecordDefault	Deletes a record

PART
five

The Well-Managed Word

13
Automated Applications

14
Document Management

Automated
Applications

W ORD'S MACRO AND MERGE FUNCTIONS can be combined to create sophisticated practical applications. Rather than limit merges to
simple form letters or invoices, you can use Word to automate complete
tasks and to manage complex word processing applications. In this chapter, you will learn how to interactively assemble personalized documents
and create a complete invoicing system that even updates the client
database.

Working with Documents in Sections

The longer your document becomes, the more time it takes to open
and save, or move from the start to the bottom. To save waiting time, you
can write and edit the document in smaller sections, each a separate file,
then merge the sections when you want to print the complete document.
(You can also assemble documents using Word's Master Document feature.)

Merging Sectional Documents

To merge documents, use the IncludeText field. For example, here is a
file called REPORT:

```
{IncludeText Intro}
{IncludeText Hypoth}
{IncludeText Method}
{IncludeText Results}
{IncludeText Summary)
```

Inserting the Field

To insert the field, press Ctrl+F9 to display the field braces, then type
IncludeText and the document name. Word will assume the file extension

is .DOC. If you used any other extension, include it with the file name. You can also use the Insert ➤ Field command. If the file name includes a path, use two backslashes to indicate directories and subdirectories, as in:

```
{IncludeText c:\\Report\\Intro.doc}
```

Selecting and Updating the Fields

When you select and update the fields, the included document will be inserted at the position of the field. If the document does not appear, press Alt+F9 to toggle off the display of field codes. When you place the insertion point in the included text, the entire document will appear shaded as a field.

 **Note**

To start an included document on a new page, insert a page break before its IncludeText field code, or at the start of the document in its original file.

Page Setup and Formatting

The page setup settings of included text, such as margins and page size, are not applied to the combined document. All of the text is formatted by the page setup settings of the document containing the fields. However, paragraph, font, and other formats in the included document will be applied.

 **Tip**

Turn on the display of codes to show just field codes. This lets you work with other text without seeing the full text of the included files. To display the text of all included documents, press Alt+F9. To display only one document, select its field code and press Shift+F9.

519

Editing and Saving Updated Text

You can edit the included text while it is displayed on the screen. However, your changes are not automatically saved in the document's disk file. To update the disk file to agree with the changes on screen, place the insertion point in the included text, or in its field, and press Ctrl+Shift+F7.

Choosing Not to Save

If you do not save the changes, they will be replaced by the original contents of the file when you update the field. For example, suppose you make extensive changes to included text. You want the changes to print with this combined document, but you do not want to change the original file. If you select the field, or the entire document, and then press F9, your changes will be lost—the included text will revert back to its original content.

Locking Fields

To prevent this from happening, lock the field by selecting it and pressing Ctrl+F11. When a field is locked, its contents do not change when updated. To later unlock the field, so you can update it, select it and press Ctrl+Shift+F11.

 **Tip**

You can also unlink a field by pressing Ctrl+Shift+F9. This deletes the field code, replacing it with the actual contents of the file.

Using Bookmarks

To include just a specific portion of a document, mark it as a bookmark, then follow the file name with the bookmark name, as in:

```
{IncludeText Results summary}
```

In this case, the contents of the bookmark named summary will be included from the file RESULTS.DOC. (See Chapter 15 for more information about working with fields.)

Designing an Interactive Document Assembly System

Using macros and merge fields, you can program an interactive assembly system. This technique allows you to specify the files to be combined each time the document is assembled. The system requires a macro that actually creates the main document, complete with merge fields.

The system described here assembles a letter to a client in the clients database. It uses a main merge document to insert the inside address and salutation, and a macro to insert the IncludeText fields for boilerplate paragraphs saved in disk files.

 **Note**   In the macros in this chapter, be certain to add the correct path for all macro commands that open files, run macros, or perform merges. Only the file names are given in these macros.

The Address Form File

Start by creating a main document file that contains the field information for the letter's address and salutation. Link the form letter with the Clients data source, enter a date field code, then insert merge fields as shown in Figure 13.1. Press Enter twice after the salutation, save the document under the name address.doc, then close the document window.

FIGURE 13.1

Merge fields for the document assembly system

```
{ DATE \* MERGEFORMAT }

{ MERGEFIELD Company }
{ MERGEFIELD Address }
{ MERGEFIELD City }, { MERGEFIELD State } { MERGEFIELD Zip }

Dear { MERGEFIELD Title } { MERGEFIELD LastName }:
```

Interactive Macro Techniques

The macro to merge the client information and insert included text should look familiar to you. The macro uses several of the techniques that you learned in Chapter 12 to select a client from the data source and to merge the client's records with the main document. It also uses techniques that you learned in Chapter 10 to change directories and to create a list box of files.

This macro, however, builds on these techniques to make your application more sophisticated and error-proof. For example, unlike the macros in Chapter 10, this macro sets up an error trap if the user entered a path that does not exist. This macro also creates a combo box, rather than a list box, so the user can either select a file name from the list or type the name in a text box.

SOLUTIONS

The Include Macro

Here's the macro we'll create for our interactive document assembly system. Create the macro under the name Include.

```
Sub MAIN
OldDir$ = DefaultDir$(0)
Goto Loop
NoPath:
Err = 0
Again = MsgBox("No such path. Try Again?",\
      "Write A Client", 4)
If Again = 0 Then
      Goto StopIt
EndIf
Loop:
Input "Enter the path", Pth$
If Pth$ <> "" Then
      On Error Goto NoPath
      ChDir Pth$
```

```
Else
    Pth$ = DefaultDir$(0)
EndIf
FileFind .SearchPath = Pth$, .Name = "*.doc"
NumFiles = CountFoundFiles() - 1
If NumFiles = - 1 Then
    Again = MsgBox("No files were located. Try Again?",\
    "Write A Client", 4)
    If Again = 0 Then Goto StopIt
    Goto Loop
EndIf
Dim ComboBox1$(NumFiles)
For x = 0 To NumFiles
ComboBox1$(x) = FileNameInfo$(FoundFileName$(x + 1),3)
Next
SortArray ComboBox1$()
Begin Dialog UserDialog 428, 216, "Include Text"
    OKButton 311, 144, 88, 21
    CancelButton 311, 168, 88, 21
    ComboBox 42, 17, 223, 181, ComboBox1$(), .ComboBox1
End Dialog
On Error Goto Endmacro
StartIt:
FileOpen .Name = "c:Clients.doc"
StartOfDocument
Mergeit$ = InputBox$("Enter the client",\
    "Write A Client")
EditFind .Find = Mergeit$
If EditFindFound() = 0 Then Goto Endmacro
FindIt:
MailIt = MsgBox("This client?", "Write A Client", 3)
    If MailIt = - 1 Then
        Goto DoLetter
    ElseIf MailIt = 1 Then
        Goto EndMacro
    ElseIf MailIt = 0 Then
        RepeatFind
    EndIf
```

```
        If EditFindFound() = - 1 Then
            Goto FindIt
        Else
            Goto Endmacro
        EndIf
        EndIf
DoLetter:
mergewith = SelInfo(14)
mergewith = mergewith - 1
client$ = Str$(mergewith)
FileClose
FileOpen .Name = "C:address.DOC"
MailMerge .Destination = 0, .MergeRecords = 1, \
            .From = client$, .To = client$, .MailMerge
EndOfDocument
Dim MyFile As UserDialog
ShowIt:
ShowFile = Dialog(MyFile)
If ShowFile = 0 Then Goto UpdateIt
If ShowFile = - 1 Then
    InsertFieldChars
    Insert "Includetext" + " " + Myfile.Combobox1
    EndOfLine
    InsertPara
    Goto ShowIt
EndIf
UpdateIt:
EditSelectAll
    UpdateFields
    LineDown
    ViewFieldCodes 0
PrintNow = MsgBox("Print the letter now?",\
    "Write A Client", 4)
If PrintNow = - 1 Then FilePrint
Another = MsgBox("Another letter?", "Write A Client", 4)
If Another = 0 Then
    Goto EndMacro
    Else
    On Error Goto EndMacro
```

```
GetName:
     Dim FS As FileSaveAs
     NameIt = Dialog(FS)
     If NameIt = - 1 Then
          FileSaveAs FS
     Else
          Goto Endmacro
     EndIf
     FileClose
     FileClose 2
EndIf
Goto StartIt
Endmacro:
     LineDown
StopIt:
     ChDir OldDir$
End Sub
```

User Input and Error Traps

The Include macro saves the current document path in the variable OldDir$, then moves to a label named Loop. It skips over a section of instructions that will be performed only when the user enters a file path that does not exist.

The user is then prompted to enter the path of the included files. If the user does not enter a path, the macro assumes the files are in the current path and assigns it to the variable Pth$. If the user does enter a path, an error trap is set up and the directory is changed. The error trap:

```
On Error Goto NoPath
```

will perform the instructions jumped over earlier if the ChDir command, which changes directories, cannot be performed.

The instructions set Err at 0 so additional errors will be detected, then display a message box asking if the user wants to try entering another path. If the user selects No, the macro ends by moving to the label Stopit. Otherwise, it performs the instructions following the Loop label.

File Finding and Sorting

The path is then searched for files having the DOC extension. If no files were found, a message box appears and the user can select to enter another path or end the macro. When matching files are located, the file names are added to the combo box array and sorted in alphabetical order.

Selecting a Client

After the dialog box is defined, the data source is opened and the user can select the client to receive the letter. The row containing the client record is then merged with the address main document to insert the inside and salutation. The dialog box is then displayed, as shown in Figure 13.2.

FIGURE 13.2

The Include Text dialog box

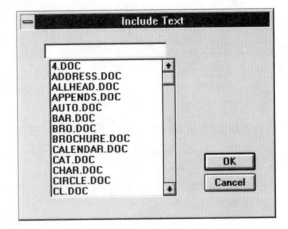

Inserting the File

When the user double-clicks on a file name, or selects it and chooses OK, or types it in the text box and chooses OK, the command InsertField-Chars inserts the field braces with the insertion point between them. The macro then enters the IncludeText field and the name of selected file, moves the insertion point out of the field braces, then inserts a carriage return to end the paragraph. The Goto command moves back to the ShowIt label, where the dialog box is displayed again so the user can select another file.

Completing and Printing the Letter

The process is repeated until the user selects Cancel from the dialog box. The document is selected, the fields are updated, then the display of field codes is turned off to display the contents of the included documents. The user can then print and save the letter, and repeat the entire process to prepare a letter to another client.

When the macro ends, the document path is returned to its previous directory.

The Boilerplate Files

Finally, create six boilerplate files that you can merge into the assembled document, as follows:

1. Enter the following paragraph, press Enter twice, save the file under the name Good, and close the window.

   ```
   You have been a valued customer and I want to personally
   thank you for your support. We are all feeling the pinch of
   these economic times, so your continued support is greatly
   appreciated.
   ```

2. Enter the following paragraph, press Enter twice, save the file under the name Overdue, and close the window.

   ```
   It has come to my attention that your account is now over-
   due. We have tried to be patient, but we are also experiencing
   cash flow problems.
   ```

3. Enter the following paragraph, press Enter twice, save the file under the name Legal, and close the window.

   ```
   Unless you pay the total amount due in 30 days, we will
   be forced to take legal action.
   ```

4. Enter the following paragraph, press Enter twice, save the file under the name Close1, and close the window.

   ```
   It has been a pleasure serving you in the past and we
   pledge to provide the best prices and service in the industry.
   ```

5. Enter the following paragraph, press Enter twice, save the file under the name Close2, and close the window.

```
        Looking forward to hearing from you regarding this matter.
```

6. Enter the following paragraph, press Enter twice, save the file under the name Close, and close the window.

```
Sincerely yours,

Alvin Aardvark
```

Using the Document Assembly System

Now let's use our system to create a customized letter.

1. Select Tools ➤ Macro, and double-click on Include. A prompt appears in the status bar asking for the path.

2. Press Enter, or type the path where you saved the boilerplate files and press Enter.

3. Type **Chandler,** then click on OK. Word will locate the record containing the name Chandler.

4. Select Yes to merge the client. The address main document is opened and merged with the client record, then the dialog box appears listing DOC files.

5. Double-click on LEGAL.DOC. The include text field is inserted and the dialog box displayed again.

6. Double-click on CLOSE2.DOC to insert it.

7. Double-click on CLOSE.DOC to insert it.

8. Select Cancel. The macro selects the document and updates the fields.

9. Select Yes or No when asked if you want to print the letter.

10. Select No when asked if you want to prepare another letter. The complete letter appears on screen.

11. Close the document without saving the letter.

Creating a Prospects and Clients Management System

By combining macros and merge files, you can design an application that performs both database management and document assembly functions at the same time.

For example, suppose that you have a database of prospective clients—companies that have requested information or applied for credit but who have not yet placed an order. You can create a system that automates the management of prospects by performing these tasks:

◆ Adds a new record to the prospects database

◆ Creates a form letter including the new client's credit limit and the name of the sales representative

To create this application, you need two new databases—one to store the address information for prospective clients, another to hold the name and telephone numbers of your sales representatives. Both databases will be used in the assembled document.

Setting Up the Databases

To create the prospect database, we only need the header record from the clients table. At first, it will not include any other records because the system will add them for you.

From Prospect to Client

When a prospect places an order, they become a client. We'll want to delete their record from the prospect data source and add it to Clients.doc. To do this efficiently, the number and size of the columns in both tables must be the same.

 **Tip**

The prospect database will include three fields that are not really needed: Due, LastAmount, and LastDate. Since a prospect has not yet placed an order, these fields will not contain any data. However, including the extra fields makes creating the databases easier, and saves time when moving the record to the clients data source.

Creating the Data Source

Unfortunately, in order to create a main document linked to the data source, the data source must contain at least one data record. So, we will temporarily use one of the client records, then delete it after we create the main document.

Follow these steps to create the data source.

1. Open Clients.Doc.
2. Select cells A1 and A2, the first cells in the first two rows.
3. Select Table ➤ Select Row to select both rows.
4. Select Edit ➤ Copy.
5. Click on the New button in the toolbar, or select File ➤ New ➤ OK.
6. Select Edit ➤ Paste Cells.
7. Select the header row that you just inserted.
8. Click on the bold button in the toolbar to turn bold off.
9. Click on the Align Left button in the toolbar.
10. Click the mouse to deselect the text.
11. Select File ➤ Save As.
12. Type **Prospect** and click on OK.

The Sales Rep Database

Next, create the database shown in Figure 13.3 to store information about your sales force. We will include only names and telephone numbers. In your own application, you can expand it to store addresses, salary, and commission information as well. Save the document under the name Reps.

FIGURE 13.3

Data source
for sales
representatives

Name	WordPhone	HomePhone
Wayne Newtown	555-1872	666-7354
Samuel Shore	555-1873	661-9836
Sarah Buchanan	555-1874	641-5661

S E C R E T S

Formatting Tips and Tricks

The ToolsAddRecordDefault, which we will later use to add a new prospect, inserts a row at the end of the data source formatted according to the previous row. If you leave the header row bold and centered, the prospect information later inserted by the macro will also appear bold and centered.

This will not affect the appearance of the prospect information in any merged documents. However, the same formats will be moved with the prospect information if it is later moved to the clients data source. To make the records in the clients table appear consistently formatted, we removed bold and centering from the prospects table.

If you want the header row bold and centered, you can leave it as it is, then manually change the format of the first prospect record.

Writing the Form Letter

The output of this system will be a letter to the prospective client. It will be addressed to them using field information from the prospect data source, but it will also include a name and telephone numbers from the reps data source.

We'll create two main documents. One will be linked with the prospect data source, the other with the reps data source. The two letters will be combined after the appropriate information is inserted by merge operations.

Creating the Main Document

Create the main document shown in Figure 13.4, linked to the prospect data source. The figure shows the field codes displayed so you can duplicate the If instructions. Save the file under the name Prolet.doc, and then close the document window.

FIGURE 13.4

Main document
for prospect letter

{ TIME \@ "MMMM d, yyyy" }

{ MERGEFIELD Title } { MERGEFIELD FirstName } { MERGEFIELD LastName }
{ MERGEFIELD JobTitle }
{ MERGEFIELD Company }
{ MERGEFIELD Address }
{ MERGEFIELD Location }
{ MERGEFIELD City }, { MERGEFIELD State } { MERGEFIELD Zip }

Dear { MERGEFIELD Title } { MERGEFIELD LastName }:
       Thank you for your interest in Aardvark Computers. We are processing your client information
now.
       { IF { MERGEFIELD Credit } <= 500 "Please contact our accounting department to arrange for a
line of credit. Until the process is complete, we will only be able to accept an order up to $ {
MERGEFIELD Credit }
" "We are pleased to provide you with a credit limit of $ { MERGEFIELD Credit }. If you would like an
additional credit line, please contact our accounting department.
" }

Next, return to the prospect data source, delete the temporary data record copied from the clients data source, then save the file. It should contain only the header record.

Now create the main document shown in Figure 13.5 and linked with the Reps data source. Save it with the name Prolet2.doc.

FIGURE 13.5

Main document
linked with
representatives

Your sales representative is { MERGEFIELD Name }. The office number is { MERGEFIELD WordPhone } and the home number is { MERGEFIELD HomePhone }. Please call your representative if you need any additional information.

{ Includetext close }

Preparing the Macros

The system requires two macros. The AddPro macro will insert new prospects into the data source. It is similar to the Add macro you created in Chapter 12 to add client records. The bulk of the work is done by the DoPro macro.

SOLUTIONS

The AddPro and DoPro Macros

You can run the AddPro macro by itself to add a new prospect without assembling the form letter. Here's how to create it:

```
Sub MAIN
Begin Dialog UserDialog 766, 352, "Prospect Data Source"
        Text 46, 21, 80, 13, "Company: ", .Text1
        Text 47, 43, 67, 13, "Address:", .Text2
        Text 47, 65, 72, 13, "Location:", .Text3
        Text 78, 88, 35, 13, "City:", .Text4
        Text 423, 89, 47, 13, "State:", .Text5
        Text 562, 89, 31, 13, "Zip:", .Text6
        Text 31, 111, 87, 13, "Telephone:", .Text7
        TextBox 130, 18, 263, 18, .Company
        TextBox 130, 41, 263, 18, .Address
        TextBox 130, 63, 263, 18, .Location
        TextBox 130, 86, 263, 18, .City
        TextBox 479, 86, 55, 18, .State
        TextBox 605, 86, 142, 18, .Zipcode
        TextBox 130, 108, 160, 18, .Telephone
        GroupBox 133, 132, 232, 101, ""
        Text 73, 144, 40, 13, "Title:", .Text11
```

```
        Text 33, 167, 87, 13, "First Name:", .Text12
        Text 35, 186, 87, 13, "Last Name:", .Text13
        Text 44, 208, 72, 13, "Job Title:", .Text14
        TextBox 141, 141, 160, 18, .Title
        TextBox 141, 162, 160, 18, .FirstName
        TextBox 141, 183, 160, 18, .LastName
        TextBox 141, 204, 160, 18, .JobTitle
        GroupBox 92, 286, 547, 45, "Credit Limit"
        OptionGroup .Credit
        OptionButton 131, 305, 67, 16, "$500", .Credit500
        OptionButton 301, 305, 76, 16, "$1000", .Credit1000
        OptionButton 489, 306, 76, 16, "$1500", .Credit1500
        OKButton 654, 7, 88, 21
        CancelButton 654, 31, 88, 21
End Dialog
FileOpen .Name = "c:prospect.doc"
Dim MyBox As UserDialog
X = Dialog(MyBox)
If X = 0 Then Goto EndMacro
ToolsAddRecordDefault
Insert MyBox.Company
NextCell
Insert MyBox.Title
NextCell
Insert MyBox.FirstName
NextCell
Insert MyBox.LastName
NextCell
Insert MyBox.JobTitle
NextCell
Insert MyBox.Address
NextCell
Insert MyBox.Location
NextCell
Insert MyBox.City
NextCell
Insert MyBox.State
NextCell
Insert MyBox.Zipcode
NextCell
```

```
Insert MyBox.Telephone
NextCell
Select Case MyBox.Credit
    Case 0
      Insert "500"
    Case 1
      Insert "1000"
    Case 2
      Insert "1500"
End Select
FileSave
EndMacro:
End Sub
```

The bulk of the work for this application is performed by the DoPro macro shown here.

```
Sub MAIN
ToolsMacro .Name = "AddPro", .Run
mergewith = SelInfo(14)
mergewith = mergewith - 1
pro$ = Str$(mergewith)
FileOpen .Name = "C:Prolet1.DOC"
MailMerge .Destination = 0, .MergeRecords = 1, \
        .From = pro$, .To = pro$, .MailMerge
FileSaveAs .Name = "Temp.Let"
FileOpen .Name = "C:Prolet1.DOC"
FileClose 2
FileOpen .Name = "c:Reps.doc"
StartOfDocument
NumRows = SelInfo(15)
Count = 0
GetRep:
    LineDown
    Count = Count + 1
    NextCell
    PrevCell
    InvoiceIt = MsgBox("Use This Rep?", \
        "Invoice Clients", 3)
    If InvoiceIt = 1 Then Stop
```

```
        If InvoiceIt = - 1 Then Goto DoRep
        If InvoiceIt = 0 Then Count = Count + 1
        If Count > NumRows Then
            StartOfDocument
            Count = 0
        EndIf
        Goto GetRep
DoRep:
    mergewith = SelInfo(14)
    mergewith = mergewith - 1
    Rep$ = Str$(mergewith)
    FileClose
    FileOpen .Name = "C:Prolet2.DOC"
    MailMerge .Destination = 0, .MergeRecords = 1, \
        .From = Rep$, .To = Rep$, .MailMerge
    EditSelectAll
    EditCopy
    FileClose 2
    FileClose 2
    FileOpen .Name = "c:Temp.Let"
    EndOfDocument
    EditPaste
    EditSelectAll
    UpdateFields
    LineDown
    ToolsOptionsView .FieldCodes = 0
GetName:
    Dim FS As FileSaveAs
    GetCurValues FS
    FS.Name = " "
    NameIt = Dialog(FS)

    If NameIt = - 1 Then
        FileSaveAs FS
    Else
        Goto Endmacro
    EndIf
FileOpen .Name = "C:prospect.doc"
FileClose
EndMacro:
End Sub
```

Running the AddPro Macro

The DoPro macro first runs the AddPro macro to insert a new prospect record. It then saves the row number of the new prospect in the variable MergeWith, opens the ProLet main document, and merges it with the record. The form document is then saved under the name Temp.let.

The FileOpen command switches back to the ProLet document, which is then closed before the Reps data source is opened. The number of rows in the data source is assigned to NumRows and the variable Count set at 0.

Selecting a Sales Rep

To enable the user to select a sales representative, we want to cycle through the rows of the data source, highlighting the name of each representative. As each is highlighted, a message box will appear asking the user if that is the rep to assign to the prospect.

 **Note** | The user must select one of the names in the data source, they cannot continue with the letter until a representative has been assigned. The GetRep label marks the start of this routine.

The routine starts with the LineDown command to move past the header record, then the variable count is incremented, indicating that we've already moved past one of the rows in the table. The cell containing the name is selected, and the message box displayed. The macro ends if the user selects Cancel. If the user selects No, the value of count is again incremented.

When the value of count is greater than the number of rows in the table, it means that the user has selected No for all of the representatives. In this case, the insertion point moves to the start of the table and the value of count is set back to zero. This is accomplished in the commands:

```
If Count > NumRows Then
        StartOfDocument
        Count = 0
EndIf
```

537

Repeating the DoRep Routine

The DoRep routine is then repeated—the insertion point moves to the next row and the message box appears. When the user selects Yes, the macro moves to the DoRep label. In this routine, the selected record is merged with the Prolet2.DOC to form the last paragraph of the letter. After the merge, the document is selected and copied, then its window and that of the Prolet2 main document are closed.

The Temp.Let document is opened and the copied text inserted at the end.

```
FileOpen .Name = "Temp.Let"
EndOfDocument
EditPaste
```

Updating the Date and Text Fields

The entire document is selected, and the date and IncludeText fields are updated. The line down command deselects the text, then the command:

```
ToolsOptionsView .FieldCodes = 0
```

ensures that contents of the fields are displayed, instead of the field codes. This is an alternative to the ViewFieldCodes 0 command.

Naming and Saving the Document

Next, the user names and saves the document. Because the active window contains the TEMP.LET document, its name will appear in the File Save As dialog box. The user could accidentally save the merged document using that name, and the document will be overwritten the next time the user runs this system. The macro clears the file name text box before the dialog box is displayed using:

```
GetCurValues FS
FS.Name = ""
```

Finally, the prospect data source is closed. Remember, the FileOpen command moves to the window already containing the opened document, so it is closed with the FileClose command.

Using the Prospect System

Let's suppose that you just heard from a prospective client. You want to add the company to the Prospect database and assemble a form letter. Here's what you do.

1. Select Tools ➤ Macro, and double-click on DoPro.

2. Type **Adam Computer Warehouse** and press Tab.

3. Now in the same way, enter the following information, pressing Tab after each field:

```
Mr
Michael
Adam
President
647 Lock Road
Philadelphia
PA
19112
676-4456
300
```

4. Click on the $500 option button in the Credit section.

5. Select OK to insert the record. The representative data source will appear, with the name of the first rep selected.

6. Select No to see the name of the next salesperson.

7. Select Yes to accept that salesperson. (The Prolet2 main document is merged, the two merged documents assembled, and the fields updated.)

Developing an Accounts Receivable System

In previous chapters, we have developed a data source of client information as well as an invoicing macro and merge file. You also have a data source of prospective clients. Let's fully automate the invoicing system to perform these functions:

◆ Determine if an order is placed by an existing client or a prospect

◆ Open the invoice and insert the address information

◆ Interactively complete and calculate the invoice

◆ Update the customer's file to contain the total and date of the order, and the total amount due

◆ Accumulate the order amount and tax in a master file for tax information

◆ If the order is placed by a prospect, move the prospect record to the clients database, then delete the record from the prospect database

S O L U T I O N S

The Receive Macro

This entire system is performed by Word using just one macro. Create the macro named Receive.

```
Sub MAIN
FileOpen .Name = "c:Clients.doc"
StartOfDocument
EndOfRow
On Error Goto EndMacro
Mergeit$ = InputBox$("Enter the client to invoice",\
    "Invoice A Client")
EditFind .Find = Mergeit$
FindClient:
If EditFindFound() = 0 Then Goto TryPro
    InvoiceIt = MsgBox("Invoice this record?", \
        "Invoice Clients", 3)
    If InvoiceIt = - 1 Then
        File = 1
        Mergethis File
        Goto Donemacro
        ElseIf InvoiceIt = 0 Then
        RepeatFind
    ElseIf Invoiceit = 1 Then
        Goto TryPro
    EndIf
```

```
Goto FindClient
TryPro:
FileOpen .Name = "c:prospect.doc"
StartOfDocument
EndOfRow
EditFind .Find = Mergeit$
FindPro:
If EditFindFound() = 0 Then Goto EndMacro
    InvoiceIt = MsgBox("Invoice this record?", \
        "Invoice Clients", 3)
    If InvoiceIt = - 1 Then
        File = 2
        Mergethis File
        Goto Donemacro
        ElseIf InvoiceIt = 0 Then
        RepeatFind
    ElseIf Invoiceit = 1 Then
        Goto Endmacro
    EndIf
Goto FindPro
Donemacro:
    EndOfDocument
    LineUp 1
    NextCell
    NextCell
    NextCell
    Total$ = Selection$()
    LineUp 1
    PrevCell
    NextCell
    Tax$ = Selection$()
If File = 1 Then
    FileOpen .Name = "C:clients.doc"
    PrepClient Total$
Else
    PrepareTable
    PrepClient Total$
EndIf
```

```
FileOpen .Name = "C:mvoice.doc"
FileClose 2
If File = 2 Then
     DelProRec
EndIf
TotDue$ = GetPrivateProfileString$("Accounts", \
          "TotalDue", "Account.ini")
     OldDue = Val(TotDue$)
     NewDue = OldDue + Val(Total$)

TotTax$ = GetPrivateProfileString$("Accounts", \
     "TotalTax", "Account.ini")
     OldTax = Val(TotTax$)
     NewTax = OldTax + Val(Tax$)

SetPrivateProfileString "Accounts", "TotalDue", \
     LTrim$(Str$(NewDue)), "Account.ini"
SetPrivateProfileString "Accounts", "TotalTax", \
     LTrim$(Str$(NewTax)), "Account.ini"
Goto Complete
EndMacro:
     MsgBox "You Did Not Complete An Invoice."
     LineDown
Complete:
     StartOfDocument
End Sub


Sub Mergethis(DSource)
mergewith = SelInfo(14)
mergewith = mergewith - 1
client$ = Str$(mergewith)
FileOpen .Name = "C:Mvoice.DOC"
If DSource = 1 Then
MailMergeOpenDataSource .Name = "C:clients.doc"
Else
MailMergeOpenDataSource .Name = "C:prospect.doc"
EndIf
MailMerge .Destination = 0, .MergeRecords = 1, \
     .From = client$, .To = client$, .MailMerge
ToolsMacro .Name = "Mergeinv", .Run
```

```
End Sub
Sub PrepClient(Tot$)
EndOfRow
PrevCell
PrevCell
OldDue = Val(Selection$())
Due = Olddue + Val(Tot$)
Insert LTrim$(Str$(Due))
NextCell
Insert Tot$
NextCell
InsertDateTime .DateTimePic = "yy/mm/dd", \
    .InsertAsField = 0
FileSave
FileClose
End Sub


Sub PrepareTable
FileOpen .Name = "C:prospect.doc"
TableSelectRow
EditCopy
FileOpen .Name = "C:clients.doc"
EndOfDocument
EditPaste
LineUp
End Sub


Sub DelProRec
FileOpen .Name = "C:prospect.doc"
TableSelectRow
EditCut
FileSave
FileClose
End Sub
```

Locating the Company

The macro begins by locating the client or prospect placing the order. It opens the clients data source, and then moves the insertion point to the end of the header row:

```
StartofDocument
EndOfRow
```

If the insertion point remained at the start of the row, a find command could stop at matching text that may be part of a field name.

Setting the Error Trap

The On Error Goto EndMacro command sets up an error trap, then the message box appears requesting the name of the company being invoiced. The error trap will end the macro if the user selects cancel instead of entering the client's name.

Searching for Matching Text

The clients data source is then opened and searched for matching text. If matching text is not located, the macro jumps to the TryPro label, which opens and searches for a matching record in the prospect data source:

```
If EditFindFound() = 0 Then Goto TryPro
```

 **Note**

The TryPro routine is also performed if the user selects No to all of the matching records in the clients data source. Notice that the FindClient and FindPro routines are almost identical.

Selecting a Record

When a matching record is found, a message box appears. If the user selects not to merge the highlighted record, the search is repeated and the macro jumps back to the start of the loop—Find Client or FindPro depending on the data source being searched.

If the user selects a record, the variable Flag is set to indicate the data source—1 if the record is from the clients data source, 2 if the record is from the prospects data source. This variable is used in several locations in the macro to determine what operations to complete.

Completing the Invoice

The macro then calls the Mergethis subroutine, sending the value of File as an argument. When the Mergethis subroutine is completed, the macro moves to the Donemacro label. We'll look at the Mergethis and DoneMacro routines soon. When the MergeThis subroutine is called, the value of the variable File is passed to Dsource. The routine first determines the row containing the selected record.

Note It doesn't matter which data source the record is from because the functions just return the row in which the insertion point is located, and then subtract one.

Linking the Invoice with the Data Source

Next, the macro opens the invoice form containing the merge fields MVOICE.DOC. When the invoice form was created, it was linked with the clients database.

Note The source of the record, however, could now be in the prospect data source. The invoice can use either data source because they have identical header records, and thus the same field names.

545

Using the Dsource variable, the macro links the invoice with the data source containing the selected company:

```
If DSource = 1 Then
MailMergeOpenDataSource .Name = "C:clients.doc"
Else
MailMergeOpenDataSource .Name = "C:prospect.doc"
EndIf
```

The MailMergeOpenDataSource command links the main document with the data source shown in the same argument. If you then save the main document, the link will be recorded with the file. This macro will later close the main document without saving it, so the main argument will remain linked with the clients data source.

The main form and the data source are then merged, and the Merge-Inv macro runs. This is the same macro described in Chapter 12 for selecting and merging a client record. This macro inputs the order items and calculates the invoice formulas. When the macro is complete, control passes back to the MergeThis subroutine, which ends and returns control to the Main routine in the macro.

Recording Invoice Totals

When the invoice is complete and calculated, the macro moves to the DoneMacro label. The insertion point is moved to the end of the document, then selects the cell containing the invoice total:

```
EndOfDocument
LineUp 1
NextCell
NextCell
NextCell
```

The contents of the cells is stored for use later

```
Total$ = Selection$()
```

then the insertion point is moved to the cell containing the sales tax.

 **N o t e**

> The LineUp 1 command moves the insertion point to the cell but does not select its contents. The contents are selected by moving the insertion point to the previous cell and then back again. The contents of the cell are stored for later use: Tax$ = Selection$()

Updating the Client Record

If the order was placed by an existing client, the record must be updated to reflect the current invoice. When the value of File is 1, the clients data source is opened, then the macro calls the PrepClient subroutine, passing it the value of the total invoice.

 **N o t e**

> Even though the macro uses the FileOpen command, the client data source is actually already open with the insertion point in the record of the selected client.

The command switches to the window containing the data source then moves to the cell containing the Due field:

```
EndOfRow
PrevCell
PrevCell
```

Current Amount Due

The current amount due is assigned to the numeric variable OldDue:

```
OldDue = Val(Selection$())
```

The Selection$() function returns the characters selected in the cell, then the Val function converts the text to a number. The total of the current invoice is then added to the previous amount due.

```
Due = Olddue + Val(Tot$)
```

The new total amount due is converted to a trimmed string and inserted back into the cell, replacing the current contents.

 **Note** Selecting the cell selects its contents. When the new value is inserted, it automatically deletes any selected text. If you turned off the Typing Replaces Selection option in the Tools ➤ Options ➤ Edit menu, the new amount will be inserted in addition to the current contents. If you are not certain of this setting, use the ToolsOptionsEdit .ReplaceSelection = 1 command before inserting the new value.

The insertion point is moved to the next cell, which contains the amount of the most recent invoice. The amount of the current invoice is inserted into the cell, replacing the previous value.

Inserting the Date

The insertion point then moves to the last cell in the table and the date is inserted. The argument:

```
.DateTimePic = "yy/mm/dd"
```

formats the date in the same format used to enter the original client records. The clients data source is saved and closed.

Updating the Prospect Record

A prospect who places an order becomes a client, and their record must be transferred to the clients data source.

When the value of the variable File is not 1, the macro passes control to the PrepareTable subroutine. In this routine, the macro changes to the window containing the prospect data sources, and then selects and copies the company's record:

```
FileOpen .Name = "C:prospect.doc"
TableSelectRow
EditCopy
```

 **Note** It would be convenient to delete the prospect record at this time. However, if the prospect were the only one in the data source, the file would then contain only a header record, and an error would be generated when the macro returns to the Mvoice document. We'll delete the record later.

The macro then opens the clients data source, moves the insertion point to the end of the table, and pastes the record from the clipboard. Finally, a LineUp command moves the insertion point into the clients record so it can be updated. When the subroutine ends, the macro returns to the main routine. The PreClient subroutine is called and the amount due, total, and date added to the new client's record.

The main invoice document is closed. If the invoice was placed by a prospect, the DelProRec subroutine is called, which deletes the prospect's record, and then saves and closes the data source.

Saving Values in INI Files

One goal of the macro is to create a file storing the total of all sales and the amount of sales tax collected. The values can be used to prepare sales reports and financial statements.

This macro stores the results in a private setting file. A private setting file is a file with the INI extension in the Windows directory. All INI files, such as WIN.INI and WINWORD6.INI have the same structure:

```
[Section]
Option1=setting
Option2=setting
```

For example, the INI file created with this macro will look like this:

```
[Accounts]
TotalDue=5.3
TotalTax=0.3
```

We will save both values in the Accounts section. However, the file can contain as many sections as you need, as in:

```
[Accounts]
TotalDue=5.3
TotalTax=0.3

[Clients]
NumberOfClients=100
MinimumCredit=500
MaximumCredit=1500

[Orders]
TotalOrders=2361
LastOrderNumber=9874
Largestorder=1870.76
```

Adding Information to a Setting File

The command to add information to a setting file is

```
SetPrivateProfileString Section$, Option$, Setting$, FileName$
```

In the previous example, [Accounts] is a section name, TotalDue is an option name, and 5.3 is a setting.

S E C R E T S

Section and Option Tips and Tricks

If the file, section, or option does not yet exist, Word will create it when it encounters the command. So, the first SetPrivateProfileString command that you use will create the setting file and add the first section and option. Later commands will add options to it or change settings. Unless you specify otherwise, Word saves the file in the Windows directory and adds the INI extension.

You can add sections and options as you need them. Word will automatically move other sections down to make room for additional options in previous sections. New options are added after those already in the section.

Section and option strings are not case sensitive. Word treats Accounts and ACCOUNTS as the same section, and TotalDue and TOTALDUE as the same option. Section and option names appear in the setting file in the format they are first written.

You can use the same option name in more than one section. Word will treat them as separate entities.

Retrieving Information from a Setting File

The command to retrieve a value from a setting file uses this syntax:

```
var$ = GetPrivateProfileString$(Sectiion$, Option$, \
    FileName$)
```

If the file, section, or option does not exist, the function returns an empty string rather than an error condition.

 **Note**

All settings are treated as strings. To write a number to the file, use the STR$() and Ltrim$() functions. To use a setting as a number, retrieve it, then convert it to a number using the VAL() function. When a positive number is converted to a string, Word adds a blank space before the number. The LTrim$() function removes any blank spaces on the left side of the string. (The RTrim$() function removes blank spaces from the end of a string.)

The Receive macro must first retrieve the current setting file values so it can add the invoice total and tax to the previous totals. The total of all previous sales is retrieved with the command:

```
TotDue$ = GetPrivateProfileString$("Accounts", "TotalDue", \
    "Account.ini")
```

Calculating the New Total

The new total amount of sales is calculated with the commands:

```
OldDue = Val(TotDue$)
NewDue = OldDue + Val(Total$)
```

These convert the previous amount to a numeric value, then add to it the value of the current invoice total.

The previous total of tax collected is retrieved and updated with the commands:

```
TotTax$ = GetPrivateProfileString$("Accounts", "TotalTax", \
    "Account.ini")
OldTax = Val(TotTax$)
NewTax = OldTax + Val(Tax$)
```

Writing the New Values to the Setting File

Then, the new values are written to the setting file:

```
SetPrivateProfileString "Accounts", "TotalDue",\
    LTrim$(Str$(NewDue)), "Account.ini"
SetPrivateProfileString "Accounts", "TotalTax",\
    LTrim$(Str$(NewTax)), "Account.ini"
```

Using the Set Private Profile String

You can also use the SetPrivateProfileString() function. It uses the same syntax as the statement but returns a value of −1 if the operation was successful, 0 if unsuccessful, as in:

```
DidIt=SetPrivateProfileString("Accounts", "TotalDue",\
    LTrim$(Str$(NewDue)), "Account.ini")
```

```
If DidIt = 0 Then
    MsgBox("Warning. The setting file was not changed",\
        "Error")
EndIf
```

Preparing an Invoice

When an order is placed, run the Receive macro. Enter the client name when prompted, then click on OK. If the client is located in the client database, a dialog box will appear asking if you want to use the displayed record. When you select Yes, the record is merged with the invoice and it appears for you to complete.

If the macro does not find a match in the client database, the prospect database is opened and a match sought. When you locate the prospect which placed the order, the record is merged and the invoice form appears for you to complete.

Automating Reports and Database Maintenance

Suppose that you have a number of database reports that you frequently print, and several macros that perform database maintenance. You can automate the entire database management process so it can be performed by someone not familiar with the merge and macro process.

Instead of specifying the name of a main document in a mail merge command, use a string variable. Allow the user to select a document name from a dialog box, then set the variable to equal the selected name. Use the same technique if you want to merge a main document with more than one data source.

Tip

You may have to modify some macros that are run by the menu. For example, the macro you wrote in Chapter 12 to delete records specifies the clients data source. To use the macro as a generic routine, delete the FileOpen command. You can then open the appropriate file in the menu program, and run the delete macro. It will delete records from whatever data source is displayed.

S O L U T I O N S

The MainMenu Macro

Here's a macro designed to display two custom dialog boxes that allow unfamiliar users to perform database maintenance, and create and print reports.

```
Sub MAIN
Begin Dialog UserDialog 644, 262, "Client Management"
GroupBox 43, 33, 204, 108, "Group Box"
OptionGroup .Source
    OptionButton 53, 45, 80, 16, "Clients", .OptionButton1
    OptionButton 53, 62, 104, 16, "Prospects", .OptionButton2
GroupBox 268, 33, 204, 108, "Group Box"
OptionGroup .Main
    OptionButton 278, 45, 99, 16, "Client List", .OptionButton6
    OptionButton 278, 62, 104, 16, "Phone List", .OptionButton7

OKButton 513, 8, 88, 21
CancelButton 513, 32, 88, 21
PushButton 513, 56, 88, 21, "Add", .Push1
PushButton 513, 80, 88, 21, "Del", .Push2
PushButton 513, 104, 88, 21, "Dup", .Push3
```

554

```
PushButton 513, 128, 88, 21, "Invoice", .Push4
PushButton 513, 152, 88, 21, "Client Let", .Push5

End Dialog

Dim Mine As UserDialog
Choice = Dialog(Mine)
If Choice = 0 Then Goto EndMacro
If Mine.Source = 0 Then
     Data$ = "clients.doc"
Else
     Data$ = "prospect.doc"
EndIf
If Choice = 1 Then
     If Data$ = "clients.doc" Then
          ToolsMacro .Name = "Add", .Run
     Else
          ToolsMacro .Name = "DoPro", .Run
     EndIf
EndIf
If Choice = 2 Then
     FileOpen .Name = Data$
     ToolsMacro .Name = "Del", .Run
EndIf

If Choice = 3 Then
     FileOpen .Name = Data$
     ToolsMacro .Name = "Dups", .Run
EndIf
If Choice = 4 Then
     ToolsMacro .Name = "Receive", .Run
EndIf
If Choice = 5 Then
     ToolsMacro .Name = "Include", .Run
EndIf

If Choice = - 1 Then
```

```
        If Mine.Main = 0 Then
            FileOpen .Name = "Clist.doc"


        Else
            FileOpen .Name = "Phone.doc"


        EndIf
MainDoc$ = FileName$()
Begin Dialog UserDialog 320, 144, "Merge Destination"
     OKButton 212, 109, 88, 21
     OptionGroup .Dest
OptionButton 69, 37, 169, 16, "To New Document", .OptionButton1
OptionButton 69, 54, 104, 16, "To Printer", .OptionButton3
End Dialog

Dim Mine As UserDialog
Loop2:
Choice = Dialog(Mine)
If Mine.Dest = 0 Then
     Mergeto = 0
Else
     Mergeto = 1
EndIf
MailMergeOpenDataSource .Name = Data$
If MailMergeMainDocumentType() = 3 And Mergeto = 1 Then
     MsgBox "Sorry. You can merge a catalog to the printer",
"Error"
     Goto Loop2


EndIf
MailMerge .CheckErrors = 1, .Destination = Mergeto,
.MergeRecords = 0, .From = "", .To = "", .Suppression = 0,
.MailMerge, .MailSubject = "", .MailAsAttachment = 0,
.MailAddress = ""
EndIf
FileOpen .Name = MainDoc$

FileClose 2
EndMacro:
End Sub
```

Defining the Dialog Box

This macro uses two custom dialog boxes, but only one is defined at any time. If you want to repeat the menu until the user selects cancel, you must redefine the dialog box with each repetition of the loop. See Chapter 14 for an example of this process. The MainMenu macro displays the dialog box shown in Figure 13.6.

The data source to use for a selected operation is chosen in an option group, then assigned to a variable based on the value of the option group identifier:

```
If Mine.Source = 0 Then
     Data$ = "clients.doc"
Else
     Data$ = "prospect.doc"
EndIf
```

(The string variable Data$ will be used in the Macro to link the selected data source with a main document.)

FIGURE 13.6

Client
Management
dialog box

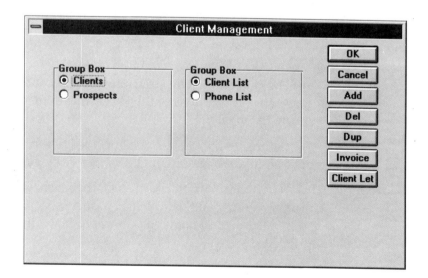

Using the Client Management Dialog Box

The selected command button determines which operation will be performed. For example, if the user clicks on the Add button, the macro selects to run either the Add macro (shown in Chapter 12 to add new clients) or the DoPro macro, shown in this Chapter to add a prospect and assemble a form letter:

```
If Choice = 1 Then
    If Data$ = "clients.doc" Then
        ToolsMacro .Name = "Add", .Run
    Else
        ToolsMacro .Name = "DoPro", .Run
    EndIf
EndIf
```

The Delete option assumes that you removed the FileOpen command from the Del macro (shown in Chapter 12). When the user clicks on Delete, the macro first opens the selected data file then runs the macro to delete either a client or prospect:

```
If Choice = 2 Then
    FileOpen .Name = Data$
    ToolsMacro .Name = "Del", .Run
EndIf
```

The Dup option will strikeout suspected duplicate records. It also assumes that you've deleted the FileOpen command from the Dup macro shown in Chapter 12.

Command buttons are also included to run the Receive macro to complete an invoice, and the Include macro to assemble a client letter.

When the OK button is clicked, the macro will merge the selected main document and data source. It does so by checking the value of the .Main identifier and opening the appropriate file:

```
If Choice = - 1 Then
    If Mine.Main = 0 Then
        FileOpen .Name = "Clist.doc"
    Else
        FileOpen .Name = "Phone.doc"
    EndIf
```

The name of the main document is stored in a variable so it can later be closed:

```
MainDoc$ = FileName$()
```

The Merge Destination Dialog Box

A second dialog box is then displayed asking the user to select the merge destination, as shown in Figure 13.7. The option selected is assigned to the MergeTo variable, then the selected data source is linked to the displayed main document:

```
MailMergeOpenDataSource .Name = Data$
```

Catalog main documents cannot be merged directly to the printer. If the user selected a catalog main document and printer destination, the macro displays a dialog box, then returns to the destination selection:

```
If MailMergeMainDocumentType() = 3 And Mergeto = 1 Then
MsgBox "Sorry. You can merge a catalog to the printer", \
     "Error"
Goto Loop2
EndIf
```

FIGURE 13.7

Merge Destination
dialog box

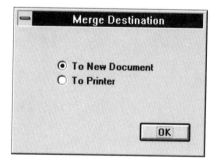

Merging Documents

When a valid destination is selected, the documents are merged. The macro then switches to the window containing the main document and closes it without saving:

```
FileOpen .Name = MainDoc$
FileClose 2
```

Retaining the Original Link

If the MailMergeOpenDataSource command names a data source not already associated with the main document, the link is actually changed. As long as you do not save the main document, however, the original link will remain intact when the document is later opened and merged.

If you are creating a macro that saves a data source, you may want to ensure that the original link is retained. Immediately after the MailMerge-OpenDataSource command, add the instruction:

```
Orig$ = MailMergeDataSource$(0)
```

This assigns the name of the linked data source to the variable Orig$. Then before saving the main document, add the command:

```
MailMergeOpenDataSource .Name = Orig$
```

CHAPTER
14

Document
Management

I F YOU'VE EVER SPENT TIME searching for a disk file, then you know the importance of proper document management. This chapter shows you how to establish a document management system using macros to standardize procedures for naming, saving, and retaining documents. You will also learn to use the File Find command, and about other ways to access files on your disk.

Working with Document Variables

A document variable is a string variable that Word stores invisibly with your document file. You can only access document variables using a macro, and only when the document is open. Three functions and one command are used to work with document variables.

The SetDocumentVar command adds a variable to the document. The syntax is:

```
SetDocumentVar Var$, Value$
```

For example, the command:

```
SetDocumentVar Client$, "Sam Watson"
```

creates a document variable named Client$ with the contents Sam Watson.

The GetDocumentVar$() function returns the value stored in a variable. So the instruction:

```
name$ = GetDocumentVar$(Client$)
```

returns the string stored in the variable Client$.

 **Tip**   The names of document variables will not appear in any built-in Word menu or dialog box. If you forget their names, however, you can still access them using macro commands.

Obtaining Variable Names

Each document variable is numbered, starting with 1. To obtain the variable name associated with a number, use the function GetDocumentVarName$().

For example, the command:

```
varname$ = GetDocumentVarName$(1)
```

returns the name of the first document variable. Once you know the name, you access the contents using the GetDocumentVar$() function.

Returning the Number of Document Variables

The function CountDocumentVars() returns the number of document variables stored with the document. Use it in an instruction such as:

```
numvars = CountDocumentVars()
```

Accessing Variables with Arrays

Because the variables are numbered, the easiest way to access them is to load an array. This macro, for example, fills an array with whatever document variables exist:

```
NumDocs = CountDocumentVars()
If NumDocs > 0 Then
Dim DocVarArray$(NumDocs - 1)
For Doc = 1 To NumDocs
    VarName$ = GetDocumentVarName$(Doc)
    DocVarArray$(Doc - 1) = GetDocumentVar$(VarName$)
Next
EndIf
```

Note
The number of document variables is assigned to NumDocs. If the document has any variable, the DocvarArray$ array is dimensioned. With each repetition of the For loop, the name of a document variable is assigned to VarName$, then the contents of the variable are assigned to another array element.

In the next section, we'll use document variables to create a revision tracking system.

Keeping Track of Revisions

One of the benefits of word processing is that you can open and edit a document as many times as you want. You may find it useful to keep track of your editing sessions using document variables.

Making Notes in Variables

In each variable, record the date you worked on the document, how much time you spent on it, and a brief note reporting what section of the document you worked on, the progress you made, or just a reminder to yourself for the next session.

Filling the Array with Variables

The For loop fills the array with the values of the document variables. If the document does not contain any variables, the array is dimensioned at 0.

The dialog box is defined to contain a list box, a text box, and the OK and Cancel button. Notice that the text box is defined first so it has focus when the dialog box is displayed. The list box is only for reference.

If the user selects Cancel in the box, the macro ends. However, if the user selects OK, the contents of the text box are assigned to the variable Revtext$.

Revision System Macro

The macro shown here creates a revision system. Each time you run the macro, it displays a list box of any current revision entries, and a text box for entering another note, as shown here. Each entry shows the date the revision was made, the total editing time devoted to the document, and a note entered in the text box. To obtain the time spent on a specific revision, just subtract its time from the time in the preceding revision.

```
                  Revision System
                  Revision  Log

10/22/94 Total Time: 23 Introduction to report
10/24/94 Total Time: 64 Introduction and section 1
10/27/94 Total Time: 132 Section 1 and 2
11/10/94 Total Time: 152 Section 2 and 3
11/16/94 Total Time: 206 Section 4




Enter Revision Note:


                         OK        Cancel
```

```
Sub MAIN
NumDocs = CountDocumentVars()
If NumDocs > 0 Then
Dim RevisionList$(NumDocs - 1)
For DOC = 1 To NumDocs
    VarName$ = GetDocumentVarName$(Doc)
    RevisionList$(Doc - 1) = GetDocumentVar$(VarName$)
```

```
Next
Else
Dim RevisionList$(0)
EndIf
Begin Dialog UserDialog 484, 256, "Revision System"
    TextBox 12, 189, 447, 18, .Revision
    Text 182, 7, 105, 13, "Revision Log", .Text1
    ListBox 10, 25, 463, 142, RevisionList$(), .ListBox1
    Text 10, 173, 159, 13, "Enter Revision Note:", .Text2
    OKButton 250, 220, 88, 21
    CancelButton 360, 220, 88, 21
End Dialog
Dim Rev As UserDialog
Choice = Dialog(Rev)
If Choice = 0 Then Goto EndMacro
RevText$ = Rev.Revision
FileSummaryInfo .Update
Dim DocStat As DocumentStatistics
GetCurValues DocStat
pos = InStr(DocStat.Time, " ") - 1
End$ = Left$(DocStat.Time, pos)
RName$ = "Edit#" + LTrim$(Str$(CountDocumentVars() + 1))
Text$ = Date$() + " Total Time: " + End$ + " " + RevText$
SetDocumentVar RName$, Text$
EndMacro:
End Sub
```

Updating the Summary Information

The command:

```
FileSummaryInfo .Update
```

updates the summary information for the document to ensure that the total editing time and other summary information fields contain the most recent information. The Document Statistics box is dimensioned, and its values assigned to the record variable DocStat.

The Document Statistics Box

The Document Statistics box contains a field called Time that contains the total editing time devoted to the document. It is stored in the format:

```
65 Minutes
```

with the number of minutes, a space, then the word Minutes.

For our system, we need to use just the number of minutes without the word "Minutes". The command:

```
pos = InStr(DocStat.Time, " ") - 1
```

locates the position of the space in the Time field, then subtracts 1 to obtain the number of characters in the time.

 **Note**

> If 65 minutes have been devoted to the document, the space character would be in the third position in the field, so the number of minutes occupies two characters. If 165 minutes had been devoted, the space would be in the fourth position and the number occupies three characters.

The number of minutes in the field is assigned to the variable End$ in the command:

```
End$ = Left$(DocStat.Time, pos)
```

The Left$() function returns a number of characters on the left side of a string.

 **Note**

> Each revision variable will start with the text Edit#, followed by the number of the variable—the first will be named Edit#1, the second will be named Edit#2, and so on.

567

Determining the Name of the Next Variable

The macro must determine the name of the next document variable to be inserted. This is accomplished in the command:

```
Name$ = "Edit#" + LTrim$(Str$(CountDocumentVars()+1))
```

Let's break this line down into its parts:

- The function CountDocumentVars() returns the number of variables in the document. When there are no variables, the value will be 0.

- One is added to the number of existing variables to obtain the number for the variable to be added.

- The Str$() function converts the variable number to a string value.

- The LTrim$() function removes any blank spaces on the left side of the string.

- The variable's number is concatenated to the end of Edit#.

Creating the String Value

Next, the macro creates the string value to be assigned to the variable, using the current date, the total number of minutes spent editing the document, and the text entered into the text box.

Storing the Variable in the Document

Finally, the variable is stored in the document:

```
SetDocumentVar RName$, Text$
```

Reviewing Revision Notes

When you want to review the revision notes in a document, use this macro to display a list box of the document variables:

```
Sub MAIN
NumDocs = CountDocumentVars()
If NumDocs > 0 Then
Dim RevisionList$(NumDocs - 1)
```

568

```
For DOC = 1 To NumDocs
    VarName$ = GetDocumentVarName$(Doc)
    RevisionList$(Doc - 1) = GetDocumentVar$(VarName$)
Next
Else
Dim RevisionList$(0)
EndIf
Begin Dialog UserDialog 484, 256, "Revision System"
    Text 182, 7, 105, 13, "Revision Log", .Text1
    ListBox 10, 25, 463, 142, RevisionList$(), .ListBox1
    OKButton 250, 220, 88, 21
End Dialog
Dim Rev As UserDialog
Choice = Dialog(Rev)
EndMacro:
End Sub
```

S E C R E T S

Summary and Statistics Tips and Tricks

The Summary Information and Document Statistics dialog boxes provide useful information about the active document. Select File ➤ Summary Info to display a dialog box listing the document name and directory, as well as text boxes for entering the title, subject, author, key words, and comments.

Summary Info	
File Name: CLIENTS.DOC	OK
Directory: C:\WINWORD	Cancel
Title: Clients data source	Statistics...
Subject: Database management	
Author: Secrets and Solutions	Help
Keywords: datasource, DBMS, clients	
Comments: Use this document for database management	

If you click on the Statistics button in the dialog box, Word displays detailed information about the document. Before displaying the box, however, Word updates the statistics, counting the number of pages, words, characters, and lines.

The FileSummaryInfo command accesses the values in the Summary and Statistics dialog boxes: All of the fields except Edit-Time are read-only, which means you can obtain their values from the dialog box but not change them through a macro.

The Document Statistics command accesses settings in the Statistics dialog box..All of the fields are read-only.

Listing Revision Notes

To create a document listing the document revision notes, use this macro:

```
Sub MAIN
Fname$ = FileName$()
NumDocs = CountDocumentVars()
If NumDocs > 0 Then
Dim RevisionList$(NumDocs - 1)
For DOC = 1 To NumDocs
     VarName$ = GetDocumentVarName$(Doc)
     RevisionList$(Doc - 1) = GetDocumentVar$(VarName$)
Next
Else
Dim RevisionList$(0)
Revisionlist$(0) = "No Revision Notes"
EndIf
FileNewDefault
CenterPara
Insert "Revision List for " + Fname$
InsertPara
InsertPara
LeftPara
For Doc = 1 To NumDocs
     Insert RevisionList$(Doc - 1)
     InsertPara
```

```
Next
EndMacro:
End Sub
```

The macro fills the RevisionList$ array with the revision notes, opens a new window, then inserts each of the notes.

Developing a File Management System

There are two keys to locating a document—knowing its name and its location on the disk. So to develop a document management system, you must design a method for naming files and placing them in an appropriate directory.

Creating Separate Directories

Start by creating a separate directory for each category of your files. For instance, suppose you have three executives in your office—Chesin, Nestle, and Smith. Create a directory named Chesin to store Mrs Chesin's files, a directory called Nestle to hold Mr. Nestle's documents, and a directory named Smith for Miss Smith's files. You would then know immediately, for example, that a document written by Mrs. Smith would be in the Smith directory.

A Numbering System

However, how do you name files? Some organizations number each file consecutively but keyed to the creator by initials. Mrs. Smith's files are SM101, SM102, and so forth, while Mr. Chesin's files are CH101 and CH102. Unfortunately, this naming convention does not make a file easy to identify. Few persons could remember the contents of SM101 while working on SM305.

A Naming System

The alternative to a numbering system is to use distinctive file names. However, as your inventory of documents grows, it becomes difficult to think of a unique and meaningful name for each document. After a while, file names become as cryptic as numbers.

571

An Indexed System

As a solution, we will develop a practical document management system using file numbers and a special index to help locate documents. The system will:

◆ Create a separate directory for each executive

◆ Maintain a file containing the last numbers used for each executive

◆ Automatically assign the next consecutive number to a file

◆ Save the file in the proper directory

◆ Maintain an index of files in each directory

◆ Allow you select and open a file in a specific directory from a list box of file names

◆ Allow you to select and open a file in a specific directory from a list box of document descriptions

◆ Enable you to delete a file and its entry in the index

Building the INI File

The document management system will store information in a private setting file. The Totals section will contain the total number of executives in the system as well as the number of indexed documents for each executive:

```
[Totals]
Execs=3
EXEC1=3
EXEC2=2
EXEC3=2
```

The executives in the system are associated with the option names EXEC1, EXEC2, and so on.

**Note**

In this instance, for example, the setting file shows that there are three executives using the system. The first executive has three documents, the other executives have two documents each.

The names section will list the last names of the executives:

```
[Names]
EXEC1=Chesin
EXEC2=Nestle
EXEC3=Smith
```

The LastNumbers section stores the last file number used for each executive:

```
[LastNumbers]
Chesin=3
Nestle=2
Smith=2
```

Chesin's last document was named CH3, Nestle's was named NE2, and Smith's named SM2.

Finally, there will be a separate section for each executive. The section will list the number of each document and a brief description:

```
[Chesin]
1=Budget report
2=Annual report memo
3=Letter to Jones

[Nestle]
1=Request for hearing
2=Deposition notice

[Smith]
1=Siravo will
2=Loan request
```

 **Tip**

While this system uses one file for the entire process, the information for each executive could be stored in a separate private setting file, either in the Windows directory or in the executive's document directory.

Using One Large File

Using one large file makes the macro a little easier to write and makes backing up the system easier. As long as you backup the one file on a floppy disk or tape, you'll maintain a catalog of all documents. However, as the file gets larger, the processing time will increase. It will take Word longer to access the file and make changes to it.

 **Warning**

If you accidentally erase or crash the file, all of your information will be lost, although you could write a macro that recreated the file from the information on the executive directories.

Using Individual Files

Using individual files will speed the processing somewhat. Also, if one file is damaged, you will still have the other executive files intact. Your macro will need some extra commands, however, to determine the name of the INI file based on the executive's name.

Preparing for the System

When an executive is added to the document system, a number of actions must be performed. A directory must be created to store the executive's files, and the related sections in the INI file must be updated. Most of the sections could be updated when the first file for the executive is saved. The only section that must be updated immediately is the total count of executives in the totals section.

S O L U T I O N S

The AddExec Macro

The macro shown here, however, updates the totals, lastnumbers and names sections. Create the macro with the name AddExec.

```
Sub MAIN
Goto GetExec
ErrorExec:
Err = 0
MsgBox "That executive is already listed", "Error"
GetExec:
    On Error Goto EndMacro
ExecName$ = InputBox$("Enter last name", \
    "Add an executive")
ExecName$ = Left$(ExecName$, 8)

    On Error Goto ErrorExec
    MkDir "C:\" + ExecName$
NumOfExecs$ = GetPrivateProfileString$("Totals", \
    "Execs", "Document.ini")
NumExec = Val(NumOfExecs$) + 1
ExecString$ = "EXEC" + LTrim$(Str$(NumExec))
SetPrivateProfileString "Totals", "Execs", \
    LTrim$(Str$(NumExec)), "Document.ini"
SetPrivateProfileString "Totals", ExecString$, \
    "0", "Document.ini"
SetPrivateProfileString "Names", ExecString$, \
    ExecName$, "Document.ini"
SetPrivateProfileString "LastNumbers", ExecName$, \
    "0", "Document.ini"
EndMacro:
End Sub
```

Error Traps and Entered Names

The macro starts by jumping around an error routine that will be performed if the user enters the name of an executive already entered into the system. The first On Error Goto command sets a trap in the event the user selects Cancel in response to the InputBox$ prompt. The InputBox$() function inputs the executive's last name, and the name is shortened to no more than eight characters—the maximum length allowed for directory names.

The next On Error statement sets a trap to determine if the executive has already been entered. The MkDir command will attempt to create a directory in the C drive using the executive's name. If the directory already exists, an error occurs and the macro jumps back to the ErrorExec label where a message box is displayed reporting the error.

When a directory is successfully created, the number of executives is obtained from the setting file, then the number incremented. This number will be used to create the option name for the executive in the totals and names sections.

Creating the Option Name

The option name is created in the command:

```
ExecString$ = "EXEC" + LTrim$(Str$(NumExec))
```

which adds the incremented number to the word EXEC. If this is the fourth person added to the system, for example, the option name will be EXEC4.

The updated total number of executives is converted to a string then trimmed of the leading blank space. It is written to the Execs option of the Totals section:

```
SetPrivateProfileString "Totals", "Execs", \
    LTrim$(Str$(NumExec)), "Document.ini"
```

Next, the option name is added to the Totals section with a value of 0, indicating that no index files have been created in the directory.

```
SetPrivateProfileString "Totals", ExecString$,
    "0", "Document.ini"
```

Saving the Executive's Name

The executive's name is saved in the Names section, and the last document number is set at 0 in the last numbers section:

```
SetPrivateProfileString "Names", ExecString$, ExecName$, \
    "Document.ini"
SetPrivateProfileString "LastNumbers", ExecName$, "0", \
    "Document.ini"
```

The INI file is now ready for the executive.

Naming and Saving Files

The macro to number and save a file, update the INI file, and add a description of the file to the index, is shown in the following sidebar. Run the macro when you want to name and save a document in an executive's directory.

S O L U T I O N S

The Savefile Macro

Enter the macro, then save it with the name SAVEFILE.

```
Sub MAIN
If IsDocumentDirty() = 0 Then
MsgBox "This document has not changed since last saved", \
        "Document Management"
    Goto EndMacro
EndIf
If FileNameFromWindow$() <> "" Then
    FileSave
    Goto EndMacro
EndIf

NumOfExecs$ = GetPrivateProfileString$("Totals",\
    "Execs", "Document.ini")
NumExecs = Val(NumOfExecs$) - 1
Dim Execs$(NumExecs)
```

```
For x = 0 To NumExecs
    EString$ = "EXEC" + LTrim$(Str$(X + 1))
    Exec$ = GetPrivateProfileString$("Names", \
        EString$, "Document.ini")
    Execs$(x) = Exec$
Next
Begin Dialog UserDialog 416, 200, "Save A Document"
    ListBox 102, 18, 160, 144, Execs$(), .ListBox1
    OKButton 305, 126, 88, 21
    CancelButton 305, 156, 88, 21
End Dialog

Dim ExecBox As UserDialog
C = Dialog(ExecBox)
If C = 0 Then Goto Endmacro
Num = ExecBox.ListBox1
LastNum$ = GetPrivateProfileString$("LastNumbers", \
    Execs$(Num), "Document.ini")
NewNum = Val(LastNum$) + 1
On Error Goto EndMacro
Input "Enter note", Note$
If Note$ = "" Then
    Note$ = "Misc Document for " + Execs$(Num)
EndIf
SetPrivateProfileString Execs$(Num),\
    LTrim$(Str$(NewNum)), Note$, "Document.ini"
SetPrivateProfileString "LastNumbers",\
    Execs$(Num), Str$(NewNum), "Document.ini"
ExecString$ = "EXEC" + LTrim$(Str$(Num + 1))
LastTot$ = GetPrivateProfileString$("Totals",\
    ExecString$, "Document.ini")
NewTot = Val(LastTot$) + 1
SetPrivateProfileString "Totals", ExecString$, \
    LTrim$(Str$(NewTot)), "Document.ini"
Pth$ = "C:\" + Execs$(Num) + "\"
Fname$ = Pth$ + Left$(Execs$(Num), 2) + \
    LTrim$(Str$(NewNum))
FileSaveAs Fname$
EndMacro:
End Sub
```

Looking for Changes

If the active document has not been changed since it was last saved, there is no need to save it again. This macro determines if the document has been changed using the IsDocumentDirty() function. When the function returns 0, it indicates that no changes have been made, the macro displays a message box and ends.

Looking for a Name

Next, the macro determines whether the document already has a name. If it does, the document is resaved using the FileSave command and the macro ends.

When the document needs to be named, the macro then displays a list box containing the names of the executives added to the system. The number of executives is obtained from the Totals section of the private setting file:

```
NumOfExecs$ = GetPrivateProfileString$("Totals",\
    "Execs", "Document.ini")
```

One is subtracted from the total so the variable NumExecs can be used as the array subscript, then the array is dimensioned. The array is filled in a for loop.

Remember that the executives' names are stored in the Names section that appears like this:

```
[Names]
EXEC1=Chesin
EXEC2=Nestle
EXEC3=Smith
```

Using the Option Name

The macro must use the option name to access the executive names. For example, to get the name of the first executive, we need an instruction like:

```
Exec$ = GetPrivateProfileString$("Names", "EXEC1", \
    "Document.ini")
```

579

The command:

```
EString$ = "EXEC" + LTrim$(Str$(X + 1))
```

concatenates the option name using the value of the loop count.

 **Note** During the first repetition of the loop, the value of X is 0. The function Str$(X+1) returns the string " 1", the value of the loop counter plus 1. The LTrim$ function removes the leading space, then the character is concatenated to "EXEC" and assigned to Estring$ as EXEC1.

Recalling a Name

The name of the executive associated with EXEC1 is recalled from the setting file with this command:

```
Exec$ = GetPrivateProfileString$("Names", EString$, \
    "Document.ini")
```

then it is assigned to the list box array element Exec$(0) with this command:

```
Execs$(x) = Exec$
```

 **Note** The loop repeats the process for each of the executives in the Names section. The elements in the array are not sorted because they must appear in the list box in the same order as they are in the Names section.

Display the Dialog Box

Next, the custom dialog box is defined, dimensioned, and displayed, as shown in Figure 14.1.

If the user selects Cancel from the box, the macro ends. Otherwise, the number of the selected executive is assigned to the variable Num,

FIGURE 14.1

Save a Document
dialog box

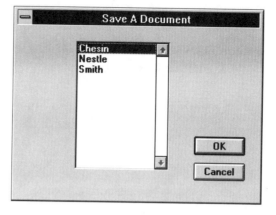

using the value of the list box identifier:

```
Num = ExecBox.ListBox1
```

Retrieving the Last Document Number

We now need to retrieve the last document number used for the executive. The numbers are stored in the Last Numbers section which uses the executive's last name as the option name.

 **Note**

We already filled an array with the last names, selected the name from a list box, and have a number representing the position of the name in the list—variable Num. The same number also represents the executive's name in the array. So, the variable Exec$(Num) contains the executive's name, which is also the name of the option containing the executive's last document number.

Obtaining the New Document Number

We can now recall the last number using the option name, and increment it to obtain the new document number:

```
LastNum$ = GetPrivateProfileString$("LastNumbers", \
```

581

```
    Execs$(Num), "Document.ini")
NewNum = Val(LastNum$) + 1
```

Inputting a Note

An error trap is set up and an input prompt is displayed so the user can enter a brief note. A status line prompt is used rather than an input box to encourage a brief note. If the user presses Enter without typing a note, a generic note is created with the words:

```
Misc Document for
```

followed by the executive's name.

The number and note for each document is stored in a section using the executive's name, like this:

```
[Chesin]
1=Budget report
2=Annual report memo
3=Letter to Jones
```

Adding the Document to the Index

The document is then added to the index in the setting file. The section name is the executive's name stored in Exec$(Num) and the option name is the number of the document:

```
SetPrivateProfileString Execs$(Num), LTrim$(Str$(NewNum)), \
    Note$, "Document.ini"
```

Updating the Sections

Next, the Last Numbers section is updated with the number of the current document:

```
SetPrivateProfileString "LastNumbers", Execs$(Num), \
    Str$(NewNum), "Document.ini"
```

The macro must then update the Totals section. It concatenates the section name, gets the previous total from the setting file, increments the number, then writes the new total to the file:

```
ExecString$ = "EXEC" + LTrim$(Str$(Num + 1))
LastTot$ = GetPrivateProfileString$("Totals",\
    ExecString$, "Document.ini")
```

```
NewTot = Val(LastTot$) + 1
SetPrivateProfileString "Totals", ExecString$, \
    LTrim$(Str$(NewTot)), "Document.ini"
```

Naming and Saving the Document

Finally, the document must be named and saved in the executive's directory. The directory path is obtained by concatenating the disk drive with the executive's name:

```
Pth$ = "C:\" + Execs$(Num) + "\"
```

The file name consists of the first two initials of the executive's name plus the document number. The path is concatenated with the name, then the document is saved:

```
Fname$ = Pth$ + Left$(Execs$(Num), 2) + \
    LTrim$(Str$(NewNum))
FileSaveAs Fname$
```

Running the Revision Macro

If you want, add a command to run the revision macro whenever you save a file. Insert the command:

```
ToolsMacro .Name = "Revision", .Run
```

before the instruction

```
If FileNameFromWindow$() <> "" Then
```

SOLUTIONS

The Getfile Macro

The macro shown here simplifies the process of opening files. Type the macro and save it with the name GETFILE.

```
Dim Shared previewfilename$
Dim Shared FoundFiles

Sub MAIN
OldDir$ = DefaultDir$(0)
```

```
NumOfExecs$ = GetPrivateProfileString$("Totals",\
      "Execs", "Document.ini")
NumExecs = Val(NumOfExecs$) - 1
Dim Execs$(NumExecs)
For x = 0 To NumExecs
     EString$ = "EXEC" + LTrim$(Str$(X + 1))
     Exec$ = GetPrivateProfileString$("Names",
          EString$, "Document.ini")
     Execs$(x) = Exec$
Next
Begin Dialog UserDialog 416, 200, "Open A Document File"
     ListBox 102, 18, 160, 144, Execs$(), .ListBox1
     OKButton 305, 126, 88, 21
     CancelButton 305, 156, 88, 21
End Dialog

Dim A As UserDialog
C = Dialog(A)
If C = 0 Then Goto Endmacro
Num = A.ListBox1
Pth$ = "C:\" + Execs$(Num) + "\"
Fname$ = Left$(Execs$(Num), 2) + "*.DOC"
FileFind .SearchPath = Pth$, .Name = Fname$
NumFiles = CountFoundFiles() - 1
If NumFiles > - 1 Then
Dim ListBox1$(NumFiles)
For x = 0 To NumFiles
ListBox1$(x) = FileNameInfo$(FoundFileName$(x + 1), 3)
Next
ChDir Pth$
SortArray ListBox1$()
FoundFiles = 1
Else
FoundFiles = 0
Dim ListBox1$(0)
ListBox1$(0) = "NO FILES"
End If

Begin Dialog UserDialog 784, 322, "File Preview", .DlgFun
     ListBox 10, 46, 303, 96, ListBox1$(), .ListBox1
```

584

```
        Text 14, 23, 101, 13, "Select a File:", .Text1
        Text 375, 19, 61, 13, "Preview", .Text2
        If FoundFiles = 1 Then
        FilePreview 375, 31, 396, 284, .Fileprev
        End If
        OKButton 92, 152, 88, 21
        CancelButton 92, 183, 88, 21
        PushButton 92, 213, 88, 21, "Open", .Push1
End Dialog

Dim MyFile As UserDialog
ShowFile = Dialog(MyFile)
If ShowFile = 1 Then FileOpen .Name = previewfilename$
ChDir OldDir$
EndMacro:
End Sub

Function DlgFun(identifier$, action, suppvalue)
If FoundFiles = 0 Then DlgEnable "Push1", 0
If FoundFiles = 1 Then
If action = 1 Then
    previewfilename$ = DlgText$("ListBox1")
    DlgFilePreview$ previewfilename$
ElseIf action = 2 Then
    If identifier$ = "ListBox1" Then
        previewfilename$ = DlgText$("ListBox1")
        DlgFilePreview$ previewfilename$
    End If
End If
End If
End Function
```

Displaying a List Box and Preview Window

Most of the commands and techniques used here should already be familiar to you. The macro displays a list box of executives using the same technique as the Savefile macro. It then uses a dialog function to create a list box and preview window to display the documents in the executive's directory. Refer to Chapter 12 if you need to review these techniques.

Finding Matching Files

After the user selects the executive's name from the list box, it determines the path of the directory and the wildcard string of the document names. Each document is stored using the first two initials of the executive's name and the DOC extension:

```
Pth$ = "C:\" + Execs$(Num) + "\"
Fname$ = Left$(Execs$(Num), 2) + "*.DOC"
```

The File Preview Dialog Box

The matching files in the directory are counted and added to a list box array. The dialog box to preview the files is then defined and displayed. The box lists the document names, as shown in Figure 14.2. The user can then preview the files and open a selected one.

FIGURE 14.2

File Preview
dialog box

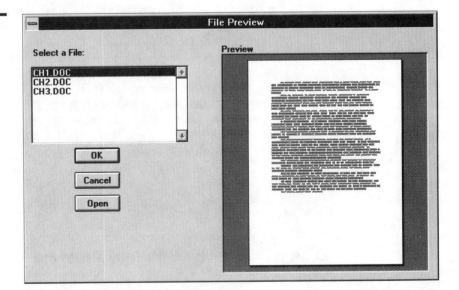

 **Note**

> The GetFile macro uses two custom dialog boxes. You can only have one custom dialog box defined at a time. To use two boxes, you must define and display the second after you close the first. If you want to close the second box and re-display the first, you must define it again.

Using Multiple Dialog Boxes

To use multiple dialog boxes, place the instructions that define and display each in a separate subroutine. Call the subroutine when you need to display the box. Remember, defining one box will automatically clear from memory any previously defined box.

Using the Find File Dialog Box

As an alternate to using a custom dialog box to display the files, you can use Word's own Find File dialog box, shown in Figure 14.3. With this dialog box, the user can open, print, delete, and sort files, and display document summary and file information. To access this dialog box from within Word, select File ➤ Find File.

FIGURE 14.3

Word's Find File dialog box

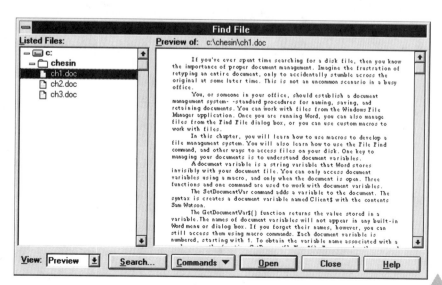

 **Tip**

Using the Find File dialog box is a useful technique only when you want the user to be able to access all of its features. If you need better control over the files, however, use a custom dialog box. In our file management system, for example, we need to delete a file in a way that also deletes its index entry in the private setting file. We do not want the user to delete the file in any other way, so a custom dialog box is more appropriate.

SOLUTIONS

Find File Macro

A macro that uses the Find File dialog box allows the user to select the executive's name, then creates strings to represent the directory path and file name. After it dimensions the Find File dialog box, it sets the path and names of the files to be displayed when the box appears:

```
Fview.SearchPath = Pth$
Fview.Name = Fname$
```

The command:

```
Fview.View = 1
```

ensures that the documents are previewed. (If the argument is omitted or 0, Word displays a line of file information for each file. An argument of 2 displays summary information for the selected file.)

The dialog box is then displayed with the command:

```
Choice = Dialog(FView)
```

Here's the entire macro:

```
Sub MAIN
NumOfExecs$ = GetPrivateProfileString$("Totals",\
    "Execs", "Document.ini")
NumExecs = Val(NumOfExecs$) - 1
Dim Execs$(NumExecs)
For x = O To NumExecs
    EString$ = "EXEC" + LTrim$(Str$(X + 1))
    Exec$ = GetPrivateProfileString$("Names",\
        EString$, "Document.ini")
    Execs$(x) = Exec$
Next
Begin Dialog UserDialog 416, 200, "Select An Executive"
    ListBox 102, 18, 160, 144, Execs$(), .ListBox1
    OKButton 305, 126, 88, 21
    CancelButton 305, 156, 88, 21
End Dialog

Dim A As UserDialog
C = Dialog(A)
If C = O Then Goto Endmacro
Num = A.ListBox1
Pth$ = "C:\" + Execs$(Num) + "\"
Fname$ = Left$(Execs$(Num), 2) + "*.DOC"

Dim FView As FileFind
Fview.SearchPath = Pth$
Fview.Name = Fname$
Fview.View = 1
Choice = Dialog(FView)
End Sub
```

Using the File Index

You might not be able to locate the document you want to open only by its name and its display in the file preview panel. As an alternative, use the entries you recorded as notes in the file index. The index entry may include several key words or phrases that identify the document.

S O L U T I O N S

SeeIndex Macro

The macro shown here displays a list of the index entries in the private setting file, along with a file preview. You'll recognize most of the routines used here from previous macros, but let's look at some of the new techniques. Create the macro with the name SeeIndex.

```
Dim Shared previewfilename$
Dim Shared FoundFiles
Dim Shared ENAME$


Sub MAIN
OldDir$ = DefaultDir$(0)
NumOfExecs$ = GetPrivateProfileString$("Totals",\
     "Execs", "Document.ini")
NumExecs = Val(NumOfExecs$) - 1
Dim Execs$(NumExecs)
For x = 0 To NumExecs
     EString$ = "EXEC" + LTrim$(Str$(X + 1))
     Exec$ = GetPrivateProfileString$("Names",\
          EString$, "Document.ini")
     Execs$(x) = Exec$
Next
Begin Dialog UserDialog 416, 200, "Select An Executive"
     ListBox 102, 18, 160, 144, Execs$(), .ListBox1
     OKButton 305, 126, 88, 21
     CancelButton 305, 156, 88, 21
End Dialog

Dim A As UserDialog
C = Dialog(A)
If C = 0 Then Goto Endmacro
Num = A.ListBox1
Pth$ = "C:\" + Execs$(Num) + "\"
ENAME$ = Left$(Execs$(Num), 2)
ExecString$ = "EXEC" + LTrim$(Str$(Num + 1))
LastTot$ = GetPrivateProfileString$("Totals",\
```

```
          ExecString$, "Document.ini")
 NumFiles = Val(LastTot$) - 1
 If NumFiles > - 1 Then
 Dim ListBox1$(NumFiles)
 Y = 1
 X = 0
 While X <= NumFiles
 CC$ = GetPrivateProfileString$(Execs$(Num),\
     LTrim$(Str$(Y)), "Document.ini")
 If CC$ <> "" Then
     ListBox1$(x) = LTrim$(Str$(Y)) + " " + cc$
     X = X + 1
EndIf
Y = Y + 1
Wend
ChDir Pth$
FoundFiles = 1
Else
FoundFiles = 0
Dim ListBox1$(0)
ListBox1$(0) = "NO FILES"
End If

Begin Dialog UserDialog 784, 322, "File Preview", .DlgFun
    ListBox 10, 46, 303, 96, ListBox1$(), .ListBox1
    Text 14, 23, 101, 13, "Select a File:", .Text1
    Text 375, 19, 61, 13, "Preview", .Text2
    If FoundFiles = 1 Then
    FilePreview 375, 31, 396, 284, .Fileprev
    End If
    OKButton 92, 152, 88, 21
    CancelButton 92, 183, 88, 21
    PushButton 92, 213, 88, 21, "Open", .Push1
End Dialog
Dim AA As UserDialog
ShowFile = Dialog(AA)
If ShowFile = 1 Then FileOpen .Name = previewfilename$
EndMacro:
ChDir OldDir$
End Sub
```

```
Function DlgFun(identifier$, action, suppvalue)
If FoundFiles = 0 Then DlgEnable "Push1", 0
If FoundFiles = 1 Then
N$ = DlgText$("ListBox1")
      pos = InStr(N$, " ")
      num$ = Left$(N$, pos - 1)
      previewfilename$ = ENAME$ + num$ + ".DOC"
If action = 1 Then
      DlgFilePreview$ previewfilename$
ElseIf action = 2 Then
      If identifier$ = "ListBox1" Then
            DlgFilePreview$ previewfilename$
      End If
End If
End If
End Function
```

Creating a Document Note Array

After accepting the name of the executive from the list box, the macro creates an array containing the document notes from the index. It obtains the total number of documents stored for the executive, then dimensions the list box.

 **Note**

If would be convenient if we could then just use a FOR loop that concatenated the option names. For example, if an executive has four documents, they would be stored under the option names 1, 2, 3, and 4. The counter variable could be converted to a trimmed string and each of the index notes written.

Programming around the Delete File Macro

Unfortunately, the process requires a few extra steps because the macro that you use later to delete a file will also delete the index entry. For example, suppose an executive has four files, named CH1 through CH4. The option names in the setting file will be 1, 2, 3, and 4. If the executive deletes the file CH3.DOC, however, the index will only contain entries like this:

```
[Chesin]
1=Budget report
2=Annual report memo
4=Letter to Jones
```

The totals section would show that there are three entries for the executive, but they are numbered 1, 2, and 4, not 1 through 3. Therefore, we cannot use the For counter variable as the option name itself.

The solution is to use a loop that continues examining the option names until they are all identified. We start by assigning two variables initial values:

```
Y = 1
X = 0
```

The variable X will count the number of option names that we successfully identify, and the variable Y will be used for the option name itself.

Next, we begin a While loop that will repeat until the value of X is larger than the number of index entries.

```
While X <= NumFiles
```

 **Note**

When X is larger than NumFiles, it indicates that we have identified all of the option names in the section. If the executive has forty documents, for example, it means that we've identified all forty option names and the loop can stop.

During the first repetition of the loop, the macro attempts to gets the option named 1 stored in the variable Y:

```
CC$ = GetPrivateProfileString$(Execs$(Num), \
    LTrim$(Str$(Y)), "Document.ini")
```

If the GetPrivateProfileString$ function does not return a null value, it means that an option named 1 exists in the section. The option name, followed by a space, and then the setting for that option are assigned to the first list box array element. Since we successfully located an option, we increment the value of X, indicating that we have found one of the executive's documents.

```
If CC$ <> "" Then
    ListBox1$(x) = LTrim$(Str$(Y)) + " " + cc$
    X = X + 1
EndIf
```

The value of Y is then incremented—to 2—and we repeat the loop looking for an option named 2:

```
Y = Y + 1
Wend
```

 **Note**   If the GetPrivateProfileString$ command returns a null value, it indicates that there is no option with the name 1. In this case, we just increment the option name to 2 and repeat the loop looking for it. Because the If condition was false, the value of X was not incremented, so we are still looking for the first option name in the section.

The process is repeated until the macro successfully identifies a number of options equal to the total number of documents indicated in the Totals section.

Displaying the Dialog Box

The dialog box is then displayed, showing the index entries for the files in the list box, as shown in Figure 14.4. When the user selects an item

FIGURE 14.4

File Preview of index entries

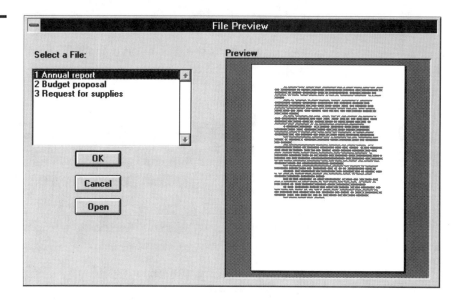

in the list, the dialog function must determine the name of the file that relates to the entry. To do this it must isolate the option number from the name. Remember, each entry appears with a space following the option number.

The command:

```
N$ = DlgText$("ListBox1")
```

returns the entire string selected in the list.

Next, the command:

```
pos = InStr(N$, " ")
```

locates the position of the space in the string. The characters representing the number are then assigned to a string:

```
num$ = Left$(N$, pos - 1)
```

The file name is concatenated using the executive's first two initials (stored previously in the string ENAME$), and the DOC extension:

```
previewfilename$ = ENAME$ + num$ + ".DOC"
```

Deleting an Indexed File

Deleting an indexed file involves erasing the file itself, as well as deleting its listing in the index and reducing the count of total documents for the executive.

S O L U T I O N S

The Erase Macro

The macro to accomplish this task is shown here. Save it under the name ERASE. (Deleting the index listing prevents anyone from selecting it accidentally.)

```
Dim Shared previewfilename$
Dim Shared FoundFiles

Sub MAIN
OldDir$ = DefaultDir$(0)
NumOfExecs$ = GetPrivateProfileString$("Totals",\
     "Execs", "Document.ini")
NumExecs = Val(NumOfExecs$) - 1
Dim Execs$(NumExecs)
For x = 0 To NumExecs
     EString$ = "EXEC" + LTrim$(Str$(X + 1))
     Exec$ = GetPrivateProfileString$("Names",\
          EString$, "Document.ini")
     Execs$(x) = Exec$
Next
Begin Dialog UserDialog 416, 200, "Delete A File"
     ListBox 102, 18, 160, 144, Execs$(), .ListBox1
     OKButton 305, 126, 88, 21
     CancelButton 305, 156, 88, 21
End Dialog

Dim A As UserDialog
C = Dialog(A)
If C = 0 Then Goto Endmacro
Num = A.ListBox1
```

```
Pth$ = "C:\" + Execs$(Num) + "\"
Fname$ = Left$(Execs$(Num), 2) + "*.DOC"
FileFind .SearchPath = Pth$, .Name = Fname$
NumFiles = CountFoundFiles() - 1
If NumFiles > - 1 Then
Dim ListBox1$(NumFiles)
For x = 0 To NumFiles
ListBox1$(x) = FileNameInfo$(FoundFileName$(x + 1), 3)
Next
ChDir Pth$
SortArray ListBox1$()
FoundFiles = 1
Else
FoundFiles = 0
Dim ListBox1$(0)
ListBox1$(0) = "NO FILES"
End If

Begin Dialog UserDialog 784, 322, "File Preview", .DlgFun
     ListBox 10, 46, 303, 96, ListBox1$(), .ListBox1
     Text 14, 23, 101, 13, "Select a File:", .Text1
     Text 375, 19, 61, 13, "Preview", .Text2
     If FoundFiles = 1 Then
     FilePreview 375, 31, 396, 284, .Fileprev
     End If
     OKButton 92, 152, 88, 21
     CancelButton 92, 183, 88, 21
     PushButton 92, 213, 88, 21, "Delete", .Push1
End Dialog

Dim MyFile As UserDialog
ShowFile = Dialog(MyFile)
If ShowFile = - 1 Or ShowFile = 0 Then Goto EndMacro
Kill previewfilename$
ExecString$ = "EXEC" + LTrim$(Str$(Num + 1))
LastTot$ = GetPrivateProfileString$("Totals",\
     ExecString$, "Document.ini")
NewTot = Val(LastTot$) - 1
```

```
SetPrivateProfileString "Totals", ExecString$, \
    LTrim$(Str$(NewTot)), "Document.ini"
Op$ = Left$(previewfilename$, Len(previewfilename$) - 4)
Op$ = Right$(Op$, Len(Op$) - 2)

ToolsAdvancedSettings .Application = Execs$(Num)\
    + " (Document.ini)", .Option = Op$, .Delete

EndMacro:
ChDir OldDir$
End Sub

Function DlgFun(identifier$, action, suppvalue)
If FoundFiles = 0 Then DlgEnable "Push1", 0
If FoundFiles = 1 Then
If action = 1 Then
    previewfilename$ = DlgText$("ListBox1")
    DlgFilePreview$ previewfilename$
ElseIf action = 2 Then
    If identifier$ = "ListBox1" Then
        previewfilename$ = DlgText$("ListBox1")
        DlgFilePreview$ previewfilename$
    End If
End If
End If
End Function
```

Displaying Executive Files

Again, most of the techniques will be familiar to you. A dialog box displays a list of the selected executive's files and a preview pane, along with command buttons OK, Cancel, and Delete.

Deleting Selected Files

The macro ends if the user selects either OK or Cancel. When the user selects the Delete push button, the selected file is deleted with the command:

```
Kill previewfilename$
```

 **Note** | Kill is Word's command for delete a file from the disk. Previewfilename$ contains the name of the file selected in the list box.

Writing the Total Back to the File

The option name in the Totals section is concatenated, the current total for the executive is read from the private setting file. One is subtracted from the total, and the number is written back to the file.

Assigning the File Name

The name of the file minus the extension is then assigned to the variable Op$. For example, if the file is CH14.DOC, the string is assigned CH14. Next, the first two characters in the string are removed, resulting in just the document number.

The command:

```
Op$ = Right$(Op$, Len(Op$) - 2)
```

takes a portion of the string on the right, two characters less than the entire string length. The string CH14 contains four characters, so the resulting string contains only the last two, the number 14.

 **Note** | The extension will always be four characters (including the period) and there will always be two initials. However, the number can be 1, 2, 3, or more characters depending on the number of files.

Deleting the Option

Finally, the option is deleted with the command:

```
ToolsAdvancedSettings .Application = Execs$(Num)\
    + " (Document.ini)", .Option = Op$, .Delete
```

The macro does not allow the file number to be reused. For example, if you delete the last file saved for Smith, the next file saved will still be the next highest number.

Using the System

The document management system includes the following macros:

- **AddExec:** Adds an executive to the system.
- **Savefile:** Assigns a file name, a description, and saves a document.
- **Getfile:** Displays a list of file names and preview to open a file.
- **SeeIndex:** Displays a list of index entries and preview to open a file.
- **Erase:** Displays a list of file names and preview to delete a file and its listing in the index.

Running the Macros

One way to use the application is to run the appropriate macro:

- To save a file, run the Savefile macro, select the executive, and enter a brief description.
- To open a file by its names, run the Getfile macro, and then select the executive's name. When the listing appears, click on a file to display a preview, and click on Open to open the file.
- To open a file by its description in the index, run the SeeIndex macro.
- To delete a file, run the Erase macro, and then select the executive's name. When the listing appears, click on a file to display a preview, and click on Delete to delete it.

Other File Management Commands

Word provides a number of other macro commands and system variables for working with documents. Here is a description of the commands and an example of their syntax.

ChDefaultDir Path$, Type—Changes the default directory to use for the current Word session. The type specifies the file type affected: 0 for documents; 1 for picture files; 2 for user templates; 3 for workgroup templates; 4 for setting files; 5 for the autosave directory; 6 for Word tools; 7 for tutorials, examples, and demos; 8 for start up files; and 15 for the style gallery templates.

DefaultDir$(Type)—Returns the current path for the specified type. In addition to the types used for the ChDefaultDir command, you can specify 9 to return the Word path; 10 for graphic filters; 11 for text converters; 12 for proofing tools; 13 for temporary files; and 14 for the current directory.

Connect [.Drive = number,] .Path = path$, .Password = string$—Establishes a connection to a network drive. For the drive number, use 0 for the first available letter, 1 for the second letter, and so on.

CopyFile Source$, Destination$—Copies a file to another directory. The destination string can also include a new file name.

CountDirectories(directory$)—Returns the number of subdirectories in the specified directory.

GetAttr(File$)—Returns a number indicating a file's attributes. The number is a sum of the following values: 0 for no attributes; 1 for read-only; 2 for hidden; 4 for system; 32 for archive. (A returned value of 6 indicates a hidden system file.)

GetDirectory$(Directory$, Count)—Returns the name of the subdirectory within the directory. The value of the count indicates the subdirectory, use 1 for the first subdirectory, 2 for the second, and so on.

**Name OriginalName$ As NewName$**—Renames a file or a directory. If you include a path in the NewName$, the file will be moved to that directory, and deleted from its current directory. You cannot use the command to move a directory, and you cannot use wildcards to rename or move multiple files.

RmDir Directory$—Deletes the named directory. An error will occur if the directory contains any files or subdirectories.

**SetAttr Filename$, Type**—Sets the attributes of a file. The types are additive and use the same values as described for the GetAttr(File$) command. An error will be generated if the file is open.

Reading and Writing Disk Files

A number of macros discussed in this book use a private setting file to store information. The setting file commands are powerful because they take care of the task of opening and closing files. In addition, private setting files provide random access capability. This means that you can get or set a specific option, no matter where it is in the file. If you add an option, Word will automatically make room for it.

WordBasic includes other commands for reading and writing text files. A text file, often called an ASCII file, contains just text, no formatting codes, styles, or other elements normally saved with a file by a word processing program.

Using these commands, your macro must first open the file and tell Word how you plan to use it. You can either open a file to read from it or to write to it. If you want to do both, you must first close the file, then re-open it.

Opening Files

To open a text file, use the Open command with this syntax:

```
Open FileName$ FOR Mode AS Number
```

as in:

```
Open "C:\ORDERS.TXT" FOR Input As #1
```

Three modes are allowed.

◆ When you open a file for *Input,* you can only read information from the file. An error will occur if the file does not exist.

◆ You open a file for *Output* to create it. If a file with the same name already exists it will be replaced by the new file, and its contents will be lost.

◆ If you open a file for *Append,* you can write new information to the end of the file, without deleting any existing contents. If the file does not yet exist, it will be created.

Because you can have as many as four files open at the same time, each file is opened with a number from #1 to #4. For each file operation you perform, you must tell Word the number of the file to use.

Closing Files

After you have finished writing to or reading from a file, you must close it. The syntax is:

```
Close #FileNumber
```

If you omit the file number, all files that you've opened with the Open command are closed.

Note

Closing a file will enable you to reopen it in another mode. For example, suppose you want to create a file, then read it back to ensure that it contains the correct information. Your macro would open the file for Output, write the information to the file, then close it. Next, the macro would open the file for Input, read the information from the file, and then close it.

Writing Information to a File

WordBasic has two commands for writing to a file, Write and Print. Both commands can write either strings or numbers, and both commands add a carriage return after each line output—each line will be on its own line in the resulting file.

The Write Command

The write command adds quotation marks around each string. If you output multiple items in one command, they will be separated by commas. Its syntax is:

```
Write #FileNumber, Item, Item, Item
```

An item can be a string variable or literal in quotation marks; a numeric value, variable or expression; or a function that returns a string or numeric value. Place a comma after the file number and between each item.

The Print Command

The Print command does not add quotation marks around strings. It uses the same syntax as Write.

```
Print #FileNumber, Item, Item, Item
```

 **Note**

If you separate items with commas, it inserts a tab between items in the file. If you separate items with a semicolon, it will leave no spaces between items in the file, although there will be a blank space before each positive number.

Output Alternatives

For example, look at this program that outputs two lines of information using the Write command:

```
Sub MAIN
Category$ = "Friend"
Open "C:\windows\friends.txt" For Output As #1
Write #1, "George",  45,  160,  Category$
Write #1, "Nancy",  46,  125, Category$
Close #1
End Sub
```

When you look at the file with the Type command from the DOS prompt, you'll see this:

```
"George", 45, 160,"Friend"
"Nancy", 46, 125,"Friend"
```

Now, if you just replace the word Write with the word Print, and run the program again, the file will appear like this:

```
George    45    160    Friend
Nancy    46    125    Friend
```

If you used semicolons with the Print commands, rather than commas, the file would appear as:

```
George 45 160Friend
Nancy 46 125Friend
```

 **Tip**

> To prevent Word from inserting a carriage return after a print command, end it with a semicolon, as in: Print #1, String$;

Planning Your Output

Before outputting information, consider how you are going to use it.

◆ Use either Write or Print if you are recording one string or numeric value per line, and you want to read the values back into variables.

◆ Use Write if you are outputting multiple values in each statement, and you want to read the values back into variables.

◆ Use Write if you want to create a delimited file to be used with a database management program, or as a data source for another word processing program that requires that format.

◆ Use Print if you are creating a generic text file that you want to read with another application.

Inputting Information from Text Files

WordBasic has several commands for reading information from a text file—Read, Input, Line Input, and Input$().

Word deals with files using a pointer. When you open a file, the pointer is at the first line. After each Read, Input, or Line Input command, the pointer moves to the next line in the file, even if the entire line was not input.

 **Note**

A line is defined as a series of characters ending with a carriage return. The carriage return is not input by the command. The Input$() reads a specific number of characters, including a carriage return, so the pointer moves to the first characters not input.

Read

The Read command is designed to input comma-delimited text information from files created with the Write command. Its syntax is:

```
Read #FileNumber, Var, Var, Var, ...
```

Use a string variable to read string values, as in:

```
Read #1, Name$, Age, Weight, Category$
```

Values in each line of the file must be separated by commas. Any quotation marks around a string will not be included in the resulting variable. (You can also use Read to input single items—one string or numeric value—written with the Print command.)

This program, for example, will read the two lines of output in the previous example with the Write command:

```
Sub MAIN
Open "C:\windows\friends.txt" For Input As #1
Read #1, Name$, Age, Weight, Category$
Insert Name$ + " " + Str$(Age)+ " " + \
    Str$(Weight)+ " " + Category$
InsertPara
Read #1, Name$, Age, Weight, Category$
Insert Name$ + " " + Str$(Age)+ " " + \
    Str$(Weight)+ " " + Category$
Close #1
End Sub
```

The information will appear on screen as:

```
George  45  160  Friend
Nancy  46  125  Friend
```

 **Note**

> If you read fewer items than are on a line, those not read will be ignored by the next Read command. If you read more items than are on a line, null values will be returned to the extra variables.

Input

The Input command is similar to Read except it does not remove quotation marks from strings in the file. If you substitute Input for the Read commands just shown, your screen will display:

```
"George"  45  160  "Friend"
"Nancy"  46  125  "Friend"
```

Line Input

The Line Input command reads an entire line, up to 65,280 characters, into a single string variable. The syntax is:

```
Line Input #FileNumber, Var$
```

The resulting variable will contain everything on the line, including quotation marks and commas inserted by a Write command, or the tabs inserted between items with a Print command. Use the file created in a previous example with the commands:

```
Line Input #1, Line$
Insert Line$
```

to display

```
"George",45,160,"Friend"
```

Input$()

This function inputs a specific number of characters, including carriage returns, using the syntax:

```
Var$ = Input$(Number_of_characters, #FileNumber)
```

You can use the command to filter out unwanted characters or delimiters. For example, these instructions would input the first 200 characters in a file but only display letters, numbers, and punctuation marks, ignoring graphic and other characters:

```
For x = 1 To 200
X$ = Input$(1, #1)
If (Asc(X$) >= 33 And Asc(X$) <= 127) \
    Or (Asc(X$) = 10) Then
Insert X$
EndIf
Next
```

 **Note**   The Asc() function returns the ANSI number assigned to a character. The character represented by ANSI number 10 will insert a carriage return.

Finding the End of the File

Word will display an error message if you attempt to read more lines or characters than are actually in the file. To avoid this error, use the EOF() function. The function returns –1 when your macro has reached the end of a file.

Reading an Entire File

To read an entire file, place your input statements within a loop like this:

```
Sub MAIN
Open "C:\windows\friends.txt" For Input As #1
While Not Eof(#1)
Read #1, Name$, Age, Weight, Category$
Insert Name$ + " " + Str$(Age)+ " " +\
    Str$(Weight) + " " + Category$
InsertPara
Wend
Close #1
End Sub
```

Uppercase to Lowercase Example

For example, this program makes a copy of a text file, converting all uppercase characters to lowercase:

```
Sub MAIN
Open "C:\windows\document.ini" For Input As #1
Open "C:\winword\lowercase.ini" For Output As #2
While Not Eof(#1)
New$ = ""
Line Input #1, x$
For Y = 1 To Len(X$)
    Letter$ = Mid$(x$, Y, 1)
    If Asc(Letter$) >= 65 And Asc(Letter$)<= 90 Then
    New$ = New$ + Chr$(Asc(Letter$) + 32)
Else
    New$ = New$ + Letter$
EndIf
Next
Print #2, new$
Wend
Close #1
Close #2
End Sub
```

Each line of the file is read by a Line Input command. The For loop then repeats once for each character in the string. The command:

```
Letter$ = Mid$(x$, Y, 1)
```

returns each character in the string.

The If condition determines if the letter is uppercase by determining if its ANSI value is between 65 (the letter A) and 90 (the letter Z). When the character is in the range, the function:

```
Chr$(Asc(Letter$) + 32)
```

returns the same character in lowercase.

 **Note** | All lowercase characters have ANSI values 32 higher than the corresponding uppercase character. All of the individual characters are concatenated into a new string, which is then written to the file opened for output. The Lof() function returns the number of characters (bytes) in the file.

Moving the File Pointer

When you open a file for input, the pointer is placed at the first item in the file. The items in the file are read sequentially, from the first item to the last.

Pointing at Certain Items

You can skip over certain items by reading them, checking their value, and then moving on. This macro, for example, opens an address file but only displays items for friends named George:

```
Sub MAIN
Open "C:\windows\friends.txt" For Input As #1
While Not Eof(#1)
Read #1, Name$, Age, Weight, Category$
If Name$ = "George" Then
    Insert Name$ + " " + Str$(Age)+ " " +\
        Str$(Weight)+ " " + Category$
    InsertPara
EndIf
Wend
Close #1
End Sub
```

Using the Seek Command

You can also move the pointer to a specific location in a file using the Seek command. The syntax is:

```
Seek #FileNumber, Position
```

where position is the location of a character in the file.

The command:

```
Seek #1, 40
```

moves the pointer just after the 40th character in the file. When you open a file for Append, you can use the command to write information at some other location other than the end of the file.

Using the Seek Function

The Seek() function, on the other hand, returns the character position where the pointer is located, as in:

```
location = Seek(#1)
```

 **Note**

You can use the command and function in a program to change information in a file using the print command. However, the print command overwrites existing characters in the file, so you must be sure that you write the same number of characters that you want to replace. End the print command with a semicolon to prevent an extra line feed after the inserted characters.

S O L U T I O N S

Seek and Replace Macro

This macro, for example, replaces the first line consisting of the name George with the same name in uppercase:

```
Sub MAIN
Open "C:\winword\friends.doc" For Input As #1
While Not Eof(#1) And test$ <> "George"
    pos = Seek(#1)
    Line Input #1, test$
```

```
Wend
Close #1
Open "C:\winword\friends.doc" For Append As #1
Seek(#1, pos)
Print #1, "GEORGE";
Close #1
End Sub
```

The Seek function is placed before the Line Input command so it returns the starting position of the string to be replaced.

If you use the Seek command, test your macro thoroughly to ensure that it will not accidentally delete text that you want to retain.

PART six

The Professional Word

Forms and Fields

A S YOU'VE LEARNED, MACROS CAN automate tasks of all types, and you've seen how date, mail merge, EQ, and SEQ fields can help solve word processing problems. In this chapter, you will learn how to use form fields to fill in forms and interactively complete form letters. You will also learn how to harness the power of Word's fields for documents of all types.

Working with On-Line Forms

It seems that the world is filled with forms. There are application forms, purchase forms, request forms, complaint forms, even forms to order more forms. With computers, many forms are completed on-line. For instance, an operator sitting at the computer will fill out a form as a customer calls in an order. The operator can then transmit the form by electronic mail to the order department for processing.

 **Tip**

An on-line form can also be used when you have pre-printed forms. Design the form on the screen exactly how it appears on the printed copy. You can complete the form on-line, then print just the information you've added on the preprinted sheet.

Automating Forms with Form Fields

In previous chapters, you read how to use a table to create an invoice form. You learned how to apply macros and merge techniques to complete the invoice. Waiting for a macro to move the insertion point from line to line, however, can be time-consuming. A faster solution is to automate forms using form fields. A form field represents a location on a form where the user must enter information. Word provides three types of form fields—text, check boxes, and drop-down lists—as illustrated in Figure 15.1.

◆ Use a text field where you want the user to type information, such as a name and address. You can limit the entry to certain types of data (such as dates or numbers), set the maximum length of entries, and you can display the results of calculations.

◆ Use a check box where you need a yes or no type of response. You can set the size of the check box, and its default status.

◆ Use a drop-down list where you want the user to select from a specific list of options.

FIGURE 15.1

Form fields

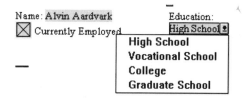

Custom Help Messages

You can also create two types of custom help messages for each field. One help message will appear in the status line whenever the field is active. The other will appear in a message box if the users presses F1 when completing the field.

Attaching Macros to Fields

If you need even further control over the form, you can attach macros to individual form fields. You can designate an *on entry* macro that will run when the user enters the form field, and an *on exit* macro that runs when the user leaves the field. For instance, you can create a macro that skips over certain fields based on the user's action in a checkbox. (You cannot use the FileClose command in a form field macro.)

 **Note** You design a form as a template and then protect it. Protecting a form ensures that the user can only access the form fields to fill in those areas that you designated. They cannot change any of the prompts or other elements of the form.

Creating the Form Template

The first step in creating an on-line form is to open a template in which to store it. The template will store the form design, its fields and help messages, and any attached macros and styles. In most cases, you'll have a word or phrase before the field as a prompt, so the user knows the type of information to enter.

The Forms Toolbar

Word provides a toolbar to help you work with forms. To display the toolbar, right-click on any other toolbar and select Forms, or select View ➤ Toolbars ➤ Forms ➤ OK. The toolbar and its button names are shown in Figure 15.2.

FIGURE 15.2

Forms toolbar

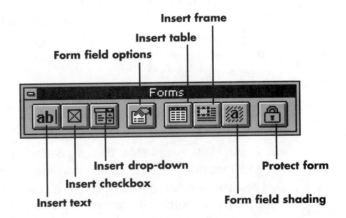

Adding a Form Field

To add a form field, place the insertion point where you want the user to enter or select information, then select Insert ➤ Form Field to display the dialog box shown in Figure 15.3. To insert a field using the default settings, select the field type and click on OK. However, you can select options to customize the field for greater control.

FIGURE 15.3

Form Field
dialog box

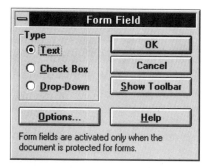

Text Field Options

To customize a text box field, select the Text type, then click on Options to display the box shown in Figure 15.4.

Select the type of entry you want the box to contain—Regular Text, Number, Date, Current Date, Current Time, and Calculation.

FIGURE 15.4

Text Form Field
Options dialog box

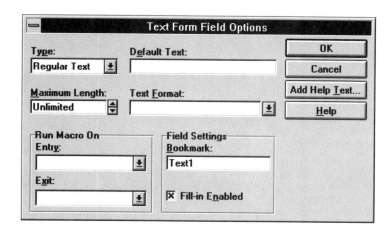

 **Note** Use the calculation type to compute a value based on other fields or table cells. If you use a regular table formula in the Table menu, you will not be able to update the fields because the template is protected.

In the Default box, enter the text, date, or number you want to appear in the field by default when the form is displayed. When you select a calculation type, the box will be labeled Expression. Type the formula for calculating the contents, using either form field bookmark names or cell references.

Use the Maximum Length box to limit the number of characters the user can enter. Choose Unlimited, or a number from 1 to 255.

The options, and label, of the Format box depend on the type selected. For regular text, you can choose uppercase, lowercase, first capital, or title case. With date and time types, you can select a date or time format. For number and calculation fields, select a numeric format from the following examples (displaying the value 12345.67):

OPTION	DISPLAY
0	12346
0.00	12345.67
#,##0	12,346
#,##0.00	12,345.67
$#,##0.00;($#,##0.00)	$12,345.67
0%	12346%
0.00%	12345.67%

Use the Macro Run On section to designate macros that you want to run when the user enters and exits the fields. We'll use these later to update the total fields in the invoice.

The Bookmark box in the Field Setting section is a name assigned to the field. You only need to assign a name if you want to reference the field in a macro command or calculation. Deselect the Fill-in Enabled box to prevent the user from accessing the field.

Creating Help Messages

You should create help messages to aid the user in completing the form. Help messages are especially important with fields that have maximum limits, or that require special formats, such as a date or time. The user can be quickly frustrated hearing warning beeps, or being unable to enter what they consider is a correct entry.

A help message in the status bar will appear automatically when the user enters the field. Use the message to tell the user the type of entry desired, a range of allowable values, or remind them to press Enter after typing the contents.

Tip

To use the same help message for a number of fields, save the message as an AutoText entry before designing the form.

To create a help message, select Add Help Text in the Field Options dialog box, then select the Status Bar tab to display the dialog box shown in Figure 15.5.

FIGURE 15.5

Status Bar tab of the Form Field Help Text dialog box

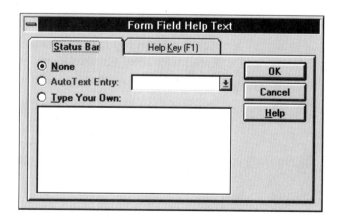

To display an AutoText entry as the help message, click on the Auto TextEntry option button, then select the entry name in the pull-down list. To display a custom message, click on Type Your Own, then enter the text in the large text box below the option.

Select the Help Key (F1) tab to create a message that will appear when the user presses F1, such as shown in Figure 15.6.

FIGURE 15.6

Custom help message for form field

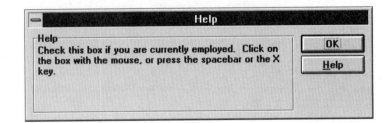

>  **Tip** To display the option menu for a field that you've already created, double-click on the field; or right-click on the field and select Form Field Options from the pull-down menu. You can also click on the Form Field Options button in the Form Field toolbar.

Check Box Fields

A check box form field appears as a checkbox, and prints as seen on screen. The Check Box Form Field Options dialog box is shown in Figure 15.7. (Note that you can set the size of the box and its default status.)

You can test the value of the field's bookmark in a macro to determine whether the box is selected or not.

FIGURE 15.7

Check Box Form
Field Options
dialog box

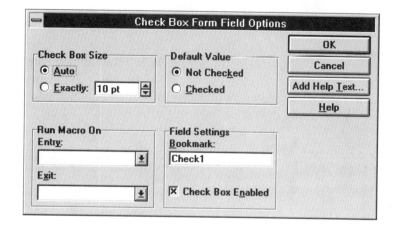

Drop-Down List Box

A drop-down list box displays a list of options. When the form is displayed, the first item in the list appears as the default value. The Drop-Down Form Field Options dialog box is shown in Figure 15.8.

You can add up to 25 items, of up to 50 characters each, to the list. To add an item to the list, type it in the Drop-Down Item text box, then click on Add. To change the position of an item on the list, select it, then click on either the up or down Move buttons.

FIGURE 15.8

Drop-Down Form
Field Options
dialog box

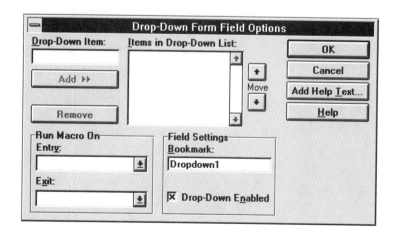

Protecting the Form

When the form is complete, protect it against changes. Select Tools ➤ Protect Document to display the dialog box shown in Figure 15.9, and click on the Forms option in the Protect Document For section. You can also assign a password to prevent unauthorized individuals from unprotecting the form.

FIGURE 15.9

Protect Document dialog box

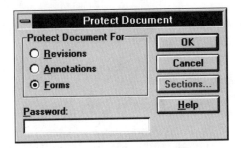

 **Tip**

If you later want to change the form yourself, display the form and select Tools ➤ UnProtect Document. Remember to protect the form again before saving and closing it. If you want the user to be able to change some portions of the document, divide the form into sections. In the Protect Document dialog box, select the Sections button, then choose the section you want unprotected.

When you protect a document:

◆ You will not be able to enter text except in form fields and unprotected sections.

◆ You cannot display the form field codes, just the results of the fields.

◆ You can only select text that you enter into text fields. You will not be able to select the whole document or any other text in protected sections.

◆ Most menu options will be dimmed.

◆ On Entry, On Exit, and form field help settings will be activated.

Using a Form

To use a form, select File ➤ New, click on the name of the template that contains the form, and then select OK.

You can only move the insertion point to form fields and unprotected sections. To move forward from field to field, press Enter, Tab, or the down arrow key. To move backward through fields, press Shift+Tab or the up arrow key. You can also click on a form field with the mouse.

To select or clear a check box, click on it with the mouse, or enter the box and press the spacebar or the X key.

To pull down a list box, click on the field, or select the field and press F4 or Alt+Down Arrow.

 **Note** If you do not want the form fields to appear shaded, display the Forms toolbar, and click on the Shading tool.

Creating an Invoice Form Step-by-Step

As an example of creating a form, look at the invoice form shown in Figure 15.10. The form is an edited version of the invoice table shown in Chapter 10.

Opening and Editing a Form

Either open and edit the form, or create it from a new template window, using these general techniques:

1. Create the first table as six rows and six columns, then merge cells and move cell borders to create the form as shown. Format the labels right-aligned in the cells.

FIGURE 15.10

Invoice form

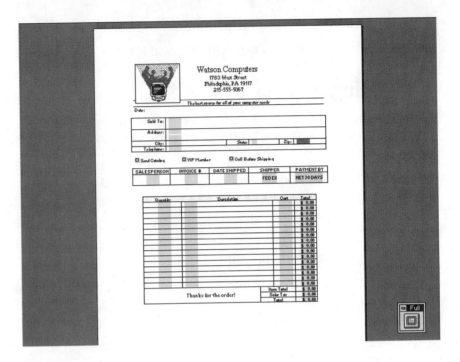

2. Leave three blank lines between the first and second tables.

3. Create the second table using two rows and five columns. Select the second row and set its height at 24 points. Format the labels centered.

4. Create the last table using four columns and twenty rows. Format the column headings and other text centered.

5. Place the insertion point in the blank cell next to the prompt Sold To in the first table, then select Insert ➤ Form Field ➤ Text ➤ Options.

6. Select Maximum Length and enter 65. This will prevent the user from entering more than one line of text.

7. Select Text Format and select Title Case.

8. Select BookMark, and enter SoldTo.

9. Select OK.

10. In the same way, enter a similar text field in the second line of the Sold To section, and then two fields in the Address section. Use a maximum length of 65 and Title Case. (You do not need to enter a bookmark name.)

11. In the cell next to the City prompt, enter a text form field with a maximum size of 25 characters and title case.

12. In the cell next to the state label, enter a text form field with a maximum of two characters and uppercase.

13. In the cell next to the zip label, enter a text form field with a maximum length of 11 characters.

14. In the cell next to the telephone label, enter a text form field with a maximum length of 65 characters.

Entering the Checkbox and List Box Fields

To enter the checkbox fields and their labels between the two tables:

1. Place the insertion point in the second blank line after the table.

2. Select Insert ➤ Form Field ➤ Checkbox ➤ OK.

3. Type **Send Catalog**, then press Tab twice.

4. In the same way, enter the VIP Member and Call Before Shipping checkboxes and labels.

Next, enter the fields in the second table, including two list box fields:

5. For the salesperson field, enter a text box form field with a maximum size of 14 characters.

6. Skip the INVOICE # field for now.

7. For Date Shipped, enter a text box field using the Date type, and select M/d/yy as the Date Format.

 **Note**

> With a data type, the user can enter the date in any valid date format. When the user exists the field, Word will convert the entry to the selected format. A warning box will appear if the user enters an invalid date.

8. Place the insertion point in the cell under the Shipper label.

9. Select Insert ➤ Form Field ➤ Drop-Down List ➤ Options.

10. In the Drop-Down Item box, type **FED EX,** and then click on Add.

11. In the same way, add the items **TRUCK, UPS,** and **U.S.P.S.**

12. Select OK.

13. Using the same technique, create a drop-down box under Payment By. Add these items: **Net 30 Days, DISCOVER, MASTERCARD, VISA, C.O.D.**

Entering the Description and Macro Fields

Add the fields required to complete the invoice. We'll start with the description field, then enter those that require calculations and macros.

1. In the first description item, add a text box form field with a maximum of 39 characters. (Instead of entering individual form fields in the rest of the cells in the description column, copy the field.)

2. Select the field you just entered, then click on the copy tool in the toolbar.

3. Place the insertion point in the description cell for the next line and click on the Paste tool.

4. Repeat step 3 to copy the field to the remaining cells in the column.

5. Move to cell D2, the first blank cell in the total column.

6. Select Insert ➤ Form Field ➤ Text ➤ Options.

7. Select Calculation in the Type section.

8. In the Expression box, enter =PRODUCT(A2,C2).

9. In the Number Format section, select $#,##0.00;($#,##0.00).

10. In the BookMark section, type **ItemTotal1,** then select OK. You'll need a bookmark to update the total as you use the form.

11. In the same manner, complete the remaining entries in the next 15 cells of that row. Enter the expressions shown here to calculate the quantity and cost amounts for that row, and increment the item total bookmark:

CELL	EXPRESSION	BOOKMARK
D3	=PRODUCT(A3,C3)	ItemTotal2
D4	=PRODUCT(A4,C4)	ItemTotal3
D5	=PRODUCT(A5,C5)	ItemTotal4
D6	=PRODUCT(A6,C6)	ItemTotal5
D7	=PRODUCT(A7,C7)	ItemTotal6
D8	=PRODUCT(A8,C8)	ItemTotal7
D9	=PRODUCT(A9,C9)	ItemTotal8
D10	=PRODUCT(A10,C10)	ItemTotal9
D11	=PRODUCT(A11,C11)	ItemTotal10
D12	=PRODUCT(A12,C12)	ItemTotal11
D13	=PRODUCT(A13,C13)	ItemTotal12
D14	=PRODUCT(A14,C14)	ItemTotal13
D15	=PRODUCT(A15,C15)	ItemTotal14
D16	=PRODUCT(A16,C16)	ItemTotal15
D17	=PRODUCT(A17,C17)	ItemTotal16

12. Enter text form fields of the calculation type that will calculate the item subtotal, tax, and grand total:

CELL	EXPRESSION	BOOKMARK
D18	=SUM(D2:D17)	SubTotal
D19	=D18*0.06	Tax
D20	=D18+D19	GrandTotal

Note The remaining form fields will either be calculated by a macro, or will require an on entry and on exit macro.

S O L U T I O N S

The SetInNum Macro

We want to fill in the Invoice # automatically by incrementing the number of the previous invoice. We'll do this with the macro shown here. Create the macro with the name SetInNum.

```
Sub MAIN
Current$ = GetFormResult$("INNUM")
If Current$ = "" Then
INNUM$ = GetPrivateProfileString$("Invoice", \
     "LASTNUM", "INVOICE.INI")
NewNum = Val(INNUM$) + 1
NewNum$ = LTrim$(Str$(NewNum))
SetFormResult "INNUM", NewNum$
SetPrivateProfileString "Invoice", "LASTNUM",\
     NewNum$, "INVOICE.INI"
EndIf
End Sub
```

Assigning the Current Value

The macro starts by assigning any current value in the field to the string Current$. The function GetFormResult$( ) returns the current contents of a field. In this case, the function returns an invoice number already in the INNUM bookmark, the name we'll soon assign to the form field.

Inserting the Invoice Number

If the contents of the field are empty, the remainder of the macro is performed to increment and insert the invoice number. Otherwise, Word will not change the number.

 **Note**

> If the macro did not check to determine if the INNUM bookmark was empty, the number in the field would be updated each time the user moves through the field. For example, suppose a user is entering item information and then realizes a mistake was made in a field before the invoice number. If the user moves through the field on the way to correcting the mistake, the invoice number would be incremented a second time when the insertion exits the field. It would then be incremented a third time if the user passes through the field to return to the invoice section of the form. The If condition, ensures that the number will remain the same once it's been filled in.

The macro then retrieves the last invoice number from a private setting file. The first invoice you complete with this macro will be numbered 1. If you want to start at some other number, say 1001, create a text file named INVOICE.INI in the Windows directory with this contents:

```
[Invoice]
LASTNUM=1000
```

The setting is converted to a number, incremented, and then converted back to a string. The SetFormResult command inserts a value into a form field. The syntax is:

```
SetFormResult Bookmark$, Value
```

In this case, the command inserts the invoice number into the form field associated with the INNUM bookmark.

Updating the Setting File

Finally, the macro, updates the private setting file with the new invoice number.

Inserting the Form Field

Once you've created the macro, follow these steps to insert the form field.

1. Place the insertion point in the cell below the Invoice # prompt, then select Insert ➤ Form Field ➤ Text ➤ Options.

2. Select a Number type, set the Number Format at 0, and then type IN-NUM in the Bookmark text box.

3. Pull down the On Entry list in the Run Macro On section, select Set-InNum, then click on OK.

The GetFormResult Function

The GetFormResult function can use either of these formats:

```
GetFormResult()
GetFormResult$()
```

With either format, the argument must be a string variable or literal in quotation marks indicating the bookmark name.

Use the function without the $ symbol to return a numeric value from a checkbox or drop-down list field. The function will return 0 if the checkbox is cleared, or 1 if the box is selected. For a drop-down list, the function returns 0 if the first item in the list is selected, 1 for the second item in the list, and so on.

Use the function with a $ symbol to return the contents of a text box field as a string, or the name of the item selected in a drop-down list box. With a checkbox field, the function returns the character "0" if the box is cleared or the character "1" if the box is selected.

The SetFormResult Command

The first argument of the SetFormResult command is always a string representing the bookmark name of the form field. The second argument is a string or number depending on the type of field. If it is a text form field, the result must be a string variable or value, even if the field has been designated as a number type. Use a numeric variable or value for checkbox and drop-down fields.

You can also add the number 1 as a third argument to indicate that the assigned result will serve as the default value.

S O L U T I O N S

The EndRow Macro

You may not always be using all 16 item lines in the invoice. Let's create a macro that will display the Save As dialog box, when the user presses Enter without entering an item quantity. Create the macro shown here with the name EndRow.

```
Sub MAIN
    Dim invoice As FormFieldOptions
    GetCurValues invoice
    RowNum$ = invoice.Name
    VALUE$ = GetFormResult$(RowNum$)
    If Val(VALUE$) = 0 Then
    EditGoTo "SoldTo"
    Dim EndForm As FileSaveAs
    Choice = Dialog(EndForm)
    If Choice = - 1 Then
        FileSaveAs EndForm
    EndIf
    EndIf
End Sub
```

Finding Empty Fields

The macro, which will be used on exit from each of the quantity form fields, must determine if the contents of the field is empty, indicating that the user did not enter a quantity and wishes to save the invoice.

To do this, the macro must determine the name of the field just exited. The bookmark name of the field is stored in the Form Field Options dialog box. The macro dimensions the dialog box and assigns its current values to the dialog record invoice. It then assigns the bookmark name of the field to the variable RowNum$ with the command:

```
VALUE$ = GetFormResult$(RowNum$)
```

FormField Options Arguments

The arguments of the FormFieldOptions command are shown here. The notation "" indicates a string setting, 0 indicates a numeric setting.

```
FormFieldOptions .Entry = "", .Exit = "", .Name="", .Enable = 1,
.TextType = 0, .TextWidth = "0", .TextDefault = "", .TextFormat =
"s", .TextWidth = "" or 0, .TextFormat = "", .CheckSize = 0,
.CheckWidth = 0, .CheckDefault= 0, .Type = 0, .OwnHelp = 0, .Help-
Text = "", .OwnStat = 0, .StatText = ""
```

Saving the Invoice

If the value of the bookmark is 0, the macro moves the insertion point to the Sold To field so the user will see the name of the company and the invoice number on the screen. The File Save As dialog box is dimensioned and displayed, and the user can save the invoice.

Creating the First Quantity Field

Write the macro, then follow these steps to create the first quantity field:

1. Place the insertion point in cell A2, and select Insert ➤ Form Field ➤ Text ➤ Options.

2. Select a Number type, set the maximum number at 4, set the Number Format at 0, and then type ITEM1 in the Bookmark text box.

3. Pull down the Exit list in the Run Macro On section, and select EndRow.

4. Now, enter a similar form field in the remaining cells in that column, but increment the bookmark name, such as Item2, Item3, and so on, up to Item16.

S O L U T I O N S

The UpRow Macro

After the user enters the cost of an item, we want to update the item total, as well as the subtotal, tax, and grand total figures. To do this, we need an exit macro that determines which cost item has just been entered. When the user enters the cost for the first item, for example, we need to update the first item total.

Create the macro shown here under the name UpRow.

```
Sub MAIN
    Dim invoice As FormFieldOptions
    GetCurValues invoice
    RowNum$ = invoice.Name
    rownum$ = Right$(RowNum$, Len(RowNum$) - 4)
    SetFormResult "ItemTotal" + LTrim$(rownum$)
    SetFormResult "Subtotal"
    SetFormResult "Tax"
    SetFormResult "GrandTotal"
End Sub
```

Obtaining the Cost Field Name

The macro uses the FormFieldOptions dialog box to obtain the name of the cost field. We will be naming the fields Cost1, Cost2, and so on. The macro uses the Right$ function to isolate the item number without the word Cost.

635

 **Note**

Subtracting 4 from the length of the bookmark returns the amount of characters in the number itself. So, the function returns all of the characters in the bookmark name, less the first four.

The Item Number Bookmark

The item total form field in each row is named ItemTotal followed by the number of the item. The value of RowNum$ is concatenated with the string ItemTotal to form the name of the bookmark to be updated.

For example, if the user exits the form field named COST12, the value of RowNum$ will be the characters "12". The item number bookmark for the row will be ItemNumber12. The macro then updates the subtotal, tax, and grand total fields using the SetFormatResult command.

Using only a bookmark name as the argument for the SetFormatResult command recalculates the expression on a calculation type form field. For example, the command:

```
SetFormResult "Subtotal"
```

recalculates the expression in the SubTotal form field.

Entering the Cost Column Fields

Once you create the macro, enter the form fields in the Cost column.

1. Place the insertion point in cell C2, and select Insert ➤ Form Field ➤ Text ➤ Options.
2. Select a Number type, set the maximum number at 7, set the Number Format at 0.00, and then type COST1 in the Bookmark text box.
3. Pull down the Exit list in the Run Macro On section, select UpRow, and then click on OK.

4. Enter a similar form field in all but the last cell in that column, but increment the bookmark name, such as Cost2, Cost3, and so on, up to Cost15.

S O L U T I O N S

The OnLast Macro

The macro used on exit from the last cost field is different than the others. It will update the item total field for the row, update the other calculations, and then display the File Save As dialog box. Because the macro is only used for the final item, which will be COST16, it does not need to determine the name of the Cost field. Create this macro with the name OnLast:

```
Sub MAIN
    SetFormResult "ItemTotal16"
    SetFormResult "Subtotal"
    SetFormResult "Tax"
    SetFormResult "GrandTotal"
    EditGoTo "SoldTo"
    Dim EndForm As FileSaveAs
    Choice = Dialog(EndForm)
    If Choice = - 1 Then
        FileSaveAs EndForm
    EndIf
End Sub
```

Note   To create the form field, follow the steps shown previously for the other fields in the Cost column, but select OnLast as the On Exit macro.

Protecting and Saving the Invoice

Finally, protect the invoice template so it cannot be changed by the user. Select Tools ➤ Protect Document ➤ Forms ➤ OK.

N o t e   Remember, you will not be able to edit the form unless you select Tools ➤ UnProtect Document.

Save the form with the name INFORM. Word already has a sample template with the name INVOICE.DOT.

Using the Invoice

To use the invoice form, select File ➤ New, and double click on Inform in the list of templates. The form will appear with the insertion point in the first field.

Enter the name of the company placing the order, then press Enter to move to the next field, the second line for the Sold To section. Fill in the remaining items in the top portion of the invoice. If you do not have information for an item, just press Enter to bypass the field.

When you enter the Invoice # field, the SetInNum macro will insert the next invoice number. The insertion point will remain at the field, however, to give the user an opportunity to override the default by entering another number.

Then, enter the quantity, description and price of each item. When the user presses Enter without typing a quantity, or enters the cost in the final item line, the invoice is updated and the File Save As dialog box appears.

Other Form Macro Commands

WordBasic includes a number of other commands and functions for working with forms. Here's a brief review.

AddDropDownItem—Adds an item to a drop-down form field using the syntax:

```
AddDropDownItem(Bookmark$, Text$)
```

CheckBoxFormField—Inserts a checkbox form field into the document at the location of the insertion point.

ClearFormField—Removes the text from the current text form field when the document is protected. When used with an unprotected document, the command only deletes selected text in the field.

DropDownFormField—Inserts a drop-down form field at the location of the insertion point. Use the AddDropDownItem to add items to the list.

EnableFormField—Enables or disables the field. The syntax is:

```
EnableFormField Bookmark$, Type
```

(For the type, use 0 to disable or 1 to enable the field.)

FormShading—Turns off or on the shading of form fields. Use without an argument to toggle the setting; use 0 to turn off shading, or 1 to turn on shading.

FormShading( )—Returns 0 if shading is turned off, –1 if turned on.

InsertFormField—Inserts a form field at the location of the insertion point. The complete syntax is:

```
InsertFormField .Entry = "", .Exit = "", .Name="", .Enable = 1,
.TextType = 0, .TextWidth = "0", .TextDefault = "", .TextFormat =
"s", .TextWidth = "" or 0, .TextFormat = "", .CheckSize = 0, .Check-
Width = 0, .CheckDefault= 0, .Type = 0, .OwnHelp = 0, .HelpText =
"", .OwnStat = 0, .StatText = ""
```

RemoveAllDropDownItems—Removes all of the items from a drop-down form field list. The syntax is:

```
RemoveAllDropDownItems Bookmark$
```

RemoveDropDownItem—Removes a specific item from a drop-down form field list. The syntax is:

```
RemoveDropDownItem Bookmark$, Text$
```

TextFormField—Inserts a text form field at the location of the insertion point.

ToolsProtectDocument—Turns on document protection. The syntax is:

```
ToolsProtectDocument .DocumentPassword="", .NoReset=0, .Type=0
```

Tip

For NoReset, enter 1 to prevent Word from resetting the fields to their default values. When a document is protected, use type 0 (or omit the argument) to allow the user to edit text but to track changes with revision marks; use type 1 to allow only annotation; type 2 to allow only changes to the form fields.

ToolsProtectSection—Turns on or off document protection of a section. The syntax is:

```
ToolsProtectSection . Section=0,.Protect=0
```

Note

Specify the section number, and set Protect at 1 to protect the section, or at 0 (or omitted) to disable protection.

ToolsUnprotectDocument—Turns off all document protection. If a password was used to protect the document, use the syntax:

```
ToolsUnprotectDocument .DocumentPassword = password$
```

S E C R E T S

Form Tips and Tricks

When you print a form, all of the table lines, prompts, checkboxes, and other text prints in addition to the contents of the form fields.

If you designed a template to match a preprinted form, you can print just the text in the form fields and the X characters in selected checkboxes. Select Tools ➤ Options ➤ Print ➤ Print Data Only For Forms. Insert the preprinted form in your printer, then print the document.

You can also save just the data from the form, not the design of the form itself. Select Tools ➤ Options ➤ Save, then select Save Data Only For Forms. The content of the fields will be saved in a comma delimited text file with strings in quotation marks. The number 1 will be saved to indicate selected checkbox, 0 for cleared checkboxes.

Form fields are not only useful for forms designed as tables. You can use form fields to automate the production of form letters as well.

```
Mr. William Watson
634 West Avenue
Altoona,  PA  19222

Dear Mr. Watson:

I am sorry to report that your account is more than 30 days
overdue. If you do not submit full payment immediat  30   we
will take legal action.                                45
                                                       60
                                                       75
                                                       90
```

In the form letter shown on the previous page, for example, the name and address information was entered using text form fields. The number of days for past due accounts is being selected from a drop down list box.

Word provides three forms already complete for your use. You'll find them in the WINWORD/TEMPLATE directory.

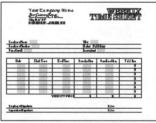

◆ INVOICE.DOT is an invoice form, similar to the form described in this chapter.

◆ PURCHORD.DOT is a purchase order form.

◆ WEEKTIME.DOT is a weekly time sheet.

Using Word Fields

Word has a number of other fields in addition to those you've learned about so far. As you have seen previously, when field codes are displayed, they have this general format:

```
{name instruction \switch}
```

Some field names are followed by one or more instructions that specify additional details about the field function. For example, the fillin field can be followed by a string indicating the prompt to appear in the fillin dialog box:

```
{fillin "Please enter your name" }
```

Most fields also have optional switches that follow the field name or instructions. Each switch starts with the backslash character. For example, in this field, the switch tells Word to display the fillin prompt only once:

```
{fillin "Enter your name" \o}
```

Other switches require arguments, as:

```
{createdate \@ "YYYY MM DD"}
```

to display the date the document was created using a custom date format. There are also general switches that can be used to format the appearance of text and numbers displayed as field results.

Inserting a Field

To insert a field, use any of these techniques:

◆ Press Ctrl+F9 to display the field braces, and then type the field and any instructions or switches.

◆ Type the field, instructions, and switches first, then select them and press Ctrl+F9. Word will insert the selected text in field braces.

◆ Select Insert ➤ Field and choose the field in the list box. If the Options button becomes selectable, click on it to see a list of instructions or switches available for the field. You can also select Help in the dialog box for additional information and a list of switches.

Updating a Field

After you insert a field, you can update its contents. Select the field and press F9, or click on it with the right mouse button and select Update Fields from the dialog box that appears.

Toggling between Codes and Results

To toggle between the display of field codes and their results, throughout the entire document, press Alt+F9, or select Tools ➤ Options ➤ View, then choose Field Codes in the View section. To toggle the display of just selected fields, press Shift+F9, or click on the field with the right mouse button and select Toggle Field Codes from the shortcut menu.

 **Note**   If Word cannot calculate or display the field results, it will display an error message, such as: Error! Bookmark not defined. Redisplay the field code and edit the field to include the proper bookmark names or syntax.

A Review of Other Word Fields

In this section, we'll discuss the fields you have not used previously. Select Help from the Insert Field dialog box for additional information.

Advance

The advance field moves the position of the text. For example, the field:

```
{advance \l36}This text starts in the margin!
```

will start the text $1/2$ inch into the left margin. As shown in Figure 15.11, the command does not change the margins or the indentation of the paragraph—wordwrap still continues lines at the margin position, only the first line is affected. The direction of the advance is given in a switch following the command. The distance is in points (there are 72 point to an inch).

FIGURE 15.11

Moving test with
the advance field

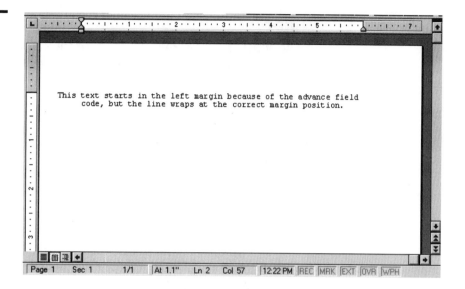

The switches are:

SWITCH	FUNCTION
\d	Moves text down.
\l	Moves text to the left.
\r	Moves text to the right.
\u	Moves text up.
\x	Moves text to a specific position from the left margin of a column or frame.
\y	Moves text to a specific position from the top of the page. The field has no affect on tables, frames, footnotes, endnotes, annotations, headers, and footers. You can see the affects of the field in Page Layout mode.

Author

The author field displays the name of the author contained in the Summary Info dialog box. You can include a string parameter to change the author name, as in:

```
{author "Jimmy Dean"}
```

You can also nest fields to input the new value, as in:

```
{author {fillin "Enter author's name"}}
```

AutoNum

Use this field to number paragraphs, similar to outlining. The first {autonum} field at an indentation level is numbered 1, the second at the same level is number 2, and so on. The numbers are followed by periods, and they reset to 1 at a new level, so this:

```
{autonum} Software
    {autonum} Word Processing
    {autonum} Database Management
```

produces this:

```
1. Software
    1. Word Processing
    2. Database Management
```

 **Note**   **Word will automatically update all autonum codes as you move, insert, or delete them in a document. You do not have to manually update the fields by pressing F9.**

As with an outline, the numbers of lower level indentations reset with a change in a higher level. However, the higher level must be numbered, as well. These codes:

```
{autonum} Software
    {autonum} Word Processing
    {autonum} Database Management
{autonum} Hardware
```

```
    {autonum} Computers
    {autonum} Printers
Supplies
    {autonum} Disks
    {autonum} Ribbons
```

result in:

```
1. Software
    1. Word Processing
    2. Database Management
2. Hardware
    1. Computers
    2. Printers
Supplies
    3. Disks
    4. Ribbons
```

(Notice that the numbers did not reset after the heading Supplies because it was not numbered.)

The autonumlgl field works the same way, but uses a legal numbering scheme:

```
1. Contracts
    1.1. Marriage
    1.2. Pre-Marital
2. Wills
    2.1. Last Will
    2.2. Living Will
```

The autonumout field uses the outlining method:

```
I. Causes of World War I
    A. Economic
        1. Trade imbalance
            a) Exports
```

AutoText

The AutoText field inserts the contents of an AutoText entry. The syntax is:

```
{AutoText entry_name}
```

Barcode

The barcode field inserts a POSTNET or FIM barcode. If you mark an address as a bookmark, you can use the zip code in the bookmark. The syntax is:

```
{barcode text, switches}
```

The text argument is the zip code to use for the barcode. When you use the /b switch, text can also be the name of a bookmark containing the address. The switches are:

SWITCH	FUNCTION
\b	Uses the zip code from the named bookmark.
\f"type"	Creates a Facing Identification Mark (FIM) code. Use type "A" for a courtesy reply mark or "C" for a business reply mark. The envelope must also contain a POSTNET code, so use the barcode field without the \f switch first.
\u	Designates a POSTNET barcode as a postal address.

Note When you create an envelope using the Tools menu, Word automatically assign the address to the bookmark ENV_ZIPCIDE1.

CreateDate

The CreateDate field displays the date the document was first created, as contained in the Document Statistics dialog box. The syntax is:

```
{createdate \@ "Picture"}
```

 **Tip**   Use the optional \@ switch to specify a picture format other than the default. Refer to "General Switches" later in this chapter to learn about format pictures.

Database

This powerful command inserts the results of an SQL query of an external database into a table. The switches are:

SWITCH	FUNCTION
\b	When used with the \l switch, determines which AutoFormat features are applied to the table. The value is the sum of these arguments: 0 for none; 1 for borders; 2 for shading; 4 for fonts; 8 for color; 16 for autofit; 32 for header rows; 64 for the last row; 128 for the first row; and 256 for the last column.
\c	Applies connection instructions for ODBC protocol.
\d	Sets the path and filename of the database.
\f	Specifies the starting data record to insert.
\l	AutoFormats the table using the specified style. The argument is equal to the position of the style in the AutoFormat list. For example, "\l "1"" applies the first style listed, Simple1; "\l "2"" applies the second style, Simple2, and so on.
\s	Sets the SQL instructions for the query.
\t	Specifies the ending record to insert.

Date

Inserts the date into the document. There are two optional switches. Use \l to insert the date in the last format selected in the Insert ➤ Date and Time dialog box, or use \@ followed by a custom date format.

649

EditTime

Displays the total editing time devoted to the document, as contained in the Document Statistics dialog box.

FileName

Displays the name of the active document. Use the optional \p switch to include the path.

FileSize

Displays the size of the document, as contained in the Document Statistics dialog box. Optional switches include \k to show the size in kilobytes, and \m to display the size in megabytes. With either switch, Word will round the size to the next whole number.

GoToButton

This command creates a hypertext jump command. When the user double-clicks on the field, the insertion point moves to a designated bookmark. The syntax is:

```
{GoToButton bookmark button}
```

Include optional button text that you want to appear in the field. You can also use a nested IncludePicture field to display the button as a graphic, as in:

```
{GoToButton summary {IncludePicture summ.bmp}}
```

(See Chapter 16 for additional information on using this field.)

IncludePicture

Displays a picture file, using the syntax:

```
{IncludePicture filename switches}
```

To include a path in the filename, use two backslash characters as in "C:\\windows\\art.bmp". Optional switches are \o to specify a graphic conversion filter file, and \d to create a link with the picture rather than embed it into the document.

IncludeText

In Chapter 13 you learned how to use the IncludeText field to assemble documents. You can also use the field to insert the contents of a bookmark from the document, rather than the entire document itself, using the syntax:

```
{IncludeText filename bookmark-name}
```

The field has two optional switches. Use the \c switch to specify a conversion format to override the automatic conversion selected by Word. Use the \! switch to prevent Word from updating any fields in the included text.

Index

Creates an index by collecting entries specified by the XE field. Here are the switches:

SWITCH	FUNCTION
\b	Creates the index from text marked as a designated bookmark.
\c	Formats the index in up to four columns, as in \c 2 for a two column index list.
\d	Indicates the characters to use for separating a page and sequence number field. See the \s switch.
\e	Indicates the separator characters between an index entry and its page number.
\f	Limits the index to a specified entry type.
\g	Determines the separator characters used in a page range.
\h	Inserts group headings formatted with the Index Heading style.
\l	Determines the separator characters used between page numbers for entries with multiple-page references.

SWITCH	FUNCTION
\p	Limits the index to the specified letters. The field {index \p b--n}, for example, created an index of entries beginning with the letters b through n.
\r	Places subentries on the same line as the main entry.
\s	Includes a sequence number with the page number.

Info

Displays information contained in the Summary Info and Document Statistics dialog boxes. The syntax is:

```
{Info argument "new setting"}
```

The word Info is optional. Possible arguments are AUTHOR, COMMENTS, CREATEDATE, EDITTIME, FILENAME, FILESIZE, KEYWORDS, LASTSAVEDBY, NUMCHARS, NUMPAGES, NUMWORDS, PRINTDATE, REVNUM, SAVEDATE, SUBJECT, TEMPLATE, and TITLE.

You can specify a new setting for the AUTHOR, COMMENTS, KEYWORDS, SUBJECT, and TITLE arguments.

Keywords

Displays the keywords contained in the Summary Info dialog box.

LastSavedBy

Displays the date the document was last saved, as contained in the Document Statistics dialog box.

Link

Creates an OLE link. The syntax is:

```
{link ClassName Filename PlaceReference Switches}
```

The ClassName is the application type, such as "ExcelChart." Use an optional PlaceReference to specify the portion of the file to be linked, such as a range of worksheet cells.

The optional switches are:

SWITCH	FUNCTION
\a	Updates the field automatically.
\b	Inserts the object as a bitmap.
\d	Links a graphic without embedding it.
\p	Inserts the object as a graphic.
\r	Inserts the object in rich-text format.
\t	Inserts the object in text-only format.

MacroButton

Inserts a button that runs a macro when double-clicked. Uses the same syntax as GoToButton. See Chapter 16 for additional information about this field.

NoteRef

Inserts the footnote or endnote number of a specified bookmark. Use the field to reference the same note in more than one location. The optional \f switch displays the number in the Footnote Reference or Endnote Reference style.

NumChars

Displays the number of characters in document, as contained in the Document Statistics dialog box.

NumPages

Displays the number of pages in document, as contained in the Document Statistics dialog box.

NumWords

Displays the number of words in document, as contained in the Document Statistics dialog box.

Page

Displays the current page number.

PageRef

Displays the page number where a specified bookmark is located. The syntax is:

```
{pageref bookmark}
```

For example, use the field to reference another location, as in:

```
Please see Page {pageref causes} for additional information on the
causes of World War II.
```

Print

Transmits control codes and PostScript instructions to the printer, using the syntax:

```
{print "Instructions"}
```

PrintDate

Displays the date the document was last printed, as contained in the Document Statistics dialog box.

Private

Word may insert this field when you open a document that was created by another word processing program. The field will internally store information that will be needed if you use Word to convert the document back to its original format.

Quote

Inserts literal text into a document.

RD

Specifies a file to include when you create a table of contents, table of authorities, or an index

Ref

Inserts the contents of a bookmark. The syntax is:

```
{Ref bookmark}
```

The name Ref is optional. Use the \f switch to include footnote, endnote, or annotation numbers, or use the \n switch to insert any paragraph numbering from the bookmark.

RevNum

Displays the revision number, as contained in the Document Statistics dialog box.

SaveDate

Displays the date the document was last saved, as contained in the Document Statistics dialog box.

Section

Inserts the section number.

SectionPages

Inserts the number of pages in the current section.

Seq

In Chapter 3, you learned how to use the Seq field to number tickets. The field can use these switches:

SWITCH	FUNCTION
\c	Inserts the last sequence number used, without incrementing it.
\h	Hides the field result so it does not appear.
\n	Increments and inserts the sequence number (the default setting).
\r	Resets the sequence number to a specified value. For example, use \r 1 to reset the number to 1.

StyleRef

Inserts text from a section of the document formatted using a speci-fied style. The syntax is:

{StyleRef "Style"}

Word begins at the location of the insertion point, and scans toward the start of the document. The first paragraph it encounters that is format-ted in the specified style is inserted at the field.

There are two optional switches. If you use the \l switch, Word will search from the end of the document to the current page. Use the \n switch to include any paragraph numbering found with the inserted text.

Subject

Displays the subject of the document, as contained in the Summary Info dialog box.

Symbol

Inserts a character from the ANSI character set. The syntax is:

{symbol Num}

The number can be the character itself, or a decimal or hexadecimal value representing the character. (Precede a hexadecimal number with the characters 0x.)

Optional switches are:

SWITCH	FUNCTION
\f	Designates the name of the font, enclosed in quotation marks.
\h	Inserts the symbol while maintaining the current line spacing.
\s	Designates the point size.

TA

Creates a table of authorities entry. The switches are:

SWITCH	FUNCTION
\b	Formats the page number in bold.
\c	Defines the entry's category number.
\i	Formats the page number in italic.
\l	Defines the entry's long citation.
\r	Includes the page range of the bookmark.
\s	Defines the entry's short citation.

TC

Creates a table of contents entry, using the syntax:

```
{tc "Text"}
```

You can use the following switches:

SWITCH	FUNCTION
\f	Specifies a specific type.
\l	Specifies the level of the entry.
\n	Prevents the page number from appearing.

Template

Displays the name of the template used for the active document. Use the optional \p switch to include the path.

Time

Inserts the current time into the document.

Title

Displays the title of the document as contained in the Summary Info dialog box. You can include a string parameter to change the title.

TOA

Creates a table of authorities, using the syntax:

```
{toa \c switch}
```

Create table entries using the TA field. You must use the \c switch to specify the category of included entries. Optional switches include \b, \d, \e, \g, \h, \l, \p, and \s as described for the Index field. In addition, you can use the \f switch to remove the formatting from the entries.

TOC

Creates a table of contents using entries defined with the TC field. Optional switches include \b and \p as described for the Index field, as well as:

SWITCH	FUNCTION
\a	Creates a figure table without labels and numbers.
\c	Creates a figure table of entries marked with a specified SEQ (Sequence) fields.
\f	Limits entries to those with a specified identifier.
\l	Limits entries to those at a specified level. For example, {TOC \l 1--3} builds the table from TC fields in levels 1 through 3.
\n	Displays the table without page numbers.
\o	Formats entries using heading styles. For example, level 1 entries will be formatted by Heading 1, level 2 entries by Heading 2, and so on.
\s	Creates the table using sequence numbers in addition to page numbers.
\t	Specifies alternate style names for formatting entries.

UserAddress

Displays the user address as contained in the Tools ➤ Options ➤ User Info dialog box. Include a literal string to change the address.

UserInitials

Displays the user initials as contained in the Tools ➤ Options ➤ User Info dialog box. Include a literal string to change the initials.

UserName

Displays the user name as contained in the Tools ➤ Options ➤ User Info dialog box. Include a literal string to change the name.

XE

Defines an index entry, using the syntax:

```
{XE "Text"}
```

The entries are used to create an index with the Index field. Use the optional \b, \I, and \r switches as described for the TA field. You can also use the \f switch to limit entries to a specified type, and the \t switch to insert the text following the switch in the place of the page number.

Formatting Field Results

You can control how the result of a field is displayed by using general format switches. The switches can be used with all fields except these:

AutoNum

Autonumlgl

Autonumout

Embed

Eq

GoToButton

MacroButton

RD

TA

TC

XE

(Use the \! to lock the results of fields included in bookmark, IncludeText or Ref fields.)

Formatting Characters

Use the * switch to format the appearance of characters in text and numbers. For example, the field:

{author * upper}

will display the name of the author in all upper case characters. There are three categories of formatting switches—case conversion, numeric conversion, character formatting.

CASE CONVERSION SWITCHES

SWITCH	FUNCTION
* caps	Capitalizes the first letter of every word.
* firstcap	Capitalizes the first character of the first word.
* lower	Displays the field in all lowercase characters.
* upper	Displays the field in all uppercase characters.

NUMERIC CONVERSION SWITCHES

SWITCH	FUNCTION
* alphabetic	Displays numbers as alphabetic. For example, if you enter the field {page * Alphabetic} on the first page of a document, the result will display as the letter A. The case of the character matches the first letter of the switch. The number 27 will be displayed as AA, number 28 as BB, and so on.
* arabic	Displays number in arabic form.
* cardtext	Displays numbers in text form. The number 14, for example, will appear as fourteen.

SWITCH	FUNCTION

* dollartext	Displays numbers in text form with decimal values. The field:
	`{quote "14.56" \* dollartext}`
	will display:
	`fourteen and 45/100`

* hex	Displays a number in hexadecimal format.
* ordinal	Displays ordinal form. The field {page * ordinal} on page 20 will display 20th.
* ordtext	Displays a number in ordinal text, such as "twentieth".
* roman	Displays a number as a roman numeral.

CHARACTER FORMATTING

SWITCH	FUNCTION
* charformat	Formats the entire result according to the format of the first character of the field. This is the default setting and can be omitted. For example, {Page } and {Page * charformat} will both display the page number in italic. You must include the switch to format quote field results.
* mergeformat	After updating a field, applies the format of the previous result.

Numeric Picture Switches

The \# switch specifies the format of numeric values using a picture clause. For example, the field:

`{ = SUM(23, 45, 76) \# $#,##0.00 }`

will display $ 144.00.

Note   You can also enclose literal text within the picture. However, the entire picture must then be enclosed in quotation marks, and the text in single-quotes as in:
{ salary \# "$#,##0.00 'debit'"}

The picture clause can contain these characters:

CHARACTER	FUNCTION
0	Required digit placeholder
#	Optional digit placeholder
x	Rounds and truncates the results
.	The position of the decimal point
,	Use a thousands separator
–	A minus sign in negative results, a space in positive results
+	A plus sign in positive results, a minus sign in negative results
'sequence'	The sequence value with the name enclosed in grave accent (`) characters

Tip   To display positive and negative results in different formats, specify each picture separated by a semicolon. For example, the field: {= net \# $#,##0.00;$#,##.00} displays negative results underlined. Use a third argument for zero results.

Date-Time Picture

Use the \@ switch for determine the format of date and time field results. For example, the field:

```
{ DATE \@ "YYYY-MMM-d dddd hh:mm AM/PM" }
```

will display the date and time in this format:

```
1994-Dec-29 Wednesday 04:38 AM
```

The possible characters are:

MONTHS CODE	DISPLAYS
M	9
MM	09
MMM	Aug
MMM	August
DAYS CODE	**DISPLAYS**
d	5
dd	05
ddd	Thu
dddd	Thursday
YEAR CODE	**DISPLAYS**
yy	95
yyyy	1995
HOURS CODE	**DISPLAYS**
h	6
hh	06
H	18
HH	01

(Use lowercase for 12 hour time, uppercase for 24 hour time.)

MINUTES CODE	DISPLAYS
m	4
mm	04

AM/PM CODE	DISPLAYS
AM/PM	AM or PM
am/pm	am or pm
A/P	A or P
a/p	a or p

CHAPTER 16

Special Applications

H OW FAR YOU AUTOMATE DOCUMENTS depends on your office procedures. At a minimum, you should create a template for each standard form or document you create containing the styles, standard headings, AutoText entries, and macros used for that document. For additional control, you can create custom forms, or design merge documents using fillin and ask fields. This chapter shows you some specialized techniques for applying Word to business in general and for setting bookmarks, creating hypertext documents, and recording and playing music and sound clips.

Creating Billable Time Applications

Consultants and professionals of all types must bill clients for their time. You should also record your time to help develop proposals and job estimates. Since it is all too easy to forget to record your time, you can use AutoOpen, AutoNew, and AutoClose macros to record time for you.

 **Tip**
If you don't want to take automation this far, give the macros other names and add them to toolbar buttons. While the macros will not run automatically, the user can easily click on a toolbar button to record the time for billing purposes.

Logging Billable Time

The system starts with this simple macro:

```
Sub MAIN
SetDocumentVar "OT", Time$()
End Sub
```

The AutoNew and AutoOpen Macros

Write the macro twice. Name one copy AutoNew and name the other copy AutoOpen. The macro saves the time that the document was opened to the document variable OT. This variable will be overwritten each time the document is opened, so it always contains the starting time of the current work session. The function Time$( ) returns the current time maintained by your system's clock, in the format 12:00 P.M.

S O L U T I O N S

The AutoClose Macro

When you close a document, you want to subtract the starting time from the closing time to determine the amount of time you spent on the document for that current session. The macro shown here will record the time as a document variable. Write the following macro under the name AutoClose:

```
Sub MAIN
Doit = MsgBox("Do you want to log this time", \
    "Time Log", 292)
If Doit = 0 Then Goto EndMacro
start$ = GetDocumentVar$("OT")
start = TimeValue(start$)
done$ = Time$()
done = TimeValue(Time$())
net = done - start
net$ = LTrim$(Str$(net))
NumDocs = CountDocumentVars()
If NumDocs < 10 Then
    addchar$ = "0"
```

```
      Else
      addchar$ = " "
  EndIf
  NewVar$ = "Rev" + addchar$ + LTrim$(Str$(NumDocs))\
      + " "
  Rev$ = NewVar$ + "S: " + start$ + " E: " + done$ \
      + " Session: " + net$
  SetDocumentVar NewVar$, rev$
  FileSave
  EndMacro:
  End Sub
```

Logging Time

The macro starts by displaying a message box asking if the user wants to log the time. If the user selects No, the macro ends. This process gives the user the choice of not recording a session as billable hours. If you want to record all time, delete the MsgBox instruction and the If command that follows it.

Next, the macro retrieves the starting time from the document variable OT and converts the time into a decimal number:

```
start$ = GetDocumentVar$("OT")
start = TimeValue(start$)
```

The parameter of the TimeValue( ) must be a time string or literal. It can be in 24-hour time, such as 14:50:00, or use the AM or PM indicator for 12-hour time, as in 1:30 AM and 10:15 PM. The digits for seconds are optional.

The function returns a decimal number that represents the time, ranging from 0 for 12:00:00 AM, to 0.99998842592593 for 11:59:59 PM. The serial number for noon is 0.5. Each minute has a time value of 0.00069444444444444.

The macro then determines the serial number for the current time, and assigns the difference between the values to the variable net, which is converted to a string.

Storing Document Variables

The document variables used to store the work session information will be saved with names that begin with the characters Rev followed by a number. The number will be equal to the number of document variables. Because you must run the AutoOpen macro first, there will always be at least one variable already in the document, OT, which stores the starting time. If that is the only existing variable, the number 1 will be used for the first session variable.

 **Note**

The numbers will not necessarily be consecutive. For example, if you have already inserted 12 document variables using the Revision macro shown in Chapter 14, the first variable created by this macro will be Rev13. If you then insert another revision note, the next macro recorded by AutoClose will be Rev15. The actual numbers are not really critical, they are just used to ensure that each entry is unique.

Word stores document variables in alphabetic order by their names. However, alphabetic order will list Rev10 after Rev1, and before Rev2, not after Rev9. To keep numbers 1 through 99 in order, the macro adds a leading 0 to numbers less than 10 by assigning the value "0" to the variable addchar$, which is concatenated with the characters Rev and the number itself to form the variable name:

```
NumDocs = CountDocumentVars()
If NumDocs < 10 Then
     addchar$ = "0"
     Else
     addchar$ = ""
EndIf
NewVar$ = "Rev" + addchar$ + LTrim$(Str$(NumDocs)) + " "
```

669

Note

When the number is 1, for example, the variable name will be Rev01. With numbers greater than 9, the variable addchar$ will contain a null value, and it will have no affect on the document variable name.

Variable Content Format

The content of the variable will use this format:

```
Rev10 S: 10:25 AM E: 10:35 AM Session: 0.0069444444444444
```

It is a concatenation of the variable name, the starting and ending times, and the difference between them in serial units. The macro creates the string and then sets the document variable.

Saving the Document

Finally, the macro saves the document. This is a needed step even if the user manually saves the document before closing it.

Note

Adding a document variable changes the document, so if the macro did not save it, a message box will appear before the document is actually cleared from the window. If the user selects No from the message box, the document will be closed without saving the newly added document variable. The FileSave command prevents this from occurring.

S E C R E T S

Time Tips and Tricks

Without a parameter, the Time$( ) function returns the current system time, but you can also use the function to display the time indicated by a serial value. For example, the command:

```
Insert Time$(0)
```

will display 12:00 AM, the time equal to serial value of 0. If you use a parameter of 1 or more, the time will cycle. For example, both Time$(0) and Time$(1) represent 12:00 AM, and both Time$(0.0006944444444) and Time$(1.0006944444444) are 12:01 AM.

You can also use the TimeSerial( ) function, which returns the serial number of a time using this syntax:

```
TimeSerial(hour, minute, second)
```

as in:

```
Insert Str$(TimeSerial(14,30,0))
```

which would return 0.60416666666667 to represent 2:30 PM.

Here are some other time functions:

- ◆ *Hour()* returns the hour (0 to 23) indicated by a serial time number.
- ◆ *Minute()* returns the minute (0 to 59) of a serial time number.
- ◆ *Second()* returns the second (0 to 59) of a serial time number.

Word also provides a number of functions for working with dates as serial numbers:

◆ *DateValue()* returns the serial number for a date using the format DateValue("1/1/95"). Word displays whole numbers, such as 34700 for the 1/1/95. Each increment of one is another day.

◆ *Date$()* returns a date as a string indicated by a serial number.

◆ *DateSerial()* returns the serial number for a date using the format DateSerial(year, month, day).

◆ *Day()* returns the day (1 to 31) indicated by a serial date number.

◆ *Month()* returns the month (1 to 12) of a serial date number.

◆ *Year()* returns the year (1899 to 4095) of a serial date number.

◆ *Weekday()* returns the day of the week (1 to 7) for a serial date number. Sunday is 1, Monday is 2, and so on.

◆ *Day360()* returns the number of days between two dates, based on a 360 day year. The syntax is Day360(Day1$, Day2$), as in Day360("10/22/94", "11/16/94").

The function Now() returns a serial number indicating the current date and time, in the format 34629.480706019. The integer portion represents the date, the decimal portion the time.

To convert the number to a date and time, you must use both the Date$() and Time$() functions. Date$() will ignore the decimal portion and only return the date. Time$() will ignore the integer portion and only display the time. (The number 34629.480706019, by the way, represents October 22, 1994 at 11:32 AM.)

> Use Now( ) if you are tracking editing sessions that run over two days, past midnight. In the AutoOpen and AutoNew macros, use the command:
>
> ```
> SetDocumentVar "OT", Str$(Now())
> ```
>
> to record the date and time.
>
> In the AutoClose macro, use these commands in place of those that use Time$( ) and TimeValue( ):
>
> ```
> start$ = GetDocumentVar$("OT")
> start = Val(start$)
> done = Now()
> done$ = str$(done)
> ```

Totaling Billable Time

Each of the session entries will be saved as a document variable. When you want to total the billable time devoted to the document, use the macro shown in the following sidebar. It adds the name of the document and the total time spent on it to a private setting file having this format:

```
[Accounting]
C:\WINWORD\BUDGET.DOC=18
C:\WINWORD\REPORT.DOC=123
```

The document name is used as the section name. You can run the macro at any time when a document is active to update the total time. Each time you run the macro it overwrites the previous setting for the same document.

Scanning Document Variables

The macro scans each document variable to determine if its name starts with Rev and its contents include the word Session. Both conditions are used to avoid accidentally listing other document variables that also start with Rev. Notice that the macro ends if it contains no document variables, or none that match the specifications.

SOLUTIONS

The Total Macro

Write this macro with the name Total:

```
Sub MAIN
Total = 0
NumDocs = CountDocumentVars()
If NumDocs = 0 Then Goto EndMacro
X = 0
For DOC = 1 To NumDocs
    VarName$ = GetDocumentVarName$(Doc)
    If Left$(VarName$, 3) = "Rev" Then
        Rev$ = GetDocumentVar$(VarName$)
        pos = InStr(Rev$, "Session: ") + 8
        If pos > 8 Then
        char = Len(Rev$) - pos
        add$ = LTrim$(Right$(Rev$, char))
        total = total + Val(add$)
        X = 1
        EndIf
    EndIf
Next
If X = 0 Then Goto endmacro
minutes = Int(total / 0.00069444444444444)
Sub$ = FileNameFromWindow$()
SetPrivateProfileString "Accounting", Sub$,\
    Str$(minutes), "BILLABLE.INI"
EndMacro:
End Sub
```

Isolating Time from Settings

The commands that isolate the time from the setting are separated in a series of instructions to make them clear. First, the ending position of the text "Session: " is located in the string to mark the start of the characters representing the time:

```
pos = InStr(Rev$, "Session: ") + 8
```

A position not greater than 8 indicates that the text is not in the string (the InStr function would return a 0 value and the variable pos would equal 8), so the variable does not contain session time information. If this occurs, the loop is repeated and the macro retrieves the next document variable.

Assigning Characters to the Variable Char

Next, the variable char is assigned the number of characters in the string that represent the number of minutes. This is done by subtracting the starting position of the number from the length of the string:

```
char = Len(Rev$) - pos
```

The variable add$ is then assigned those characters from the right end of the string:

```
add$ = LTrim$(Right$(Rev$, char))
```

Next, the characters are converted to a numeric value and accumulated in the total:

```
total = total + Val(add$)
```

The loop repeats to retrieve the next document variable.

Converting Serial Units to Minutes

The variable total is in time serial units, so fifteen minutes, for example, would appear as 0.010416666666667. The total is converted to minutes by dividing it by the serial unit for a minute and removing any decimal remainder:

```
minutes = int(total / 0.00069444444444444)
```

Recording the Total Time

Finally, the total time spent on the document is recorded in the Accounting section of a private setting file. The document name becomes the option name.

Designing a Client Accounting System

By combining elements of the macros discussed in this and previous chapters, you can create a client billing system. Rather than store the billable times in one large section, for example, use separate sections for each client. The section will include the name of each document, and the time spent on it. You can then use sections to prepare invoices, or to analyze your efforts.

Adding Clients

You will need a private setting file listing the names of each client and the number of clients. The macro you need to create is similar to the one you created in Chapter 14 to add executives to the document management system.

S O L U T I O N S

The AddClient Macro

Create the following macro with the name AddClient:

```
Sub MAIN
NumOfClients$ = GetPrivateProfileString$("Total", \
    "Clients", "clients.ini")
NumClients = Val(NumOfClients$)
Goto GetClient
ClientError:
Choice = MsgBox("Client already entered or improper name", \
    "Add a client", 1)
    If Choice = 0 Then Goto EndMacro
GetClient:
On Error Goto EndMacro
```

```
ClientName$ = InputBox$("Enter last name", "Add a client")
ClientName$ = UCase$(ClientName$)
PTH$ = Left$(ClientName$, 8)
pos = InStr(ClientName$, " ")
If pos > 0 Then PTH$ = Left$(ClientName$, pos - 1)
Flag = 0
For x = 1 To Len(PTH$)
  If Mid$(PTH$, x, 1) < "0" Or Mid$(PTH$, x, 1) > "Z" \
  Or (Mid$(PTH$, x, 1) > "9" And Mid$(PTH$, x, 1) < "A") \
    Then

          Flag = 1
Next
If Flag = 1 Then Goto ClientError
On Error Goto ClientError
    MkDir "C:\" + PTH$
NumClients = NumClients + 1
NumClients$ = LTrim$(Str$(NumClients))
CString$ = "CLIENT" + Numclients$
SetPrivateProfileString "Total", "Clients", NumClients$, \
    "clients.ini"
SetPrivateProfileString "Names", CString$, ClientName$, \
    "clients.ini"
EndMacro:
End Sub
```

Creating Client Directories

The macro creates a directory for each client by using the first eight characters in the client name:

```
PTH$ = Left$(ClientName$, 8)
```

Because directory names cannot include spaces, the macro shortens the name up to the first space, if one exists:

```
pos = InStr(ClientName$, " ")
If pos > 0 Then PTH$ = Left$(ClientName$, pos - 1)
```

Error Trap and Path Name Checks

An On Error statement will trap an attempt to create a directory that already exists, but it will not trap an improper directory name. So the macro checks the path name for any characters not allowed in directory names, accepting only uppercase characters and numbers. (Lower case characters are allowed in directory names, but the client name has already been converted to uppercase anyway.) The directory is then created to store the client's files.

Creating a Setting File

The macro then creates a setting file in this format:

```
[Total]
Clients=3

[Names]
CLIENT1=COMPUTERS ARE US INC.
CLIENT2=WATSON AND COMPANY
CLIENT3=SMITHSON ENGINE COMPANY
```

Saving to a Directory

The AutoClose macro shown previously displays the File Save As dialog box if the document has not been named before closing. If you store your client files in separate directories, the AutoClose macro must let the user choose the client name from a list box, then set the path to the proper directory before saving the file, as in this macro:

```
Sub Main
Doit = MsgBox("Do you want to log this time", "log", 292)
If doit = 0 Then Goto EndMacro
start$ = GetDocumentVar$("OT")
start = TimeValue(start$)
done$ = Time$()
done = TimeValue(Time$())
net = done - start
net$ = LTrim$(Str$(net))
NumDocs = CountDocumentVars()
If NumDocs < 10 Then
    addchar$ = "0"
    Else
    addchar$ = ""
```

```
EndIf
NewVar$ = "Rev" + addchar$ + LTrim$(Str$(NumDocs)) + " "
Rev$ = NewVar$ + "S: " + start$ + " E: " + done$ + " Session: " +
net$
SetDocumentVar NewVar$, rev$
If FileNameFromWindow$() = "" Then
NumOfClients$ = GetPrivateProfileString$("Total", \
 "Clients", "clients.ini")
NumClients = Val(NumOfClients$) - 1
Dim Clients$(NumClients)
For x = 0 To NumClients
    CString$ = "CLIENT" + LTrim$(Str$(X + 1))
    CName$ = GetPrivateProfileString$("Names", CString$, \
    "clients.ini")
    Clients$(x) = CName$
Next
Begin Dialog UserDialog 416, 200, "Microsoft Word"
    ListBox 102, 18, 160, 144, Clients$(), .ListBox1
    OKButton 305, 126, 88, 21
    CancelButton 305, 156, 88, 21
End Dialog

Dim A As UserDialog
C = Dialog(A)
If C = 0 Then Goto Endmacro
Num = A.ListBox1
OldDir$ = DefaultDir$(0)
PTH$ = Left$(Clients$(Num), 8)
pos = InStr(Clients$(Num), " ")
If pos > 0 Then PTH$ = Left$(Clients$(Num), pos - 1)
PTH$ = "C:\" + PTH$ + "\"
ChDir Pth$
Dim FSA As FileSaveAs
Choice = Dialog(FSA)
If Choice = - 1 Then FileSaveAs FSA Else Goto EndMacro
ChDir OldDir$
Else
FileSave
EndIf
EndMacro:
End Sub
```

If you study the macro, you'll see that it combines techniques from the previous AutoClose macro with standard routines that you've used in a number of macros already. For example, it contains the routine for displaying and selecting clients from a list box that you've used for a number of macros. It also uses the routine for determining the directory from the client name as in AddClient.

Nothing in the macro is a new technique, it simply uses previous routines as building blocks.

Recording Billable Time Data

When you are ready to record the active document's billable time in the setting file, let a macro determine the section name using the document's path.

To determine the section name, first use the FileInfoName$( ) function to return the path. Next, scan all of the names in the setting file, converting each name to the client's path. When the path of the document matches the path determined from the client's name in the setting file, you know which section to record the billable time.

S O L U T I O N S

Time Recording Macro

A macro that determines the client's directory is shown here. It is similar to the Total macro shown previously, however, it replaces it by determining the client section to insert the item. The macro also displays a list box of billable time entries.

```
Sub MAIN
dir$ = FileNameInfo$(FileNameFromWindow$(), 5)
NumOfClients$ = GetPrivateProfileString$("Total", \
  "Clients", "clients.ini")
NumClients = Val(NumOfClients$) - 1
For x = 0 To NumClients
    CString$ = "CLIENT" + LTrim$(Str$(X + 1))
    CName$ = GetPrivateProfileString$("Names", CString$, \
    "clients.ini")
    PTH$ = Left$(CName$, 8)
    pos = InStr(CName$, " ")
    If pos > 0 Then PTH$ = Left$(CName$, pos - 1)
```

```
      PTH$ = "C:\" + PTH$ + "\"
      If PTH$ = dir$ Then FoundIt$ = CName$
Next
Total = 0
NumDocs = CountDocumentVars()
If NumDocs > 0 Then
RevN = 0
x = 0
For DOC = 1 To NumDocs
      VarName$ = GetDocumentVarName$(Doc)
      If Left$(VarName$, 3) = "Rev" Then
            Rev$ = GetDocumentVar$(VarName$)
            pos = InStr(Rev$, "Session: ") + 8
            If pos > 8 Then
            X = X + 1
            EndIf
      EndIf
Next
Dim RevisionList$(x - 1)
For DOC = 1 To NumDocs
      VarName$ = GetDocumentVarName$(Doc)
      If Left$(VarName$, 3) = "Rev" Then
            Rev$ = GetDocumentVar$(VarName$)
            pos = InStr(Rev$, "Session: ") + 8
            If pos > 8 Then
            RevisionList$(RevN) = Rev$
            char = Len(Rev$) - pos
            add$ = LTrim$(Right$(Rev$, char))
            total = total + Val(add$)
            RevN = RevN + 1
            EndIf
      EndIf
Next
Else
Dim RevisionList$(0)
EndIf
Begin Dialog UserDialog 484, 256, "Microsoft Word"
      Text 182, 7, 105, 13, "Revision Log", .Text1
      ListBox 10, 25, 463, 142, RevisionList$(), .ListBox1
      OKButton 250, 220, 88, 21
```

```
End Dialog
Dim Rev As UserDialog
Choice = Dialog(Rev)
minutes = total / 0.00069444444444444
If FileNameFromWindow$() = "" Then
    Input "Enter subject name", Sub$
    If Sub$ = "" Then Sub$ = "Misc " + Date$() + " " +
Time$()
Else
    Sub$ = FileNameFromWindow$()
EndIf
SetPrivateProfileString FoundIt$, Sub$, Str$(minutes),
"Time.Ini"
EndMacro:
End Sub
```

Creating a List Box of Variables

The macro creates a list box of document variables with names starting with Rev and whose contents include the word "Session." Both conditions are used to avoid accidentally listing other document variables that
also start with Rev. Notice that the macro ends if it contains no document
variables, or none that match the specifications.

For Loop Procedures

Two complete passes are made through the document variables using
For loops. In the first For loop, the number of variables meeting the conditions are counted. The array is then dimensioned, and a second pass is
used to actually add the elements to the list. The variable RevN is used as
the list box array subscript.

 **Note**

If may seem a waste of time to use two complete passes through the document variables when one loop could fill the array. For example, you can dimension the array to store the total number of document variables: Dim RevisionList$(NumDocs -1). You could then delete the first For loop and load the array using the second loop exactly as it appears in the macro. However, some memory set aside for array elements will not be assigned values. The empty array elements will "appear" as blank entries in the list box. You will be able to scroll the list and highlight blank lines in the box. It is best not to have empty list elements.

Printing a Client Summary

The billable time information stored in the setting file can be used in a variety of ways. For example, you can use the data to prepare invoices, or to analyze your efforts by client or project.

One way to access the file, is to use the GetPrivateProfileSetting command. You can retrieve the total number of clients to load an array with the client names. However, to access the individual options in each client section, you would need a count of the items for each client, in much the same way the document management macros in Chapter 14 recorded the number of documents for each executive.

The Macro Report

The macro would produce a report as shown in Figure 16.1.

The private setting file TIME.INI consists only of sections using the client names, such as [COMPUTERS ARE US INC.]. All of the options on that section are items of billable time.

SOLUTIONS

The Report Macro

As an alternative to adding these instructions, access the setting file as a sequential text file using the Line Input command. The trick is to isolate the individual client sections, as shown in this macro, named Report:

```
Sub MAIN
     Open "C:\windows\time.ini" For Input As #1
     Line Input #1, Sting$
     size = Len(Sting$) - 2
     client$ = Mid$(Sting$, 2, size)
     While Not Eof(#1)
     X = 0
     Total = 0
     Underline 1
     Insert "Billable time for " + Client$
     Underline 0
     InsertPara
     InsertPara
     While Not Eof(#1) And X = 0
          Line Input #1, Sing$
          If Left$(Sing$, 1) = "[" Or Sing$ = "" Then
          X = 1
          Else
          pos = InStr(Sing$, "=")
          prolen = pos - 1
          project$ = Left$(Sing$, prolen)
          timelen = Len(Sing$) - pos
          billable$ = Right$(Sing$, timelen)
          Insert project$ + Chr$(9) + billable$
          total = total + Val(billable$)
          InsertPara
          EndIf
          Wend
     Italic 1
     Insert "Total for " + Clients$ + " is " \
          + Str$(total)
```

```
      Italic 0
      InsertPara
      InsertPara
      grandtot = grandtot + total
      If Sing$ = "" And Not Eof(#1) Then
      Line Input #1, Sing$
      EndIf
      If Not Eof(#1) Then
      size = Len(Sing$) - 2
      client$ = Mid$(Sing$, 2, size)
      EndIf
Wend
InsertPara
InsertPara
Bold 1
Insert "Total billable time is " + Str$(grandtot)
Bold 0
End Sub
```

FIGURE 16.1

Billable time report

Billable time for COMPUTERS ARE US INC.

C:\COMPUTER\PROPOSAL.DOC=25
C:\COMPUTER\BUDGET.DPC=18
Total for COMPUTERS ARE US INC. is   43

Billable time for WATSON AND COMPANY

C:\WATSON\REPORT.DOC=123
C:\WATSON\INVOICE.DOC=2
Total for WATSON AND COMPANY is   125

Total for SMITHSON ENGINE COMPANY is   0

Total billable time is   168

Determining the Client Name

The macro reads the first section name, then determines the client name by removing the brackets. It does so by taking a middle section of the string, starting at the second position (past the opening bracket) and less than two characters of the entire length.

The first While loop will read through the entire file until its end. But within that loop, we use another While loop to read the options for each client. The next Line Input command reads another line from the file.

If the line starts with a bracket or is blank, then we do not want to process it as a billable item. The If command bypasses the processing lines. If the line is blank and we have not yet reached the end of the file, the macro reads the next line from the file, which will be another section name:

```
If Sing$ = "" And Not Eof(#1) Then
Line Input #1, Sing$
EndIf
```

If we have not yet reached the end of the file, the last line read—either as a result of the If command or in the second While loop—will be another section name, and the macro determines the client:

```
If Not Eof(#1) Then
    size = Len(Sing$) - 2
    client$ = Mid$(Sing$, 2, size)
EndIf
```

Listing the Client Items

The first while loop is then repeated to list the items for the client.

If the line does not start with the [character, and it is not a blank line, then it contains a document name and time, in the format:

```
C:\COMPUTER\BUDGET.DOC=18
```

The macro locates the position of the equal sign, then assigns the characters on its left to the variable project$:

```
pos = InStr(Sing$, "=")
prolen = pos - 1
project$ = Left$(Sing$, prolen)
```

686

(For example, if the equal sign is in position 23, then the document name is contained in the first 22 characters of the string.)

Assigning Time Characters

Next, the macro assigns the characters that represent the amount of time to the string billable:

```
timelen = Len(Sing$) - pos
billable$ = Right$(Sing$, timelen)
```

The time is contained in the right portion of the string—in the characters past the position of the equal sign.

Inserting a Detail Line

The macro then inserts a detail line reporting the project and time, then converts the time to a numeric value and accumulates it to the total.

Displaying the Grand Total

When all of the clients have been processed, the grand total of billable time is displayed and the macro ends.

Automating the Legal Office

Modern law offices rely heavily on computers and word processors for managing a large number of forms, such as wills, pleadings, leases, and contracts. Because the forms use standard headings, layout, and boiler-plate text, their production can easily be automated using macros and merge files. Use the applications shown in previous chapters as a guide.

The Pleading Wizard

Word includes a wizard named Pleading that creates a document as shown in Figure 16.2. The address information is contained in a text box drawing object in the text layer. The line numbers and vertical lines are stored in drawing objects in the header and footer layer. The wizard makes it easy to create a pleading but the process can take some time, depending on the speed of your system.

FIGURE 16.2

Sample Pleading
Wizard document

Attorney Name
Company Name
Street Address
City, State/Province Zip/Postal Code
Telephone: (888)888-8888
Fax:(888)888-8888

Attorney For: Secrets and Solutions

UNITED STATES DISTRICT COURT
CENTRAL DISTRICT OF CALIFORNIA

Creating a Pleading Template

As an alternative to using the wizard to generate each copy, you can create the pleading paper as a form in a template. You can either design your own form, or run the wizard and use the completed document as the basis for the template.

Using the Wizard's Format

To use Word's pleading format, run the wizard to display the completed document on the screen. Convert it to a template by saving the document with the DOT extension in the WINWORD\TEMPLATE directory. Next, replace the text that will change with each copy with form fields.

Unfortunately, you cannot insert a form field in a text box drawing object. Instead, delete the box, insert form fields as shown in Figure 16.3, and protect the document as a form. You can then prepare a document without going through the wizard procedure.

FIGURE 16.3

Edited pleading
paper

{ FILLIN "Enter Attorney's Name" }
{ FILLIN "Enter Company Name" }
{ FILLIN "Enter Address Name" }
{ FILLIN "Enter City, State, and Zip" }
{ FILLIN "Enter Telephone Number" }
Fax: { FILLIN "Enter Fax Number"}

Attorney For: { FILLIN "Enter Client's Name" }

UNITED STATES DISTRICT COURT
CENTRAL DISTRICT OF CALIFORNIA

Creating Your Own Form

If you do not like Word's pleading format, create your own form. Figure 16.4, for example, shows a form using a table. The shaded areas indicate text form fields. The text in some areas appears as default text, serving as a prompt to the user. Possible second lines for the defendant and plaintiff names contain no default text so the user can just bypass the field without entering any information.

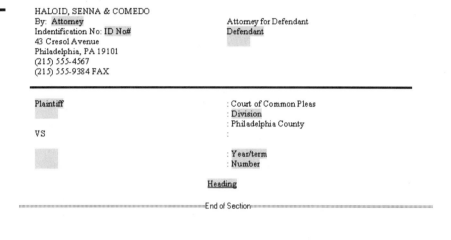

FIGURE 16.4

Custom pleading form

The first line of the defendant's name will automatically appear in the first field under VS, because of this OnExit macro for the Defendant field:

```
Sub MAIN
De$ = GetFormResult$("Defendant")
SetFormResult "Defend", De$
End Sub
```

When the user exits the first defendant's name field (using the bookmark Defendant) in the top section, the macro assigns its contents to the field in the bottom section (using a bookmark Defend). A similar macro will copy the contents of the second defendant field name to the other field.

Note The template contains two sections, but only the first is protected. After completing the top portion of the form, the user can type the text of the pleading in the unprotected section.

Combine the pleading template with the document management and billable time macros for a complete system.

Academic Word

If you've ever had to write a term paper or dissertation, then you know the exacting demands of academic documents. Most institutions have fixed layout requirements and strict rules for formatting footnotes, endnotes, bibliographies, outlines, and so on.

Because of the need to consistently adhere to formatting requirements, macros can be of invaluable help.

Creating Footnotes

Most colleges and universities provide or sell a stylebook that shows the required format. Still, it can be time-consuming to refer to the stylebook each time you have to enter a footnote or bibliographic entry.

Many stylebooks show different formats when referring to books, articles, compilations, works of a series, newspapers, encyclopedia entries, radio and television programs, plays and poems, scriptural references, legal citations, manuscript collections, and interviews. In addition, each style may vary with the number of authors or other specifics about the reference.

 **Tip**

While you can automate the process somewhat using a macro; a macro which handles all possibilities would be rather long and complex. One alternative would be to create a series of macros, one for each type of reference.

S O L U T I O N S

Footnote Macro

This macro formats a very standard footnote when referencing pages from a book. Run the macro when you are ready to enter a footnote.

```
Sub MAIN
Author:
Input "The primary author", Author$
If Author$ = "" Then Goto Author
Insert Author$
Input "How many additional authors", More
If More > 2 Then
    Insert ", "
    Italic 1
    Insert "et al, "
    Italic 0
EndIf
If More = 1 Then
    Input "The second author", Author2$
    Insert " and " + Author2$ + ", "
EndIf
If More = 2 Then
    Input "The second author", Author2$
    Insert ", " + Author2$ + ", and "
    Input "The third author", Author3$
    Insert Author3$ + ", "
EndIf
```

```
If More = 0 Then Insert ", "
Work:
    Work$ = InputBox$("Enter the title", "Footnote")
    If Work$ = "" Then Goto Work
    Underline 1
    Insert Work$
    Underline 0

Place:
    Input "Enter the city of publication", Place$
    If Place$ = "" Then Goto Place
    Insert " (" + Place$ + ": "

Publish:
    Input "Enter the published", Pub$
    If Pub$ = "" Then Goto Publish
    Insert Pub$ + ", "

GetDate:
    Input "Enter the date of publications", PubDate$
    If PubDate$ = "" Then Goto GetDate
    Insert PubDate$ + ") "

Input "Did you reference more than one page. Press Y or N",
Pages$
If Pages$ = "y" Then Pages$ = "Y"
If Pages$ <> "Y" Then
    Input "Enter the page referenced", PageRef$
    Insert "p. " + PageRef$ + "."
Else
    Input "Enter the starting page referenced", PageRef1$
    Insert "pp. " + PageRef1$ + "-"
    Input "Enter the ending page referenced", PageRef2$
    Insert PageRef2$ + "."
EndIf

End Sub
```

Creating Tests

By combining outlines with merge commands, you can create multiple choice and true-false tests and answer keys. For example, the data file in Figure 16.5 includes a record for each test question. Note that the fields include the question, four choices, and the answer.

FIGURE 16.5

Test data file

question	choice1	choice2	choice3	choice4	answer
How many bytes in 1K?	one	one million	one thousand	1024	4
What are two common disk sizes?	3 and 5	3.5 and 5.25	8 and 9	4 and 6	2
What is Windows?	A graphic interface	An operating system	Building supplies	All of the above	1

The Test Form Document

The form document for printing the test is shown in Figure 16.6.

FIGURE 16.6

Main document
for tests

    1.   «question»
      1.   «choice1»
      2.   «choice2»
      3.   «choice3»
      4.   «choice4»
        «answer»
    2.

To write the document, use this procedure:

1. Create a catalog form document associated with the data file of questions and answers.

2. Select View ➤ Outline to enter the outline mode. The outlining tool bar will appear.

3. Select Format ➤ Heading Numbering ➤ Modify.

4. Adjust the first two levels to use the 1,2,3 style, then select OK to return to the document. The number 1 will appear for the first level.

5. Click on the Insert Merge Field button and select the Question field.

6. Press Enter and then Tab to insert number 1 for the next level.

7. Click on the Insert Merge Field button, select the Choice1 field, and then press Enter.

8. In the same way, enter the Choice2, Choice3, and Choice4 fields.

9. After you press Enter after inserting the Choice4 field, click on the Demote To Body Text button in the outlining toolbar.

10. Click on the Insert Merge Field button, select the Answer, and then press Enter.

11. Click twice on the Promote button in the toolbar to insert the outline level 2.

12. Select the Answer field, and format it as hidden text.

13. Save the form document.

Merging the Test Files

When you merge the files, the questions will be numbered consecutively. To print a copy with the questions, select to display hidden text. You can also create a separate answer bank using a main document To create an answer key, use a primary document with these two lines:

```
1.     <<answer>>
2.
```

Insert the number using the outline feature.

Setting and Using Bookmarks

Setting and using bookmarks can help you work with long documents. When you are reading a book, a bookmark holds your place. When you start to read, you open the book at the location of the mark to find your place. A Word bookmark serves the same purpose. You set bookmarks at locations where you might need to quickly return, such as to edit a section of text, to check a reference, or to begin an editing session.

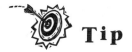

Tip

Each time you close a document, Word sets a special bookmark marking the position of the insertion point. When you open the document, press Shift+F5 to jump to your last editing position. Word actually sets bookmarks at the last four positions— continue pressing Shift+F5 to move to the previous position, even if it is in another open document.

Creating a Bookmark

To create a bookmark, place the insertion point at the desired location in the document, then select Edit ➤ Bookmark to display the dialog box shown in Figure 16.7. Enter an identifying name for that location in the document, then click on Add.

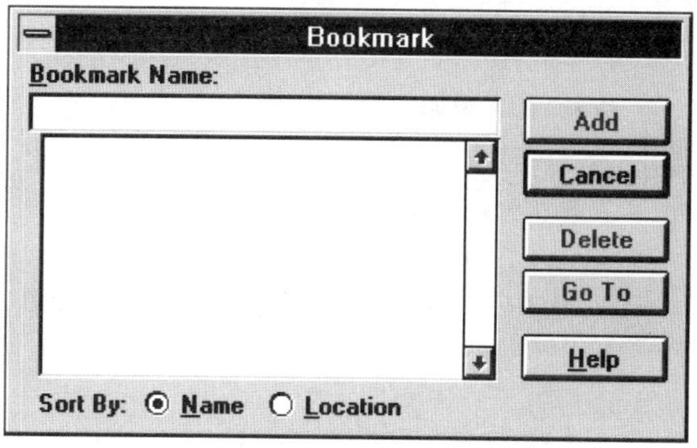

FIGURE 16.7
Bookmark dialog box

 **Tip**

If you select text and then create a bookmark, the same text will be selected when you jump to the bookmark. You can also insert the same text elsewhere in the document by using the bookmark name in field braces. To display the text, select the field and press F9, then toggle on the display of field results with Alt+F9. Naming a bookmark for selected text has the same affect as using the Set field.

Moving a Bookmark

To move to a bookmark, select Edit ➤ Bookmark, select the name of the bookmark, then choose Go To. If the text was selected when you created the bookmark, it will appear selected on the screen.

Bookmark Macros

Here is a review of other macros that are useful when working with bookmarks.

BookmarkName$( )

Word internally numbers bookmarks starting with 1. This function returns the name of the bookmark indicated by the number, as in Insert BookmarkName$(1).

CmpBookmarks( )

Compares the contents of two bookmarks, using the syntax:

```
CmpBookmarks(Bookmark1, Bookmark2)
```

The parameters must be bookmark names in quotation marks, or string variables. The returned values are shown in Table 16.1.

TABLE 16.1: Returned values from the CmpBookmark macro

VALUE	INDICATES
0	The bookmarks contain the same text.
1	The first bookmark starts below the end of the second.
2	The first bookmark ends before the start of the second.
3	The first bookmark begins within the second, but extends past its end.
4	The first bookmark starts above the second, but extends into the second bookmark.
5	The first bookmark encloses the second.
6	The second bookmark encloses the first.
7	The bookmarks start at the same position, but the first bookmark is longer.
8	The bookmarks start at the same position, but the second bookmark is longer.
9	The bookmarks end at the same position, but the first bookmark is longer.
10	The bookmarks end at the same position, but the second bookmark is longer.
11	The first bookmark is below and adjacent to the second.
12	The first bookmark is above and adjacent to the second.
13	One or both bookmarks do not exist.

CopyBookmark

Assigns the position or selected text of one bookmark to another, using the syntax CopyBookmark(Bookmark1, Bookmark2). When executed, Bookmark2 will be set to refer to the same text or position as Bookmark1.

CountBookmarks( )

Provides the number of bookmarks in the active document. To list the names of your bookmarks, use the macro:

```
For X = 1 to CountBookmarks()
    Insert BookmarkName$(x)
    InsertPara
Next
```

EditBookmark

Inserts, deletes, or jumps to a bookmark, using the syntax:

```
EditBookmark .Name = "bookmark_name", .SortBy = number, .Add,
.Delete, .Goto
```

 **Note**

The SortBy argument determines how the bookmarks are listed in a dialog box. Use 0 to sort the list by name, 1 by location. Use one of the remaining arguments to determine the action performed: .Add a bookmark at the location of the insertion point, .Delete the bookmark, or .Goto the bookmark. Add is the default.

EditGoTo

Jumps to a bookmark, using the syntax:

```
EditGoTo "bookmark_name"
```

EmptyBookmark( )

Returns –1 indicating whether the bookmark is empty (marking only the location of the insertion point) or returns 0 if it marks selected text or does not exist. The syntax is EmptyBookmark("Bookmark_name").

ExistingBookmark( )

Returns –1 if the bookmark exists, 0 if it does not exist.

GetBookmark( )

Returns the contents of a bookmark. Returns the string "FORM TEXT" if the bookmark marks a text form field.

GoBack

Moves the insertion point to the previous editing position.

SetEndOfBookmark

Sets the end of a bookmark at the insertion point position, using the syntax:

```
SetEndOfBookmark "Bookmark_name"
```

You can also use the command to mark the end of one bookmark with another bookmark name, using the form:

```
SetEndOfBookmark "Bookmark_name1", "Bookmark_name2"
```

SetStartOfBookmark

Marks the start of a bookmark.

Creating Hypertext and Help Systems

Hypertext takes the concept of bookmarks even further. With Hypertext, you create links to bookmarks, macros, and other documents on your disk. You can then move to a bookmark position, run a macro, or open another document by double-clicking on text or a button on the screen.

Word does not provide built-in hypertext functions, but you can create hypertext links using the GoToButton and MacroButton fields.

The GoToButton Field

The GoToButton field uses this syntax:

```
(GOTOBUTTON Destination DisplayText}
```

The destination refers to a bookmark in the same document. The display text will appear at the position of the field. When the user double-clicks on the displayed text, or places the insertion point in it and presses Alt+Shift+F9, Word moves to the named bookmark.

 **Note** The displayed text argument can also be the name of another bookmark, an includepicture field, or an included picture. The text or graphic must appear on one line in the result.

Figure 16.8 for example, shows a bookmark field and its display results.

FIGURE 16.8
GoToButton field
and results

Double-click on the icon to read the summary: { GOTOBUTTON summary }

Double-click on the icon to read the summary:

The MacroButton Command

The MacroButton command uses the same arguments but executes a macro when double-clicked.

```
{macrobutton MacroName DisplayText}
```

(The macro must be located in the active or a global template.)

Use a macro button, for example, to create a hypertext link to another document. If you know the name of the document, you can use a simple macro like this:

```
Sub MAIN
FileOpen .Name = "Help.DOC"
End SUB
```

Word will execute the macro, opening the document, when the user double-clicks on the macrobutton field.

Extending Hypertext with Macros

An efficient hypertext system, however, will allow the user to jump to one document, then back again to the original document. You can create this system using two macros.

The JumpTo Macro

Write the first macro, named JumpTo:

```
Sub MAIN
If FileNameFromWindow$() = "" Then
     Dim Saveit As FileSaveAs
     Doit = Dialog(Saveit)
     If Doit = -1 Then
          FileSaveAs Saveit
     Else
     Goto EndMacro
     EndIf
     EndIf
Back$ = FileNameFromWindow$()
Input "Enter file to jump to", JUMPTO$
FileOpen .Name = JUMPTO$
SetDocumentVar "Returnto", Back$
End Sub
```

The ReturnTo Macro

Next, create this macro called ReturnTo:

```
Sub MAIN
Back$ = GetDocumentVar$("ReturnTo")
FileOpen .Name = Back$
End Sub
```

How the Macros Work

The JUMPTO macro ensures that the current document has a filename so it can be returned to with the FileOpen command. It assigns the file name to the variable Back$, then inputs the name of file the user wants to jump to.

The FileOpen commands opens, or switches to, the document, then the macro creates a document variable containing the name of the document from which the user just jumped. The ReturnTo macro retrieves the name of that document and jumps back to it.

 **Tip**   Create the macros, then add tools for them on a toolbar. The user can jump to a document by clicking on the JUMPTO tool (or a macrobutton), then return to the original document by clicking on the ReturnTo tool.

Using the Macros

You can use the macros to move through a series of documents, not just between two. The user can run JUMPTO to move from one document to a second, then run it again to move from the second document to a third, and so on. Each time the user runs ReturnTo, the macro opens the previous document in the series.

The Sound of Word

If your computer has a sound device installed (such as SoundBlaster), you can add sound clips to your documents. The sound clip can contain a musical interlude, a sound effect, a message to another user, or a reminder to yourself.

Adding a Sound Clip

To add a sound clip, select Insert ➤ Object ➤ Sound to display the Windows Sound Recorder application, as shown in Figure 16.9.

Recording Sound

If you have a microphone, you can record a sound clip to insert. Click on the record button, speak into the microphone, then click on stop. To insert an existing WAV file, select Edit ➤ Insert File, select the file from the dialog box that appears, then select OK.

FIGURE 16.9
Windows Sound
Recorder

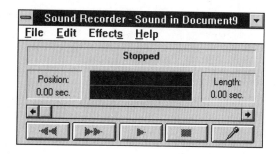

To return to the document, select File ➤ Update and then select File ➤ Exit to insert a link to the file. If you select File ➤ Exit without first updating, Word will display a dialog box asking if you want to update the sound file. Select Yes to embed the sound clip into the document.

Embedding a Sound

Word adds the clip as an embedded field. With field displayed, it will appear as:

{EMBED SoundRec}

With the results displayed, the field appears as an icon of a microphone, as shown in Figure 16.10.

FIGURE 16.10
Recorded sound
object icon

 Please listen to this announcement!

Playing and Editing Sounds

To play the sound, use any of these techniques:

◆ Double-click on the microphone icon

◆ Right-click on the icon or the field and select Play Sound from the shortcut dialog box

◆ Select the icon or field, then select Edit ➤ Sound Object ➤ Play.

To edit the sound in the Sound Recorder, select Edit Sound from the shortcut menu, or Edit ➤ Sound Object ➤ Edit.

Sound Clip Macros

Here's a macro that will move to and play the next embedded sound clip:

```
Sub MAIN
EditGoTo "o'SoundRec'"
ActivateObject
End Sub
```

To play a recorded message whenever the user starts Word, save the sound clip in a document named SAYIT.DOC and create this macro named AUTOEXEC:

```
Sub MAIN
FileOpen("SAYIT.DOC")
EditGoTo "o'SoundRec'"
ActivateObject
FileClose 2
End Sub
```

S E C R E T S

Sound Recorder Tips and Tricks

Sound Recorder operates just like a tape recorder, letting you play, record, and edit sound files with the WAV extension. From left to right, the buttons in the Sound Record application are:

- ◆ Rewind button
- ◆ Forward button
- ◆ Play button
- ◆ Stop button
- ◆ Record button

To play a file that you recorded or inserted, click on the Play button. The Wave box will display a pattern representing the portion of the file being played. Use the scroll bar to move to another position in the sound file. Clicking on the scroll bar or arrows moves backward or forward 1 second.

The options in the Edit and Effects menu let you:

- Insert the contents of one sound file into another
- Mix sound files together
- Delete a portion of the sound file
- Increase or decrease the volume
- Change the speed of the file
- Add an echo
- Reverse the sound

When you access the Sound Recorder from Word, you cannot use the File ➤ Open command to embed a sound clip in a document.

Index

Note: **Boldfaced** numbers indicate pages where you will find the principal discussion of a topic or the definition of a term. *Italic* numbers indicate pages where a topic is illustrated in a figure.

Symbols

* (asterisk), in form documents, 448
$ (dollar sign), in macro variables, 302
= (equal to), assigning values to macro variables, 302–303
? (question mark), in form documents, 448
" " (quotation marks)
    assigning string values to macro variables, 303
    AutoCorrect feature and, 10, 14
    AutoFormat feature and, 17

A

academic applications, **690–694**
    footnote macro, 690–692
    test form document, 693–694
accented characters, 181–182
accessing
    document variables with arrays, 563–564
    equation editor, 188–189
accounts receivable systems. *See* applications
Action arguments, in dynamic dialog boxes, 396–398

adding
    captions, 145–146
    columns to tables, 235–236
    form fields to form templates, 619
    graphics to envelopes, **76**
    information to .INI files, 550–551
    list boxes
        to dialog boxes, *378*, 386
        to forms, *623*, 627–629
    rows, 235–236
    text
        to envelopes, **76**
        to templates, 56
Advance field, 644–645, *645*
Align dialog box, *169*, 170
aligning
    borders with margins, **117–118**
    drawing objects, 169, 170
    text with macro commands, 294
anchoring frames to paragraphs, **126**, *126*
AND operator, in If commands, 313, 447
applications, **518–560, 666–705**. *See also* database management; document management; form documents; forms; macros
    academic applications, **690–694**

Help, for macro commands, 287–288
help messages, for form fields, 617, 621–622, *622*
hiding, screen elements, 27
horizontal lines, 108
hot keys. *See* shortcut keys
hypertext systems, **699–702**
hyphens, 182–183

I

.ID fields, in dialog boxes, 385
If command, **312–316**. *See also* macro commands
    AND and OR operators in, 313
    conditional If commands, 313–314
    in form documents, 443–446
    for message and dialog box selection, 315
    in mortgage payment calculator macro, 360
    multiple If commands, 315
    nested If commands, 314
    string variables in, 313
    Yes, No, Cancel options, 315–316
IncludePicture field, 650
IncludeText field, 651
indentation, borders and, 108
Index field, 651–652
indexed files
    deleting, 596–600
    using, 589–595
indexes
    RD field, 654
    XE (index entry) field, 659
Info field, 652
Information dialog box, dialog editor, 379–381, *380*
.INI files
    in accounts receivable system
        adding information to, 550–551

        retrieving information from, 551–552
        saving values in, 549–550
        writing new values to, 552
    in file management system, **572–574**
inline equations, **201–202**, *201. See also* equations
Input$() function, 607–608
Input command, 304–305, 354, 607
Inputbox$() function and dialog box, 306–307, *306*
Insert AutoText button, 5, 8
Insert Cells dialog box, 235–236, *235*
Insert Field dialog box, 644
Insert macro command, 305
Insert menu
    Break command, 30
    Caption command, 145
    Field command, 201
    Frame command, 119
    Object command, 131
    Picture command, 240
    Symbol command, 180
Insert Postal Bar Code dialog box, 437–438, *437*
Insert Table command, Table menu, 224, 236, 237
Insert Word Field: Fill-in dialog box, 453–455, *454*
Insert Word Field: IF dialog box, 443–446, *443*
inserting
    AutoText entries, 8–9
    cells, 235–236
    dates in accounts receivable system, 548
    fields, 643
    form fields in inline equations, 201–202
    pictures, *141*
    section breaks, 30–31

M

727

U

Word 6 for Windows Secrets & Solutions

GET A FREE CATALOG JUST FOR EXPRESSING YOUR OPINION.

Help us improve our books and get a *FREE* full-color catalog in the bargain. Please complete this form, pull out this page and send it in today. The address is on the reverse side.

Name _____ Company _____

Address _____ City _____ State ____ Zip _____

Phone ( )_____

1. How would you rate the overall quality of this book?

❑ Excellent
❑ Very Good
❑ Good
❑ Fair
❑ Below Average
❑ Poor

2. What were the things you liked most about the book? (Check all that apply)

❑ Pace
❑ Format
❑ Writing Style
❑ Examples
❑ Table of Contents
❑ Index
❑ Price
❑ Illustrations
❑ Type Style
❑ Cover
❑ Depth of Coverage
❑ Fast Track Notes

3. What were the things you liked *least* about the book? (Check all that apply)

❑ Pace
❑ Format
❑ Writing Style
❑ Examples
❑ Table of Contents
❑ Index
❑ Price
❑ Illustrations
❑ Type Style
❑ Cover
❑ Depth of Coverage
❑ Fast Track Notes

4. Where did you buy this book?

❑ Bookstore chain
❑ Small independent bookstore
❑ Computer store
❑ Wholesale club
❑ College bookstore
❑ Technical bookstore
❑ Other _____

5. How did you decide to buy this particular book?

❑ Recommended by friend
❑ Recommended by store personnel
❑ Author's reputation
❑ Sybex's reputation
❑ Read book review in _____
❑ Other _____

6. How did you pay for this book?

❑ Used own funds
❑ Reimbursed by company
❑ Received book as a gift

7. What is your level of experience with the subject covered in this book?

❑ Beginner
❑ Intermediate
❑ Advanced

8. How long have you been using a computer?

years _____

months _____

9. Where do you most often use your computer?

❑ Home
❑ Work

❑ Both
❑ Other _____

10. What kind of computer equipment do you have? (Check all that apply)

❑ PC Compatible Desktop Computer
❑ PC Compatible Laptop Computer
❑ Apple/Mac Computer
❑ Apple/Mac Laptop Computer
❑ CD ROM
❑ Fax Modem
❑ Data Modem
❑ Scanner
❑ Sound Card
❑ Other _____

11. What other kinds of software packages do you ordinarily use?

❑ Accounting
❑ Databases
❑ Networks
❑ Apple/Mac
❑ Desktop Publishing
❑ Spreadsheets
❑ CAD
❑ Games
❑ Word Processing
❑ Communications
❑ Money Management
❑ Other _____

12. What operating systems do you ordinarily use?

❑ DOS
❑ OS/2
❑ Windows
❑ Apple/Mac
❑ Windows NT
❑ Other _____

13. On what computer-related subject(s) would you like to see more books?

_____

_____

_____

_____

14. Do you have any other comments about this book? (Please feel free to use a separate piece of paper if you need more room)

_____

_____

_____

_____

- - - - - - - - - - - - PLEASE FOLD, SEAL, AND MAIL TO SYBEX - - - - - - - - - - - - - -

SYBEX INC.
Department M
2021 Challenger Drive
Alameda, CA
94501

SYBEX®

To program macros with WordBasic commands, see Chapter 9.

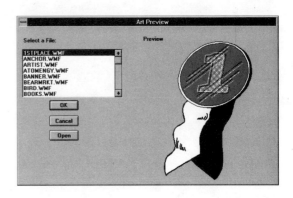

To use advanced WordBasic commands to create special applications and custom dialog boxes, see Chapter 10.

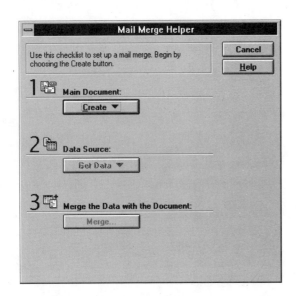

To merge letters, envelopes, labels, and database reports, see Chapter 11.

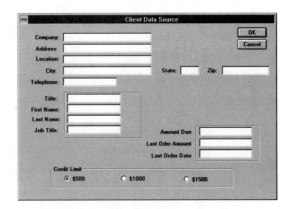

To manage database applications, see Chapter 12.